The Letters of
GUSTAVE FLAUBERT
1857–1880

The Letters of

GUSTAVE FLAUBERT
1857–1880

---<◈>---

SELECTED, EDITED, AND TRANSLATED

BY

Francis Steegmuller

THE BELKNAP PRESS OF
HARVARD UNIVERSITY PRESS
CAMBRIDGE, MASSACHUSETTS
AND LONDON, ENGLAND
1982

Library of Congress Cataloging in Publication Data

Flaubert, Gustave, 1821–1880.
    The letters of Gustave Flaubert.

    Includes bibliographies and indexes.
    Contents:[1] 1830–1857 — [2] 1857–1880.
    1. Flaubert, Gustave, 1821–1880—Correspondence.
2. Novelists, French—19th century—Correspondence.
I. Steegmuller, Francis, 1906-   . II. Title.
PQ2247.A23E57 1980   843'.8   79–13505
ISBN 0-674-52636-8 (v. 1)   AACR2
ISBN 0-674-52640-6 (v.2)

As before,
to
Jean Bruneau
and
Norbert Guterman

ACKNOWLEDGMENTS

IN PREPARING this volume I have been greatly helped by the cooperation of Professor Alphonse Jacobs and his publisher, Flammarion, who have allowed me to use portions of the texts and notes of his *Gustave Flaubert—George Sand, Correspondance* (Paris, 1981). Once again I am indebted to Professor Jean Bruneau—this time for sharing with me some of his preparations for the forthcoming third and fourth volumes of his *Flaubert Correspondance* (Bibliothèque de la Pléiade), and, as before, for his patient clarification of many details. (I have included his initials and those of Professor Jacobs in a number of my notes.) My thanks go also to the National Endowment for the Humanities for its generous grant-in-aid. I am grateful to Madame Léo d'Erlanger for hospitality in the region of Carthage; to Steele Commager for clarifying many of Flaubert's references to Latin writers; to David Marcus for elucidating certain terms in *Salammbô* and in Flaubert's notes for that novel; to Camille Smith for her editorial help; to Monsieur and Madame Olivier Ziegel for research and information; and, as always, to Shirley Hazzard for—everything.

My warm thanks go also to the following: Lucien Andrieu, Mohammed K. Annabi (Attaché de Recherches, Conservation du site de Carthage, Institut National d'Archéologie et d'Art de Tunisie) and Madame Chedlia Annabi, Max Aprile, Jacques Barzun, Jeanne Bem, Mr. and Mrs. Steven Bosworth, Erse Breunig, Leroy C Breunig, Victor Brombert, Anita Brookner, Cavaliere Alfonso Cavolli (Chief Concierge of the Hotel Excelsior, Naples) and his staff, Natalie Datlof, Comtesse Catherine Donin de Rosière, Dr. Henry R. Erle, Everett Fahy, William B. Goodman, Lily Gravino, David Hamilton, Edgar Johnson, Carlo Knight, Serge Lancel (Directeur de la Mission Française, Carthage), Monsignor Andrew P. Landi, Harry Levin, Georges Lubin, Kenneth Martin, Stanley Martin, Mark Piel, Jeanine Parisier Plottel, Gordon N. Ray, Jasper Ridley, Edward Said, Dr. Alvin A. Schaye, Douglas Siler,

Dorle Soria, Alex Szogyi, F. Firat Topçuoğlu (Deputy Turkish Consul-General in New York), and Marietta Tree.

The French texts of Flaubert's letters used for translation have been, whenever possible, those provided by Jean Bruneau in his edition mentioned above. Also used have been the edition published by Louis Conard (1926–1933) with Supplement (1954), and that of the Club de l'Honnête Homme (1971–1975), together with a number of articles in professional publications correcting the dating of certain letters. For the correspondence with Turgenev, I have used chiefly the texts edited by Gérard Gailly (1946).

Contents

ILLUSTRATIONS

Following page 126

George Sand, portrait drawing by Thomas Couture
Photo, Bibliothèque Nationale, Paris

Flaubert, portrait drawing by E. Liphart
Photo, Bibliothèque Municipale, Rouen

Ernest Commanville
Photo, Bibliothèque Municipale, Rouen

Caroline Commanville
Photo, Bibliothèque Municipale, Rouen

Flaubert, caricature by E. Giraud
Photo, Bibliothèque Nationale, Paris

The last Saint Polycarp dinner
Photo, Les Amis de Flaubert, Rouen

INTRODUCTION

Reflections: Gustave Flaubert's Correspondence

THE POPULAR and literary success of Gustave Flaubert's first published novel, *Madame Bovary*, brought him notoriety but did not greatly change his daily life. Already thirty-six when the book appeared in 1857, he continued to live as he had lived for the past dozen years or so—with his mother in her country house at Croisset on the banks of the river Seine below Rouen in Normandy. Earlier, his father, an eminent surgeon, had tried to force him into a career in the law; and only the sudden onset of morbid physical symptoms—a series of epileptiform attacks, which unfitted him for so active a profession—had made it possible for him to achieve the quiet he found essential for the writing of fiction, his passion since childhood. The attacks diminished in strength and frequency after the doctor's death when Flaubert was twenty-five, but by that time the pattern of his existence had been set and with the rarest of interruptions was never to change. Following the acclaim of *Madame Bovary* his acquaintances inevitably became more numerous; nevertheless, his stays in the Paris apartment he had leased during the composition of the novel were seldom prolonged. He never ceased to value quiet above all else, although in his last years he sometimes found the solitude of Croisset a high price to pay for it.

Flaubert's greatest departure from existence as the "hermit of Croisset" was an eighteen-month tour of Egypt and the Near East in 1849–1851 with his friend Maxime DuCamp. In the spring of 1858 he visited Tunisia briefly in preparation for his second novel, the exotic *Salammbô*, but otherwise he seldom strayed far from home. When he reached his early fifties the modest financial independence he had enjoyed was undermined by the assistance he gave his niece's husband during years of business failure, but he scrupulously retained his literary independence. Although his later works were often harshly reproached at publication with their dissimilarity to *Madame Bovary*, and although material rewards from his books were meager, his reputation as a writer of high seriousness and great style never diminished. Flaubert always generated a respect which at difficult moments earned him a degree of indulgence. "This morning the newspapers vie with one another in trying to cushion Flaubert's fall," Edmond de Goncourt wrote in his diary following the disastrous reception of Flaubert's only produced play, *Le Candidat*. A curious and growing public sympathy was extended to this uncompromising artist who held himself aloof.[1]

If melancholia and misanthropy—or rather a supreme irritation with human folly—intensified in Flaubert during his later years, events appeared to justify that development. He lived through the Franco-Prussian War of 1870–1871 and the subsequent catastrophe of the Commune. These conflicts wrung him, both for their larger meaning and in the sorrow and turmoil they brought to his secluded existence. Under their influence, too, he became—if not quite a patriot—more overtly a Frenchman. We find Flaubert—of all people—drilling the local company of the National Guard and going to Rouen "to take lessons in military art." The occupation by Germans of his mother's house at Croisset polluted it in his eyes: "If [it] belonged to me, I would certainly have it demolished."

Flaubert suffered with the victims of famine and privation and endured the humiliations of defeat; embittered by the tragic divisions between his countrymen, he was indignant with both Right and Left. And he marked, with habitual prescience, the onset of a new chaos in which technology, political and social fluctuation, and gigantic wars would overwhelm the claims of civilized order and fatally reduce the possibilities for imagination and reflection in human affairs. Having ever despised "current opinion" and its insistent purveyors, he watched its contagion spread, under the impetus of events, into the domain of intellect, scholarship, and art; infecting all concepts of quality and excellence, and of truth itself, and blighting his closest associations. Before the war he walked out of one of the Magny dinners—those gatherings of literary men and scholars founded by Sainte-Beuve and a few friends—because the other guests insisted on discussing politics, "an indecency among intellectuals"; and in 1874 he wrote to George Sand: "The men of my profession are so *little* of my profession! There is scarcely anyone except Victor Hugo with whom I can talk about what interests me. Two days ago he quoted to me by heart from Boileau and Tacitus. It was like receiving some gift, the thing is so rare."

The great "Realist" refused to exalt "modernism," and retained to the end his vision of the long individuality of art: "This mania for thinking . . . that you're more true than your predecessors exasperates me . . . There is no 'True.' There are only ways of perceiving . . . Down

1. See my earlier volume, *The Letters of Gustave Flaubert, 1830–1857* (henceforth referred to as Volume I), and *Flaubert in Egypt*, in Works of Related Interest.

with Schools, whatever they may be! Down with words devoid of sense!
. . . Material truth (or what is so called) must be only a springboard, to
help one soar the higher." At such moments Flaubert—who had once
declared himself "a rabid old Romantic"—brings to mind the Leopardi
of "La Ginestra."

In 1872 his mother's death dissolved Flaubert's strongest emotional
tie. Seclusion was intensified by the deaths of most of his close friends
and became, at times, isolation: "Almost all human beings are endowed
with the gift of exasperating me, and I breathe freely only in the desert."

Exhorted—in a fine exchange—by George Sand to acknowledge the
beneficence of "mercy" and "humanitarianism," Flaubert emphatically
declined, labeling them "sentimental" and calling instead for justice—
"the blood of the wounded Themis"—and the spirit of inquiry. On the
modern ideal of material and social "progress" he was similarly un-
yielding: "The entire dream of democracy is to raise the proletariat to
the level of bourgeois stupidity." His views were arrived at not through
animus or posturing, but with immense suffering: "Everything moves
me, everything lacerates and ravages me, and I make every effort to
soar." Flaubert had painfully earned his right to the despair that often
possessed him.

Together with despair there were close affections, great generosity of
spirit toward younger writers, an ebullient sense of absurdity, and a
generally fastidious code of private behavior. It is the astringent Edmond de Goncourt who records, at their final meeting, Flaubert's "kind
face." The remark is unexpected, but somehow not surprising. It is notable that Flaubert did not often or frivolously speak ill of others in his
letters, or indulge in trivial gossip and mockery. Men of stature liked
and respected him. He cultivated no little court of inferiors to whom he
might hold forth without contradiction; and to those who disagreed
with him he was not vengeful. He recognized—and indeed held sacred—the private bonds of tenderness, loyalty, goodwill; of shared experience and common suffering; and of an ultimate humility before the
great creations of art.

Two significant instances, during the period covered by the present
volume, in which Flaubert violated his own standards derive from
"bourgeois" considerations of the kind he himself most savagely condemned. His harmless infatuation with the world of society and court
influence was brief—although his friendship with Princesse Mathilde
Bonaparte survived. But his role in allowing his beloved niece to be
forced into a loveless marriage with a seemingly prosperous bourgeois,
a union that later brought him immeasurable grief, was undertaken for
thoroughly unworthy reasons. "I'd rather see you marry a millionaire

philistine than an indigent genius": those are the words not of a petty or grand bourgeois, of Monsieur Homais or Monsieur Dambreuse, but of Gustave Flaubert. The consequences were to cost him a precious friendship and to plunge him into mercenary wrangles of the kind his soul had always abhorred: "I feel spiritually *soiled* by all these sordid concerns, by all this commercial talk; I feel I'm being turned into a shopkeeper. Imagine a virtuous woman made to prostitute herself in a brothel, or a fastidious person being dragged about in a garbage cart, and you have my situation."

These curious episodes make uneasy reading—if only because we seek from genius a consistency greater than our own. They may, without too much insistence, be linked to endless manifestations of the greater dichotomy of Gustave Flaubert's spirit. Kindliness and misanthropy; the quandary of a novelist who debated whether his next work would deal with Thermopylae or a pair of nineteenth-century copyclerks; the genius who sought, in his work, "to be like a God"—and the man who declared he would "die of suppressed rage at the folly of my fellow men."

FOR THE MOST PART these later letters of Flaubert's are less well known than their predecessors; nevertheless, some are individually renowned. One might mention the pair to the critics Sainte-Beuve and Froehner rebutting their objections to *Salammbô*—letters of which Jacques Barzun has said: "Flaubert had his fingers rapped by authoritative pedants, but he knew his subject and crushed their knuckles with the finality of a sledge hammer." There are the two analytical letters to Taine; the moving congratulations to his young "disciple," Guy de Maupassant, on having produced a masterpiece in "Boule de Suif"; the passages on the German occupation; and almost any of the letters to George Sand. Each reader will make his own selection. Flaubert's genius as a correspondent was immune to the fluctuations of fortune and expresses itself with equal force under every variety of circumstance.

The difference between the younger and the older Flaubert is perhaps most manifest in the contrast between the sensual outpourings to Louise Colet in Volume I and what can be thought of as their *pendant* in the present pages—the celebrated series to George Sand, infused with a riper sentiment. Unlike the Flaubert-Colet correspondence, that between Flaubert and Madame Sand survives almost intact on both sides. A number of their exchanges, particularly illuminating of Flaubert's character, life, and work, have been included here.[2]

2. The entire corpus, as recently edited by Alphonse Jacobs (with acknowledgments to Georges Lubin and Jean Bruneau), invites integral translation into any number of languages. (*Gustave Flaubert—George Sand, Correspondance*, Paris: Flammarion, 1981.)

WHEN THE FOURTH and last volume of the first edition of Flaubert's general correspondence was published by Charpentier early in 1893 (the volumes having been issued separately over a period of several years), a long review of the whole, by Henry James, was printed in *Macmillan's Magazine*. James's immediate concern was, he claimed, for the ethical aspects of this disclosure of Flaubert's private circumstances, feelings, and statements, as contrasted with Flaubert's own attitude to such revelations. " 'May I be skinned alive before I ever turn my private feelings to literary account,' " James quoted from a letter dated 1854; whereas "Flaubert's niece, Madame Commanville" (who edited the series) had given the letters to the world "without attenuation and without scruple ... In our merciless age," James went on, "ineluctable fate has overtaken the man in the world whom we most imagine gnashing his teeth under it."

James had no way of knowing how inapposite were his words "without attenuation and without scruple." In fact, Mme Commanville had been sparing, to say the least, when it came to inserting the series of dots which, in a quoted text, signify ellipsis. (In 1906 she would edit a fifth volume, composed entirely of letters from her uncle to herself, entitled *Lettres à sa nièce Caroline:* here the indications of omission would be much more frequent—although, as we know today, still not frequent enough to meet the case.)

Mme Commanville's censorship took several forms. Most obviously superfluous, in her view, were the passages, very numerous in the later letters to her, in which her uncle—fond of her as he was—complained of ill-treatment by her, or, more frequently, by her unlucky and rapacious husband. The image of a niece always affectionate and considerate had to be preserved. (That she had deep cause, if not justification, for the imperfections of her devotion, the reader of the present volume will discover.)

The next category of her omissions related to unflattering, or possibly libelous, references to persons then still alive.

Third, there was Flaubert's tendency to be obscene, profane, and scatological. In these realms he was fluent and, particularly in youth, linguistically inventive. In France phrases of the kind have always been in somewhat wider use than in English speaking society; and here Mme Commanville—who, though genteel, was thoroughly Gallic—sometimes surprises us by her permissiveness. She might have been yet more liberal in this respect had it not been for her "spiritual director," the Reverend Father Didon. "In publishing your uncle's correspondence," this Dominican priest wrote her, "you have not pledged yourself to say everything, and your private conscience must guide you in using judgment as to what you allow to be printed—since it is through you that these letters will be made public. You are responsible before God and man for the moral result of this publication."[3]

FLAUBERT SOMETIMES commented on the letters of other artists and writers. On New Year's Eve, 1876, he wrote to Caroline:

> I have read Balzac's Correspondence. Well, for me it was edifying reading. Poor man! What a life! How he suffered and worked! What an example! It would be indecent ever to pity oneself when one knows the tortures he underwent—and one loves him for it. But what an obsession with money! And so little concern for Art! *Not one single time does he talk about it!* Fame was the goal of his ambition, not Beauty. And such limitations!—legitimist, Catholic, dreaming of the Chamber of Deputies and the French Academy! With all that, ignorant as a pot, and provincial to the marrow of his bones: luxury dazzled him. His greatest literary admiration was for Walter Scott. I prefer Voltaire's correspondence. The compass spreads wider there!

There were also the letters of Hector Berlioz, for whose tormented life Flaubert expressed a similar pity. (Flaubert and Berlioz had known each other, and Berlioz had written Flaubert of his admiration for *Salammbô*, which he had thought of making the subject of an opera.) Once again to Caroline, in April 1879:

> Reading Berlioz's *Unpublished Correspondence* has revived me. Read it, I beg you. There's a man for you! and a true artist! What a hatred of mediocrity! What marvelous anger against the vile bourgeois! What scorn for "Them"! It beats Balzac's letters hollow! I'm no longer surprised that we found each other so congenial. Would I had known him better! I'd have adored him!

Even though he enjoyed those letters written by other artists, and expressed no scruples over their publication, it is conceivable that Flaubert might nonetheless have been aghast at the thought of his own letters in print. Who is an exception if not oneself? And Flaubert was a man of contradictions. We cannot be certain. Like everyone else acquainted with the Goncourt brothers, Flaubert knew that they kept a journal intended for publication; nevertheless, in the Goncourts' presence he often spoke openly about the most intimate aspects of his own life and told some of his most scabrous stories—as he did in letters to them. It would hardly have surprised Flaubert to learn that these remarks were

---

3. Over the years more and more of Flaubert's letters have come to light. The four-volume first edition, plus the volume of letters to Caroline, included something over two thousand letters. The Pléiade edition of the correspondence (Paris: Gallimard), edited and annotated by Jean Bruneau and at present in the course of publication, will include about five thousand.

commemorated in the journal. In response to queries from Hippolyte Taine, who was writing his treatise *On Intelligence*, he discussed his thoughts concerning the creation of his fictional characters and even described the hallucinations preceding his own epileptiform attacks. We see today what James could not: that Flaubert's remark, "May I be skinned alive before I ever turn my private feelings to literary account," refers predominantly to his novels rather than to his letters. Caroline Commanville's prime motive for publishing the letters was financial— that consideration was always prominent with her and her husband; and it is true that in her day it was customary to remove anything "unseemly" from letters before publication. Nevertheless, we, at this distance, inevitably find her culpable—not because she sent her uncle's letters to the printer, but because she censored them before doing so.

(In the present volume—a selection from Flaubert's thousands of letters—dots of omission indicate passages which in the editor's opinion reiterate Flaubert's already expressed views or are less revelatory than other passages of his personality and opinions.)

EVEN IN THEIR truncated condition, the early printed volumes of Flaubert's correspondence immediately fascinated readers. The several fuller editions that have been published since Caroline's series have led some critics to hail the correspondence, with varying degrees of enthusiastic exaggeration, as "the best of Flaubert's novels." There have also been dissenting voices. James himself, in addition to stating his "ethical" objection, was so repelled by Flaubert's personality as revealed in the letters that the prose in his long review became opaque: he found Flaubert, if "impossible as a companion, [yet] deeply refreshing as a reference"; and the letters themselves he pronounced productive of a "compassion ... full of mystifications and wonderments."

Marcel Proust, in his essay "On Flaubert's 'Style'" (the quotation marks around "Style" are Proust's own), expressed astonishment that whereas most writers whose books are written badly (as, in his judgment at the time, was the case with Flaubert) *improve* their style immensely when writing spontaneously in letters, Flaubert's epistolary style is "even worse" than that of his novels. Proust—who paid a late tribute, in his own novel, to *Madame Bovary*—disagreed with the critic Albert Thibaudet, who found in Flaubert's correspondence "the expression of the ideas of a first-rate intellect."

The art and the private correspondence of a great writer are not in rivalry. Yet there will always be those who enjoy setting the one against the other. In an ironic passage dealing with such literary pretentions in *The Guermantes Way*—and included only in recent editions of Proust's novel—the Comtesse d'Arpajon converses with the Narrator:

"As a matter of fact I find that old correspondences have a peculiar charm," the lady who was well up on literature and had such fascinating letters in her château went on ... "Have you noticed how often a writer's letters are superior to the rest of his work? What's the name of the author who wrote *Salammbô?*"

I should have liked not to have to reply in order not to prolong the conversation, but I felt it would be disobliging to the Prince d'Agrigente, who had pretended to know perfectly well who *Salammbô* was by and out of politeness to be leaving it to me to say, but who was now in a painful quandary.

"Flaubert," I ended up by saying, but the vigorous signs of assent that came from the Prince's head smothered the sound of my reply, so that my interlocutress was not exactly sure whether I had said Paul Bert or Fulbert, names which she did not find entirely satisfactory.

"In any case," she went on, "how intriguing his correspondence is, and how superior to his books! It explains him, in fact, because one sees from everything he says about the difficulty he has in writing a book that he wasn't a real writer, a gifted man."[4]

Few readers will now share the reservations of either the American mandarin or the French concerning Flaubert's letters. For many, the correspondence is fundamental. Jean Bruneau, in the preface to his first volume, quotes André Gide: "For more than five years his correspondence took the place of the Bible at my bedside. It was my reservoir of energy. It made me realize that the force impelling me could be consecrated in a new way."

4. *Remembrance of Things Past*, trans. C. K. Scott Moncrieff and Terence Kilmartin (New York: Random House, 1981), II, 508.

The Letters of
GUSTAVE FLAUBERT
1857–1880

I

The Writing of
Salammbô
1857–1862

O N ITS PUBLICATION in two volumes in April 1857, *Madame Bo-vary* was an immediate "success." That is, it sold widely and was soon reprinted—partly, no doubt, because of the scandal of the prosecution following its serialization in Maxime DuCamp's *Revue de Paris*. On a more serious plane, thoughtful critics recognized the book's importance; and a penetrating review by Baudelaire contributed to the general acceptance of *Madame Bovary* as a masterpiece that depicted human existence with a degree of realism hitherto unknown in fiction.

Unlike many a writer who has achieved immediate fame with his first published work, Flaubert did not remain a man of that one book, or even of one kind of book. He went on to produce a variety of extraordinary works. *Salammbô*, his Carthaginian story, was his second published book—aloof (as contrasted with *Madame Bovary*) from the study of human character; rather, a richly colored historical and imaginative reconstruction of a vanished civilization. Guy de Maupassant has evoked the nature of what he calls Flaubert's "Homeric tale":

> Is it a novel? Is it not rather a kind of opera in prose? The tableaux unroll with prodigious magnificence, with astonishing splendor, color, and rhythm. The sentences sing and shout with the fury and resonance of trumpets; they murmur like oboes, surge like cellos; they are as flexible as violins, delicate as flutes.
>
> The characters, heroic in their stature, give the impression of being always on a stage; they speak superbly, with an elegance now mighty, now charming; they seem to move in a décor antique and grandiose.
>
> This book, written by a giant, and plastically the most beautiful of all his works, creates the impression of a magnificent dream.
>
> Did the events related by Gustave Flaubert really occur in this way? Certainly not. Exact though the facts may be, the brilliance of the poetry he showers on them displays them to us in a kind of apotheosis, whose lyric art envelops everything it touches.[1]

The writing and reception of *Salammbô*, the "magnificent dream" of a nineteenth-century novelist in love with antiquity, would be one of the subjects of his correspondence for the next several years.

EVEN BEFORE *Madame Bovary* was published, Flaubert had known what his next book would be.

Abandoning his thought of preparing at that time a definitive version of his early extravaganza, *The Temptation of Saint Anthony*, most of which remained in manuscript (a few revised sections had been printed in Théophile Gautier's magazine *L'Artiste* during the excitement about *Madame Bovary*), he deliberately chose a subject equally exotic. Distance from his own life and times was essential, for *Madame Bovary*, he told Mlle Leroyer de Chantepie, his literary spinster correspondent in Angers, had filled him with "a long disgust" for anything to do with the French bourgeoisie. The new book, he wrote her on March 18, 1857, would be a historical novel whose action took place "in one of the least known periods of antiquity . . . three centuries before Christ." More precisely, its subject would be the bloody revolt and annihilation of the unpaid polyglot mercenary army of Carthage, following that city's first defeat by Rome in 241 B.C.—and the end of the first Punic war. He wanted, he told the Goncourt brothers, to "write something purple."

Such would be *Salammbô*. The immense difference between Flaubert's first and second novels is proclaimed in their titles, the names of their heroines: Madame Bovary, the bourgeois wife of a provincial French health officer, and Salammbô, daughter of the Carthaginian general Hamilcar—"a daughter," Flaubert wrote to a friend, "invented by your humble servant." (The historian Polybius, writing in the second century B.C., mentions a daughter of Hamilcar but does not name her; Flaubert baptized her from the Babylonian and Syrian pantheons, where the goddess whose name can be transcribed as "Salambo"—we shall see that Flaubert's spelling is specifically French—corresponds to the Greek Aphrodite, or, more particularly, to the mourning Venus of the legend of Venus and Adonis.)

In reply to a letter from Flaubert now lost, Louis Bouilhet, his old friend and literary counselor, who was now librarian in the town of Mantes, wrote in warning on July 18, 1857:

> Either you misunderstood me, or I expressed badly my feelings about your future book. Like you, I not only think it possible, but hope it will be splendid. However, I see it as being so difficult that it alarms me, and I was surprised from the start to see you throw yourself so blithely into so scabrous a subject. That's all. Now, what is of lesser, indeed not of the slightest, importance, from the artistic point of view, is, in my opinion, the inopportuneness of the book at this critical point of your reputation. I may be mistaken, but I think it would be more astute, whatever you may say, to write

another work of close observation, making it your last production of that kind. This is certainly the case as far as money is concerned, and also from the standpoint of reputation. At least, such is my sincere opinion. I hope I may be wrong. I'm not afraid that what you propose doing will be a fiasco, but even assuming the same level of excellence it will never, because of its very subject, make the sensation that *Bovary* did, and I'd like you to fire two cannon-balls in rapid succession, both of them red-hot.

Everything I'm saying is silly and useless, but I wanted to explain my lack of enthusiasm. *This has nothing to do with the book itself, which will certainly be very fine.* It has to do with its *timing.*

From now on there must be no turning back, and besides I may be making quite a blooper. One never knows how the public will react. So: get to work, start writing as soon as possible. Don't wear yourself out making new notes; digest your old ones; take up your pen, and if something turns up that has to be researched, then research it.

Some years before, during his travels in Egypt, Flaubert had written to Bouilhet: "Let's not get lost in archaeology": and with typical inconsistency it was into archaeology that he himself now deeply plunged. He is said to have had a Carthaginian subject in mind since his schoolboy reading of Michelet's *Histoire Romaine:* almost the entire background of his story, and most of its military incidents, are based (as is Michelet's account) on Polybius's narrative in his *History.* Until he was well into his new novel, Flaubert sometimes referred to it as *"Carthage,"* or *"The Mercenaries."* Though he was not deterred by Bouilhet's doubts, his letters of 1857 and early 1858 tell of dread caused by Bouilhet's injunction to *begin*—and of near despair, followed by resolve.

1. From Maupassant's preface to *Lettres de Gustave Flaubert à George Sand* (Paris: Charpentier, 1884).

◇–◇–◇–◇–◇

To Ernest Feydeau[1]

[Croisset, July 26 (?), 1857]

I am sick with fear, filled with terrors of all kinds: I'm about to start to write. No, my friend, I'm not so stupid: I'll not show you any part of *Carthage* until the last line is written, because I already have enough doubts of my own without adding those you would give me. Your remarks would drive me crazy. As for my archaeology, it will be "probable," that's all. As long as no one can *prove* that I've written absurdities, that's all I ask. As for the botanical side, I have no worries; I've seen with my own eyes all the plants and trees I need.

Besides, that's of little importance: it's a secondary matter. A book

3

can be full of enormities and blunders and be no less splendid for that. Such a doctrine, once admitted, would be deplorable, I know, especially in France, where pedantry and ignorance reign. But in the opposite tendency (which is mine, alas!) I see a great danger. Concentration on costume makes us forget the soul. I would give the demi-ream of notes I've written during the last five months and the ninety-eight volumes I've read, to be, for only three seconds, really moved by the passion of my heroes.

· · ·

1. Flaubert had met Ernest Feydeau (1821–1873, father of the playwright Georges Feydeau), through Théophile Gautier, at the time when Feydeau had begun his archaeological study, *Histoire des usages funèbres et des sépultures des peuples anciens*. In 1858 Feydeau would publish his first novel, *Fanny*, which enjoyed a popular and, in some quarters, even critical success equal to that of *Madame Bovary*, but which is forgotten today along with most of Feydeau's subsequent fiction. Flaubert envied him the financial aspect of his success (the publisher Lévy had paid only 800 francs for five years' rights to *Madame Bovary*, plus a voluntary extra 500 francs when it had sold widely); but he greatly liked Feydeau, and spent much time and effort granting his pleas for help in the composition of his novels. Although they were the same age, Flaubert sometimes addressed Feydeau as "nephew."

❖❖❖❖

Flaubert apparently lamented similarly to Bouilhet, who wrote him on September 19, 1857: "Consider especially that given the milieu and period you have chosen, the book can never be as living as *Bovary*. That is impossible. I'll go further: it would be wrong if it were. Over distant subjects there should always be a haze: the stump is better than the hard pencil, and real life should appear only at rapid intervals, like flashes of lightning on a very distant horizon. That is the danger, but also the beauty and the originality, of your subject."[1]

1. As *Salammbô* advanced, Flaubert would ask Bouilhet for help at a number of delicate moments. Most of his letters to Bouilhet are lost; many of Bouilhet's replies survive, in the Bibliothèque Lovenjoul at Chantilly. Salammbô's betrothal to the Numidian chieftain, Narr' Havas, despite her broken ankle-chain; the substitution of the slave boy for the child Hannibal; the forced combat between two groups of Theban friends: Flaubert's treatment of all these scenes, and others, owes something to Bouilhet's suggestions. The episodes were conceived by Flaubert, but Bouilhet assisted in their realization. Benjamin F. Bart has written an interesting exposition of Bouilhet's role in his article "Louis Bouilhet and the Redaction of Salammbô," *Symposium*, Fall 1973.

❖❖❖❖

To Ernest Feydeau

[Croisset,] Thursday night [August 6, 1857]

· · ·

For the past six weeks I've been shying away from *Carthage* like a coward. I'm accumulating reams of notes, and reading book after book,

4

for I don't feel ready to begin writing. I don't see my objective clearly. In order for one's book to *sweat* truth, one has to be stuffed to the ears with its subject. Then the color comes quite naturally, like a result decreed by fate, and like a flowering of the very idea.

. . .

◇◇◇◇◇

By early October he took a somewhat more hopeful tone in a letter to Jules Duplan, a businessman who performed various friendly services for him in connection with his books: "Finally I'm beginning to have an erection. That's the important thing. But how hard it's been to get it up! Will it stay?"

◇◇◇◇◇

To Mademoiselle Leroyer de Chantepie

[Croisset, November 4, 1857]

. . .

The more experience I acquire in my art, the more tormenting that art becomes. The trouble is, imagination remains stationary while taste matures. Few men, I think, will have suffered as much as I for literature. Now I am going to spend two months in complete solitude, with no company except that of the yellow leaves as they fall on the flowing river . . . Have you noticed how we love our miseries? You cling to the religious ideas that cause you such suffering, and I to the chimera of style, which consumes me body and soul. But perhaps we are worth something only because of our sufferings, for these are all aspirations. There are so many people whose joys are so ignoble and whose ideals so shallow, that we must bless our troubles if they make us more worthy.

. . .

To Ernest Feydeau

[Croisset, about November 20, 1857]

Oh, I'm done for, my friend, done for! . . . Let me tell you confidentially that for the past month I've found it impossible to write. I can't find a single word. I'm horribly bored, and keep staring at the fire. Voilà.

I'm being punished for wanting, like a fool, to begin to write a book before carrying it long enough in my belly. I assure you I'm not very gay . . .

. . .

5

To Ernest Feydeau

[Croisset,] Tuesday night [November 24 (?), 1857]

· · ·

At last I've finished, for better or worse, my first chapter, and am preparing the second. I have undertaken something bold, my boy, something very bold, and I may well break my neck before reaching the end. Never fear, I'll not shirk it. Sombre, grim, desperate, but no coward. But just think, intelligent nephew, of what I've let myself in for: trying to resuscitate an entire civilization with nothing whatever to go on!

How difficult it is to write something that has substance and at the same time *moves!* This is essential, however. On every page there must be food and drink, action and color.

· · ·

To Ernest Feydeau

[Croisset,] Saturday [December 12, 1857]

· · ·

I'm not going ahead, which is better than continuing to make mistakes. I stopped because I felt I was on the wrong track. I'm baffled by the psychology of my characters. So I'm waiting, and sighing.

I'll be in Paris Tuesday or Wednesday of next week, Christmas Eve at the latest . . . Once there, I swear I'm going to go in for some monstrous debauches, to restore my morale. I'm longing for them. Perhaps by sticking something up my ass I can give my brain a good fucking. I hesitate between the column in the Place Vendôme and the obelisk [in the Place de la Concorde.] I'm laughing—but I'm not merry. It's true that I've gone through similar periods before, and come out of them all the livelier. But this one is lasting too long, too long!

◇◇◇◇◇

Flaubert became increasingly dissatisfied with what he was doing. Might it help if he were to see for himself the site and surroundings of Carthage? One of the basic difficulties was, as he had said, that there was "nothing to go on": the city had been all but obliterated by Rome following the end of the second Punic war in 147 B.C. On January 23, 1858, he wrote to Mlle Leroyer de Chantepie:

I absolutely must make a trip to Africa; so, toward the end of March I'll return to the land of dates. I'm thrilled at the prospect. Once again I'll live on horseback and sleep under a tent. What deep breaths of air I'll treat myself to when I board my ship at Marseilles! But this trip will be a short one. I need to go only to El-Kef[1] (thirty leagues from Tunis), and explore the environs of

Carthage within a radius of twenty leagues, in order to acquaint myself thoroughly with the landscapes I'll be describing. My outline is done, and I'm a third of the way through the second chapter. The book will have fifteen. As you see, I've barely begun. Under the best of circumstances, I'll not be finished for two years.

Leaving Croisset, the village on the Seine near Rouen where he lived with his widowed mother and his motherless niece, Caroline Hamard (now twelve years old), he took ship at Marseilles on April 16, 1858. He went ashore at Stora, Algeria, for a preliminary look at Philippeville and Constantine; at Bône (for Bizerta, the ancient Hippo); and on the twenty-fourth debarked at Tunis, close to the site of Carthage. He was well supplied with notebooks. His earliest known letter from this voyage is to Louis Bouilhet.

1. The antique Sicca.

◇◇◇◇◇

To Louis Bouilhet

Midnight [April 23–24, 1858]
Night of Friday–Saturday, aboard the *Hermus*, abreast
Cap Negre and Cap Serat. Latitude 37°10—longitude
6°40—(look at the map and you'll see where I am!!!)

Mon Vieux,

It's a beautiful night, the sea flat as a lake of oil; old Tanit[1] is shining, the ship's engine panting, the captain smoking beside me on his sofa, and the deck packed solid with Arabs Mecca-bound. Barefoot, swathed in their white burnouses, their faces covered, they look like shrouded corpses. There are women, too, with their children. The entire lot of them are sleeping, or wretchedly vomiting; we are skirting the Tunisian coast, visible in the mist. Tomorrow morning we'll be at Tunis; I'm not going to bed—I want to miss none of this lovely night. Besides, my impatience to see Carthage would keep me awake.

From Paris to Constantine, in other words from Monday to Sunday, I scarcely exchanged a word with a soul. But at Philippeville we took on some fairly agreeable passengers, and since then I've been having various conversations—some quite philosophical and very indecent. I am initiating a young Russian gentleman into the arcana of pederasty . . . though I suspect that as a Scyth he may know more than I about such matters.

At Marseilles I saw the well-remembered house where eighteen years ago I fucked Mme Foucaud, née de Langlade.[2] All changed! The ground floor, then the salon, is now a bazaar, and upstairs is a barbershop. I went there twice to be shaved. I spare you any Chateaubriandesque comments and reflections on the flight of time, on falling leaves

7

and falling hair. No matter: it's a long time since I have thought—or is it *felt?*—so deeply . . .

I was extremely solitary during my two days in Marseilles. I went to the museum, to the theatre. I visited the brothel streets, I sat and smoked in sailors' cafés, looking out at the sea.

The only important place I have seen so far is Constantine, Jugurtha's city. It is surrounded by an immense ravine, tremendous, vertiginous. I walked along its edge and rode a horse along its floor. It was the evening hour, when lines begin to form outside the little theatres on the Boulevard du Temple.[3] Vultures were wheeling in the sky, etc.

In the realm of the ignoble, I have never seen anything better than the three Maltese and an Italian who were with me in the coach from Constantine—drunk as Polacks, stinking like corpses, roaring like tigers. These gentlemen excelled in obscene jokes and gestures, accompanied by farts, belches, and much chewing of garlic, their pipes glowing in the dark. What a journey! What company! It was Plautus to the twelfth degree, lowlife par excellence.

At Philippeville, in a seaside garden full of roses in full bloom, I saw a fine Roman mosaic of two women, one riding a horse and the other a sea monster. The place was filled with exquisite silence: nothing could be heard but the sound of the sea. The gardener, a Negro, brought an old watering-can and sprinkled the mosaic to bring out the lovely fresh colors. And then I left.[4]

And you, old chap, what are you up to? Are you beginning something? My greetings to Léonie[5] and the old bridge at Mantes with the mill creaking beside it. My next letter will be longer. I expect one from you at the end of the week, and I embrace you tenderly, mon pauvre vieux.

1. The Carthaginian moon goddess, a great presence in *Salammbô*.
2. See Volume I. Flaubert considered Mme Foucaud his true sexual initiatress, when he was nineteen. She was the inspiration for his early novel, *Novembre*, published only posthumously.
3. Where Flaubert had his Paris apartment, at no. 42.
4. Flaubert's notebook gives a few more details: "Arrived at Philippeville 6 A.M. [April 19, 1858]. Visited the garden belonging to Mr. Nobeli, overlooking the sea. Fragrant with rosebushes in bloom. A mosaic, found on the site, shows two women, one seated and driving an eagle-beaked sea monster, another seated on and driving a horse, iris between its ears like red flames; a third, a dancer, with anklets; feet and legs remarkable for their form and movement, the right crossing over the left; the background dotted with fish. The Negro gardener who showed it to me goes to fill a watering can and sprinkles the mosaic to make it brighter. I am filled with tender feelings here in this garden. The weather hazy, soldiers on the terrace opposite playing fanfares."
5. Léonie Leparfait, Bouilhet's companion. Bouilhet adopted her illegitimate son, Philippe Leparfait, whose father was believed to be Philippe de Chennevières (1820–1899), directeur des Beaux-Arts in the 1870s. (J.B.)

To Ernest Feydeau

Tunis, Saturday, May 8, 1858

It's very good of you to write to me, but I'm *exhausted*, and unless you long for my death don't ask for letters. This week I was at Utica, and I spent four entire days at Carthage, from eight to fourteen hours on horseback every day. At five this afternoon I leave in a caravan for Bizerta, riding a mule: I scarcely have time to make notes. Don't worry about me: there's nothing to be afraid of in Tunisia. The worst of the inhabitants hang around the city gates; it isn't a good idea to frequent those regions at night, but I think the European residents here are egregious cowards. I discharged my dragoman because he was similarly afflicted, trembling at every bush—not that that kept him from robbing me at every step. His successor, beginning today, is a hideous Negro, very black.

I miss you greatly. You'd enjoy it here—we'd enjoy it together. The sky is splendid. At evening and in the morning the lake of Tunis is covered with flocks of flamingos: when they fly off they're like a mass of little pink and black clouds.

I spend my evenings in Moorish cafés listening to Jewish singers and watching the obscenities of Karagöz.[1]

The other day, on my way to Utica, I slept among dogs and chickens in a Bedouin douar, between two walls made of cow dung; all night I heard jackals barking. In the morning I hunted scorpions with a gentleman addicted to that form of sport. And with a whip I killed a snake a yard or so long that was coiling itself around the legs of my horse. Such is the sum of my exploits.

I shall probably leave here for Constantine *by land*—it is feasible—with two of the Bey's horsemen. At the [Algerian] frontier, four days from here, the commanding officer at Suk Ahras will give me some men to take me on to Constantine. This journey is easier going from Tunis to Constantine than from Constantine to Tunis, yet few Europeans have done it, so far. In this way I'll have seen *all* the places I'll be writing about in my book.

. . .

1. Karagöz ("Black Eye") is the Turkish name both of the traditional Turkish-Arab-Egyptian shadow-theatre (puppets manipulated behind a transparent lighted screen), and of one of its two principal stock characters—much like "Punch and Judy." Its popularity began in the seventeenth century. Even by Flaubert's time it was declining; today it is occasionally revived, usually on television. In his Carthaginian notes, Flaubert describes the performance he saw:

"[When we arrived] in the long, narrow, very crowded theatre there was as yet nothing taking place behind the transparency. In the narrow space between two of the benches a man was performing a rhythmic walk, lifting his knees very high, or dancing without flexing his knees, shaking his belly Egyptian style (very inferior version). What was good was the three musicians, who from time to time, at regular intervals, took up what he was saying, or rather *reflected* it quite loudly, like a chorus; that was very dramatic, and made me feel I understood. As for Karagöz, his penis is about the size of a wooden beam; it soon ceases to seem indecent. Karagöz has several identities: I think the type is falling into decay. The whole thing is to display the penis as much as possible. The biggest had a bell at the tip, which rang with every movement of the haunches; that aroused much laughter. What a deplorable spectacle for a man of taste! and for a gentleman with principles!"

◇-◇-◇-◇-◇

For two more weeks Flaubert remained close to the site of Carthage, filling his notebooks; then he returned westward, bound for Constantine, this time traveling overland as he had announced in his letter to Feydeau. Riding with armed escorts, sleeping outdoors or in native inns, devoured by fleas but happy in his adventure, he spent a week in the mountains and valleys of the Atlas, continuing to make notes on encounters and on the topography he would later describe, in *Salammbô*, in his narrations of the marches of the Mercenaries. On June 2 he took ship at Stora, reached Marseilles on the fourth, and within a week, after spending a few days in Paris, was back at Croisset.

There he "slept for three days" and went over the notes he had brought back. Notes on the vestiges of Carthage, on the colors of North African land and sea, and on wayside encounters, with details that he might or might not use. On eating lion, for instance:

> [*Bizerta.*] Father Jérémie, jovial . . . chéchia on the back of his head, hair ruffled, witty, very comical, setting a great value on "bons vivants" (his word). Formerly curate at Boufarik. He has eaten lion, jackal, panther, hyena; he claims that lion is excellent fare. He is raising a wild boar, "having only four parishioners," and is much occupied with silkworms.

Or on entertainment, much inferior to what he had enjoyed in Egypt:

> [*Tunis,*] *Thursday,* [*May*] 20. Evening party at the house of M. de Kraft. Jewish musicians, whom I had already seen in a café. M. de Montès, Colonel Caligaris, Dubois, Cavalier. In the patio . . . a high torch standing in the middle, like a church candelabrum. Ra'hel, small, thin, long nose, eyebrows completely joined by copper-red paint. The toad dance. Ass smaller than all the rest. Very free behavior. Marsen's servant in red vest, combines both tastes. Left at 2 A.M.
> Friday. Visit to Ra'hel near the leather souk. Stairs. Shit. One room at the back, one to the left. The whores in the salon! A handsome gold necklace of large rings, very flat. My room! Stones! Two stones to hold the door shut; thin calico curtain at the back. Shout-

10

ing of Jews outside. The women block the window with a pillow. Big bed with mosquito netting, horrible sheets, red-striped blanket. Filthy mattress. Daylight visible through the walls—fear of bringing the house down while fucking. Continuous frying-pan movement. Cavalier arrived ten minutes after me—laughter! And Marsen had been there just before us.

He added more notes,[1] and ended the whole with an invocation:

Midnight, Saturday–Sunday, June 12–13, [1858]

Oh, may I be suffused with all the energies of nature I have inhaled, and may they breathe forth in my book! Powers of artistic emotion, come to my aid! Help me! Beauty must guide my pen, but all must be living and true! Have pity on my purpose, oh God of all souls! Give me Strength—and Hope![2]

1. A visitor to the region of ancient Carthage who is familiar with Flaubert's Tunisian notebooks (now in the Bibliothèque Historique de la Ville de Paris) is impressed by the accuracy of their topography and archaeology. Today, recent excavations of the upper part of the city, particularly of its principal ascending street, confirm other details in the novel, which Flaubert took from ancient authors. Following the death, in 1931, of his niece and heir, Mme Caroline Hamard Commanville Grout, the notes of his reading were sold at auction in several lots and widely dispersed. A portfolio in the Pierpont Morgan Library, New York, includes some of these notes, as well as replies to Flaubert from correspondents in Tunisia and France to whom he wrote for information.

The history of the region, together with the literary nostalgia of the former French protectorate, has produced place-names evocative of Flaubert's brief visit. A station on the railway line which serves those suburbs of Tunis now occupying the site of ancient Carthage is named Salammbô. Another, Amilcar, recalls not only the first chapter of Flaubert's novel, but particularly its opening sentence: "It was a Mégara, suburb of Carthage, in the gardens of Hamilcar." Amilcar is, in fact, close to the present site of beautiful private gardens between that stop and the next—the picturesque Arab village of Sidi-Bou-Saïd. The ancient Mégara is now La Marsa, an adjacent community.

2. "Que toutes les énergies de la nature que j'ai aspirées me pénètrent et qu'elles s'exhalent dans mon livre. A moi, puissance de l'émotion plastique! resurrection du passé, à moi! à moi! Il faut faire, à travers le Beau, vivant et vrai quand même. Pitié pour ma volonté, Dieu des âmes! donne-moi la Force—et l'Espoir!"

❖❖❖❖❖

TO MADEMOISELLE LEROYER DE CHANTEPIE

Croisset, July 11 [1858]

.   .   .

Living in a house is one of the sadder aspects of civilization. I think we were made to sleep on our backs, looking up at the stars. In a few years mankind (thanks to new developments in locomotion) will revert to its nomadic state. People will travel the world from one end to the other, as they used to cross prairies and mountains: this will calm their spirits and inflate their lungs . . .

I thought of you from time to time down on the African coast, where I enjoyed myself thinking a lot of historical thoughts and meditating on the book I am going to write. I breathed deeply of the air, and stared long at the sky, the mountains, and the sea. I needed to! I've been stifling since my return from the East six years ago.[1]

I made a thorough exploration of the country around Tunis and the ruins of Carthage, I crossed the Regency from east to west, reentering Algeria via the frontier at El Kef, and crossed the eastern part of the province from Constantine to Philippeville, where I reembarked. I was alone the whole time, very well, on horseback, and in high good spirits.

And now, everything I had done on my novel has to be done over: I was on the wrong track entirely. So it turns out that a little over a year since I first had the idea for the book, and after working hard on it most of that time, I am still only at the beginning. It will be a weighty thing to execute, I assure you. For me, at least. It's true that my intentions are not middling. I am tired of ugly things and sordid environments. *Bovary* inspired me with a long disgust for bourgeois ways. Now I'm going to live, perhaps for several years, in a splendid subject, far from the modern world I'm fed up with. What I am undertaking to do is insane, and will have no success with the public. No matter! One must write for oneself, first and foremost. Only that way does one stand a chance of producing something good . . .

1. It was in June 1851 that Flaubert had returned from France after his eighteen-month "voyage en Orient" with Maxime DuCamp.

To Ernest Feydeau

[Croisset,] Saturday night [August 28, 1858]

. . .

You send me news of the arts: let me repay you with an item from the country.

The Croisset baker has, as assistant breadmaker, a lad of considerable corpulence. Maestro and servant bugger. They knead each other in the heat generated by their oven. But (and here begins the nice part) the aforesaid baker has a wife, and the two gentlemen, not satisfied with ——ing[1] each other, join forces in beating the poor woman. They go at it so lustily—both for fun and out of cunt-hatred (*système Jérôme*)[2]—that the lady is sometimes bedridden for days. Yesterday, however, for the first time, she turned on them with a knife, and the arms of both of them are in horribly sliced condition. Such are the ways of our good rustics—charming, no?

. . .

You ask me what I'm doing. During the past two weeks I have read, without interrupting my work, and *for* my work, six *Mémoires* of the Academy of Inscriptions, two volumes of Ritter,[3] Samuel Bochart's *Chanaan*,[4] and various parts of Diodorus.[5] I can't possibly be finished before two years at the earliest, and once again everybody will have it in for me.

No matter. I think this is going to be a very lofty enterprise, and since our aspirations weigh more heavily in the scale of values than our works, and our desires more heavily than our actions, I may acquire considerable merit—who knows?

1. Dubiously effective censoring of the autograph or editorial copy here, perhaps by Flaubert's niece. The autograph, like those of most of the letters to Feydeau, has disappeared.

2. The reference is to "L'Histoire de Jérôme," in Sade's *Justine*.

3. Karl Ritter, German geographer (1779–1859): *Die Erdkunde im Verhältnis zur Natur und zur Geschichte des Menschen* [Geography in Relation to Nature and World History], 20 vols., 1817–1858. Only the volumes on Africa, doubtless those read by Flaubert, had been translated into French.

4. Samuel Bochart, French scholar (1599–1667). The *Chanaan* is part of his *Geographia Sacra*.

5. Diodorus Siculus, Greek historian of the age of Julius Caesar and Augustus.

◇◇◇◇◇

The reader will hereafter be temporarily spared further annotation of Flaubert's vast, continuous reading for *Salammbô*. Indication of its extent will be copiously afforded in Chapter II.

◇◇◇◇◇

To Ernest Feydeau

Croisset, Sunday [December 19, 1858]

You ask me what I'm up to. Here's your answer.

I get up at noon and go to bed between three and four in the morning. I take a nap about five in the afternoon. I scarcely see the daylight—a horrible way to live in winter—and am thus totally unable to distinguish the days of the week or day from night. My existence is extravagantly unsociable; I love its uneventfulness, its quiet. It is complete and objective nothingness. And I am not working too badly, at least for me. In eighteen days I have written ten pages, read *The Retreat of the Ten Thousand*[1] in its entirety, and analyzed six treatises by Plutarch, the great hymn to Ceres (in the Homeric poems, in Greek), and Erasmus's *Encomium moriae*; plus Tabarin[2] at night, or rather in the morning, in bed, for diversion. So there you are. And in two days I'll begin Chapter III. This will be Chapter IV if I retain the preface; but no—no preface, no explanation. Chapter I took me two months last summer. Nevertheless I shan't hesitate to scrap it even though in itself I'm very fond of it.

I'm in a terrific funk because in Chapter III I'm going to repeat an effect already used in Chapter II.[3] Clever writers would think up tricks to conjure the difficulty away, but I'm going to plunge straight into it, like an ox. Such is my system. But how I'll sweat! And how I'll despair while putting said passage together! Seriously, I think that no one has *ever* undertaken a subject so difficult as regards style. At every line, every word, language fails me, and the insufficiency of vocabulary is such that I'm very often forced to change details. It will kill me, my friend, it will kill me. No matter: it begins to be tremendous fun.

I've finally achieved the erection, Monsieur, by dint of self-flagellation and masturbation. Let's hope there's joy to come . . .

1. Xenophon's *Anabasis.*
2. Tabarin was a seventeenth-century Parisian street comedian. A collection of farces and dialogues attributed to him had recently been reprinted.
3. Max Aprile points out that this refers to Flaubert's numbering of chapters in early drafts, not in the volume as published: "Flaubert's fear of repetition therefore refers to the Hannon and Giscon episodes, Chapters II and IV." (Personal communication.)

To Ernest Feydeau
[Croisset] Tuesday evening [January 11, 1859]

No, my friend! I do not admit that women are competent to judge the human heart. Their understanding of it is always personal and relative. They are the hardest, the cruelest, of creatures. "Woman is the desolation of the righteous," said Proudhon. I have little admiration for said gentleman, but that aphorism is nothing less than a stroke of genius.

As far as literature is concerned, women are capable only of a certain delicacy and sensitivity. Everything that is truly sublime, truly great, escapes them. Our indulgence toward them is one of the reasons for the moral abasement that is prostrating us. We all display an inconceivable cowardice toward our mothers, our sisters, our daughters, our wives, and our mistresses. Never has the tit been responsible for more kinds of abject behavior than now. And the church (Catholic, Apostolic, and Roman) has given proof of the greatest good sense in promulgating the dogma of the Immaculate Conception—it epitomizes the emotional life of the nineteenth century. Poor scrofulous swooning century, with its horror of anything strong, of solid food, its fondness for lolling in the laps of women, like a sick child!

"Woman, what have I to do with thee?"[1] is a remark that I find more splendid than any of the celebrated sayings of history. It is the cry of the pure intellect, the brain's protest against the womb. And it has this to be said for it: it has always aroused the indignation of idiots.

Our "mother-cult" is one of those things that will inspire future generations to helpless laughter. So too our reverence for "love": this will be thrown into the same trash-bag with the "sensibility" and "nature" of a hundred years ago.

Only one poet, in my opinion, understood these charming animals—namely, the master of masters, Shakespeare the omniscient. His women are *worse* or *better* than his men. He portrays them as overenthusiastic beings, never as reasonable ones. That is why his feminine characters are at once so ideal and so true.

In short, *never* pay any attention to what they say about a book. For them, temperament is everything—the occasion, the place, the *author*. As for knowing whether a detail (exquisite or even sublime in itself) strikes a false note in relation to the whole—no! A thousand times no!

I note with pleasure that printer's ink is beginning to stink in your nostrils. In my opinion it is one of the filthiest inventions of mankind. I resisted it until I was thirty-five, even though I began scribbling at eleven. A book is something essentially organic, a part of ourselves. We tear out a length of gut from our bellies and serve it up to the bourgeois. Drops of our hearts' blood are visible in every letter we trace. But once our work is printed—goodbye! It belongs to everybody. The crowd tramples on us. It is the height of prostitution, and the vilest kind. But the platitude is that it's all very fine, whereas to rent out one's ass for ten francs is an infamy. So be it! . . .

1. John 2:4.

To Mademoiselle Leroyer de Chantepie

Croisset, February 18, 1859

. . .

It's a sad story about your relative, the girl driven insane by religious ideas, but not an uncommon one. A robust constitution is needed if one is to scale the peaks of mysticism without losing one's head. And then the whole thing involves (especially for women) questions of temperament, which complicate the malady. Don't you see that they are all in love with Adonis? The eternal bridegroom is what they yearn for. Whether ascetic or lustful, they dream of love, *le grand amour*; and in order to be cured (at least temporarily) what they need is not an idea, but something tangible—a man, a child, a lover. That may sound cynical to you. But human nature is not my invention. I am convinced that the most raging material appetites express themselves unwittingly in

15

outbursts of idealism, just as the most obscene carnal excesses are engendered by pure desire for the impossible, ethereal aspiration toward supreme bliss. Besides, neither I nor anyone else knows the meaning of those two words: "soul" and "body"—nor where one leaves off and the other begins. We are aware of certain *drives*, and that is all. Materialism and spiritualism still weigh too heavily on the study of man to permit an impartial investigation of all these phenomena. The anatomy of the human heart is as yet uncharted. So how can you expect it to be cured? To have embarked on such studies will remain the nineteenth century's sole claim to fame. The historical sense is a very new thing in the world. Ideas will now be studied like facts; beliefs dissected like organisms. There exists an entire school that is quietly working on these things, and it will bring results, I am sure.

Do you read Renan's splendid books? Do you know Lanfrey's, or Maury's?[1]

I have had occasion recently to return to those psychomedical studies that so fascinated me ten years ago, when I was [first] writing my *Saint Anthony*. In connection with my *Salammbô* I have been investigating hysteria and mental derangement. There are treasures to be discovered in those fields. But life is short and Art is long, indeed nearly impossible when one is writing in a language that is worn to the point of being threadbare, so worm-eaten that it frays at every touch. What discouragement, what anguish, the love of Beauty brings! Besides—I have undertaken something that is unachievable. No matter: if I stimulate a few noble imaginations I'll not have wasted my time. My task is about a quarter done. Still two years' work ahead.

1. Pierre Lanfrey (1828–1877), French historian and politician, republican, author of works of an anticlerical and rationalizing tendency.

Alfred Maury (1817–1892), professor at the Collège de France, who wrote studies of psychology and religion and collaborated with Napoleon III on the latter's biography of Julius Caesar. He was later appointed Director General of the National Archives. (See Flaubert's letter to Maury of August 20, 1866.)

To ERNEST FEYDEAU

[Croisset, early August 1859 (?)]

. . .

I don't think that everything can be said well. Some ideas are impossible (for example those which are hackneyed, or radically wrong), and since *style is merely a manner of thinking*, if your conception is weak your writing will never be strong. For instance: I have just recorrected my fourth chapter. It is a tour de force (I think) of conciseness and clarity if one examines it sentence by sentence; which doesn't keep said chapter from being utterly boring and seeming very long and very dim, because the concept, the basis, or the plan (I don't know what, exactly) has a hidden defect—which I will ferret out. Style *underlies* words as much as it is embodied in them. It is as much the soul of a work as its flesh.

Tonight I am going to begin my sixth chapter. I have thus reached the end of my first third; and yet there still remains much in it that will have to be changed, I'm sure.

Oh, my friend, don't fall into that easy old cliché that is such a plague to me: "You're lucky to be able to work without pressure, thanks to having private means." My fellow writers are constantly throwing in my face the few francs of income that keep me from starving. It's easier to do that than to imitate me. I mean, to live as I do: (1) in the country three-quarters of the year; (2) without a wife (a rather delicate little point, but considerable), without friends, horse, or dog—in short, without any of the attributes of human life; (3) and then, for me everything outside the work itself counts for nothing. Success, time, money, publication, are relegated to the lowest level of my mind, off in some very vague horizons that are of no concern to me whatever. All that seems to me dull as dishwater, and unworthy (I repeat the word, *unworthy*) of exciting one's brain about.

The impatience of literary folk to see themselves in print, acted, known, praised, I find astonishing—like a madness. That seems to me to have no more to do with a writer's work than dominoes or politics. Voilà.

Anybody can do as I do—work just as slowly as I, and better. All you have to do is rid yourself of certain tastes, and sacrifice a few pleasures. I am not at all virtuous, but I am consistent. And though I have great needs (which I never mention), I would rather be a wretched monitor in a school than write four lines for money. I could have been rich; I said fuck all that, and I continue to live like a Bedouin, in my desert and my pride. Shit, shit, *shit:* such is my motto. And I embrace you tenderly.

To Mademoiselle Amélie Bosquet[1]

Wednesday morning [November (?), 1859]

You mistook the *sense* of my last letter. And I doubtless overdid my reproaches, since you ask me to excuse you. One thing is sure: the pleasure afforded by the amends is greater than the pain caused by the offense. Only women know how to wound and how to caress! We men are heavy-handed in comparison.

My liaison with Mme Colet left me with no lasting "wound," in the usual emotional and deep sense of the word. What remains is rather the memory (and, even now, the sensation) of prolonged irritation. Her book has been the crowning touch. Add to it the comments, questions,

17

jokes, and allusions I have been subjected to since the publication of said work. When I saw that you, too, were joining in the game I lost my patience a little, I admit, because in public I keep my dignity. Don't you see? Don't think I hold it against you. No, I embrace you warmly for the nice things you say to me. Please believe me.

Why *did* you join in the taunts? Why did you act like the others? "They" have a cut-and-dried opinion of me that nothing will eradicate (it's true that I do nothing to undeceive them), namely: that I'm utterly devoid of feeling, that I'm a buffoon, a womanizer (a kind of Romantic Paul de Kock),[2] something between a bohemian and a pedant. Some even suspect me of being a habitual drunkard, etc. etc.

But I think I am neither a hypocrite nor a poseur. No matter: people always take me for something I'm not. Whose fault is that? Mine, no doubt? I am more elegiac than people think: I pay a price for my five feet eight inches[3] and my ruddy complexion.

I am still as timid as an adolescent, and quite capable of preserving withered bouquets as keepsakes. In my youth I *loved*, inordinately— loved without any return, deeply, silently.[4] Nights spent gazing at the moon, dreams of eloping with a beloved, of travels in Italy, dreams of conquering fame for *her* sake, spasms at the scent of a perfumed shoulder, sudden blanchings when eye met eye—I have experienced all that, and know it well. In the heart of each of us there is royal chamber. I have walled mine up, but it is there.

Everyone has talked *ad nauseam* about the prostitution of women. But not a word about that of men. I have suffered the tortures of a whore, as has every man who after loving long has wanted to love no longer.

And then one reaches the age when one is *afraid*, afraid of everything—of a liaison, of being shackled, interfered with: one longs for happiness, yet dreads it. Isn't it so?

And yet it would be so easy to live a tolerable life! But we seek emotions that are intense, excessive, unqualified, whereas only the composite, the grayed, is practicable. Our grandfathers, and especially our grandmothers, had more sense than we, no?

It seems to me that our little disagreement has made us even better friends than before. Is this an illusion? No: you have learned that I am more serious than I seem, and I have come to know how very good you are. So let us exchange a long, firm handshake.

Tell me about yourself, when you have nothing better to do. Work as much as you can: that is still the best way. The moral of *Candide*, "we must cultivate our gardens," must be the rule for people like us, those "who haven't found the answer." Does one, in fact, ever find it? And when one does, one seeks something else.

1. A feminist writer in Rouen. Louise Colet, the mistress with whom Flaubert had broken in 1855, and who had thereupon depicted him unfavorably in a novel, *Une His-*

toire de Soldat (1856), now in 1859 had renewed the attack in another novel, *Lui*. Mlle Bosquet was indiscreet enough to refer to this in a letter to Flaubert. His sharp reply to which he alludes here is missing from the collection of his letters that she gave to the Municipal Library of Rouen in 1892.

In August 1859, Flaubert wrote to Ernest Feydeau, whose novel, *Fanny*, Louise Colet had recently reviewed: "As for the widow Colet, she has plans, I don't know just what. But she has plans. I know her through and through. Her praising *Fanny* was done for a *purpose*. Now that you've written to her she'll invite you to come to see her. Go, but be on your guard. She's a pernicious creature. If you want a good laugh, read her *Histoire de Soldat* ... You'll recognize your friend in it, painted in odious colors—an attempt to smear. And that's not all. She has made me the subject of an unperformed play and a number of short pieces. All because I withdrew *my* 'piece' from her ..."

2. Charles-Paul de Kock (1794–1871), the author of best-selling humorous novels about the French bourgeoisie.

3. At this height Flaubert was so conspicuously taller than most Frenchmen of his time that he was sometimes called a "giant" or a "gendarme."

4. Flaubert is probably thinking of Elise Schlesinger (see Volume I and pages 293–294 and 442–445 below).

To Madame Roger des Genettes[1]

[1859 or 1860?]

.   .   .

I pity you on the death of your friend. It's no light matter to lose those we love. I myself have wrapped one after another in their shrouds, sat through many a wake. The body of the man I loved best in the world practically fell apart in my hands.[2] Once you have kissed a corpse on the forehead, something of it always remains on your lips— an infinite bitterness, an aftertaste of annihilation that nothing ever effaces. One must look up at the stars, and say "There perhaps I will go." But I am repelled by the way all religions speak about God—they treat him with such certainty, such nonchalance and familiarity. I am especially revolted by priests, who have his name on their lips incessantly. It's like a chronic sneeze with them: "God's goodness," "God's anger," "an offense against God." That's the way they talk. It means thinking of him as a man, and, what's worse, as a bourgeois. They still persist in bedecking him with attributes, the way savages put feathers on their fetish. Some paint infinity in blue, others in black. It's all at the level of cannibals. We're still at the stage of browsing on grass and going on all fours, despite our balloons. The idea of God that mankind has made for itself doesn't go beyond that of an oriental monarch surrounded by his court. The religious concept is thus several centuries behind the social, and there are plenty of clowns pretending to swoon with admiration before it.

1. Mme Edma Roger des Genettes, so graceful that she was known as "La Sylphide," had become for a time the mistress of Louis Bouilhet after reading aloud from his poem *Melaenis* in Louise Colet's salon in 1852. Later she became Flaubert's friend and corre-

spondent. His letters to her exist chiefly in the form of copies in her hand, undated and incomplete.

2. A reference to Flaubert's helping enshroud his friend Alfred Le Poittevin in April 1848 (see Volume I, p. 94).

To Madame Roger des Genettes

[1861?]

. . .

A good subject for a novel is one that comes all at once, in a single spurt. It is a matrix idea, from which all the others derive. An author is not at all free to write this or that. He does not choose his subject. That is what the public and the critics do not understand. Therein lies the secret of masterpieces—in the concordance of the subject and the author's temperament.

You are right: Lucretius must be spoken of with respect. I see only Byron as comparable with him, and Byron has neither his seriousness nor his sincerity in sorrow. The melancholy of the antique world seems to me more profound than that of the moderns, all of whom more or less imply that beyond the dark void lies immortality. But for the ancients that "black hole" was infinity itself; their dreams loom and vanish against a background of immutable ebony. No crying out, no convulsions—nothing but the fixity of a pensive gaze. With the gods gone, and Christ not yet come, there was a unique moment, from Cicero to Marcus Aurelius, when man stood alone. Nowhere else do I find that particular grandeur. But what makes Lucretius intolerable is his physics, which he presents as certainty. It is because he didn't *doubt* enough that he is weak: he wanted to explain, to conclude. If he had had only the *spirit* of Epicurus, without his system, all aspects of his work would have been immortal and *radical*. No matter: our modern poets are meager thinkers compared with such a man.

To Charles Baudelaire

Croisset, Monday [June 25, 1860]

You are very kind, my dear Baudelaire, to have sent me such a book.[1] Everything about it pleases me—the topic, the style, even the paper. I have read it very attentively. But first of all I must thank you for introducing me to so charming a man as le sieur De Quincey! How one loves him!

Here—to get the "but" over with quickly—is my sole objection: it seems to me that with a subject you have treated so loftily, in a study that marks the beginning of a new science, a work of observation and induction, you have (and repeatedly) insisted too much (?) on "the Spirit of Evil." One senses something like a leaven of Catholicism here and there. I would have preferred you not to condemn hashish, opium, overindulgence. How do you know what may ultimately come of all that?[2]

But note that this is merely my personal opinion, which I do not insist on at all. I refuse utterly to admit the right of criticism to substitute its opinion for another's. And what I object to in your book is perhaps what constitutes its originality and the very mark of your talent. Not to resemble one's neighbor: that is everything.

Now that I have confessed the sum of my grievance, I can scarcely begin to tell you how excellent I found your book from beginning to end. The style is very lofty, very assured, very incisive. In "Le Poëme du haschisch" I deeply admire pages 27–33, 51–55, 76,[3] and everything that follows. You have found the way to be classical while remaining the transcendent Romantic we love.

As for the part called "Un mangeur d'opium," I don't know what you owe to De Quincey, but in any case it is a *marvel*. I know of no figure more sympathetic than he, to me at least.

These particular drugs have always raised great longings in me. I even own some excellent hashish, prepared by Gastinel, the pharmacist. *But I am afraid of it.* For which I blame myself.[4]

Do you know, in Escayrac de Lauture's *Soudan*,[5] an entire particular theogony and cosmogony invented by an opium-smoker? I remember it as being "quite something," but I prefer Mr. De Quincey. Poor man! What became of Miss Ann?[6] Thanks are due you, too, for the little note about moral critics. I for one was touched, or rather flattered in my sensitive spot.

I impatiently await the new *Fleurs du mal.**[7] How hard you work! and how well!

Adieu—here's a handshake that will dislocate your shoulder.

* Here my objection is not valid, for the poet has the perfect right to think what he likes. But a scientist? Perhaps I'm talking nonsense? Nevertheless I think I know what I mean. We'll talk about it another time.

1. Baudelaire's new volume, *Les Paradis artificiels*, whose two principal parts are "Le Poëme du haschisch," a prose poem about hashish taking, its effects and aftereffects; and "Un mangeur d'opium," an adaptation and partial translation of Thomas De Quincey's *Confessions of an English Opium-Eater* and *Suspiria de Profundis*. There are interesting discussions of *Les Paradis artificiels* in Enid Starkie's *Baudelaire* (London: Faber and Faber, 1957; New York, New Directions, 1958), and in Alethea Hayter's *Opium and the Romantic Imagination* (London: Faber and Faber, 1968).

2. Flaubert means "Who knows what beautiful works of art may result from taking opium and hashish?" (J.B.)

3. Pages 27–33 of the first edition of *Les Paradis artificiels* provide a description of hashish, the circumstances under which it is most safely taken, and some of its effects. Pages 51–55 treat of hallucinations that may be caused by hashish. On pages 76 et seq. Baudelaire describes the human type "whom the eighteenth century called *l'homme sensible* [the

sensitive man], whom the Romantic school dubbed *l'homme incompris* [the incomprehensible man], and whom bourgeois families and the bourgeoisie in general commonly stigmatize with the epithet *original.*" For the impression made on Flaubert by the terms in this last passage, see his letter to Laure de Maupassant, p. 34.

4. Flaubert is responding self-consciously to a passage in which Baudelaire says: "The man who has long been addicted to opium or hashish and is enfeebled by his long bondage, and who nevertheless has been able to find the energy necessary to free himself, seems to me like an escaped prisoner. He inspires me with more admiration than the prudent man who has never succumbed, having always been careful to avoid temptation."

J. B. Gastinel was professor of pharmacology in Cairo, author of works on hashish and opium.

5. *Le Désert et le Soudan,* by Comte d'Escayrac de Lauture (Paris, 1853).

6. The fifteen-year-old girl who was De Quincey's companion in the night streets of London, who brought him "port wine and spices" when he fainted, and whom he sought in vain on his return from Oxford. Baudelaire's words, in his paraphrase of De Quincey, are similar to Flaubert's: "Mais la pauvre Ann, qu'en est-il advenu?" De Quincey's are: "Meanwhile, what had become of Ann?"

7. Flaubert had seen, in his copy of *Les Paradis artificiels,* that the publisher advertised the first edition of *Les Fleurs du mal* as being "sold out" and announced the second as being in press. It was published in 1861. Actually, most of the first edition had been destroyed by court order following Baudelaire's conviction for "offense against public morality."

CHARLES BAUDELAIRE TO FLAUBERT

June 26, 1860

My dear Flaubert:

I thank you most heartily for your excellent letter. I was much struck by your observation, and after delving very sincerely into the memory of my daydreams I saw that I have always been obsessed by the impossibility of accounting for certain precipitate human actions or thoughts without the hypothesis of the intervention of an exterior evil force. That is a mighty confession, for which the entire confederated nineteenth century will not make me blush. Note, however, that I do not renounce the pleasure of changing my ideas or of contradicting myself.

One of these days, if I may, on my way to Honfleur I will stop at Rouen, but since I presume you are like me and hate surprises, I will give you ample notice.

You tell me that I work a great deal. Are you making fun of me? Many people, myself included, consider that I do very little. To *work* is to work ceaselessly, to renounce the senses, never daydream—and to be *pure will,* always in motion. Perhaps I shall reach that point.

All yours—your very devoted friend.

I have always dreamed of reading the *Temptation of Saint Anthony* in its entirety, and also another singular book which you have never published even in part (*November*).[1] And how goes *Carthage?*

1. Baudelaire had read the portions of *The Temptation of Saint Anthony* printed in Théophile Gautier's magazine *L'Artiste* for December 1856 and January 1857, and in his

review of *Madame Bovary* had called *The Temptation* "the secret chamber" of Flaubert's mind, "clearly the more interesting for poets and philosophers." Baudelaire did not live to see the final version, which was not published until 1874. Flaubert's short, youthful, very Romantic novel *November*, written when he was twenty, he would occasionally read to friends, but its publication would be only posthumous.

To Edmond and Jules de Goncourt

Croisset, July 3 [1860]

Since you are worried about *Carthage*, here is what I can tell you about it:

I think my eyes were bigger than my stomach. "Reality" is almost impossible with such a subject. There remains the dodge of "going poetic." But that would mean rehashing old stuff, familiar from *Télémaque* to *Les Martyrs*. I don't speak of the archaeological research, which mustn't call attention to itself or of the language to fit the form—a near impossibility. To be authentic I'd have to be obscure, talk gibberish, and stuff the book with notes; whereas if one sticks to "Ye Olde Frensh" literary tone one becomes banal. "Problème!" as Père Hugo would say.

Despite all that, I press on, though devoured by worries and doubts. I console myself with the thought that I'm attempting something worthwhile. That's the whole story.

The standard of the Doctrine[1] will be boldly unfurled this time, you may be sure. For this book proves nothing, states nothing. It is neither historical, nor satirical, nor humorous. However, it may be stupid.

I am now beginning Chapter VIII. After which there will remain seven to be done: I shan't be finished for at least another eighteen months.

It was not out of mere politeness that I congratulated you on your last book[2] and on the kind of work you do. I love history, madly. The dead are more to my taste than the living. Whence this lure of the past? Why have you made me fall in love with Louis XV's mistresses? This kind of love, incidentally, is something new in mankind. The historical sense dates from yesterday. And it is perhaps the best thing about the nineteenth century.

What are you going to do now? As for me, I am giving myself over to the Cabala, to the Mishna, to the military art of the ancients, etc. (a mass of reading that is of no service to me but which I undertake through excess of conscience and also, a little, for the fun of it); and I keep being distressed by the assonances I come upon in my prose. My life is as flat as the table I write on. Day follows day, and outwardly, at least, each is like the other.

In my periods of despair I dream of travel—a poor remedy.

The two of you seem to be virtuously bored in the bosom of your family, amid the delights of the country. I understand this condition, having very often endured it myself . . .

1. The doctrine of "Art for art's sake"—"L'Art pour l'art."
2. *Les Maitresses de Louis XV.*

◇-◇-◇-◇-◇

Flaubert's correspondence is slimmer concerning the progress of *Salammbô* than was the case with *Madame Bovary* (or will be, with *L'Éducation sentimentale*). During these years there is lacking any intimate correspondence with a woman to whom he could pour out his thoughts and his news as he once had to Louise Colet; most of his letters to Louis Bouilhet are lost, and, besides, the two friends saw each other at Croisset almost every Sunday. When Flaubert was not writing *Salammbô* he was reading for it. After three years of work the Carthaginian novel had inevitably become a kind of intoxication, and as in all intoxications tristesse was one of its elements. "I'm on a spree with antiquity, the way others gorge themselves on wine"; *"In order not to live*, I plunge into art, like a man in despair; I make myself drunk with ink as others do with wine" were two of the messages he sent to friends as the book advanced. "The things I'm reading," he told Ernest Feydeau, "weren't written to be amusing—Mosander, the Emperor Leo, Vegetius, Justus Lipsius"; and also among his authors were "Cedrenus, Socrates, Sozomen, Eusebius, and a treatise by M. Obry on the immortality of the soul among the Jews." "When people read *Salammbô* they won't think of the author, I hope. Few will suspect how depressed one had to be to undertake the resuscitation of Carthage: it's a Thebaid I was pushed into by my disgust with modern life."

In letters to friends he groaned about climactic scenes:

I shall soon be in the middle of my Chapter VIII (The Battle of the Macar) . . . The narration and description of a battle of antiquity is no small task, for one keeps falling into the eternal "epic battle" that all your high-toned writers have imitated from translations of Homer. There's no end to the asininities I keep skirting with this damned book. There will be a pretty weight off my mind when it's finished. If only I were at the end of my tenth chapter: that's where the fucking's about to begin.

At the moment, I'm overwhelmed with fatigue. I'm carrying two entire armies on my shoulders—thirty thousand men on one side, eleven thousand on the other, not counting the elephants with their elephantarchs, the camp followers, and the baggage!

Let's be ferocious ...! Let's pour brandy onto this century of sugar water. Let's drown the bourgeois in a grog eleven thousand degrees strong, and may his mouth burn! May he roar with pain!

My determination doesn't weaken, and as background the thing is becoming quite dainty: my men have already begun to *eat* each other. But imagine my anxiety: I am just now composing a sex scene—*the* sex scene of the book. It must be at once lewd, chaste, mystical, and realistic. A slavering such as was never seen, and yet the reader must see it.

The ferocities he was inventing, or gathering from old sources, stimulated Flaubert's habitual impatience with niceties. Writing to the Goncourts to congratulate them on their novel *Soeur Philomène*, he nevertheless complained, as one familiar with doctors and medical students, of the insipidity of its hospital scenes. "In the Rouen asylum there was an idiot known as 'Mirabeau,' who *for a cup of coffee* would copulate with dead women on the dissecting table. I'm sorry you couldn't have introduced this little episode into your book: it would have pleased the ladies. It's true that 'Mirabeau' was a coward, and unworthy of such an honor, for one day he funked it badly when faced with a woman who had been guillotined."

Indeed the composition of his Carthaginian slaughterings seems to have turned his thoughts back more often than usual to the hospital where his father had been surgeon-in-chief (his brother Achille was now codirector), and where he and his sister, as children, had peered through windows into the dissecting room at "the cadavers on their slabs."

<>-<>-<>-<>-<>

To Ernest Feydeau

[1861 (?)]

It's a strange thing, the way I'm attracted by medical studies. That's the way the intellectual wind is blowing nowadays. I long to dissect. If I were ten years younger I'd do just that. In Rouen there is an excellent man, the medical director of the insane asylum, who is giving a very curious little course for his close friends on hysteria, nymphomania, etc. I haven't the time to attend, and yet I've long been meditating a novel on insanity, or rather on how one becomes insane. I'm furious at being so slow a writer, at being stuck in all kinds of reading and revising. Life is short and Art is long! And then, what's the use? No matter: "We must cultivate our gardens." The day before his death Socrates in his prison asked a musician to teach him an air on the lyre. "What's the use," said the man, "since you're about to die?" "To know it before I die," answered Socrates. That is one of the loftiest things, morally speaking, that I know of, and I would rather have said it than taken Sebastopol.

. . .

◇-◇-◇-◇-◇

During the labors on *Salammbô* there was printed in Brussels and more or less openly "smuggled" into France a new book of ultra-Romantic poetry by one of Flaubert's old heroes, a political self-exile who was denied French publication—a book whose sonority, sweep, and blazing imagery, although Flaubert claimed it made him despair about his own work, quite clearly had the opposite effect, rousing him from his fatigue and giving him new wind. "Something magnificent has just been published," he wrote Mlle Leroyer de Chantepie, "*La Légende des siècles*, by Hugo. This colossal poet has never been so lofty. To you who love the ideal, and recognize it, I recommend the tales of chivalry in the first volume. Such enthusiasm, such strength, such language! It makes one despair, to write in the wake of such a man. Read this, gorge yourself on it, for it is beautiful and salutary."

To Ernest Feydeau, on the same theme: "What a poet! Good God, what a poet! I have just swallowed both volumes at one gulp. I miss you! I miss Bouilhet! I long for intelligent ears, since I feel like shouting three thousand lines such as have never before been written! And when I say shouting—No! *Yelling!* I'm beside myself! Tie me up! Ah, I feel better! Old Hugo has driven me mad!"

And to Jules Duplan: "What a tremendous, marvelous man! Never has anyone written poetry like *Les Lions!*"

When *Salammbô* was almost complete, Flaubert was willing to read parts of it to friends:

◇-◇-◇-◇-◇

To Edmond and Jules de Goncourt

Paris [shortly before May 6, 1861]

The solemn event will take place on Monday, grippe or no grippe. And I beg your pardon for having made you wait so long. Here is the program:

1. I'll begin my bellowing at four o'clock sharp. So come about three.

2. At seven, *dîner oriental.* You will be served human flesh, bourgeois' brains, and tigresses' clitorises sautéed in rhinoceros butter.

3. After coffee, resumption of Punic caterwauling until listeners' last gasp.

Does this suit you?

P.S. *Punctuality!* And *mystery!*

◇◇◇◇◇

The Goncourt brothers describe the "solemn event" in one of the worst-written entries in their immense *Journal* (that of May 6, 1861). The following is an attempt to render into readable English the opinions expressed in the unwieldy French of their first paragraphs:

> At four o'clock we arrive chez Flaubert, who has invited us to a grand reading of *Salammbô*, along with a painter whom we find there, Gleyre . . .
> From four to six, Flaubert reads in that resounding, bellowing voice of his, which has the lulling effect of a purr, but a *bronze* purr. At seven we dine . . . Then, after dinner and a pipe, the reading is resumed. Certain portions he doesn't read completely, but summarizes, and we go all the way through to the last completed chapter, Salammbô's fornication with Mâtho. By this time it is two in the morning.
> I am going to set down here what I sincerely think of this book by a man whom I love—there are few of whom I can say that—a man whose first book I admired.
> *Salammbô* does not come up to what I expected of Flaubert. His personality, so very carefully concealed in *Madame Bovary* as to be in fact absent from that very impersonal book, is here revealed—inflated, melodramatic, declamatory, luxuriating in overaccentuation and in crude, almost garish, colors. Flaubert sees the Orient, and the antique Orient, in the guise of present-day Algerian decor. Some of the effects are childish, others ridiculous. His struggle with Chateaubriand is the great defect, and deprives the book of originality: the reader is constantly put in mind of *Les Martyrs*.
> Immensely fatiguing are the eternal descriptions, the minute, button-by-button itemizations of every character and every costume, which destroy any possibility of grand group effects. All the effects are minuscular, concentrated on a single point; faces are obscured by trappings, feelings are lost in landscapes.
> Unquestionably, immense effort, infinite patience, and rare talent have gone into this attempt to reconstruct a vanished civilization in all its detail. But this project—in my opinion doomed from the start—Flaubert has not been able to illuminate. There are none of those revelations by analogy which enable one to discover something of the soul of a nation no longer in existence.
> . . . The feelings of his characters . . . are the banal feelings of mankind in general, not of Carthaginian mankind; and his Mâtho is basically nothing but an operatic tenor in a barbaric poem.

The Goncourts' verdict was prophetic.

With the end of *Salammbô* in sight, Flaubert was again exhausted and prey to depression. Again he confided in Ernest Feydeau.

◇◇◇◇◇

To Ernest Feydeau

Croisset, July 15, 1861

You say you're not very cheerful: well, I'm not precisely joyful, my-self. *Carthage* will make me die of fury yet. I am now full of doubts about the ensemble, about the general plan: I think there are too many military men about. That is historical, I know. But if a novel is as boring as a scientific book, *bon soir!* Good-bye Art! In short, I pass my time telling myself I'm an idiot, and my heart is full of sadness and bitter-ness.

But my will is as strong as ever, and I press on. Now I'm beginning the siege of Carthage. I'm lost in battle-engines—ballistas and scor-pions[1]—and it all passes my understanding as well as everybody else's. There has been a lot written about such things, but nothing very clear. To give you an idea of the nice little preparatory work that certain pas-sages call for, I have read since yesterday sixty pages (folio, double-column) of Justus Lipsius's *Politicorum*.

． ． ．

1. "Scorpions": the ancient name for a kind of catapult.

To Ernest Feydeau

Croisset, September 16, 1861

If I don't write, my friend, blame only my extreme lassitude. There are days when I haven't the strength to lift the pen. I sleep ten hours a night and two during the day. *Carthage* will be the end of me if it goes on, and I'm not yet at the end of *it*. Still, by the beginning of next month I'll have finished my siege; but it will take all of October to reach my Chapter XIV, which will be followed by a single short one. It's taking a long time, and the *writing* is becoming more and more impossible. In short, I'm like a toad squashed by a paving-stone, like a dog with its guts crushed out by a shit-wagon, like a clot of snot under a police-man's boot, etc. The military art of the ancients makes my head swim; I'm stuffed with it; I vomit catapults, have hoisting machines up my ass, and piss scorpions.

As for what everybody is going to say, do you want to know how I really feel? As long as they don't say it to my face, that's all I ask.

． ． ．

To Jules Duplan

Croisset, September 25, 1861

I'm physically tired, my muscles are sore. The poisoning of Bovary made me throw up into my chamber pot; the assault on Carthage is giving me aches and pains in my arms—such, nonetheless, is one of the more agreeable effects of my profession!—and then the thought of all the ineptitudes I'm going to hear offered about my book depresses me in advance. That prospect I found rather entertaining when I was in the middle of the book, but now it nauseates me.

. . .

To Jules de Goncourt

Croisset, Friday [early October 1861]

. . .

I'm at the end of my tether! The siege of Carthage, which I'm just finishing, has been the end of me. War machines are sawing my back in half, I'm sweating blood, pissing boiling water, shitting catapults and farting slingsmen's stones . . . I've succeeded in introducing, into the same chapter, a shower of shit and a procession of pederasts. I've stopped there. Am I being too sober? . . .

◇-◇-◇-◇-◇

For one of his last scenes he read treatises on the eating of human flesh, by Plutarch and by "Dr. Savigny, the doctor of the raft of the *Méduse*";[1] and in his 1862 New Year letter to the Goncourts: "I'm about half way through my last chapter. The funfair I'm producing will make honest citizens vomit with disgust. I'm piling horror on horror. Twenty thousand of my characters have just died from starvation and cannibalism; the rest will end up trodden by elephants and devoured by lions."

On April 24, 1862, he wrote from Paris to Mlle Leroyer de Chantepie: "Last Sunday, at seven in the morning, I finally finished my novel *Salammbô*. Corrections and copying will take another month, and I'll return here in mid-September to watch over publication, which will be in late October. But I'm at the end of my tether. I run a temperature every evening, and can scarcely hold a pen. The end was heavy work, very hard to bring off."

Only at the beginning of July could he write to the Goncourts: "*Salammbô* is finally off my hands. The fair copy went to Paris last Monday . . . The work was interminable, but I finally resigned myself to considering it finished. Now the umbilical cord is cut."

About publication, he had written to Mlle Leroyer de Chantepie in January 1862: "I don't know whether I'll publish immediately or wait until October, because of the great Hugo's *Les Misérables*, the first two volumes of which will appear next month. This colossal publication will continue until May (two volumes are to appear each month), and after May is a bad season for books. I think it would be a bit imprudent and impudent to risk appearing alongside something so great. There are certain people to whom one has to bow, and say 'Après vous, Monsieur.' Hugo is one of them."

But then he read *Les Misérables*.

1. The raft (made famous by Géricault's painting, exhibited in the Salon of 1819) carrying survivors of a shipwreck off the west coast of Africa in 1816.

◇-◇-◇-◇-◇

To Madame Roger des Genettes

[Croisset, July 1862]

[. . .][1] such threadbare stuff as *Les Misérables*. But it is not permitted to say anything against it. One would have the air of a police spy.[2] The author's position is impregnable, unassailable. I, who have spent my life adoring him, am at the present moment *indignant!* I have to explode.

I find neither truth nor greatness in this book. As for the style, it strikes me as deliberately incorrect and low. It's a way of flattering the populace. Hugo is taking pains to be nice to everybody: Saint-Simonians, Philippistes, and even innkeepers—the lot. [. . .] Let truth take care of itself, if it can. Where are there prostitutes like Fantine, convicts like Valjean, and politicians like the stupid cocos of the A.B.C.? Not once do you see them *suffer*, in the depths of their souls. They are puppets, figures made of sugar, beginning with Monseigneur Bienvenu. In his socialist mania Hugo slanders the church just as he slanders the poor. Where will you find a bishop who asks a *conventionnel*[3] for his blessing? Where will you find a factory that would discharge a girl for having had a baby? Etc. And the digressions! So many! So many! The passage about fertilizers must have enchanted Pelletan.[4] This book is designed for the catholic-socialist rabble, for all the philosophical-evangelical vermin. What a charming character is Monsieur Marius, living three days on a cutlet.[5] And Monsieur Enjolras, who has given only two kisses in his life,[6] poor chap! As for what they say, they talk very well, but all alike. Old Gillenormand's drivel, Valjean's last ravings, the humor of Cholomiès and Gantaise—it's all from the same mold. Innumerable quips and jokes, artificial high spirits, and never anything comic. Endless explanations of irrelevancies, and none whatever of things indispensable to the subject. But instead, sermons to show that universal suffrage is a very fine thing, that the masses must be educated: this repeated *ad nauseam*. Despite its good passages, and they are rare, this book is decidedly infantile. Observation is a secondary quality in literature, but a contemporary of Balzac and Dickens hasn't the right to depict society so falsely. The subject was certainly a very good one. But it called for such unemotional handling, such broad, scientific consideration! It's true that Père Hugo despises science. And he demonstrates just that . . .

Posterity will not forgive this man for wanting to be a thinker—a role contrary to his nature. What has he been brought to by his mania for posing as a philosopher! And such philosophy! That of Prud'homme, of Poor Richard, or Béranger.[7] He is no more a thinker than Racine or La Fontaine, of whom his opinion is not very high. That is, like them he summarizes the drift and substance of the banal ideas of his time, and with such persistence that he forgets his own work, and his art. That is my opinion [. . .] I am keeping it to myself, needless to say. Everyone who touches a pen must be too grateful to Hugo to allow himself to criticize. But—privately—I think the gods are growing old. What lack of regard for beauty! Just quote *one page* of the kind he used to write [. . .]

1. The autograph is mutilated here and at other spots marked [. . .].

2. That is, of siding with the government of Napoleon III against Hugo, who was in self-imposed political exile.

3. A member of the revolutionary National Convention of 1792–1795.

4. In this passage, a portion of the long introduction to Jean Valjean's journey through the Paris sewers, Hugo calls on French agriculturists, in the name of "progress," to learn to use human excrement as fertilizer. Eugène Pelletan, a left-wing politician, author of a work called *Le Monde marche,* was a leading celebrant of "progress"—a concept anathema to Flaubert.

5. "The first day he ate the meat, the second day he ate the fat, the third day he gnawed the bone" (third part, book 5, ch. 1: "Marius Indigent").

6. And both to a corpse (that of M. Mabeuf) (fourth pt. bk. 14, ch. 2; and fifth pt. bk. 1, ch. 22).

7. Joseph Prud'homme is the quintessential bourgeois, as invented by the writer and caricaturist Henri Monnier. Poor Richard is Benjamin Franklin's sayer of maxims, and Pierre-Jean Béranger was a popular versifier whom Flaubert despised.

<><><><><>

Worse than *Les Misérables,* from Flaubert's point of view, was soon to come from Hugo. In 1864 he would publish his magnificent *William Shakespeare,* full of explicitly socialistic pages, culminating in the famous sentence that one hopes Flaubert never saw: "Art for art's sake is perhaps splendid, but art for the sake of progress is more splendid still."

Salammbô was published on November 24, 1862.

One of Flaubert's gift copies went to Laure LePoittevin de Maupassant, sister of the long-dead friend of his youth, Alfred LePoittevin. After fifteen years, Laure's marriage to Gustave de Maupassant had disintegrated; she had obtained an agreement of separation and was now living with her two sons, Guy, twelve, and Hervé, six, in the seaside village of Étretat, near Le Havre, whence she wrote Flaubert her thanks.

<><><><><>

Etretat, December 6, 1862

I am very grateful to you, my dear Gustave, for sending me *Salammbô*, and my pleasure in first opening the book was a double one. It was proof that I was remembered by an old friend whose affection and regard I hold ever dear; and then the book, just out, was already famous, and I knew I would spend charming hours in the ancient Carthage you have so painstakingly resurrected. My first thought should have been to thank you, but I was drawn at once to your pages, and felt a compulsion to read and reread them before taking up my pen.

Here in the depths of my hermitage I lead a very active life: my sons' education, for which at the moment I am solely responsible, takes up much of my time; there are long walks, necessary to their health; and in addition, my mother is here just now. All this keeps me excessively busy, and my free moments become fewer and fewer. Still, I have pared away a bit here and there, and can now say that I know this novel, so much and so loudly spoken of in Paris that our Etretat cliffs ring with the echo. Before expressing the humble opinion of this provincial lady, before burning my bit of incense, let me say that your successes of today, as well as those of yesterday, invariably carry me back into the past, to memories of our poor Alfred, whom you too have never forgotten. Do you not feel, as I do, that he has had his part in all this, that some of it goes back to him, and to his praise—the first you had—of your early efforts? I can say things like this to you, and I am sure you agree with me that there are fond memories which occupy an increasingly greater place in our lives, instead of disappearing with time. My mother and I enjoy reliving all the past these long autumn evenings, and our hours together pass a bit sadly, but not without a certain charm. For the last few days, however, *Salammbô* has left us no time to chat: as soon as dinner is over, we sit around the fire, I take up the book, and begin to read aloud. My son Guy is by no means the least attentive member of the group: his eyes flash at your descriptions, some of them so charming and others so terrible, and I swear he hears the din of your battles and the trumpeting of your elephants. It goes without saying that my first reading was complete and for myself alone; now I am rereading it for the others as well as for myself, and very probably I shall go through it several times more. Your heroine is in my opinion a strikingly original creation: I think you fashioned her out of moonbeams. Around this woman—almost a goddess, and suffused with a mysterious perfume—the action develops, powerful, grandiose, terrible. We are present at the scenes you describe, we touch them with our fingers; and when at the end we see Mâtho fall, and see his living heart offered to the sun, we close our eyes against the unspeakable horror. It is Ribera, I think, who lent you his brush, and you will do well to keep it, for no one will be able to use it as you do. The few summer people

still here are besieging me with requests to lend them *Salammbô*; everyone wants to read it; so far, I have given it to no one—to avoid stirring
up jealousy.

Your dear mother has already learned from mine of some of the
troubles I have had; but to all you dear friends of other days I want to
say a little more. I have suffered greatly—I know you understand that:
but I am one of those who can make, and keep, a resolution, and I hope
you know and esteem me sufficiently to make it unnecessary for me to
say that this resolution is absolutely irrevocable, and that I shall know
how to preserve the dignity of my life. I am quite well situated here in
my pretty village, in my modest house, and in this new-found tranquillity there is a kind of happiness. My sons are growing up and devel-
oping; the elder is almost a man in his intelligence, and I have to work
hard to keep up with him—I who have grown so ignorant. I have
plunged into being a student again: I enjoy it, and it does me good. I
have greatly improved the appearance of my house this year—painted
it white, and made a garden that goes down to the Fécamp road. I
greatly hope that Madame Flaubert won't fail to pay us a visit next
summer; my mother is counting on all of you, and you must not deprive us of the joy your presence here would bring us.

.   .   .

To Laure de Maupassant

Paris [January 1863]

Your good letter touched me deeply, my dear Laure; it stirred old
feelings, old feelings that are perennially young. It brought back to me,
like a breath of fresh air, all the fragrance of my youth, in which our
poor Alfred had so large a place. That memory never leaves me. Not a
single day passes, I dare to say almost not an hour, without my thinking
of him. I am now acquainted with what are commonly called "the most
intelligent men of the day," and I compare them with him and find
them mediocre. Not one of them has ever dazzled me as your brother
used to. What excursions into the empyrean he used to take me on, and
how I loved him! I think I have never loved anyone, man or woman, as
much. When he married, I suffered torments of jealousy: it was a rupture, an uprooting. For me he died twice, and I carry his memory with
me constantly, like an amulet, like something private and intimate.
How often, in the weariness of my work, or during an interval in some
Paris theatre, or alone beside the fire at Croisset on a long winter evening, I am carried back to him—see him and hear him! With delight
and sadness mingled I think of our interminable conversations, talks
made up of everything from farce to metaphysics—the books we read,
our dreams, our high aspirations! If I am worth anything, it is certainly

because of those things. I have retained a great respect for that part of the past: we were not commonplace, and I have done my best not to fall short.

I can see all of you at your house in the Grande-Rue,[1] strolling in bright sunshine on the terrace, beside the aviary. I arrive, you greet me with the "Garçon's" great laugh,[2] etc. How I would love to talk about all that with you, dear Laure! It's a long time since we've seen each other. But I have followed your life from a distance, and have sensed and inwardly shared some of your sufferings. I have "understood" you, in sum. That's an old-fashioned word, a word from our day, from the school of the Romantics. It expresses everything I mean, and I hold to it.[3]

Since you mention *Salammbô*, you will be glad to hear that my Carthaginian girl is making her way in the world. My publisher announces the second edition for Friday.[4] Big and little newspapers are speaking about me; I'm the occasion for large quantities of stupid talk. Some critics vilify me, others exalt me. I have been called a "drunken helot," charged with "poisoning the air" around me, compared to Chateaubriand and Marmontel, accused of trying to get myself elected to the Institute; and one lady who had read my book asked a friend of mine whether Tanit wasn't a devil. Voilà! Such is literary fame. Gradually the mentions come at longer and longer intervals, then you're forgotten and it's over.

No matter: I wrote the book for a very limited number of readers, and it turns out that the public is snatching it up. Blest be the god of the book trade! I was very glad to know that you liked it, for you know how I value your intelligence, my dear Laure. You and I are not only old friends from childhood, but almost schoolmates. Do you remember our reading the *Feuilles d'automne*[5] together at Fécamp, in the little upstairs room? Please give my excuses to your mother and sister for not sending them the book, but I had a very limited number of copies, and many presents to make. Besides, I knew that Mme LePoittevin was with you at Etretat, and counted on your reading it aloud. Hug your sons for me—and to you, dear Laure, a double, long, hand-clasp, and fondest thoughts, from your old friend,

Gustave Flaubert

---

1. In Rouen.

2. A grotesque character, with a particularly revolting loud laugh, invented by the adolescent Flaubert and his school friends.

3. Cf. page 22, note 3.

4. The second printing of *Salammbô* was announced for January 10, 1863.

5. This volume of Victor Hugo's poems had been a bible for the young, Romantic Flaubert and his friends.

◇◇◇◇◇

Flaubert would always be proud of his "Carthaginian girl." "People don't sufficiently realize the trouble it takes to produce a well-made sentence," he wrote to Mme Roger des Genettes in 1873. "But what a joy when everything turns out right! I mean color, relief, harmony. You were speaking to me the other day about the Banquet of the Mercenaries. I can tell you I sweated over that chapter, but [when I finished reading it to you] you gave a cry of satisfaction that I can still hear. Ah, that little flat in the Boulevard du Temple was the scene of some great literary feasts!"

II

The Battle of
Salammbô
1862–1863

A S FLAUBERT wrote to Laure de Maupassant, *Salammbô* was
greeted with high praise and with vituperation. Victor Hugo,
Hector Berlioz,[1] Jules Michelet, George Sand, and Eugène Fromentin
were among those who sent him splendid letters about it; and to
Théophile Gautier, who praised the book in the newspaper *Le Moniteur
Universel,* Flaubert wrote: "If someone had told me, twenty years ago,
that the Théophile Gautier who filled my imagination would write such
things about me, I'd have gone mad with pride."[2] The book's detrac-
tors, a less distinguished group, proclaimed themselves disgusted by its
bloodiness, its eroticism, its "obscenity," its pictorial extravagance. Its
erudition made them uneasy; some called it exhibitionistic, others cast
doubt on its authenticity.

Flaubert's defense of *Madame Bovary* in a court of law in 1857 had
been a necessity, forced on him by the public prosecutor. Now, he was
to defend his new book twice—on both occasions voluntarily: first in a
personal letter to the literary critic Sainte-Beuve (who later printed the
letter, with Flaubert's permission); and second in a letter of rebuttal to a
scholar, written for publication in a newspaper.

These were the last occasions in Flaubert's career when he allowed
himself to reply in writing to adverse published comments on his work.
Both letters are noteworthy, and are included here as examples of Flaubertian polemics, as illustrations of Flaubert's code of literary morality,
and to suggest the extraordinary extent of his research for *Salammbô.*
They bring to mind what he had written to Ernest Feydeau just before
beginning his first pages: that in the realm of fiction it is possible to consider archaeological accuracy a "secondary" matter, whereas the opposite tendency, Flaubert's own, to "concentrate on costume," tends to
make one "forget the soul." My extensive annotation of these two letters is intended to illuminate the habits of research applied by Flaubert
to all his books published after *Madame Bovary.*[3]

As SOON AS his publisher, Michel Lévy, had proof sheets of *Salammbô*, Flaubert sent a set to Charles-Augustin Sainte-Beuve.

By far the most influential critic in France, Sainte-Beuve had in 1857 confirmed the respectability of *Madame Bovary* by making it the subject of one of his weekly *Causeries du Lundi*, his "Monday chats"—reviews of new books or articles on aspects of literature—in *Le Moniteur Universel*. The review of *Madame Bovary*, apparently written with some reluctance at the particular request of the paper's editor, could scarcely be called enthusiastic or perceptive. Nevertheless, by its very appearance it had contributed to the book's success, and Flaubert had written his thanks to Sainte-Beuve. Since then the two men had become—if not quite friends—friendly acquaintances, and they would soon be meeting at the "Magny Dinners," literary evenings at the Restaurant Magny, which Sainte-Beuve and a few friends inaugurated about that time, and which Flaubert would be invited to attend. Sainte-Beuve's *Lundis* were now appearing in the newspaper *Le Constitutionnel*.

With the proof sheets Flaubert sent the critic a note:

Mon cher Maître

Here is my Carthaginian girl at last. I send her to you in fear and trembling. Now I have nothing further to do except discover printers' errors, mistakes in style, mistakes in grammar, etc.—in short, undergo the usual humiliations.

I am impatient to know what you think. When you finish reading this big bundle, send me a note to tell me the day and time you can see me, and I'll come at once.

Sainte-Beuve wrote in the margin of that letter: "Grammatical mistakes not very important! The essential is that a book should have life and interest, catch hold of the reader, *bite* him—be absorbingly real, or magic."

He and Flaubert apparently had a conversation about the novel; and Sainte-Beuve's long critique, one of its chief points being that *Salammbô* did not do what his marginal note said a book should, appeared in *Le Constitutionnel* on three successive Mondays, December 8, 15, and 22. The first installment contained a prefatory paragraph: "This long-awaited book, on which M. Flaubert has worked for several years, is now published. We intend to forget our connection with the author, even our friendship with him, and to pay his talent the greatest possible tribute: namely, a verdict based on careful reading; impartial, and unrestricted by conventional rules of politeness."

After reading those words and the text of the comparatively mild first installment, Flaubert sent Sainte-Beuve a brief note of thanks; and then, remaining cordial with him despite the severity of the second and third articles, prepared a long letter of justification. It is included here in full translation. The charges made by Sainte-Beuve in his review are for the most part sufficiently indicated by Flaubert's specific ripostes.

1. Berlioz, whose opera *The Trojans at Carthage* had been completed four years before and was still awaiting production, wrote Flaubert on November 4, 1862:

My dear Monsieur Flaubert,
I wanted to run over to see you today; that has proven impossible, but I cannot wait any longer to tell you that your book has filled me with admiration, astonishment, and even terror . . . It frightened me: I've been dreaming about it these last few nights. Such style! Such archaeological knowledge! Such imagination! Oh! Your mysterious Salammbô and her secret love—ungovernable and so full of horror—for the enemy who has violated her is an invention of the highest poetry, and yet true to supreme truth.
Let me clasp your powerful hand and sign myself your devoted admirer,
Hector Berlioz
P.S. *Now* let anyone slander our native tongue!

A few months later, on July 6, 1863, with his opera finally scheduled for production, Berlioz wrote Flaubert again:

Learned Poet:
I stopped by today to ask a service of you. At this moment we are busy staging my opera, *The Trojans at Carthage*. The manager of the Théâtre Lyrique [Léon Carvalho] and I would be grateful if you would be willing to give us a little advice concerning the Phoenician and Carthaginian costumes. Certainly there is no one who knows more about this than you. When you return, would you be good enough to let me know when we might see each other? Carvalho will come with me and we shall both listen to you as to the Delphic Oracle.
All admiration from your devoted
Hector Berlioz

As Jacques Barzun points out in his *Berlioz and the Romantic Century*, "Flaubert insisted on being the one who should call on the other"; and on July 15 Berlioz wrote to thank him for the "precious notes" he had sent him.
2. For more on Gautier and *Salammbô*, including a discussion of his possible role in its genesis, see Joanna Richardson, *Théophile Gautier* (listed in Works of Related Interest).
3. Flaubert had of course carefully verified details of topography, medicine, fashion, and so on for *Madame Bovary*. But the setting and timing of that novel—in Flaubert's native Normandy, less than a generation before the years of its composition—had made the task less onerous. He had done extensive research for the first, unpublished *Temptation of Saint Anthony*, and would do more for the final version.

❦❦❦❦❦❦

TO CHARLES AUGUSTIN SAINTE-BEUVE

[December 23–24, 1862]

Your third article on *Salammbô* has mollified me (I was never very outraged). My friends were a bit annoyed by the two others; but remembering how frankly you told me what you thought of my big tome, I am grateful to you for the leniency of your criticism. Therefore, once again, and very sincerely, I thank you for the marks of affection you show me; and now, bypassing the usual compliments, I begin my "Apologia."

Are you quite sure, first of all, that your general judgment isn't a little overinfluenced by your emotional reaction? The world I depict in my book—barbarian, Oriental, Molochian—is displeasing to you *in itself*. You begin by doubting the verisimilitude of my reproduction of it, and then you say: "After all, it *may* be true"; and, in conclusion, "So much the worse if it *is* true!" You keep being surprised, and hold it against me that you should be. But that I cannot help! Should I have embellished the picture, sweetened, distorted, frenchified it? But you yourself reproach me for having written a poem, for being classical in the unfavorable sense of that word, and you use *Les Martyrs*[1] as a stick to beat me with.

Now, Chateaubriand's system seems to me diametrically opposed to mine. He started from a completely ideal viewpoint: he was thinking of the martyr as a certain type. Whereas I, by applying to antiquity the technique of the modern novel, wanted to capture a mirage, and I tried to be simple. Laugh as much as you like! Yes, I say *simple*, and not sober. Nothing is more complicated than a Barbarian.

But now for the points you make. I defend myself: I fight you inch by inch.

From the outset, I clash with you head-on about Hanno's *Periplus*,[2] which Montesquieu admired and I do not. Who can be persuaded to believe today that it is an "original" document? It is obviously translated, shortened, pruned, and arranged by a Greek. Never did an Oriental, whoever he might be, write in that style. Witness the inscription of Eshmunazar,[3] so bombastic and redundant. People who have themselves called "son of God," "eye of God" (see Hamaker's inscriptions)[4] are not simple in the way you mean. And then you will grant me that the Greeks understood nothing about the barbarian world. If they had understood something about it, they would not have been Greeks. The Orient was repugnant to the Hellenic spirit. What travesties they made of everything that came to them from abroad! The same is true of Polybius. He is for me an incontestable authority as to facts; but for anything he has not seen (or which he omits intentionally, for he too had a preconceived framework and belonged to a "school") I am perfectly entitled to look elsewhere. Hanno's *Periplus* is thus not a "Carthaginian monument," let alone the "only one," as you say it is. One true Carthaginian monument is the inscription at Marseilles,[5] written in real Punic. That one is "simple," I admit, because it is a list of charges; and even so, it is less "simple" than the famous *Periplus*, in which a touch of the marvelous comes through the Greek—to mention only those gorilla-skins, mistaken for human skins, that hung in the temple of Moloch (i.e. Saturn), and whose description I spared you. (You can thank me for that.) So: one point settled. I will even tell you, entre nous, that Hanno's *Periplus* is completely odious to me, the result of my having read and reread it together with Bougainville's four dissertations (in the *Mémoires* of the Academy of Inscriptions), not to mention many a doctoral thesis, the *Periplus* being a thesis subject.[6]

As for my heroine, I do not defend her. According to you, she resembles a "sentimental Elvire," Velléda, Mme Bovary.[7] No: Velléda is active, intelligent, European; Mme Bovary is the prey of many passions; Salammbô, on the contrary, remains adamantine, immobilized by her obsession. She is a maniac, a kind of Saint Teresa. No matter! I am not sure how real she is; for neither I, nor you, nor anyone, whether ancient or modern, can understand the Oriental woman, for the reason that association with her is impossible.

You accuse me of lacking logic, and you ask: "Why did the Carthaginians massacre the Balearics?" The reason is very simple: they hate all the Mercenaries; they happen to have that one group of them, the Balearics, in their power; they are stronger, and they kill them. But, you say: "The news could reach the camp from one moment to the next." How? Who would have brought it? The Carthaginians? What would have been their purpose? Or some of the Barbarians? But there were none left in the city. Foreigners? Persons unconcerned? But I was careful to show that there was no communication between Carthage and the army.

As for Hanno[8] . . . (The "bitches' milk," let me say in passing, is not a "joke." It was, and *still is*, a remedy against leprosy. See the *Dictionnaire des sciences médicales*, article "Leprosy"—a poor article, by the way: I corrected parts of it from my own observations in Damascus and Nubia.) Hanno escapes because the Mercenaries deliberately let him escape. They are not yet "unleashed" against him. They become indignant later, when they reconsider the matter: they are slow to grasp all the perfidy of which the Elders are capable. (See the beginning of my Chapter IV.) Mâtho "prowls like a madman" around Carthage. "Madman" is the right word. As conceived by the ancients, wasn't love a madness, a curse, a sickness sent by the gods? Polybius would be "astonished," you say, to see his Mâtho so depicted. I do not think so, nor would M. de Voltaire have shared this astonishment. Remember what he has the old woman in *Candide* say about the violence of passions in Africa: "Like fire, vitriol, etc."

Concerning the aqueduct: "Here the reader is up to his neck in improbability." Yes, cher maître, you are right, and even more so than you think; but not in the way you think. I will tell you further along what I think about this episode, introduced not to describe the aqueduct itself (which gave me a lot of trouble), but to enable my two heroes to enter Carthage. Actually, it is taken from an anecdote recounted by Polyaenus[9] (*Strategica*)—the story of Theodorus, the friend of Cleon, at the capture of Sestos by the people of Abydos.

"One needs a dictionary." This is a reproach that I consider supremely unfair. I could have bored the reader to death with technical terms. Far from doing so, I was careful to translate everything into French. I used not a single special term without immediately furnishing an explanation. I except the names of coins, measurements, and the months, which are indicated by the context. But surely, when you encounter on a page such words as "kreutzer," "yard," "piastre," or "penny," they are not beyond your understanding? What would you have said had I called Moloch "Melek," Hannibal "Han-Baal," Carthage "Karthadhadtha," and if instead of saying that the slaves in the mill wore muzzles, I had written "pausicapes"?! As for the names of perfumes and precious stones, it is true that I had to take names that are in Theophrastus, Pliny, and Athenaeus. For plants, I used Latin names—'commonly accepted names"—instead of Arab or Phoenician. Thus I said "Lausonia" instead of "Henneb," and I was even considerate enough to write "Lausonia" with a "u," which is wrong, and not to add "inermis," which would have been more precise. The same for "Rokh'eul," which I call "antimony," sparing you "sulphide," oh ungrateful one! But out of respect for the French reader I cannot write "Hannibal" and "Hamilcar" without the "H" (since there is a "rough breathing" on the *alpha*), and remain faithful to Rollin.[10] Be a bit gentle with me, please!

As for the temple of Tanit, I am confident that I reconstruct it correctly, on the basis of the treatise on the Syrian Goddess,[11] the duc de Luynes' medals, our knowledge of the temple at Jerusalem, a passage from St. Jerome quoted by Selden[12] (*de Diis Syriis*), the plan of the temple at Gozo[13] (which is certainly Carthaginian), and the ruins of the temple of Thugga,[14] which I have seen with my own eyes and which, so far as I know, is mentioned by no traveler or antiquarian. "No matter," you will say, "it is a strange-sounding place." Granted. The description itself, from the literary point of view, I find perfectly comprehensible. And it does not impede the action: Spendius and Mâtho remain in the foreground; the reader never loses sight of them. The descriptions in my book are never isolated or gratuitous: they all serve some purpose relating to my characters, and sooner or later they are seen to play a role in the plot.

Nor do I accept the word "chinoiserie" as applied to Salammbô's bedroom, despite the "exquisite" you add to take the curse off it (like "devouring" applied to "dogs" in the famous Dream),[15] because I have not included a single detail that is not in the Bible or not still to be seen in the Orient. You tell me more than once that the Bible is not a guide to Carthage (a debatable point); but surely the Hebrews were closer to the Carthaginians than were the Chinese! Besides, there are climatic considerations, which are eternal. For furniture and costumes, I refer you to the texts included in the twenty-first dissertation by the Abbé Mignot (*Mémoires* of the Academy of Inscriptions, Volume LX or XLI, I forget which).

As for everything in the book having a flavor of "opera, pomp, and bombast," why should you think that things were not like that then, considering that that is how they are now? Ceremonies, state visits, obeisances, panegyrics, and all the rest were not invented by Mohammed, I suppose.

The same applies to Hannibal. Why do you maintain that I have made his childhood "fabulous"? Because he kills an eagle? A miracle indeed, in a land where eagles abound! If the scene had been Gaul, I would have made it an owl, a wolf, or a fox. Being French, you are accustomed, automatically, to think of the eagle as a noble bird, more symbol than living thing. However, eagles do exist.

You ask me where I derived "such an idea of the Council of Carthage." But in all situations of the kind, in periods of revolution, from our own Convention to the American Parliament,[16] where until quite recently there were duels with canes and pistols, said canes and pistols (like my daggers) were brought in hidden in coatsleeves. And even my Carthaginians were more seemly than the Americans, since the public was not admitted to the Council. Against me you quote a weighty authority: Aristotle. But Aristotle lived more than eighty years before my period, and carries no weight here. Besides, the Stagirite is grossly mistaken when he states that "in Carthage there was never an uprising or a tyrant." Would you like a few dates? Carthalo's conspiracy in 530 B.C.; the usurpation of the two Magos, 460; Hanno's conspiracy, 337; Bomilcar's conspiracy, 307. But here I go beyond Aristotle's time. On to something else.

You scold me about the "carbuncles formed by lynxes' urine." That is from Theophrastus, *On Stones.* So: poor Theophrastus![17]

I was forgetting Spendius. No, cher maître, his stratagem is neither "bizarre" nor "strange." It is almost a stereotype. I took it from Aelianus (*History of Animals*) and Polyaenus (*Strategica*). In fact, it was so well known following the siege of Megara by Antipater (or Antigonus) that pigs were deliberately fed alongside elephants in order that the larger animals not be frightened by the smaller. In short, it was a common device, probably often used in Spendius's day. I didn't have to go back as far as Samson, because I avoided, as much as possible, details belonging to legendary periods.

Now I come to Hamilcar's treasure. This description, whatever you say, is not in the foreground: Hamilcar himself is the dominant figure, and I think the description is well warranted. The magistrate's anger gradually increases as he sees the depredations made in his house. Far from being "continuously beside himself," he doesn't explode until the end, when he is insulted personally. That he "does not gain in stature from this visit" is quite all right with me, since I am not writing his panegyric; but I do not think that in this scene I "caricature him, to the detriment of the rest of his characterization." The man who later kills the Mercenaries in the way I have shown (his son Hannibal went in for the same charming behavior, in Italy), is very much the same man who orders his merchandise to be adulterated and his slaves to be whipped unsparingly.

You quibble about the "eleven thousand three hundred ninety-six men" who form his army, asking me "How do you know this number? Who told you?" But you have just seen that for yourself, since I mentioned the number of men in the different corps of the Punic army. It is simply the sum total: not a figure recklessly invented to create an effect of precision.

There is nothing "sly" or "depraved" in the scene of the serpent, no "bagatelle."[18] This chapter is a kind of rhetorical precaution, to attenuate the effect of the chapter about the tent. The latter has not shocked readers; but it would have, had it not been preceded by the snake. I preferred a salacious scene with a snake (if there is salaciousness here) to one with a man. Before leaving her house, Salammbô embraces the genius of her family, the very religion of her country and its most ancient symbol. That is all. Quite possibly it would be "unseemly in an Iliad or a Pharsalia"; but I make no claim to be writing the Iliad or the Pharsalia.

Nor is it my fault if there are frequent storms in Tunis at the end of the summer. Chateaubriand no more invented storms than he did sunsets; and both, it seems to me, are everyone's property. Besides, please note that the heart of this story is Moloch—Fire, Thunder. Here the god himself acts, in one of his forms: he subdues Salammbô. Thus the thunder is appropriate: it is the voice of Moloch, speaking from without. Furthermore, you must admit that I spared you the "classic description of a storm." Besides, my poor storm occupies only *three lines*—separated, at that. The fire that follows was inspired by an episode in the story of Massinissa,[19] by another in the story of Agathocles,[20] and by a passage in Hirtius[21]—all three in analogous circumstances. As you see, I don't stray from the milieu, from the very country in which my action takes place.

About Salammbô's perfumes: you credit me with more imagination than I possess. Just take a whiff of Judith and Esther in the Bible. They literally soaked themselves, poisoned themselves, with perfumes. Which is what I was careful to say at the beginning, as soon as there was a question of Salammbô's sickness.

Why do you object to "the disappearance of the zaïmpf being a factor" in the loss of the battle, since the army of Mercenaries included men who believed in the zaïmph? I indicate the principal reasons (three military movements) for this defeat; then I add the other, as a secondary, final reason.

To say that I "invented tortures" at the funeral of the Barbarians is not true. Hendrich (*Carthago, seu Carth. respublica,* 1664) assembled texts to prove that it was a custom of the Carthaginians to mutilate the corpses of their enemies. And you are surprised that the Barbarians, defeated, desperate, enraged, should retaliate in kind, doing so on this one occasion only? Must I remind you of Mme de Lamballe, of the Garde Mobile in '48, and what is taking place this very moment in the United States?[22] In fact I have been moderate and very considerate.

And since you and I are exchanging truths, I confess to you frankly, cher maître, that your "element of sadistic imagination" wounded me a little. Every word you write is serious. Such words from you, when they are printed, become almost a stigma. Are you forgetting that I once sat on a bench in Criminal Court, accused of offences against public decency, and that fools and knaves use any weapons that come to hand? So do not be surprised if one of these days you read in the *Figaro*[23] some such words as these: "M. G. Flaubert is a disciple of Sade. His friend, his sponsor, a master critic, has said so himself, quite clearly, although with that finesse and laughing good humor which, etc." What would I reply—or do?

I bow before the following. You are right, cher maître: I did add finishing touches; I did do violence to history; as you so well say, I had "made up my mind to depict a siege." But with a military subject, what is wrong with that? And then I did not completely invent this siege. I merely laid it on a bit thick. That is my only sin.

But concerning the "passage in Montesquieu" about immolating children, I rebel. This horror does not "raise a doubt" in my mind. (Remember that human sacrifices were not completely abolished in Greece at the time of the battle of Leuctra, 370 B.C.) Despite the condition imposed by Gelon (480), in the war against Agathocles (392) two hundred children were burned, according to Diodorus; and as for later periods, I refer you to Silius Italicus, to Eusebius, and especially to St. Augustine, who states that such things sometimes took place in his day.

You regret that among the Greeks I have not included a philosopher, a dialectician who would be portrayed as giving a course in morals, or as performing good actions—a gentleman, in short, who "feels as we do." Come, now! Would that have been possible? Aratus,[24] whom you mention, was in fact the very person I thought of when imagining Spendius. He was a man of ruses and sudden assaults, capable of killing sentinels at night, and a man who had attacks of vertigo in broad daylight. True, I sidestepped a contrast, but such a contrast would have been a facile one, forced and false.

So much for your "analysis." Now as to your "judgment."

You are perhaps right in your reflections concerning the historical novel as applied to antiquity, and quite possibly I have failed.[25] However, judging from my own impressions, it seems to me quite probable that the picture I have painted does resemble Carthage. But that is not the question. I care nothing for archaeology. If the color is not unified, if details jar, if the ways of life I depict are not what can be derived from what we know of the religion, or the action from what we know of human passions, if the delineations of character are not consistent, if the costumes are inappropriate to the life of the people and the architecture to the climate—if, in a word, harmony is lacking—then my book is wrong. If not, not: it is all of a piece.

But you find the milieu itself detestable. I know you do, or rather I sense that you do. Instead of continuing to regard it from your viewpoint, your viewpoint as a man of letters, as a modern, a Parisian, why not come and look at it from mine? The human soul is not the same everywhere, whatever M. Levallois[26] may say. The briefest glance at the world provides sufficient proof of the opposite. Actually, I think I have been less hard on humanity in *Salammbô* than in *Madame Bovary*. The curiosity and love that impelled me to deal with religions and people that are no more has something moral and sympathetic about it, I think.

As to style, I sacrificed less in this book than in the other to rounding out my phrases and my periods. Metaphors are few, and epithets are factual. If I put "blue" beside "stones," it is because "blue" is the right word, believe me; and you may be equally sure that it is indeed possible to distinguish the color of stones by starlight. Ask any traveler in the Orient, or go and see for yourself.

And since you reproach me for certain words—"*énorme*," for example, which I will not defend (even though excessive silence does give the effect of clamor)—let me in turn object to some of your expressions. I did not understand the quotation from Désaugiers,[27] or why you included it. Your "Carthaginian knickknacks" made me frown, as did your calling the zaïmph "a kind of crazy cloak," your speaking of Salammbô's "romping with the snake" as being a kind of "spicy come-on," your calling my Libyan a "handsome rogue" when he is neither handsome nor a rogue, and your reference to Schahabarim's "libertine" imagination.

One last question, oh maitre—an unseemly question. Why do you find Schahabarim [the high priest] almost comic, and yet take your friends at Port-Royal[28] so seriously? For me, your M. Singlin is deadly, compared with my elephants. I regard the tattooed Barbarians as less inhuman, less "special," less ludicrous, less exceptional, than men living a communal life who address each other as "Monsieur" to the end of their days. And it is precisely because they are remote from me that I admire your talent for making me understand them. For I *believe* your picture of Port-Royal, and I would enjoy living there even less than in Carthage. Port-Royal, too, was an exclusive group, unnatural, forced, all of a piece—and yet true. Why will you not allow two truths to exist, two diametrically opposed examples of excess, two different monstrosities?

I am almost done. Be patient a bit longer! Are you curious to know the *enormous* defect ("*énorme*" is used properly here) that I find in my book? It is this:

1. The pedestal is too big for the statue. Or rather, since "too little," rather than "too much," is the great sin, there should have been a hundred pages more, devoted to Salammbô alone.

2. A few transitions are lacking. I had them, but removed them or overpruned them, for fear of being boring.

3. In Chapter VI, everything relating to Gisco is of the same tonality as the second part of Chapter II (Hanno). The situation is the same, and the effect is not enhanced.

4. Everything from the battle of the Macar to the serpent, and all of Chapter XIII, up to the enumeration of the Barbarians, sink out of sight, vanish from the reader's memory. These are areas of middle ground, dull and of ephemeral effect. Unfortunately I could not avoid them, and they give a heaviness to the book despite my best efforts at briskness. Those are the parts that gave me the most trouble; I like them the least, and yet they are the ones I am proudest of.

5. The aqueduct. A confession! My *secret* opinion is that there was no aqueduct at Carthage at that period, despite the ruined aqueduct we see today. Therefore I was careful to anticipate possible objections with a hypocritical sentence intended for archaeologists—a clumsy reminder that aqueducts were a Roman invention, new at the time, and that the aqueduct one sees now was a new construction, on the foundations of an older one. I was obsessed by the memory of Belisarius cutting the Roman aqueduct at Carthage;[29] and besides, it made such a splendid entrance for Spendius and Mâtho! But no question, my aqueduct *is* an evasion. *Confiteor!*

6. One more, final, fraud: Hanno. For the sake of keeping the picture clear, I falsified the story of his death. He was indeed crucified by the Mercenaries, but in Sardinia. The general crucified at Tunis, opposite Spendius, was named Hannibal. Think of the confusion that would have caused the reader![30]

Such, cher maître, are what I consider the worst features of my book. I will not tell you what I think the good ones. But you may be sure that my Carthage is no mere fantasy. Documents on Carthage exist, and not all of them are in Movers.[31] They must be sought for a bit further. For example, Ammianus Marcellinus[32] provided me with the exact form of a gate; a poem by Corippus[33] (the *Johannis*) with many details about African tribes, etc.

And besides: few will be following my example. So where is the danger? The Leconte de Lisles and the Baudelaires are less to be feared than the Nadauds and the Clairvilles[34] in this dear land of France, where superficiality is a *quality* and where the banal, the facile, and the foolish are invariably applauded, adopted, and adored. One does not risk corrupting anyone when one aspires to greatness. Am I forgiven?

I end by thanking you once again, mon cher maître. You have clawed me, but you have also given me the handshake of affection; and though you have mocked me a little, you have nevertheless given me three great salutes—three long articles, very detailed, very distinguished, which must have been more painful for you than they are for me. It is for that, especially, that I am grateful. Your closing advice[35] will not be forgotten, and you will see that you have not been dealing with a fool or an ingrate.

1. Chateaubriand's Romantic prose epic, *Les Martyrs, ou le Triomphe de la réligion chrétienne* (1809).

2. The *Periplus* is an account of a voyage around Africa, written in the Punic language by a Carthaginian (Hanno was a common Carthaginian name) and later translated into Greek.

3. Eshmunazar (the name means "the god Eshmun has helped") was a king of Sidon, about the early fifth century B.C. The inscription is on his sarcophagus, discovered in 1855.

4. Hendrik Arent Hamaker, a Dutch orientalist (1789–1835), published works on Phoenician and Punic inscriptions.

5. The so-called Marseilles Tariff, a third- or second-century B.C. stone inscription in Punic listing sacrifices and dues, found at Marseilles in 1845 and thought to have come from Carthage.

6. That is, permitted as a subject for theses in French universities.

7. Elvire is Lamartine's idealized heroine in his Romantic *Méditations poétiques* (1820). Velléda is a druidess in *Les Martyrs*.

8. This Hanno is a Carthaginian general and magistrate, a character in the novel.

9. Greek author of a book on military stratagems.

10. Charles Rollin (1661–1741), historian, Rector of the University of Paris, where he reintroduced the study of Greek. "Rough breathing" and "smooth breathing" are terms referring to the pronunciation of ancient Greek.

11. Lucian: *De dea syria*.

12. John Selden (1584–1654), English jurist and oriental scholar. The book consulted by Flaubert was his *De dis syris syntagmata II* (London, 1617). Flaubert would later be scolded for his misspelling of the title (see letter to Froehner, January 21, 1863, note 14).

13. The second-largest island in the Maltese group.

14. In Tunisia. Sometimes written Dougga. When Sainte-Beuve published Flaubert's letter, with permission, as a note to his review as reprinted in a volume of *Nouveaux Lundis*, he appended the following footnote: "M. Flaubert, whom I asked to reread this

passage of his letter, has agreed that he was neither the first nor the only writer, as he had previously thought, to speak of the temple of Thugga."

15. The dream in Racine's *Athalie*, II, 5.

16. One supposes Flaubert means the Congress. The reference might be to the beating of Charles Sumner in the Senate in 1856.

17. Sainte-Beuve had jeered at Flaubert's description of Hamilcar's collection of gems: "Here we have to do with an auctioneer, amusing himself in this underground treasure house by reeling off for us a list of all the mineralogical marvels imaginable, even including 'carbuncles formed by lynxes' urine.' This is too much, and shows up the author as a dilettante who is making sport of us."

André Gide wrote more understandingly of this aspect of *Salammbô* in his *Journal* (April 9, 1908): "It seems to me that in the texts he used as sources, Flaubert was seeking less for documentation than for authorization. In his horror of daily reality, he was enchanted by everything in these texts that differed from it. Did he really believe that carbuncles were 'formed by lynxes' urine'? Certainly not! But he was delighted that a passage in Theophrastus authorized him to pretend to believe so; and so on throughout the book."

This inner, or secret, way of the artist, Flaubert would not, or perhaps could not, explain to someone who, like Sainte-Beuve, did not sense it.

18. "Bagatelle" in the eighteenth-century sense: the act of coition.

19. King of Numidia (c. 238–149 B.C.), vassal and ally of Carthage, who was married to Sophinisba, daughter of the Carthaginian Hasdrubal, transferred his allegiance to Rome.

20. Sicilian tyrant (d. 289 B.C.).

21. Roman historian (d. 43 B.C.).

22. The Princesse de Lamballe, friend of Queen Marie-Antoinette, met an atrocious end at the hands of a mob during the September massacres of 1792. The Garde Mobile (a portion of the National Guard) mowed down demonstrating workmen during the "June Days" of 1848; Flaubert refers to the National Guard again in his letter of September 29, 1868, to George Sand, and it plays a large role in *L'Education sentimentale*. Bulletins concerning the events of the American Civil War were appearing in the newspapers Flaubert read.

23. "in the *Figaro*." Responding to Flaubert's request that in his letter as printed the name of the newspaper be omitted, Sainte-Beuve substituted "in some little scandal sheet."

24. Achaean general, ally and then enemy of Philip of Macedon.

25. In his review, Sainte-Beuve had written: "On this subject chosen by M. Flaubert, little information is provided either by monuments or by books. What he tried to accomplish was thus a complete tour de force, and it is little wonder that, in my opinion, he has failed."

26. Jules Levallois (1829–1903), Sainte-Beuve's former secretary, had written unfavorably about *Salammbô* in the *Opinion Nationale*.

27. Antoine Désaugiers (1772–1827), composer of light songs. Sainte-Beuve, whose taste in humor was not always the most appropriate, had quoted, quite ineptly, some jolly lines from Désaugiers "as a relief from the solemnity and monotony" of *Salammbô*.

28. The reference is to Sainte-Beuve's *Port-Royal*, his study of the community of seventeenth-century Jansenists.

29. In A.D. 534—approximately eight hundred years after the events recounted in *Salammbô*.

30. That is, they would probably have thought that Flaubert was speaking of the younger, greater, Hannibal.

31. Franz Karl Movers (1806–1856), German orientalist. His *Die Phönizier*, one of Flaubert's sources for Carthaginian names and other particulars, was published in two separate parts: Bonn, 1841, and Berlin, 1856.

32. Roman historian in the age of Julian.

33. Flavius Cresconius Corippus, Roman epic poet of the sixth century A.D.

34. Gustave Nadaud (1829–1893), composer of light songs; and Louis-François Nicolaie, called Clairville (1811–1879), composer and *vaudevilliste*. Flaubert was probably unaware, when writing his "Apologia," that a few months later a vaudeville by Clairville and a collaborator, entitled *Folammbô, ou les Cocasseries carthaginoises*, would open at the Théâtre du Palais-Royal, then as now the home of the farce.

35. Sainte-Beuve's "closing advice" to the author of *Salammbô* had been:

"A new book by him is due us, and let us hope that this time we shall not have to wait so long. To men—even to the most genuine talents—few years of fertility are granted: one must know how to make use of them, in order to establish oneself before it is too late—anchor oneself in the hearts and memory of one's contemporaries. Besides, that is the surest route to posterity. So let him give us, without too much delay, and without excessive concern for that style of which he is such a master that he can afford to relax a little, a strong, powerful, well-observed, vital work. Certainly it must have some of the bitter, refined qualities of his first novel; it must be earmarked with his originality and his inimitable nature (no one wishes him to abdicate!); but one hopes it will contain at least one vein that will please all of us, if only as a measure of consolation."

Perhaps Flaubert was referring to that "closing advice" when he wrote to his niece, on Sainte-Beuve's death seven years later: "I wrote *L'Éducation sentimentale* in part for Sainte-Beuve."

The text of Flaubert's "Apologia" used for this translation is chiefly that printed by Sainte-Beuve in the fourth volume of his *Nouveaux Lundis* along with his own reply to it (translated below). Notice has been taken of the corrections pointed out by Benjamin F. Bart in "Lettres Inédites de Flaubert à Sainte-Beuve," in *Revue d'histoire littéraire de la France*, 64 (1964), which contains also the texts of Flaubert's two shorter letters. For the identification of certain persons, places, and works mentioned in this letter and the next, and for the proper anglicization of certain terms and names, I am particularly grateful to David Marcus.

CHARLES-AUGUSTIN SAINTE-BEUVE TO FLAUBERT

December 25, 1862

My dear friend,

I was waiting impatiently for the promised letter. I read it last night, and have reread it this morning. I no longer regret having written those articles, since by doing so I induced you to bring out all your reasons. The African sun has had the singular effect of causing the humors of all of us, even our secret humors, to erupt. *Salammbô*, independently of the lady, is from now on the name of a battle, of several battles. I plan to do the following: when I reprint my articles, I will keep them as they are, and will place, at the end of the volume, what you call your "apologia," with only these few words of reply from me. I had my say; you responded; attentive readers will judge. What I appreciate especially, and what everyone will feel, is the high-mindedness and nobility of character which enabled you quite naturally to tolerate my contradictions, and which increase the esteem in which you are held. M. Lebrun (of the Academy), a just man, said this about you to me the other day: "After all, he comes out of this a more considerable person than before. That will be the general, and definitive, impression . . ."[1]

1. Those last dots of deletion were substituted by Sainte-Beuve, in the published text of his letter, for the closing words of the autograph. Those words, or their sense, can be deduced from Flaubert's brief note of reply: " 'Less good friends than before,' cher maître? Come: *better!* What a charming man you are. This time I don't shake your hand: I embrace you."

◇◇◇◇◇

In connection with one particularly infuriating review of *Salammbô* Flaubert wrote to Jules Duplan on January 13, 1863:

> I had taken all imaginable precautions to keep my mother from learning about the article in *Le Figaro*, but two of her women friends (it's always friends, in such a case) found nothing better to do than recite the article to her by heart. She was very upset about it on Sunday night, and whenever I go out she imagines I'm on my way to fight a duel. So you see my life at home is disturbed by those bastards. Such are the rewards of literature. Lévy is rubbing his hands and printing the third edition.

The newspaper notices emphasizing the novel's "horrors" were indeed helping the sale, and Flaubert was persuaded by Bouilhet not to reply to any of them.

However, Flaubert would not agree to ignore one magazine article, signed "G. Froehner," which he viewed as belonging to an order of its own. The author, a twenty-seven-year-old German (naturalized French, hence the "G" for "Guillaume" rather than "W" for his baptismal "Wilhelm"), was not a literary critic but an assistant curator in the Department of Antiquities at the Louvre, and the provocation of his remarks was undeniably acute. When couched in a certain tone, *all* accusations of error can be equally maddening, whether justified or not. Those made in Froehner's article were of both kinds; and its author, who held a degree from the University of Bonn, excelled in a Teutonic variety of tactlessness which always offends—most of all, perhaps, when it condescends to praise. Flaubert's reply appeared in the newspaper *L Opinion Nationale* for January 24, 1863, and was reprinted in the magazine *La Revue Contemporaine* (where the attack had appeared) for February 15. As in the case of the letter to Sainte-Beuve, the critic's objections are for the most part made evident by Flaubert's ripostes.

◇◇◇◇◇

To Guillaume Froehner

Paris, January 21, 1863

Monsieur:

I have just read your article on Salammbô[1] in the Revue Contemporaine of December 31, 1862. Despite my practice of never replying to reviews, I find yours unacceptable. It is very courteous, and contains many things extremely flattering to me; but since it casts doubt on the sincerity of my studies, you will kindly allow me to use this space to challenge a number of your assertions.

Let me first ask you, Monsieur, why you so obstinately link me with the Campana collection,[2] claiming that it was my source, my continual inspiration. The fact is that I completed Salammbô last March, six weeks before the opening of that museum. Already an error, you see: we shall be finding others, more serious.

I have, Monsieur, no pretensions to archaeology. My book is presented as a novel, without preface and without notes, and I marvel that a man of your eminence should waste his time and effort on such light literature! However, I know enough to risk saying that you err completely, from the beginning of your article to the end, on every one of your eighteen pages, in every paragraph, and in almost every line.

You reprimand me for not having consulted either Falbe or Dureau de la Malle,[3] from whom I "might have profited." A thousand pardons! I have read them—more often than you, perhaps, and amid the ruins of Carthage itself. It is indeed quite possible that you "know of no satisfactory work dealing with the configuration of the city or with its principal districts"; others, however, better informed, do not at all share your skepticism. We may lack information as to the whereabouts of the suburb Aclas, or the place called Fuscianus, or concerning the exact sites of the principal gates whose names we have, etc.; but we do know, and quite well, the position of the city, the architectonic construction of the walls, the Taenia, the Mole, and the Cothon.[4] We know that the houses were faced with tar and the streets paved with blocks; we have an idea of the Ancô,[5] described in my Chapter XV; we have heard about Malqua, about Byrsa, about Megara, about the Mappalia and the Catacombs, and about the temple of Eshmun, situated on the Acropolis, and that of Tanit, a little to the right as one stood with one's back to the sea. All that is to be found (not to mention Appian, Pliny, and Procopius) in that same Dureau de la Malle whom you accuse me of not knowing. So it is really regrettable, Monsieur, that you did not, as you put it, "go into tedious detail" to prove that I had no idea of the situation and plan of ancient Carthage—"even less than Dureau de la Malle," you add. What is one to believe? On whom is one to rely?—since you have so far not had the kindness to reveal your own system with respect to Carthaginian topography.

It is true that I can quote no text to prove that there existed a street of the Tanners, or of the Perfumers, or of the Dyers. Still, you must agree that it is a likely hypothesis. But I most certainly did not invent Kinisdo and Cynasyn—"names," you say, "whose structure is foreign to the spirit of the Semitic languages." Not so foreign as all that, however, since they are in Gesenius.[6] Almost all my Punic names ("disfigured," according to you) were taken from Gesenius (*Scripturae lingaeque phoeniciae* [*monumenta quotquot supersunt*]) [1837], or from Falbe, whom I assure you I did consult.

An orientalist of your erudition, Monsieur, should have been a bit more indulgent concerning the Numidian name Naravasse, which I write Narr'Havas, from Nar-el-haouah, *feu du souffle*.[7] You could have guessed that the two *m*'s in Salammbô were put there on purpose, so that the name would be pronounced Salam and not as in Salan;[8] and you might have had the charity to suppose that Égates, instead of Ægates, was a typographical error—corrected, incidentally, in the second edition of my book, which appeared a fortnight before the article in which you offer me advice. The same goes for Scissites, instead of Syssites, and for the word Kabires, which has always been printed without an *h* (horrors!) even in the most serious works, such as Maury's *Les Religions de la Grèce antique*. As for Schalischim, if I did not write (as I should have) Rosh-eisch-Schalischim, it was to shorten a name that I found too forbidding—it not having occurred to me that I would be quizzed by philologists. But since you choose to descend to these chicaneries about words, I will take you up on two (among others) of your own: (1) *Compendieusement*, which you employ in the opposite sense from its meaning, making it signify "abundantly," "prolixly"; and (2) *carthachinoiserie*,[9] an excellent jest, but not your own: you took it from the little newspaper in which it appeared early last month. As you see, Monsieur, if you are sometimes unacquainted with my authors, I know yours. But it might have been better had you passed over "those minutiae," as you so properly call them, "which do not survive critical examination."

One more such, however. Why did you underline the *and* in this sentence (a little shortened) from my page 156: "Buy me some Cappadocians *and* some Asiatics"? Was it because you wanted to impress a few ignoramuses, to make them think that I don't distinguish Cappadocia from Asia Minor? But I know the country, Monsieur: I have seen it, I have ridden through it![10]

You have read me with so little care that almost always you quote me incorrectly. Nowhere did I say that the priests formed a particular caste, nor, on page 109, that the Libyan soldiers "were possessed by the desire to drink iron," but that the Barbarians threatened to make the Carthaginians "drink iron";[11] nor, on page 108, that the guards of the Legion "wore, in the middle of the forehead, a silver horn to make them look like rhinoceroses," but that *their great horses* were so adorned; nor, on page 29, that the peasants amused themselves one day by crucifying two hundred lions. The same goes for those unfortunate Syssites,[12] which, according to you, I spoke of "doubtless not knowing that the term signified special guilds." Your "doubtless" is charming. But doubtless I did know what those guilds were, and the etymology of the word, since I translate it into French the first time it appears in my book, on page 7: "Syssites, companies (of merchants) who ate together." Furthermore, you have falsified a passage from Plautus: his *Poenulus* does not at all prove that "the Carthaginians knew all languages" (which would be a curious privilege for an entire nation); the prologue reads simply (line 112): *"Is omnes linguas scit,"* which must be translated as *"This man* knows all languages"—the Carthaginian in question, not all Carthaginians.

It is not true to say that "Hanno was not crucified in the war of the Mercenaries, since he was still commanding armies long afterward": for you will find in Polybius, Monsieur, Book I, Chapter XVII, that he was indeed captured by the rebels and crucified (in Sardinia, it is true, but at this same time). Thus it is not a question of "that gentleman" having "grounds for complaint against M. Flaubert," but rather of Polybius having grounds for complaint against M. Froehner.

As for the sacrificing of children, it is very far from "impossible" that they were being burned alive at the time of Hamilcar, since they were still being so sacrificed at the time of Julius Caesar and Tiberius, if one is to trust Cicero (*Pro Balbo*) and Strabo (Book III). "The statue of Moloch," you say, "does not resemble the hellish device described in *Salammbô*. This figure, composed of seven compartments, one above the other, for the confinement of victims, belongs to the Gallic religion. M. Flaubert has no pretext for making the analogy: his audacious transposition is unjustified." No! I have no *pretext*: quite true. But I have a *text*, namely *the* text, the actual description by Diodorus,[13] which you may recall, and which is the source of mine—as you may verify should you care to reread, or read, Book XX in Diodorus, Chapter IV, to which please add the Chaldean paraphrase by Paul Fage,[14] which you do not mention, and which is quoted by Selden, *De diis syriis*, pp. 164–170, along with Eusebius, *Preparatio evangelica*, Book I.

How can it be that "history makes no mention of the miraculous mantle,"[15] since you yourself state that "it was exhibited in the temple of Venus, but much later, and only at the time of the Roman emperors"? Now I find in Athenaeus, XII, 58, a very minute description of this mantle of which "history makes no mention." It was bought from Dionysius the Elder for 120 talents, brought to Rome by Scipio Aemilianus, returned to Carthage by Caius Gracchus, brought again to Rome under Heliogabalus, and then again returned to Carthage. All of which is found also in Dureau de la Malle, from whom I most decidedly did "profit."

Three lines further down, you affirm, with the same—candor, that "most of the other gods invoked in *Salammbô* are completely invented," and you add: "Who has ever heard of an Aptouknos?" Who? D'Avezac[16] (in his *Cyrénaique*), in connection with a temple near Cyrene.— "Of a Schaoûl?" But that is a name I give to a slave (see my page 91).— "Or of a Matisman?" He is mentioned as a god by Corippus.[17] (See his *Johannis* and *Mémoires de l'Académie des Inscriptions*, Vol. XII, p. 181). "Who doesn't know that Micipsa was not a divinity, but a man?" But that is what I say, Monsieur, and very clearly, on that same page 91, when Salammbô calls her slaves: "Help! Help! ... Kroûm, Ewa, Micipsa, Schaoûl!"

You accuse me of taking Astareth and Astarté to be two distinct divinities. But early in the book, page 48, when Salammbô invokes Tanit, she invokes her by all her names at once: "Anaïtis! Astarté! Derceto! Astareth! Tiratha!" And I was even careful to say, a little further on, page 52, that she repeated "all these names, which had no distinct meaning for her." Are you perhaps like Salammbô in this? I am tempted to think so, since you make Tanit the goddess of war rather than of love, of the female, humid, fecund element: you do so despite Tertullian, and despite the very name Tiratha, of which you will find the scarcely decent, but very explicit, explanation in Movers,[18] *Phénic.*, Book I, page 574.

Next, you are astonished by my apes consecrated to the moon and horses consecrated to the sun. "These details"—you are sure—"are found in no ancient author nor in any authentic monument." But let me remind you, Monsieur, that baboons were consecrated to the moon in Egypt, as one still sees on the walls of the temples, and that Egyptian cults had penetrated into Libya and the oases. As for the horses, I do not say that they were consecrated to Aesculapius, but to Eshmun— who was assimilated to Aesculapius, Iolas, Apollo, the Sun. Horses consecrated to the sun are mentioned in Pausanius (Book I, Chapter I), and in the Bible (II Kings 23:11). But perhaps you will deny that the Egyptian temples are authentic monuments, and that the Bible and Pausanias are ancient authorities?

Apropos of the Bible, I will take another vast liberty, Monsieur, and draw your attention to Volume II of Cahen's translation,[19] page 186, where you will read this: "Around their necks they wore, suspended from a gold chain, a small figure made of precious stones, which they called The Truth. Debates opened when the president set before himself the image of The Truth." That is a text from Diodorus. Here is another, from Aelian:[20] "The eldest among them was their chief, and the judge of all; around his neck he wore an image carved in sapphire. This image was called The Truth." So be it, then, that [as you say], "this 'Truth' is a very pretty invention by M. Flaubert."

But everything surprises you: malobathrum, which is quite properly written (if you have no objection) either "malobathrum" or "malabathrum"—the gold powder that is still gathered today, as in the past, on Carthaginian beaches; the elephants' ears painted blue; the men who daub themselves with vermilion (cinnabar) and eat vermin and apes; the Lydian men in women's dress, the carbuncles formed by lynxes' urine;[21] the mandragoras (which are in Hippocrates); the ankle-chainlet[22] (which is in the *Song of Songs*—Cahen, Volume XVI, 37); the sprinkling of pomegranate trees with silphium; bound beards; crucified lions, etc.—everything!

Well, no, Monsieur, I did *not* "borrow all those details from the negroes of Senegambia." I refer you, concerning the elephants, to the work by Armandi,[23] page 256, and to the authorities he indicates, such as Florus, Diodorus, Ammianus Marcellinus, and other such Senegambian Negroes.

As for the nomads who eat apes, munch lice, and daub themselves with vermilion: since you might be "asked from what source the author has drawn these precious bits of information," and would be, as you confess, "very embarrassed as to know what to say," let me humbly give you a few hints that may help you in your research.

"The Maxyans . . . paint their bodies with vermilion." "The Gyzantians all paint themselves with vermilion, and eat apes." "Their women [the women of the Adyrmachidae] . . . if they are bitten by a louse, take it up, bite it, etc." You will find all this in the Fourth Book of Herodotus, Chapters CXCI, CXCIV, and CLXVIII.[24] (I feel no "embarrassment" in telling you this.)

It was Herodotus from whom I learned (in his description of Xerxes' army) that the Lydians wore women's dress. Athenaeus, also, in his chapter on the Etruscans and their resemblance to the Lydians, says that they wore women's dress. Finally, the Lydian Bacchus is always portrayed in feminine costume. Is that enough about the Lydians and their garb?

Beards bound up as a sign of mourning are mentioned in Cahen (Ezekiel 24:17),[25] and are found on Egyptian colossi, such as those at Abu Simbel; carbuncles formed by lynxes' urine, in Theophrastus's treatise *On Stones* and in Pliny, Book VIII, Chapter LVII. And as regards the crucified lions (you increase their number to two hundred, no doubt to impute to me an absurdity not my own), do me the favor of consulting Pliny yet again—same book, Chapter XVIII—where you will learn that Scipio Aemilianus and Polybius, riding together in the countryside near Carthage, saw several strung up in that position. *"Quia ceteri metu poenae similis absterrerentur eadem noxa.*"[26] Are those, Monsieur, some of the passages taken indiscriminately [as you suggest] from the *Univers pittoresque*, and "which the higher criticism has tellingly used against M. Flaubert"? What is the "higher criticism" you speak of? Your own?

You make very merry about the pomegranate trees sprinkled with silphium. But this detail is not my invention, Monsieur. It is in Pliny, Book XVII, Chapter XLVII. And I am very sorry to have to spoil your joke about the hellebore that "should be grown at Charenton";[27] but as you yourself say, "the most penetrating mind cannot make up for the lack of acquired knowledge." Of which, by the way, you display a complete lack in affirming that "among the precious stones in Hamilcar's treasury more than one properly belongs to Christian legend and superstition." No, Monsieur: they are *all* in Pliny and Theophrastus.

The emerald steles at the temple entrance, which make you laugh (you have a delightful sense of humor), are mentioned by Philostratus (*Life of Apollonius*) and by Theophrastus (treatise *On Stones*), whom Heeren[28] (Volume II) quotes as follows: "The largest Bactrian emerald is at Tyre, in the temple of Hercules. It is a column of considerable size." Another passage from Theophrastus (Hill's translation): "In their temple of Jupiter there was an obelisk composed of four emeralds."

Despite your "acquired knowledge," you confuse jade, which is a greenish-brown nephrite and comes from China, with jasper, a variety of quartz found in Europe *and* in Sicily. Had you chanced to open the *Dictionnaire de l'Académie française* at the word *jaspe*, you would have discovered without looking further that there is black, red, and white jasper. You would then perhaps have moderated your marvelous mirth and not heaped hilarious reproaches on my master and friend Théophile Gautier for giving a woman (in his *Roman de la Momie*) "green feet"—when the feet he gives her are white. Thus it is not he, but you, who have made "a ridiculous error." If you were a bit less disdainful of travel,[29] you could have seen in the Turin museum the very arm of this mummy, brought from Egypt by M. Passalacqua, and in the gesture described by Th. Gautier—"a gesture" which, according to you, "is certainly not Egyptian."[30]

Even without being an engineer you would have learned the functioning of the saklehs which carry water into the houses, and would have been convinced that I was not mistaken in speaking of black clothing: it is generally worn in those countries, where women of the upper classes never go out except swathed in black. But since you prefer written testimony, let me recommend, in the matter of women's clothing, Isaiah 3:18–24; the Mishna ("de Sabbatho"); Samuel 13:18; St. Clement of Alexandria, *Paedagogus*, II, 13; and Abbé Mignot's dissertations in the *Mémoires de l'Académie des Inscriptions*, Vol. XLII. And as for that abundance of ornamentation which so astonishes you, I am certainly correct in attributing it to a people who encrusted the floors of their apartments with precious stones. (See Cahen, Ezekiel 28:14). But you are unlucky, as regards precious stones.[31]

In closing, let me thank you, Monsieur, for your charming manners—a rare thing nowadays. I have called attention to only the grossest of your inaccuracies, those relating to specific points. As to your vague criticisms, your personal allusions, and your consideration of my book from a literary point of view, I have left them unmentioned. I have kept strictly to your own territory—erudition; and I repeat once more that there I am but middling strong. I know neither Hebrew, nor Arabic, nor German, nor Greek, nor Latin, and I make no boast of knowing French. I have often used translations; on occasion, the originals. In my uncertainties I have consulted the men who in France are considered the most competent, and if I have not been "better guided" it is because I have not had the honor, the advantage, of knowing you: forgive me! Had I taken advice from you, would I "have been more successful"? I doubt it. In any case, I would have been deprived of those proofs of benevolence which you display throughout your article, and I would have spared you the kind of remorse which you express at the close. But let me reassure you, Monsieur: though you seem to be terrified of your own strength, and though you seriously think that you have "torn my book to shreds," have no "fear": set your mind at rest! For you have not been "cruel": you have merely been—trivial.[32]

1. More accurately, the article, entitled "Le Roman archéologique en France," was "on" three publications: principally *Salammbô*, but also Théophile Gautier's *Le Roman de la Momie*, and Ernest Desjardins' *Promenade dans les galeries du Musée Napoléon III*.

2. Le Musée Campana, also called Le Musée Napoléon III, was an assemblage of antiquities bought by the French state from an Italian collector, the Marchese Campana, and opened to the public in Paris in April 1862. For complex legal reasons it was forced to close, amid some scandal, after only a few months. It was dispersed, and some of its contents are now in the Louvre.

Froehner had strangely called *Salammbô* "the natural daughter of *Les Misérables*"—a work of which we have already heard Flaubert's opinion—"and of the Campana collection." Flaubert's riposte has been questioned because of what he wrote to Mlle Leroyer de Chantepie on April 24: "Last Sunday . . . I finally finished my novel *Salammbô*." But a novel is apt to be "finished" several times. Flaubert possibly meant something like: "Six weeks before the Musée Campana opened, everything that would appear in *Salammbô* was down on paper." Indeed in that same letter of April 24 he mentions that the Musée Campana has opened.

3. Christian Tuxen Falbe, *Recherches sur l'Emplacement de Carthage, avec le plan topographique du Terrain et des Ruines de la Ville* (Paris, 1833); Adolphe-Jules-César-Auguste Dureau de la Malle, *Recherches sur la topographie de Carthage* (Paris, 1835).

4. These and the following are identifiable sections or landmarks of Punic Carthage. The Taenia ("ribbon") was the strip of land, south of the city, dividing the present Lake of Tunis from the sea; the Cothon was the military harbor, and so on.

5. The Ancô, which is not mentioned by name in Chapter XV or elsewhere in the

novel, is identified by Flaubert in one of his working notes as the dungeon, hollowed in the rock of the Acropolis, where Mâtho is held in solitary confinement and from which he emerges, on the day of his execution, "bowed almost double, with the bewildered air of wild beasts when they are suddenly released from captivity."

6. Heinrich Friedrich Wilhelm Gesenius (1786–1842), German orientalist and biblical scholar.

7. On introducing Narr'Havas, the Numidian prince, in the early pages of *Salammbô*, Flaubert emphasizes his "blazing, staring eyes." *Feu du souffle* can be translated "fire of the breath," or perhaps "fiery current." One wonders whether Flaubert was aware that *haouah* is also a form of a word meaning "passion." It seems likely that had he known this he would have profited from the word's double intensity.

8. Meaning that the *m* should be pronounced hard, rather than merely giving the syllable a nasal sound, as when *m* or *n*, preceded by a vowel, is written singly.

9. A humorous word coined from the French *chinoiserie*, literally "Chinese knick-knacks," but in common use as "foolish intricacies," "stuff and nonsense." This was one of many journalistic lampoonings of *Salammbô*.

10. The point here seems to be a distinction between Cappadocia, the name of the Roman province north of Cilicia, and the narrow antique application of the name "Asia" to the country around Ephesus. Flaubert had ridden through both regions with Maxime DuCamp in 1850.

11. Probably a metaphor: "to cut their throats." But the more literal "to make them drink [molten] iron" would not be out of place in the *Salammbô* torture repertoire.

12. The Syssites were doubly unfortunate in the printed French spellings of their name. There was the misprint in the first edition, already alluded to; and furthermore, as Froehner had properly shown (a point ignored by Flaubert), the correct French spelling would be "Syssities" (from the Greek *Syssitia*). In English it is usually written "Syssitia." Flaubert's definition of the term is correct. (D.M.)

13. Diodorus Siculus, Greek historian of the first century B.C.

14. Froehner, in his riposte, makes fun of Flaubert's gallicization of the name of the seventeenth-century German scholar "Paulus Fagius"—which was, he says, in itself a latinization of the original "Paul Bucheim." Froehner also corrects Flaubert's "De diis syriis" to "De dis syriis." Selden's title page says "De dis syris."

15. The "zaïmph," the sacred veil, or mantle, of the goddess Tanit, stolen, in the novel, from her temple by the giant Mâtho and retrieved by *Salammbô* in Mâtho's tent at the price (ecstatically paid) of her virginity.

16. Marie-Armand-Pascal d'Avezac-Macaya (1799–1875), French geographer.

17. See letter to Sainte-Beuve, note 33.

18. For Movers see letter to Sainte-Beuve, note 31. The "explanation," as given in Movers' original German text (p. 583), is left in Latin: *pudendum muliebre*.

19. The hebraicist Samuel Cahen (1796–1862) published his French translation of the Old Testament in eighteen volumes (1831–1851). They include the Hebrew text and ample notes by Cahen. The passages from Diodorus and Aelian quoted by Flaubert are in Cahen's "supplementary notes" to Exodus 28:30 ("I have just read Cahen's book from one end to the other," Flaubert had written Ernest Feydeau in August 1857. "I know perfectly well that it's very faithful, very good, very scholarly: no matter! I prefer the old Vulgate, because of the Latin! How it rumbles, beside this poor little puny consumptive French! I'll even show you two or three mistranslations, or embellishments, in the Vulgate, which are much finer than the true meaning.")

20. The anecdotal *Various History* of Claudius Aelianus (Aelian), Roman rhetorician of the age of Hadrian.

21. See letter to Sainte-Beuve, note 17.

22. This is the gold chainlet joining Salammbô's ankles, first described by Flaubert as

worn "pour régler sa marche," and which later snaps when she is in Mâtho's arms. Cahen, in his note to a variant of the Song of Songs 2:7, refers to "the chainlets attached to both legs, to prevent accidents that might befall girls taking overlong strides. This kind of fetter served as a sign of virginity—a sign whose absence could give rise to great scandal at the time of marriage."

23. Pierre-Damien Armandi, *Histoire militaire des éléphants* (Paris, 1843); L. Florus (other names and exact identity uncertain), Latin historian of the age of Hadrian and Trajan: *Epitome de T. Livio Bellorum omnium annorum DCC Libri duo;* for Marcellinus, see letter to Sainte-Beuve, note 31.

24. George Rawlinson's translation of Herodotus, IV, 168 reads: "Their women . . . when they catch any vermin on their persons, bite it and throw it away."

25. Cahen's translation, ". . . ne fais pas de deuil; . . . ne te voile pas le menton" is closer to Flaubert's "beards" than is the King James: "cover not thy lips."

26. Flaubert's slightly faulty Latin has been corrected here. The meaning is: "because the others might be deterred from the same mischief by fear of the same penalty." The "Univers pittoresque" (begun in 1844) was a popular series of seventy illustrated volumes describing the countries of the world.

27. Charenton is a famous mental hospital of seventeenth-century origin in a suburb of Paris, popularly thus called by the name of its location; now officially named L'Hôpital Esquirol. The expression "bon pour Charenton" ("fit for the loony bin") is still current. Froehner's jeer at the "pomegranate trees sprinkled with silphium" reads: "I know that an infusion of this plant was a well known herbal drink . . . What would we say of a gardener who sprinkled his orange trees with linden tea? We would probably send him to grow hellebore at Charenton." (In ancient times hellebore was thought to cure madness.)

28. Arnold Hermann Ludwig Heeren (1760–1842), German author of numerous works on ancient history. It is not certain to which of them Flaubert refers. As to the huge "emeralds," both Theophrastus himself and John Hill, in his notes to his translation (London, 1746), say that they are the stuff of legend and cannot possibly be true emeralds. Flaubert had apparently read Hill carelessly. Froehner, in his riposte, continued to jeer at Flaubert's "emeralds."

29. Froehner had written of some of Flaubert's details that "they smack of the modern traveler, who is perhaps an excellent recounter of traditions picked up along the way, but whose testimony has not the slightest value when it comes to reconstituting the society of ancient Carthage." Flaubert, of course, was "the modern traveler." For example, in connection with Flaubert's mention (a few lines further on) of sakiehs, which he had seen in Egypt, Froehner had expressed doubt that they could raise water to the upper floors of Carthaginian houses, some of which were six stories high.

30. Gautier himself says, in the novel, that the gesture of his beautiful Tahoser, "celle de la Vénus de Milo," is "peu fréquent chez les momies."

31. Flaubert himself seems "unlucky" in this reference. Ezekiel 28:14 does not speak of the floors of apartments. The King James reads: ". . . thou hast walked up and down in the midst of the stones of fire." Cahen's French translation is almost identical.

32. Flaubert's word is *léger*.

◇◇◇◇◇

Froehner defended himself, and counterattacked, in a second article, in which he spoke of his own "urbanity" as contrasted with Flaubert's bad manners. He granted Flaubert "a certain talent for light literature" and urged him not to stray again, in his novel writing, from his native Normandy. The Flaubert-Froehner engagements in what Sainte-Beuve had called the "battle" of *Salammbô* ended with a letter from Flaubert to the editor of *L'Opinion Nationale:*

❖❖❖❖❖

To Adolphe Guéroult

[Paris,] February 2, 1863

Mon cher Monsieur Guéroult:

Forgive me for bothering you once again. But since M. Froehner is to publish in *L'Opinion Nationale* what he has just printed in the *Revue Contemporaine,* I venture to draw his attention to the following:

I did, in fact, commit a *very* grave error. Instead of Diodorus, Book XX, Chapter IV, read Chapter XIX. Another error: I forgot a text concerning the statue of Moloch, in Dr. Jacobi's *Mythologie,* Bernard's translation, page 322, where M. Froehner will once again find the seven compartments that so arouse his indignation.

Also, although he has not deigned to give me a single word of reply concerning (1) the topography of Carthage; (2) the mantle of Tanit; (3) the Punic names I "travestied"; (4) the gods I "invented"; and though he has maintained the same silence regarding (5) the horses consecrated to the Sun; (6) the statuette of The Truth; (7) the bizarre customs of the nomads; (8) the crucified lions; (9) the sprinkling with silphium; along with (10) the lynx carbuncles and (11) the Christian superstitions regarding precious stones; keeping similarly silent about (12) jade, and (13) jasper; making no mention of anything concerning (14) Hanno; (15) women's costumes; (16) the dresses of the Lydian men; (17) the fantastic gesture of the Egyptian mummy; (18) the Campana museum; (19) his quotations (inaccurate) from my book; and (20) my Latin, which he urges you to consider incorrect, etc., I am nonetheless quite ready, concerning all that and all the rest, to admit that he is right, and that antiquity is his private property. Let him therefore enjoy himself in peace, "destroying my edifice," and proving that I know nothing at all . . . For I will not answer him. I will pay no further attention to this gentleman.

I withdraw a word that seems to have displeased him. No: M. Froehner is not *léger.* He is just the opposite. And if I "chose him as a victim, from among so many writers who have disparaged my book," it was because he had seemed to me the most serious. I was certainly mistaken.

Finally, since he interests himself in my biography (as though I troubled myself about his), affirming twice (he *knows!*) that I was six years writing *Salammbô,* I will confess to him that I am not entirely sure, by now, that I was ever at Carthage.

It remains, Monsieur, for both of us to thank you: I, for your having spontaneously offered me such generous hospitality in your newspaper; and as for M. Froehner, he must be infinitely grateful to you. You have given him the opportunity to apprise many people of his existence. This foreigner[1] desperately wanted to become known. Now he is: to his—advantage.

A thousand greetings.

1. Readers of Volume I may nevertheless recall his assertions that he cared nothing for "the idea of a fatherland, that is, a certain portion of the earth's surface drawn on a map and separated from others by a red or blue line," and that "I am as Chinese as I am French."

❖❖❖❖❖

About *Salammbô*, André Malraux once said that what Flaubert wanted it to be was "a series of poetic moments."[1] Surely *Salammbô* is that: a concentrated essence, distilled by Flaubert's imagination from observation and research. Sainte-Beuve, in objecting to Flaubert's method and hating the subject, and Froehner, picking flaws in the research, do not touch the heart of the matter. It is as though one of Delacroix's paintings—say one of his Arab horsemen disemboweling a wild beast—were to be disparaged on the grounds of technique, subject, and some "incorrect" details. Whereas it is Delacroix's fire that counts. Is there fire—one might say "the sacred fire"—in *Salammbô?* Readers have always been, and continue to be, divided in their opinions. The burden of these two chapters has been to display, chiefly in Flaubert's own words, his struggle to light such a fire and keep it burning, and the alternations in his own estimates of what he had accomplished. Even so, his prodigious effort will be considered in conjunction with the observation he himself made when he was beginning the novel: "I would give the demi-ream of notes I've written during the last five months and the ninety-eight volumes I've read, to be, for only three seconds, really moved by the passion of my heroes."

1. André Malraux, "Professions délirantes," in *L'Homme précaire et la littérature* (Paris: Gallimard, 1977). Translated by Jeanine Parisier Plottel in *New York Literary Forum*, 1979.

III

Interlude:
Society
1863–1866

IN JANUARY 1863, two months after the publication of *Salammbô*, there opened in Flaubert's life a curious new episode which is perhaps best introduced by a series of short letters, all of them dated in that month and having to do with a great house in Paris, in the rue de Courcelles.

◇◇◇◇◇

TO EUDORE SOULIÉ

[Paris,] Tuesday [January 13, 1863]

My dear Soulié

We should like to know—Saint-Victor, the Goncourts, and myself—what is customary regarding the staff in the rue de Courcelles. What does one give as New Year's presents? And to whom does one give them? You will be going there tomorrow, Wednesday . . . It would be kind of you to find out about this from Giraud or Mme de Fly . . .[1]

---

1. Eudore Soulié (1817–1876), curator of the Musée de Versailles, was a member of the "inner circle" surrounding Princesse Mathilde Bonaparte; it is not clear why he, presumably au courant with the customs of the princess's household in the rue de Courcelles, should have to seek information from the artist Eugène Giraud (1806–1881), the princess's instructor in watercolor painting, and Mme de Fly, the princess's lady-in-waiting.

Paul de Saint-Victor was a critic of literature and art. He and Flaubert were friendly until he refused to write an article about *L'Éducation sentimentale*, which he disliked.

CAMILLE DOUCET TO FLAUBERT[1]

January 18, 1863
Ministère d'État Théâtres

Mon cher Confrère et Ami,

Here is a letter I promised to hand you myself, but I am a little unwell and send it to you instead.

You are definitely expected on Wednesday, 9 o'clock.

Confidentially, the Emperor and Empress will be there, and—this I whisper in your ear—have expressed the desire to see you.

I have promised you will be there: don't let me down.

All yours,
Camille Doucet

I am writing to Bouilhet today, sending him 2000 francs.

1. Camille Doucet (1812–1895), in addition to being a bureaucrat charged with certain responsibilities regarding ceremonies and the dispensing of grants-in-aid to needy dramatists like Louis Bouilhet, was himself a dramatist, characterized as follows in Larousse, *Grand Dictionnaire Universel:* "His temperament was devoid of those vigorous hatreds felt by genius . . . and this smoothed his path to the Academy." This amiable man succeeded to Alfred de Vigny's chair in the French Academy in 1865.

To Théophile Gautier

[Paris, January 19, 1863]

Mon vieux Théo,

Don't come on Wednesday. I'm invited that evening to Princesse Mathilde's, and we wouldn't have time for a leisurely talk after dinner. Come on Saturday instead. I have alerted DuCamp . . .

Agreed? Till Saturday.

To Félicien de Saulcy[1]

[Paris,] Saturday morning [January 24, 1863]

Mon cher Ami

. . . Do you remember showing me, two or three years ago, a gold repoussé plaque that was brought back from Kamiros by Salzmann?[2] This plaque represented the figure of a woman, which served me for one of Salammbô's costumes. I need to see it again. Where is it? Do you have a drawing of it, or a detailed description?

I have had a request from a very high source, on behalf of a great lady of your acquaintance, for Salammbô's costumes[3] (there are four in my book, including the one taken from the plaque). I am having them drawn by Bida, and shall add an explanatory note, as clear as possible. Such are my occupations at the moment . . .

1. Félicien de Saulcy, archaeologist and numismatist, had published the discovery of the Punic "Marseilles Tariff" (see page 48, note 5). Flaubert had met him in Constantinople in 1850.
2. August Salzmann, another archaeologist, would publish his *Nécropole de Kamiros* in 1865. Alexandre Bida was a well-known painter of Oriental subjects and illustrator of

the Bible. Maxime DuCamp says in his memoirs that Bida declined the commission to design *Salammbô* costumes.

3. Sainte-Beuve wrote to Matthew Arnold on January 13, 1863: "*Salammbô* is our great event! The Empress is so struck by it that she wants to dress as Salammbô at some court masquerade or other, and has expressed a wish to know the author."

❖❖❖❖❖

In 1863 Princesse Mathilde Bonaparte, niece of the great Napoleon, daughter of his brother Jerome, was forty-three years old. In youth she had been spoken of as a bride for her first cousin, Louis Napoleon, now Emperor Napoleon III (there was in reality no blood tie, the Emperor's illegitimacy being well known); but she had married, instead, the wealthy Russian Count Anatole Demidoff. Mistreated by him, she had successfully petitioned Czar Nicholas to order her husband to grant her a legal separation and a large financial settlement; and now she reigned in Paris as what might be called her imperial cousin's unofficial—but subsidized—cultural representative. Her love of society and her taste, of sorts, for the arts, brought her a pension from the civil list, the government favoring her salon in the belief (which proved to be well founded) that it might win the support, or at least moderate the opposition, of members of the "liberal" professions, seduced by the princess's charm and flattered to mingle with ministers and courtiers.

With memorable exceptions, writers have historically been far from immune to the appeal of official pomp, whether royal, republican, or totalitarian; and by 1863 Flaubert was regularly attending the princess's evenings in the rue de Courcelles during those few months of the year he spent in Paris—along with the Goncourts, Sainte-Beuve, Taine, Renan, and others. In addition to being able to help them, Princesse Mathilde—"Notre Dame des Arts," she was sometimes called by her familiars—was capable of true friendship with the artists and writers among her guests, and Flaubert was not the only one to reciprocate. Despite the constant mention of her in memoirs and letters of the time, and the efforts of biographers, the princess remains rather a figure of "a lady of position" than a distinct personality.

Her older brother, Prince Jerome Napoleon, the so-called republican member of the imperial family, nicknamed "Plon-Plon" and married to Princesse Clothilde (Clotilda, daughter of King Victor Emmanuel of Italy), was also interested in the arts. He was said to have tried to stop the government's prosecution of Flaubert as the author of *Madame Bovary* in 1857, and since then the two men had become acquainted. Flaubert came to know, also, one of the prince's many mistresses, the beautiful courtesan Jeanne de Tourbey, and wrote her a number of letters, rather forced in their gallantry and of insufficient interest to include here. His activities in imperial society lasted a few years, ending with the collapse of the regime in 1870. The friendship with Princesse Mathilde was the chief survival.

A passage from a letter he wrote to his niece Caroline in January 1864 is typical of his references—half boastful, half abashed—to this side of his life: "Saturday I dined chez la Princesse Mathilde, and last night (Saturday-Sunday) I was at the Opera Ball until five in the morning (!) with Prince Napoleon and the Ambassador from Turin, in the big imperial box. Voilà. The following should be read as spoken by the sheik: 'How different from our dull life in the provinces!' "[1]

1. "The sheik," a character invented by Flaubert and Maxime DuCamp, was the type of pompous French bourgeois to whom they attributed all possible clichés (see Volume I).

❖❖❖❖❖

To Jules Duplan

Palais de Compiègne,[1] corridor de la Pompe
Second floor, no. 85
[November 12 (?), 1864]

My dear Jules,

Do me the following service pronto. Get yourself to the Passage de l'Opéra and order a bouquet of white camellias[2] from Mme Prévost—the finest possible; I insist that it be ultra-chic. (One has to cut a fine figure when one belongs to the lower orders of society.) The box must arrive here on Monday morning, so that I can present the flowers that evening. The florist can post the bill to me here or you can pay it, as you prefer. Don't forget, for Christ's sake—I'm counting on you. Immediate reply, please. Je t'embrasse.

1. From the following description of imperial weekends at the Château de Compiègne, given in the Larousse *Histoire de France*, it will be seen that at least as far as the date of his visit is concerned, Flaubert was a particularly honored guest:

"During the three weeks of the Compiègne season (from All Saints' Day to the opening of the legislature), five groups of guests were entertained at the château, each group staying for four days, not including the evening of arrival and the morning of departure. It was a particular favor to be invited for November 15, the fête de l'Impératrice . . . For each series, the Empress herself supervised the assignment of rooms, with the guest's name on a card on each door. She did not always manage to satisfy everyone. The painter Couture has been quoted as replying to the sovereign, when she asked him whether he was comfortably installed: 'All the more so, Madame, since my room reminds me of the garret I lived in when I was beginning my career.'

"The guests arrived at four o'clock. The chamberlains took them to their apartments, and they foregathered at 7:15, the ladies in ball gowns, the men in tails and either knee-breeches or narrow trousers, in the grand salon, where the sovereigns soon made their appearance. Dinner was served at 7:30. After dinner, before half past eight, everyone returned to the salon, where there were charades, card games, and dancing. The next day there was a shoot, and in the evening a gala theatrical performance, serious or light as the case might be. The second day, rides in the forest and excursion to Pierrefonds [the nearby medieval château recently restored by Viollet LeDuc]. The third day, riding to hounds; and the fourth, small-game shooting, in which the ladies joined. The following day, after lunch, the guests left, driven to the railway station in the château carriages."

Maxime DuCamp has written about Flaubert at Compiègne:

"He did not dislike grandeur, and wherever he was, he was always himself. Into that society, so subservient and right-thinking, he carried the spirit of literary independence, which he of all men possessed to the highest degree. One night, in a group gathered around the Empress, someone spoke irreverently of Victor Hugo: I don't know whether sincerely or in an attempt to flatter the imperial pair. [Victor Hugo was a political exile at this time.] Gustave Flaubert interrupted in no uncertain terms: 'Stop right there! That man is the master of us all. Hats off when his name is mentioned!' The other persisted: 'Still, you would agree, Monsieur, that the man who wrote Les Châtiments . . .' Flaubert glared: 'Les Châtiments! Magnificent poetry! I'll recite it, if you like!' The subject was quickly changed."

2. White camellias were the favorite flower of the Empress, whose celebrated beauty and grace were not lost on Flaubert. He was ordering the flowers to arrive for her fête on the fifteenth. (Readers of Volume I may recall his broadside at poor Louise Colet when she reproached him for never sending her flowers.) On a later occasion, after seeing the Empress, Flaubert asked Jules Duplan to give Mme Cornu (see page 144, note 1) a message, clearly meant to be passed on, which included the words "I love Her," the capitalization—"Je L'aime"—reverentially identifying the object of his affection.

But by 1869, in a letter to Caroline telling her of seeing the Emperor at a ball given in his honor by Princesse Mathilde, he adds ruefully: "His spouse seems to have forgotten me." By that time, having finished L'Éducation sentimentale, for which he had immersed himself in the history and politics of the past several decades, he was referring ironically to the Emperor as "our Savior."

To His Niece Caroline

[Paris,] Wednesday [February 22, 1865]

What do you want me to tell you about the Prince's ball?[1] It was a very big affair, and very luxurious as far as the decoration of the apartments was concerned. What surprised me most was the number of salons—twenty-three, each opening into the next, not counting the smaller side-rooms. "Monseigneur"[2] was astonished by the number of people I knew. I must have spoken with two hundred. In the midst of this "brilliant society," what did I see? Several mugs from Rouen! Old Lédier, old Corneille, old Barbet, old Rouland, the four of them together. Horrified, I put a distance between myself and that group and went and sat on the "steps of the throne," beside Princesse Primoli. On Saturday said princess sent me her album, for me to inscribe some mighty thoughts therein. I wrote one thought—but it wasn't mighty. Half the ladies who attended the ball are now in their beds, having caught cold on leaving: the confusion in the cloakroom and in the calling of carriages was staggering. I gazed with admiration at the Régent[3] (15 millions) on my Sovereign's head; it's quite a pretty thing. I was never very close to her, but her little spouse passed so near me that if I

67

had chosen to greet him I'd have fallen on his nose.[4] Princesse Clothilde, seeing me with Mme Sandeau[5] on my arm, asked her cousin
[Princesse Mathilde] if that was my wife—inspiring many pleasantries
by both princesses at my expense. Such are the witty cancans I have to
report to you.

.   .   .   .

1. A fête given by Prince Jerome Napoleon at his Paris residence, the Palais Royal.
2. Louis Bouilhet. So called, according to Flaubert's niece Caroline, because of his
"imposing appearance and slightly unctuous manner."
3. The 136-carat diamond (reduced from 410 carats by cutting) bought by Thomas
Pitt (grandfather of William Pitt the elder, earl of Chatham) when he was Governor of
Madras and sold in 1717 to the duc d'Orléans, regent of France. It remained "the property of the French crown" and is now in the Louvre.
4. Napoleon III was considerably under Flaubert's "gigantic" height of 5'8".
5. Mme Sandeau's husband, the novelist Jules Sandeau, had been an early lover of the
young Baronne Dudevant, who had appropriated part of his name to become George
Sand. Sandeau was now librarian at the Palais de Saint-Cloud and a member of the
French Academy.

To Princesse Mathilde

Caude-Côte, near Dieppe, August 16 [1866]

Madame et Princesse,

How kind of you to write me at once! A sign of your large heart.

I don't doubt the good will of M. Duruy,[1] but I imagine that the idea
was somewhat suggested to him by someone else? So the red ribbon[2] is
for me more than a favor, almost a memento. I did not need that, to
have Princesse Mathilde often in my thoughts.

. . . Awaiting the pleasure and the honor of seeing you, Princesse, I
kiss your hands and beg you to believe me your very grateful, devoted,
and affectionate

Gustave Flaubert

1. Victor Duruy (1811–1894), Minister of Education.
2. The red ribbon of the Légion d'Honneur.

To Charles-Augustin Sainte-Beuve

Caude-Côte, near Dieppe, August 16, 1866

Cher Maître,

I have received M. Duruy's letter along with your note. Thank you
for the one and especially for the other. But I am long accustomed to
your way of doing things.[1]

Haven't friends had a little hand in this affair? I mean *un ami* or *une
amie?* The latter has been very kind also: it was from her that I first
learned of my nomination.[2]

A thousand thanks from your sincerely devoted

G. Flaubert

P.S. This should be the occasion for thinking of something witty or heartfelt to say. But my mind is a blank. So—another handshake.

1. Sainte-Beuve was Flaubert's chief proposer for the Légion d'Honneur.

2. A fortnight later Flaubert wrote again to Princesse Mathilde, who had told him that she herself was sending him the cross that is the emblem of the Légion d'Honneur. (The crosses the princess gave her protégés were diamond-studded.) "The present from you will be more precious to me than the nomination in itself. For the honor is shared by many, but not this."

◇-◇-◇-◇-◇

It has been said that Flaubert persuaded himself that he had "fallen in love" with Princesse Mathilde, and that on one occasion he was about to declare himself to her but was overcome by timidity and rushed from the room; and Enid Starkie has noted that in one of his letters to the princess he told her he wished she were a simple bourgeoise so that he could speak to her more easily. The tone of certain of his letters about the court, and some of his language in those to the princess (formulas he used in writing to no one else—"Je me mets à vos pieds"; "Votre très humble, très devoué et très affectionné") bring to mind Voltaire's letters to Catherine the Great.

No doubt to himself, and defensively to at least one friend, Flaubert insisted that favor at court did not soften his memory of his earlier prosecution by the regime, or—by implication—cause him to swerve from his principles. Mlle Amélie Bousquet, the Rouen novelist who had been tactless about Louise Colet's "portrayals" of him (and whose continued presumptions would eventually put an end to their friendship) had now teased him about his acceptance of the Légion d'Honneur; he replied in August 1866:

> What gives me pleasure about the red ribbon is the joy it causes those who love me: that is the best part of it, I assure you. Ah! if one had been given it when one was eighteen! As to forgetting my trial and no longer feeling resentment—not at all! I am made of slate when it comes to receiving impressions, and of bronze when it comes to retaining them; with me, nothing is ever effaced; all is cumulative.

In writing certain of those lines, Flaubert was perhaps remembering the lack of confidence his family had shown in him as a youth, with his father a famous surgeon, his elder brother already studying medicine, and he himself, in their eyes, with aptitude for nothing but scribbling. Had some honor, or at least recognition, befallen him at that time, it would have carried far greater weight than now.

IV

The Beginning of
L'Éducation sentimentale
1863–1866

SHORTLY AFTER the publication of *Madame Bovary*, and when he had already begun to make notes for *Salammbô*, Flaubert had written to Mlle Leroyer de Chantepie (March 18, 1857): "I feel the need to step out of the modern world, which I've dipped my pen into too much; and besides, I find it as wearying to reproduce as disgusting to contemplate." But readers who have become acquainted with Flaubert through his letters will not be surprised to learn that as early as June 1859, before he had reached even mid-point in the Carthaginian novel, he was writing to Ernest Feydeau: "The deeper I plunge into antiquity, the more I feel the need to do something modern, and inside my head I'm cooking up a whole crew of characters."

Who were those modern characters whom he was pondering even while struggling with the Mercenaries of the third century B.C.?

Most probably they were the provisional cast of what would, in fact, be his next—what he would call his "Parisian"—novel: *L'Éducation sentimentale*.[1] But at this same time he was considering a different novel—one about a pair of "bonshommes" whom he referred to as "my two copy-clerks," or "my two troglodytes." (This novel, eventually to be called *Bouvard and Pécuchet*, would be postponed and would be his last work, unfinished at his death.) An entry in one of his notebooks, dated "Today, December 12, 1862, my 41st birthday"—that is, two weeks after the publication of *Salammbô*—contains the first mention of the "Parisian" novel:

> Stopped by at M. de Lesseps to leave a copy of *Salammbô* for the Bey of Tunis. Also left copies for [Jules] Janin, Ed[ouard] Delessert, H[ector] Berlioz. At the Palais Royal, signed the Prince's visitors' book.. Bought two Carcel lamps. Received a letter from B[ouilhet]. And applied myself seriously to the outline of the first part of my modern Parisian novel.

For some time he hesitated between the two projects. "I'm slaving at my Parisian novel, which doesn't advance at all," he wrote Jules Duplan at the end of March, 1863. "It's stupid, stale stuff, nothing sharp or new about it. I haven't thought up a single major scene; I'm not *caught* by this book. I can't manage an erection, and keep masturbating my poor brain in vain. I'm attracted by the story of my troglodytes, and have been working at an outline for that, as well. *It* is good, I'm sure, despite what would be frightful difficulties in varying the monotony of the effect. But I'll be hounded out of France and Europe if I write it!" And to the Goncourts: "I'm working on the outlines of two novels. So far, I don't know which of them to harness myself to."

He kept appealing to Louis Bouilhet to help him make up his mind. "If you really don't feel yourself primed for the sentimental novel, then go full steam ahead with your two clerks," Bouilhet wrote him about this time. And again: "If your Parisian subject is definitely not ripe, that's no cause for despair—it will come later; and in the meantime you have another project, very tart and original, to get to work on."[2]

In early April he was busy at the "sentimental" novel. "I'm working uninterruptedly on the outline of my *Éducation sentimentale*," he wrote to Jules Duplan. "Perhaps it's beginning to take shape. But its general design is bad! It doesn't form a pyramid! I doubt that I'll ever become enthusiastic about this idea. I'm far from cheerful." A week later, also to Duplan:

> "I'm not in a state of grace," as pious folk say; "I can't get it up," as pigs put it. *L'Éducation sentimentale* doesn't move. I lack *facts* . . . In short, I'm disgusted with it. Very probably I'm going to fall back on *The Two Troglodytes*. It's an old idea that I've had for years, and perhaps I should get it off my chest. I'd rather write a book about passion, but one doesn't choose one's subjects: one submits to them. Tomorrow I expect Monseigneur: we're going to talk about all this, and I'll make up my mind, but I feel very empty and very tired, and quite glum.

Once again he wrote to Duplan: "Decidedly, I wasn't born to write modern things; I pay too high a price for dealing with them. After *Salammbô* I should have immediately set to work on *Saint Anthony:*[3] I was all set for it, and it would be done now. At the moment, I'm bored to death: my idleness (which isn't idleness: I keep racking my brains like a poor wretch), my nonwriting, rather, weighs heavy on me. A cursed state!" To the Goncourts he wrote again lamenting his dilemma: "Besides, spring is giving me wild longings to take off for China or the Indies, and Normandy with its greenery sets my teeth on edge like a dish of bitter sorrel. To cap it all, I'm having stomach cramps . . ."

It was in this state of indecision that he wrote his first letter to a new friend, a Russian now living in France, whom he had met at one of the Magny dinners.

1. Flaubert had given this title to a novel written in his twenties. He had wisely put it aside, and it would be published only posthumously, as an example of his juvenilia. "Sentimental Education," the literal and usual translation of "L'Éducation sentimentale," is somewhat ambiguous. "The Story of a Romantic Passion" would be closer to the theme of both books. In spirit, Flaubert's title is related to Goethe's *Die Wahlverwandt-schaften* [Elective Affinities]. Both versions of *L'Éducation sentimentale* treat of love and its illusions: not, as the English title might suggest, of sentimental schooling.

2. Benjamin F. Bart has written about Bouilhet's role in "Louis Bouilhet, Flaubert's 'Accoucheur,'" in *Symposium,* Fall 1963.

3. Except for the few extracts printed in *L'Artiste* during the first excitement over *Madame Bovary, The Temptation of Saint Anthony* was still in manuscript.

◇–◇–◇–◇–◇

To Ivan Turgenev

Croisset, near Rouen, March 16 [1863]

Dear Monsieur Turgenev,

How grateful I am for your present! I have just read your two volumes, and cannot resist telling you that I am enchanted by them.

For me, you have long been a Master. But the more I study you, the more I marvel at your talent. I admire your manner, at once intense and restrained: that sympathy which extends even to the humblest beings and endows landscapes with reflection. We see, and we dream.

Just as when I read *Don Quixote* I long to ride a horse along a road white with dust and eat olives and raw onions in the shade of a rock, so your *Scènes de la vie russe*[1] makes me want to be jolted in a telega among snow-covered fields, listening to the howling of the wolves. Your works emanate a perfume at once sweet and pungent, a charming sadness that reaches to the depths of my soul.

What art you possess! What a mixture of tenderness, irony, observation, and color! And how they are all combined! How you bring off your effects! What sureness of touch!

You are *particular,* and at the same time general. How many things that I have felt and experienced myself I find and recognize in you! In "Trois Rencontres," among others; in "Jacques Passynkof," in the "Journal d'un homme de trop," etc.—everywhere.

But what has been insufficiently praised in you is *heart*—that is, ever-present *feeling,* some profound, secret sensibility.

I was very happy to make your acquaintance a fortnight ago and to shake your hand. Now I do so again, more firmly than ever, and beg you to think of me, *cher confrère,* as

All yours—
G^{ve} Flaubert

1. "Scenes from Russian Life," an early collection of Turgenev's short stories in French translation. Of those mentioned by Flaubert in this letter, "Journal d'un homme de trop" is recognizable as the tale known in English translation as "Diary of a Superfluous Man"; but other titles seldom correspond to their English versions.

◇◇◇◇◇

Still hesitating between the two novels, Flaubert spent the next few months working on an unlikely theatrical piece, *Le Château des coeurs* [The Castle of Hearts], in collaboration with Louis Bouilhet and another Norman friend, a witty politician, Charles d'Osmoy. This was undertaken in the hope of earning some money: *Madame Bovary* and *Salammbô* had both sold well, but the agreements Flaubert had signed with Michel Lévy were much in the latter's favor. Belonging to the French theatrical genre called *féerie*—a spectacle with supernatural characters (fairies, wizards, and so on), requiring special scenic effects—*Le Château des coeurs* is an allegory, a contest between good impulses (fairies) and bad (gnomes) for possession of the human heart. Flaubert would keep tinkering with it, and proposing it to producers, for many years. Never performed, it was the first of his several theatrical misadventures. Later in his life it was printed in installments in a magazine.

Introductory paragraphs of a letter to Bouilhet about this *féerie*, written during a July vacation in Vichy, are more Flaubertian than the unfortunate piece itself:

> I don't know whether it's hot in the Celestial Empire [Bouilhet was studying Chinese], but here the heat is one great fart-blast. Mercury plus humidity means sweat-through-clothes; underwear wringing wet; trickle-trickle between ass-cheeks; underarms, phew!; shoes hell on feet; skin scorched; air stifling, gasp-making, murderous. Frantically oppressive; the only breeze the panting of human breasts; every bourgeois metamorphosed into a hot-air furnace . . . In short, the brain melts and animal spirits are disordered. I feel as flabby as a dog's prick after coitus . . . I have read Renan's *Life of Jesus*, a work about which, between you and me, I am none too enthusiastic . . .

Late in 1863 Flaubert's much loved, motherless, seventeen-year-old niece, Caroline Hamard, who lived with him and her grandmother, and whom he had helped educate, was under family pressure to accept her suitor, Ernest Commanville, a Rouen lumber-merchant, for whom she felt no affection. In writing her the following letter, rather than encouraging her to resist, Flaubert—the self-professed enemy of the bourgeois—incurred a responsibility that was to cost him dear (see Appendix I).

◇◇◇◇◇

To His Niece Caroline

Paris, Wednesday, 3 o'clock [December 23, 1863]

. . . Now let's talk about the big thing.

So, my poor Caro, you're still in the same uncertainty, and perhaps now, after a third meeting, you've advanced no further? It's such a serious decision to make that I'd be in exactly the same state of mind were I in your pretty skin. Look, think, explore yourself heart and soul; try to discover whether this gentleman can offer you any chance of happiness. Human life feeds on more than poetic ideas and exalted sentiments. But on the other hand if bourgeois existence kills you with boredom, what to do? Your poor grandmother wants you to marry, fearing to leave you alone in the world, and I too, dear Caro, should like to see you united with a decent young man who would make you as happy as possible. The other night, when I saw you crying so bitterly, your distress nearly broke my heart. We love you dearly, my darling, and the day of your marriage will not be a merry one for your two old companions. Little jealous though I am by nature, I shall begin by having no liking for the fellow who becomes your husband. But that's not the question. As times goes on I'll forgive him, and I'll love him and cherish him if he makes you happy.

So you see I can't even pretend to advise you. What speaks well for M. Commanville is the way he has gone about things. Moreover, we are acquainted with his character, his background and connections, things it would be next to impossible to know in a Parisian milieu. Here in Paris you might perhaps find young men who are more brilliant; but charm—*l'agrément*—is almost exclusively the property of bohemians. Now the idea of my poor niece being married to a man without means is so dreadful that I won't consider it for a moment. Yes, my darling, I declare I'd rather see you marry a millionaire philistine than an indigent genius. For the genius wouldn't be merely poor; he would be brutal and tyrannical, and make you suffer to the point of madness or idiocy.

The bugbear of living in Rouen has to be considered, I know; but it's better to live in Rouen with money than to be penniless in Paris; and for that matter why shouldn't you move to Paris later if the business goes well?

I am like you, you see; I don't know what to think, I keep saying white one moment and black the next. It's hard to see straight in questions that concern one too deeply.

It will be hard for you to find a husband who is your superior in mind and upbringing. If I knew one who had those qualifications and met all other requirements I'd set off and secure him for you very quickly. So you are faced with having to take a young man of good character who is nevertheless inferior. But will you be able to love a man whom you'll inevitably look down on? Will you be able to live happily with him? That's the whole question. You'll doubtless be badgered to give a quick answer. Don't do anything in a hurry. And whatever happens, my poor Loulou, you know you can depend on the affection of your old uncle, who sends you a kiss.

Take good care of your grandmother. Kiss her for me.
Write me long letters with many details.

❖-❖-❖-❖-❖

Caroline married Ernest Commanville on April 6, 1864. By the time she was off on her melancholy wedding journey, Flaubert had ended his indecision between the two novels: the "sentimental" one, the "livre de passion,"[1] had won out. "I'm hard at work on the outline of my big Parisian novel," he wrote Caroline in Venice. "I'm beginning to see it clearly, but never have I so belabored my poor brain. Ah! How I'd rather be floating on the Grand Canal or strolling on the Lido!" On May 4, after Caroline's return to France: "Yesterday I worked all day with Monseigneur on the outline of my book ... The principal theme has emerged, and the course is now clear. I don't intend to begin writing before September." Meanwhile he studied the historical background for the scenes he would invent: the novel would be laid in the 1840s, and research for it made him more concerned with politics than in the past.

1. *"Inactive* passion," as Flaubert himself would qualify it (see letter to Mlle Leroyer de Chantepie, October 6, 1864).

❖-❖-❖-❖-❖

To Madame Roger des Genettes

[Croisset, summer 1864]

... Before long I'll be able to give a course in socialism; at least I know its spirit and meaning. I have just swallowed Lamennais, Saint-Simon, and Fourier, and am now going over all of Proudhon. If you want to know *nothing* about these people, then read the critiques and résumés written about them; they have always been refuted or praised to the skies, never expounded. One salient feature is common to them all: hatred of liberty, hatred of the French Revolution and of philosophy. All those people belong to the Middle Ages; their minds are buried in the past. And what schoolmasters! What pedants! Seminarians on a spree, bookkeepers in delirium! The reason for their failure in '48 was that they stood outside the mainstream of tradition. Socialism is one face of the past, just as Jesuitism is another. Saint-Simon's great teacher was M. de Maistre, and how much Proudhon and Louis Blanc owe to Lamennais has never been sufficiently told. The Lyons school, the most active, is entirely mystical, like the Lollards. The bourgeois understood nothing of all this. They instinctively sensed what stands at the core of all social utopias: tyranny, antinature, the death of the soul ...

76

◇◇◇◇◇
For Part One of his novel, Flaubert visited the scenes of his hero's birth and education.
◇◇◇◇◇

To Jules Duplan

Sens, Hôtel de l'Ecu de France
Wednesday, 9.30 P.M. [August 17, 1864]

. . . What weather! Miséricorde! I was so soaked at Corbeil that I took a hot bath while my clothes were hung to dry. The aquatic establishment of that wretched locality is staffed by fifteen-year-old girls and a woman who half-opens the door of your bath cabin with unparalleled decorum—never did I see anything so discreet as that arm stretching out along the wall to take my duds . . .

After nearly coming to blows with two coal men and the proprietor of a livery stable, I took the omnibus for Melun in the company of two highly alcoholized masons and a farmhand who kept guzzling brandy and garlic; and reached Melun at 9 P.M., dying of hunger and cold. Beware the Hôtel de Commerce! Then, this morning, I had an *exquisite* drive from Melun to Montereau along the river, past rocky slopes covered with vineyards, in bright sunshine. My driver wore four military decorations on his lapel, which brought me salutations from people in passing vehicles. Arrived here at two o'clock. I visited the collège, austere retreat that saw the education of our great dramatic poet, him whom decency forbids me to name and who is giving himself over to a Richard Darlington kind of existence, as you will see from the enclosed piece of bumf.[1] The concierge of the collège is a woman of about forty, big tits, brunette, good-natured. While she was showing me the dormitory, the idea occurred to me of pushing her down on to one of the beds and skewering her in honor of Doucet. But I reflected that that might have serious consequences, and therefore abstained.

Oh! the lovely sacristan in the cathedral! What an Onuphre![2] A fortnight's growth of beard, a hump on each shoulder blade, turd-shaped proboscis, and a mug! a mug! He showed me the coronation robe of Charles X, various heads of saints, clothes belonging to Thomas à Becket, etc., and "recognized me at once for an art lover." I also saw a tremendous candle, presented by the Pope to Monseigneur;[3] it weighs twenty pounds and is used only once a year. To make it last, it is *never* lit; a seminarian carries it in procession, ahead of Monseigneur.

Think of me on two consecutive evenings "going to the café"![4] Yesterday, to the café favored by Messieurs the military; today, to that preferred by Messieurs the traveling salesmen. They repeat lines from *Lambert*[5] and laugh over items in the *Charivari*.[6] Oh, France!

77

Adieu, little one. I expect to be back in Paris on Saturday, during the day or in the evening. Je t'embrasse.

Ton vieux.

1. In the second chapter of *L'Éducation sentimentale* we learn that Frédéric Moreau, born in Nogent-sur-Seine and eighteen years old when the novel opens in 1840, had been a boarder at the Collège de Sens. In real life the collège had been attended by the "great dramatic poet" Camille Doucet, whom we have already met as a bureaucrat. Richard Darlington, in the play of that name by Alexandre Dumas (the elder) and a collaborator, is ambitious for official posts and honors. The enclosed bumf was, of course, a newspaper clipping.

2. A hypocrite in LeBruyère's *Caractères*.

3. Here not Louis Bouilhet, but the Archbishop of Sens.

4. Elsewhere in the correspondence Flaubert speaks with shame of being on some occasion "reduced" to sitting in a café. He considered it a low and stupid pastime.

5. A play, *Lambert Simnel*, by Scribe and Mèleville.

6. A popular satirical journal.

To Charles-Edmond[1]

[August 1864?]

I'm very sorry that you can't make the little trip to Villeneuve with me. I get so fed up on a train that after five minutes I'm howling with boredom. Passengers think it's a neglected dog; not at all, it's M. Flaubert, sighing. Such is my reason for desiring your company, my dear chap. The which said, *passons* (as Hugo might put it).

I will send your letter to Mme Regnier, and I have no doubt that in her longing to "see herself in print" she'll succumb to your exhortations; but if she asks my opinion in the matter I'll advise her to tell you to go straight to blazes (even admitting that you may be right). Yes, my friend, that I shall do—out of conviction, stubbornness, pride, and were it only to uphold my principles.

Ah! How right I am not to write for periodicals, and what deadly emporiums they are! Their mania for "correcting" manuscripts submitted to them results in everything they print having the same absence of originality. If five novels are published per year in a newspaper or magazine, since all five are "corrected" by one man or by a like-minded committee, the result is five books that are all the same. Look for example at the style of the *Revue des Deux Mondes.* Turgenev told me recently that Buloz cut something from his last story. By that alone, Turgenev has lowered himself in my esteem. He should have thrown his manuscript in Buloz's face, with a couple of slaps added and a blob of spit as dessert. Mme Sand also lets herself be advised and cut. I have seen Chilly open up aesthetic horizons to her! Whereupon she rushed to adopt his suggestions! It was the same with Théo[phile Gautier] at the *Moniteur* in Turgan's time, etc. Good God! In my opinion this condescension on the part of such geniuses comes close to corruption. Because the moment you offer something you've written, it means, if you're not a rascal, that you think it good. You have presumably put all your effort into it, all your soul. One individuality isn't to be substituted for another. A book is a complicated organism. Any amputation, any change made by a third party, denatures it. It may be less bad: no matter—it won't be *itself*.

This is not a plea for Mme Regnier, but I assure you, my friend, that you're on a downward path, and that all you newspapermen are contributing to the further debasement of human character—to the degradation, greater every day, of intellectual matters.

I will show you the manuscript of *Bovary*, adorned with the corrections and cuts made by the *Revue de Paris*. It's a curiosity. To calm me, they urged on me the examples of Frémy and Delessert.

It is certain that Chateaubriand would have spoiled a manuscript by Voltaire; nor could Mérimée have "corrected" Balzac. In short, the *Revue* and I quarreled to such a point that the result was my trial. Those gentlemen were wrong, and yet how shrewd! Laurent-Pichat, my good friend DuCamp, old Kauffmann the silk merchant from Lyon, Fovard the notary.

At which point, mon vieux, I blow you a kiss and say farewell.

1. Charles-Edmond Chojecki (1822–1899), the Polish-born editor of the Parisian newspaper *La Presse*, did not use his family name in his French career as journalist and dramatist. Mme Regnier (1840–1887), wife of Dr. Raoul-Emmanuel Regnier of Mantes, had submitted a novel, *Un Duel de salon*—apparently through Flaubert—to *La Presse*; and the editor's insistence on "corrections" rekindles Flaubert's memories of the battle of *Madame Bovary*. His eloquence renders unnecessary the identification of obscure names. *Un Duel de salon* apparently remained in manuscript. Mme Regnier later published several novels, using the nom de plume "Daniel Darc."

◇◇◇◇◇

Launched on his novel at last, Flaubert revealed its theme and character as he had come to see them:
◇◇◇◇◇

To Mademoiselle Leroyer de Chantepie

Croisset, October 6, 1864

No, chère Demoiselle, I have not forgotten you. I think of you often, of your mind, which is so distinguished, and of your sufferings, which seem to me utterly without remedy.

Our existences are perhaps not as different as they appear to be on the surface and as you imagine them to be. Between the two of us there exists something amounting to a bit more than mere literary sympathy, I believe. My days are spent in solitude, somber and arduous. It is thanks to work that I am able to stifle the melancholy I was born with. But often the old dregs resurface, the old dregs that no one knows of, the deep, secret wound.

Here I am, harnessed now and for the past month to a novel about modern life, which will be laid in Paris. I want to write the moral history of the men of my generation—or, more accurately, the history of their *feelings*. It's a book about love, about passion; but passion such as can exist nowadays—that is to say, inactive. The subject as I have conceived it is, I believe, profoundly true, but for that very reason probably not very entertaining. Facts, drama, are a bit lacking; and then the action is spread over a too extended period. In short, I'm having a good deal of trouble and am full of anxieties. I shall remain here in the country for part of the winter, in order to push ahead a little with this long task.

· · ·

To Madame Roger des Genettes

[Croisset, December 1864]

Just now I am in complete solitude. A fog has been gathering, deepening the silence and seeming to shroud me in a great whitish tomb. I hear no sound except the crackling of my fire and the ticking of my clock. I work by lamplight ten hours out of the twenty-four, and time passes. But I waste so much of it! What a dreamer I am, in spite of myself! I'm beginning to be a little less discouraged. When you next see me, I'll have done almost three chapters—three, not more. But I thought I'd die of disgust during the first. One's faith in oneself is worn down with the years, the flame dies, strength declines. I have a fundamental reason for being depressed—the conviction that I'm writing something useless; I mean contrary to the goal of Art, which is exaltation, of one kind or another. But with the scientific requirements of today, and a bourgeois subject, that goal seems to me altogether impossible. Beauty is not compatible with modern life. So this is the last time I'll deal with it: I've had enough.

· · ·

◇◇◇◇◇

After Flaubert had shown him the beginning of the book, Bouilhet wrote him, late in 1864: "What is particularly serious and strange about your new novel is 'le pavé de Paris.'[1] The first pages are in line with your usual literary habits—descriptions, psychological longings, the birth of love. I am sure in advance that you have found, in general, the right tone, whether your opinion be more or less favorable about any particular passage. And you seem to me quite excited and clairvoyant about what's to come. Weigh the thing, peer into it . . ."

The Goncourts, who dined with Flaubert at Croisset on January 6, 1865, on their way back to Paris from a visit to Le Havre, wrote (with some exaggeration) in their Journal: "He certainly works fourteen hours a day. That goes beyond work; it's the life of a Trappist." Over a year after Flaubert's announcement to Mlle Leroyer de Chantepie that he had begun Part One of the novel, he wrote her, on January 23, 1866, that he had finished it. "When will the whole book be done? That's what I don't know." Soon he was writing Caroline about being "holed up in porcelain factories," and about reading treatises on faience, and Paris newspapers for the year 1847—research which readers of the novel will recognize as underlying sections of Part Two. "Could you tell me what I should read to learn something about the neo-Catholic movement of around 1840?" he asked Sainte-Beuve in March. "My story extends from 1840 to the Coup d'État [December 1851]. I need to know everything, of course, and must get into the atmosphere of the period before writing about it." Several times he mentioned long sessions with Bouilhet, who was continuing his role of literary "midwife," and he sought information from Jules Duplan about laws regulating businesses in 1847, as he wanted to show his entrepreneur Arnoux to be "only a demi-crook—chiefly rattlebrained."

His doubts about the novel persisted.

1. "The streets of Paris," as we might say "the sidewalks of New York"—that is, the atmosphere, the life, of the city. Bouilhet finds it "serious and strange" that Flaubert, no Parisian, should undertake a Parisian novel.

◇-◇-◇-◇-◇

To Alfred Maury

Croisset, near Rouen, August 20, 1866

. . .

You are too kind, my dear friend. I do not share your hopes concerning the novel I'm now writing. On the contrary, I fear it may prove to be a mediocre work, because the conception is faulty. I want to depict a psychological state—an authentic one, in my opinion—which has not yet been described.[1] But the ambience in which my characters live and move is so crowded and teeming that time after time they barely manage to avoid disappearing into it. Thus I am forced to relegate to a middle ground precisely those things that are the most interesting. I skim over many subjects that one would like to see treated more deeply. My purpose is complex—a bad aesthetic method: in short, I think I have never undertaken anything more difficult. We must trust in God, after all!

1. The state of "inactive passion" mentioned earlier.

V

Enter George Sand.
The Completion and Reception
of *L'Éducation Sentimentale*
1866–1869

OF THE COPIES of *Madame Bovary* which Flaubert or his publisher had sent to prominent literary people, one was inscribed "To Madame Sand, Hommage d'un inconnu." This may well have been more advertisement than tribute. Although at the age of eighteen Flaubert had written Ernest Chevalier, "I have read few things as fine as *Jacques*," his opinion of George Sand's writing had changed in the intervening years. "I read some G. Sand every day, and regularly remain indignant for a quarter of an hour," he wrote to Louis Bouilhet in May 1855, when Mme Sand's *Histoire de ma vie* was being serialized in *La Presse*. At that time they had apparently not met.

Shortly after receiving *Madame Bovary*, Mme Sand noted in her diary for April 30, 1857, that "G. Flaubert" had been at a theatrical opening she had attended; he had perhaps been presented to her there. The following September 29, an article about literary realism, paying particular attention to *Madame Bovary*, was printed in a series she was contributing to the newspaper *Le Courrier de Paris*.[1] Learning of it, Flaubert wrote to Jules Duplan: "Send me Mme Sand's article. Wouldn't it be 'the proper thing' for me to write a little word of thanks to that latter-day Dorothée? The comparison is perhaps irreverent. Still, isn't it widely said of her that she 'ejaculates like a man'? For she, too, has her 'philosophy.'"[2]

If Flaubert read the article in question, he discovered a new defender. Though finding *Madame Bovary* "desolating," and dismayed by its pessimism, George Sand recognized "the hand of a master" and "great talent": the novel was "a brilliant debut," and not at all immoral. It is not known whether Flaubert wrote to her at this time, but it is certain that he never again wrote scabrously about her.

Two years later, after seeing her occasionally, he wrote to Ernest Feydeau: "I gather you idolize la mère Sand. I find her personally a charming woman. As for her doctrines, as expressed in her writings— beware! A fortnight ago I reread *Lélia*. Read it. I beg you, read that book again!"[3] Even when their friendship came to full flower Flaubert would have trouble reconciling the George Sand who was so "charming"—as well as good, wise, and adorable—with the George Sand of the inadmissible "doctrines."

La Presse published Mme Sand's laudatory review of *Salammbô* in January 1863, and she replied to Flaubert's letter of thanks (now lost):

1. "Le Réalisme," posthumously reprinted in *Questions d'Art et de Littérature* (1878).

2. Dorothée, Mme d'Esterval, in Sade's *La Nouvelle Justine*, is endowed with a physical trait which makes her (like other women in Sade's pages) "more man than woman." In this respect she resembles the Comtesse Gamiami, the chief character in a later pornographic novel, *Gamiami ou deux nuits d'excès* (1833–1835), by "Alcide de M . . ." (widely thought to be Alfred de Musset, writing spitefully about George Sand after their rupture). The "philosophy" refers to the peculiar moral doctrines professed by characters in Sade's *La Philosophie dans le boudoir.*

3. One of George Sand's lifelong "doctrines," preached with particular explicitness in her early novel *Lélia*, was "reciprocity"—woman's right to experience, rather than merely provide, physical and spiritual ecstasy in love. "Where liberty and reciprocity do not exist," she would write in one of her letters to Flaubert, "there is outrage against holy nature."

◇◇◇◇◇

GEORGE SAND TO FLAUBERT

Nohant, January 28, [18]63

Mon cher frère,

You must not be grateful to me for having done a duty. Whenever the critics do theirs I will keep silent, for I prefer producing to judging. But everything I had read about *Salammbô,* before reading *Salammbô* itself, was unjust or inadequate. Silence would have seemed to me cowardice—or laziness, which closely resembles it. I don't at all mind adding your adversaries to my own. A few more, a few less . . .

I must ask you to forgive my rather puerile criticism regarding the Defile of the Axe. If I let it stand it was because a reservation added to the sincerity of my admiration.

We are but slightly acquainted. Come and see me when you have time. It's not far, and I am always here. But I am an old woman;[1] don't delay until I'm in my second childhood.

Help me solve a puzzle. In September I received an interesting dried plant in an anonymous envelope. It seems to me today that the handwriting is yours. But that is unlikely: how would you know that I have a keen interest in botany?

What stays with me, in your thanks, is the tone of friendship, and this I know I merit.

1. Now in her sixtieth year and a grandmother, George Sand (born, in 1804, Amandine Lucile Aurore Dupin) was known for the placidity—some called it heaviness or tor-

por—that masked her habitual and formidable industry. (Her collected works constitute over one hundred volumes.) Her nature was paradoxical: she once said of herself, "My soul is impatient, sombre, haughty; my temper withdrawn, indolent, calm." Few writers, and perhaps no woman, have had more biographers. Her chroniclers never tire of recounting her descent on the paternal side, through many misalliances, from Frédéric Auguste de Saxe, seventeenth-century king of Poland, and the eighteenth-century Maréchal de Saxe; her mother was a Parisian bird-seller. The story continues with her marriage to the rustic Baron Casimir Dudevant, the birth of their two children, their separation, her "liberation" and literary beginnings in Paris, including her adoption of a new name (see page 68, note 5); and her affairs with Musset, Chopin, and several others. The range of the writings by which she made her living was as wide as that of her friendships; she was a pamphleteer in the Revolution of 1848, during which she was de facto Minister of Propaganda until the June Days. Then came years of laborious rural existence with household, farm tenants, and guests, and above all her pen (it was her habit to write twenty pages during the night hours) in the charming old country house inherited from her grandmother at Nohant. The house, about 175 miles south of Paris, is little changed and may be visited today.

To George Sand

[January 31, 1863]

Chère Madame,

It's not that I'm grateful to you for having performed what you call a duty. I was touched by your goodness of heart; and your sympathy made me proud, that's all.

Your letter, which I have just received, adds to your article and goes beyond it, and I don't know what to tell you other than, quite frankly, that I love you for it.

M. Aucante has asked me to get you a copy of *L'Opinion Nationale*.[1] You will receive it at the same time as this letter.

No, it wasn't I who sent you a flower in an envelope last September. But what is strange is that at that same time I was sent a leaf, in the same fashion.

As for your very cordial invitation, I answer neither yes nor no, like a true Norman. Perhaps I'll surprise you some day this coming summer. Because I greatly long to see you and talk with you.

All my affection. I kiss both your hands, and am

All yours,
G^ve Flaubert

Boulevard du Temple 42; or Croisset, near Rouen

P.S. I should very much like to have your portrait to hang on the wall of my study in the country, where I often spend long months quite alone. Is the request indiscreet?[2] If not, I send you my thanks in advance. Accept them along with the others, which I reiterate.

1. The issue containing Froehner's article on *Salammbô*. Emile Aucante was Mme Sand's man of business.
2. Mme Sand replied that she would send her portrait later. "Thank you for wanting

to have my face, so insignificant in itself as you well know. What counts for more is the understanding inside the head, and the appreciation in the heart."

◇◇◇◇◇

During the next few years their paths sometimes crossed when Mme Sand was in Paris, usually for the opening of a play drawn, either by herself or by a collaborator, from one of her novels. On February 29, 1864, they were together at the triumphant first performance of *Le Marquis de Villemer* in the Théâtre de l'Odéon, where she was the wildly applauded "Author! Author!" and he a guest with her in Prince Napoleon's box. "You were so good and so sympathetic to me at the première of *Villemer* that I no longer merely admire your admirable talent," she wrote him a fortnight later, "I love you with all my heart."

Finally, in 1866, they truly discovered each other. It was at one of the Magny dinners—the first to which she (the only woman present) was invited. "Dinner chez Magny, with my little friends," she wrote in her diary for February 12. "They gave me the warmest possible welcome. They are all very brilliant, except the great scholar Berthelot.[1] Gautier, constantly sparkling and paradoxical; Saint-Victor charming and distinguished. Flaubert, impassioned, I find more sympathetic than the others. Why? I don't yet know." From then on the friendship developed rapidly. In May she asked Flaubert to accept the dedication of the novel she had just finished, *Le Dernier amour*; in August, after a weekend visit to Alexandre Dumas on the Normandy coast, she spent a few days at the Flaubert house in Croisset. "She is always very natural, not at all a bluestocking," Flaubert wrote to Princesse Mathilde. "I'm experienced in that line, you know"—a reference to poor Louise Colet. And for the first time in years he made favorable mention of one of Mme Sand's novels—the one dedicated to him. "I think you're very severe about *Le Dernier amour*," he told the princess. "In my opinion there are some quite remarkable things in this book."[2]

From then on there was a constant exchange of letters between Croisset, or Paris, and Nohant. In one dated September 12, 1866, George Sand marveled at the diversity of Flaubert's work—the contrasts between *Madame Bovary* and *Salammbô*, and certain scenes from *The Temptation of Saint Anthony* that he had read to her during the Croisset visit. "You are a singular being," she wrote him, "very mysterious, and at the same time gentle as a lamb. I greatly wanted to question you, but felt too much respect for you to do so . . . Sainte-Beuve, though he loves you, claims that you are frightfully dissolute. But perhaps Sainte-Beuve sees with eyes that are none too pure?"

1. Marcelin Berthelot (1827–1907), the chemist.
2. Perhaps Flaubert was accustoming—or resigning—himself to George Sand's free-

flowing style, so different from his own. Stendhal once said, thinking of his own very limited public: "If the *Chartreuse* were translated into French by Mme Sand, it would be a success, but would require three or four volumes to express what it now does in two."

Mme Sand was well aware of her own tendency. "I wonder why I couldn't have said in twenty lines what has already covered as many pages," she says of herself in *A Winter in Majorca.* And in her novel *Elle et Lui* [She and He], based on her affair with Alfred de Musset, the painter Laurent says to the heroine, Thérèse: "I wasn't born like you, with a little steel spring in my brain, so that I'd have only to press the button to set the will to work. *I* am a creator!"

◇-◇-◇-◇-◇

To George Sand

[Croisset,] Saturday night [September 22, 1866]

I, "a mysterious being"! chère maître,[1] come now! On the contrary, I find myself revoltingly banal, and am often thoroughly bored by the bourgeois I have under my skin. Sainte-Beuve, between you and me, doesn't know me at all, whatever he may say.

I even swear to you (by your granddaughter's smile)[2] that I know few men less "dissolute" than I. What deceives superficial observers is the dissonance between my feelings and my ideas. If you want my confession, I'll make you a full one.

The sense of the grotesque has kept me from slipping into a disorderly life. I maintain that cynicism confines one to chastity. We'll have a great deal to say to one another about this if you're willing, the next time we meet.

Here is the program I propose. This house will be cluttered and uncomfortable for a month, but toward the end of October or the beginning of November (after the opening of Bouilhet's play), I hope nothing will prevent your coming back here with me, not for a day, as you say, but for a week at least. You will have your room, "with a table and everything needed for writing." Is it agreed? There will be just the three of us, counting my mother.

. . . . .

I have read, straight through, the ten volumes of your *Histoire de ma vie* (I already knew about two-thirds of it, but only in fragments.) What struck me most is the convent life. I have many thoughts about it, which I'll remember to tell you . . . What wish shall I make for you? *My* wish is to see you . . . My mother and I speak of you every day. She'll be happy to see you again.

1. Flaubert's customary salutation to Mme Sand would be this double tribute—the combination of the feminine form of the adjective, *chère* ("dear"), with the masculine *maître* ("master").

2. The infant Aurore, born January 19, 1866, daughter of Maurice Sand and his wife, Carolina ("Lina") Calamatta.

George Sand to Flaubert

Nohant, La Châtre, Indre, September 28, [18]66

. . . I have packed and sent by express a good proof of the drawing by
Couture, signed by the engraver, my poor friend Manceau.[1] It's the best
one I have, and it was down here. I have added a photograph of a
drawing by Marchal, which was also a good likeness; but one changes
from year to year. Age constantly gives another character to the face of
people who think and seek; that is why their portraits don't look alike
and don't resemble them for very long. I dream so much, and live so
little, that sometimes I'm only three years old. But the next day I'm
three hundred, if the dreaming was sombre. Isn't it the same with you?
Doesn't it seem to you, at times, that you're beginning life, without
even knowing what it is, and at other times don't you feel the weight of
several thousand centuries, with a vague memory of them, and an impression of pain? . . .

1. Alexandre Manceau, thirteen years George Sand's junior and a friend of her son
Maurice, had begun his long role as her secretary, confidant, and lover in 1849. His continued presence at Nohant made difficulties between Mme Sand and Maurice, however,
especially after the latter's marriage in 1862; and in 1864 Mme Sand had left Nohant to
live briefly with the ailing Manceau in Palaiseau, near Versailles. He died there the next
year, nursed by her to the end. Soon thereafter she returned to Nohant, using the house
at Palaiseau only occasionally. She sold it a few years later.

To George Sand

Croisset, Saturday night [September 29, 1866]

So now I have that beautiful, beloved and famous face! I'm going to
have a wide frame made for it, and hang it on my wall. Like M. de Talleyrand to Louis-Philippe, I can say, "This is the greatest honor ever
paid my house." But that's a poor phrase, you and I being worth something more than those two fellows.

Of the two portraits, I prefer the drawing by Couture. Marchal saw
only the "good woman" in you; but for me, old Romantic that I am, the
other is the "portrait of the author" that so often set me dreaming in my
youth . . .

To George Sand

Croisset, Saturday night [September 29, 1866]

I do not experience, as you do, that sense of a life that is beginning,
the stupefaction of an existence freshly unfurling. It seems to me, on
the contrary, that I have always existed! And I am *possessed* by memories

that go back to the Pharaohs. I see myself at different moments of history, very clearly, in various guises and occupations. My present self is the result of all my vanished selves. I was boatman on the Nile, *leno* [procurer] in Rome at the time of the Punic wars, then Greek rhetorician in Suburra, where I was devoured by bedbugs. I died, during the Crusades, from eating too many grapes on the beach in Syria. I was pirate and monk, mountebank and coachman—perhaps Emperor of the East, who knows?

Many things would be explained if we could know our *real* genealogy.[1] For since the elements that make a man are limited, mustn't the same combinations reproduce themselves? Thus "Heredity" is a correct principle that has been incorrectly applied. So it is with that word as with many others. Everybody takes hold of it from a different end, and nobody understands anybody else. The psychological sciences will remain where they are today—that is, at a dim and foolish stage—as long as there is no precise nomenclature, and as long as it is permitted to use the same expression to signify the most diverse ideas. When categories are confounded, farewell Morality!

Don't you find that *basically* we've lost the track since '89? Instead of continuing along the highroad, which was broad and splendid, like a triumphal way, we have wandered off along little by-paths and are floundering in quagmires. Perhaps it would be wise to return to d'Holbach for a time? Before admiring Proudhon shouldn't we know Turgot?

But in that case, what would become of CHIC, that modern religion? Chic opinions: being *for* Catholicism (without believing a word of it), being *for* slavery, being *for* the House of Austria, wearing mourning for Queen Amélie, admiring *Orpheus in Hades*, taking part in Agricultural Fairs, talking Sport, cultivating a cold demeanor, being an Idiot even to the point of regretting the treaties of 1815: such are the very latest.

Ah, you think that because I spend my life trying to write harmonious sentences, avoiding assonances, I don't have my own litle judgments on things of this world. Alas, I do; and I'll die mad from not having uttered them . . .

---

1. Flaubert can scarcely have seen Gregor Mendel's *Principles of Heredity*, published in German the previous year. It received little attention until 1900.

TO MADAME ROGER DES GENETTES

[Croisset, November 12, 1866]

I'm so exhausted from having been called out to a fire last night[1] that I can scarcely hold a pen. Actually I don't regret the labor: I was repaid by the spectacle of bourgeois and administrative stupidity in all its splendor. To maintain order, the authorities sent for troops, who proceeded to cross bayonets *against* the firefighters, and also some cavalry, who blocked all the streets of the village. It's inconceivable, the element of confusion that power injects everywhere.

My illustrious friend, Mme Sand, left Saturday afternoon. There was never a better woman, more good-natured and less of a bluestocking. She worked all day, and at night we chattered like magpies until three in the morning. Though she's a bit too benevolent and benign, she has insights that evince very keen good sense, provided she doesn't get on to her socialist hobbyhorse. Very reserved concerning herself, she talks freely about the men of '48[2] and frankly stresses their goodwill rather than their intelligence. I showed her the sights of Rouen. My mother finds her delightful. Now I must settle down to a steady grind, for every distraction upsets me. What an absurd life mine is, and I want no other! . . .

1. A civic duty—for which there was plenty of water, as the Seine flowed past the village.
2. Mme Sand wrote happily in her diary about her week at Croisset. Her entry for Wednesday, November 7, records in part: "Flaubert reads me the first part of his novel. It is good, good. He reads from ten to two. We talk till four." Apart from the sessions with Bouilhet, this is the first mention of any reading aloud from *L'Éducation sentimentale*. Mme Sand would continue to supply Flaubert with memories of 1848 for what are some of the best scenes in the novel.

To George Sand

[Croisset,] Monday night [November 12–13, 1866]

You are sad,[1] pauvre amie et chère maître. It was you I thought of on learning of Duveyrier's death. Since you loved him, I am sorry for you. This loss adds itself to the rest. How many of the dead we have in our hearts! Each of us carries his necropolis within him.

I've been all at odds since you left: I feel I haven't seen you for ten years. My mother and I speak only of you; everyone here loves you. What constellation were you born under, to be endowed with so many qualities, so diverse and so rare? I don't know what to call the feeling I have for you: it's a very particular kind of affection, such as I have never felt for anyone until now. We got along well together, didn't we? It was nice.

It was so very good, in fact, that I don't want to let others enjoy it. If you make use of Croisset in one of your books, disguise it, so that it won't be recognized. That would oblige me. The memory of your presence here is for the two of us, for me. Such is my selfishness.

I missed you particularly last night at ten o'clock. There was a fire at my woodseller's. The sky was pink and the Seine the color of red-currant syrup. I worked at the pumps for three hours and came home as tired as the Turk and the giraffe.[2]

... A Rouen newspaper (*Le Nouvelliste*) reported your visit to Rouen, with the result that on Saturday, after leaving you, I ran into several bourgeois who were indignant with me because I hadn't exhibited you. The best thing was said to me by an ex-Magistrate: "Ah! If we'd known she was here ... We'd have ..."—pause for five minutes while he hunted for the phrase—"we'd have ... *given her a smile!*" That would have been little enough, no?

... To love you "more" is difficult for me. But I do embrace you fondly. Your letter of this morning, so melancholy, went deep. We parted at the moment when many things were rising to our lips. All the doors between us are not yet open. You inspire me with great respect, and I dare not ask you questions.

Adieu. I kiss your good and lovely face, and am

Your

G^{ve} Flaubert[3]

1. George Sand had written: "On my arrival in Paris I had some sad news. Last night while you and I were talking—and I think that the day before, we had talked about him—my friend Charles Duveyrier died, a man of most tender heart and candid spirit. He will be buried tomorrow. He was a year older than I. My generation is disappearing, one by one ... I give you the part of my heart that he had: added to what you already have, that makes a very large portion. I wept all night ... Love me *more* than before, since I'm suffering." Charles Duveyrier was a Saint-Simonian lawyer, journalist, and dramatist.

2. An allusion to an old vaudeville skit about the first live giraffe brought to France, in 1827. (A.J.)

3. The present editor has followed the example of earlier French editors in not including Flaubert's signature at the end of all his letters. Unlike Mme Sand, who often omitted her "G. Sand," Flaubert always affixed his "G^{ve} Flaubert."

TO GEORGE SAND

[Croisset,] Saturday morning [November 17, 1866]

Don't torment yourself regarding information about the newspapers [of the 1840s]. They will take up little space in my book and I am in no hurry.

But when you have nothing to do, jot down for me on a scrap of paper what you remember about '48. Then you can fill it out when we talk. I'm not asking you for a treatise, needless to say—just a few of your own recollections.

.   .   .

If your little engineer has made a vow,[1] and if that vow comes easily to him, he is right to keep it; otherwise, it's pure folly, between you and me. Where is liberty to exist, if not in passion? Catholicism, whose only idea has been to inhibit sexual enjoyment—that is, to repress Nature—

has overaccustomed us to setting a high value on chastity. We give such things a grotesque importance! One must no longer be spiritualist or materialist, but *naturalist*. Isis seems to me superior to the Virgin, as well as to Venus. No! "In my day" we made no such vows. We made love! And boldly! But it was all part of a broad eclecticism. And if we kept away from the "Ladies," as I did, absolutely, for two years (from 21 to 23), *it was out of pride*, out of self-defiance, as a show of strength. After which, we would give ourselves over to excesses of the opposite kind. We were Romantics, in short—reds, utterly ridiculous, but in full flower. The little good left in me comes from those days!

Adieu, ma chère maître. I love and embrace you tenderly.

G^{ve} Flaubert

Do you know, you're spoiling me with all the sweet things you say to me in your letters.

1. Mme Sand had written him of a young friend who had promised his fiancée to remain chaste during the four years that must elapse before their marriage. "You would tell him he's stupid, but I preach him *my* morality, that of an old troubadour." From now on Flaubert and Mme Sand would sometimes refer to themselves as "two troubadours," perhaps with overtones relating to their Romantic pasts and present chaste affection. (See following letter, note 3.)

To George Sand

Croisset, Tuesday, 5 o'clock [November 27, 1866]

You are lonely and sad down there;[1] it's the same with me, here. Where do they come from, these waves of black depression that engulf one from time to time? It's like a rising tide. You feel you're drowning, you have to flee. At such moments I lie flat on my back. I do nothing—and the flood recedes.

My novel is going very badly for the moment. Add to that the deaths I have learned of: that of Louis de Cormenin (a friend for twenty-five years), of Gavarni,[2] and then all the rest. But this will pass.

You don't know what it is, to spend an entire day with your head in your hands, taxing your poor brain in search of a word. With you, the flow of ideas is broad, continuous, like a river. With me it's a tiny trickle. I can achieve a cascade only by the most arduous artistic effort. I know them well, the Pangs of Style! In short, I spend my life racking my heart and my brain: such is the true essence of your friend.

You ask him if he sometimes thinks of "his old troubadour of the clock."[3] Doesn't he, though! And he misses her. They were very sweet, our nighttime chats. There were moments when I had to restrain myself from giving you little kisses, as though you were a big child! Your ears must have burned last night. I dined at my brother's with all his family.

We spoke only of you, and everyone sang your praises. Except me, of course: I disparaged you to the limit, beloved chère maître.

Apropos of your last letter (and by a natural train of ideas), I reread old Montaigne's essay called "Some Lines of Virgil." What he says about chastity is precisely what I believe.[4] It's the Effort that is virtuous, and not the Abstinence in itself. Otherwise one would have to curse the flesh, like Catholics. God knows where that leads! So, at the risk of always harping on the same string, and of being a Prud'homme, I repeat that your young man is wrong. If he's celibate at twenty, he'll be an ignoble old rake at fifty. Everything has its price! Large natures (and those are the good ones) are above all prodigal, and don't keep such strict account of how they expend themselves. We must laugh and weep, love, work, enjoy and suffer—*vibrate* as much as possible, to the whole extent of our being. Thus it is, I believe, to be truly human.

Try to maintain your serenity. Soon you'll be seeing your granddaughter. That will do you good. And think of this old man, who sends you all his affection.[5]

1. Mme Sand had written from Palaiseau, where, she said, she was "sharing her solitude with a dead man [Alexandre Manceau], whose life ended here, like a lamp extinguished but still present."

2. Louis de Cormenin had been one of the editors of *La Revue de Paris* during its serialization of *Madame Bovary*. Gavarni, the caricaturist, had been one of the founders of the Magny dinners.

3. "At Croisset do you sometimes think of your old troubadour of the inn clock, who always sings, and always will sing, of perfect love?" Mme Sand had written to Flaubert on November 22. Had they perhaps seen, in some inn, a Romantic-period clock with the figure of a troubadour painted on its case? In *A Winter on Majorca*, Mme Sand had written: "Like all southern people, the Majorcans are born musicians and poets, or, as their ancestors called them, 'troubadours,' *trobadors*, which we might translate as 'improvisers.'"

4. "I guard myself from temperance as I formerly did from volupté—it draws me too far back, even to dullness. I desire to be master of myself in every way. Wisdom has its excesses, and has no less need of moderation than does folly."

5. Replying on November 30, Mme Sand, after defending her young man and his vow of chastity—since his fiancée is in agreement, why dissuade him?—goes on to speak of sex and the artist:

"I don't believe in those Don Juans who are Byrons at the same time. Don Juan didn't write poems; and Byron, they say, made love very badly. He must sometimes—one can count such emotions in one's life—have experienced complete ecstasy of heart, mind, and senses; he knew enough about that to be one of the poets of love. No more is required by the instruments of our sensibility. The continual gust of petty appetites would destroy them."

And she naively urges Flaubert to try to write more easily, confessing that she does not at all understand the "anguish" he experiences in his work. She wishes that some day he would "write a novel in which the artist (the real artist) is the hero . . . The artist is such a fine type to portray . . . You should paint yourself."

There exists a somewhat similar letter written by her to Flaubert the previous day and never sent, perhaps because she sensed the ineptitude of her "advice." (A.J.)

To George Sand

[Croisset,] Wednesday night [December 5–6, 1886]

····

I'm not a bit surprised that you fail to understand my spells of literary anguish. I don't understand them myself. They exist, however, and
are violent. At such times I no longer know how to go about writing,
and after infinite fumbling I succeed in expressing a hundredth part of
my ideas. Nothing spontaneous about your friend! Far from it! These
last two days, for example, I've been casting and recasting a paragraph,
and still haven't solved it. At times I want to weep. I must seem pitiable
to you. How much more so to myself!

····

As for our subject of discussion (apropos of your young man), what
you write me in your last letter is so much my way of viewing things
that I've not only put it into practice, but preached it. Ask Théo! Let's be
clear, however. Artists (who are priests) risk nothing by being chaste.
On the contrary! But bourgeois—what's to be gained by their being so?
Some people have to remain within the human race. Happy indeed are
those who never stir beyond it!

My view—contrary to your own—is that nothing good can be done
with the character of the "ideal Artist." Anything of the kind would be
monstrous. Art isn't intended to depict exceptional beings.[1] I feel an
unconquerable aversion to putting anything of my heart on paper. I
even think that a novelist *hasn't the right to express his opinion* on anything
whatsoever. Has God ever expressed his opinion? That is why there are
so many things that make me gag—things I long to spit out, and which I
choke down instead. Indeed, what would be the use of uttering them?
Any Tom, Dick, or Harry is more interesting than Monsieur G. Flaubert, because they are more *general* and consequently more typical.

There are days, nevertheless, when I feel I'm at a level lower than
cretinism. I now have a bowl of goldfish. And they entertain me, they
keep me company while I eat my dinner. Imagine taking an interest in
anything so inane!

Adieu—it's late and I have a headache. I kiss you fondly.

1. So says the depictor of Salammbô, St. Anthony, St. Julian, and Hérodias!

George Sand to Flaubert

[Paris, December 7, 1866]

Not put anything of your heart into what you write? I don't understand at all, oh, but not at all. To me it seems that you can't put anything else into it. Can you separate your mind from your heart? Is it
something different? Can feeling limit itself? Can one's being split itself

in two? In short, not to give of yourself entirely in your work seems to me as impossible as to weep with something other than your eyes or to think with something other than your brain. What was it you meant? Answer when you have time.

To George Sand

[Croisset,] Saturday night [December 15–16, 1866]

. . .

I expressed myself badly when I told you "one must not write with one's heart." What I meant was: don't put your own personality on stage. I believe that great art is scientific and impersonal. What is necessary is, by an intellectual effort, to transport yourself into your Characters—not attract them to yourself. Such at least is the method—which amounts to this: try to have a lot of talent, and even genius, if you can. What vanity, all Poetics, all works of criticism! The complacency of the gentlemen who produce such things flabbergasts me! Oh! nothing daunts those numbskulls!

. . .

❖-❖-❖-❖-❖

Flaubert had recently thanked Hippolyte Taine for sending him the second volume of his Italian travels, *Florence et Venise*. Taine replied, mentioning certain unfavorable reviews of the book, and sending Flaubert the following questionnaire in connection with the study he was now preparing, the celebrated *De l'intelligence*:

I need some hypertrophic cases to illustrate what I have to say about imagination and images. I am seeking information from such cases, and you are one of them.

1. When you have reached the point of imagining, in minute detail, a landscape, a character, such as Emma's face and figure, or the horde trapped in the Defile of the Axe, are there moments when you might confuse the intensive imagination with the real object?

2. Having imagined a character or a place with intensity and at length, have you ever become obsessed by it, as by a hallucination, with the character spontaneously changing shape before your eyes?

3. Ordinarily, after looking at a wall, a tree, or a face, when you recall it do you see, with exactitude, its irregularities, the uneven details of its surface—completely, integrally? Or do you perceive merely such and such a gesture, angle, effect of light—in short, three or four fragments, no more?

You are doubtless familiar with the intense but quiet images, and the pleasant hallucinations, which precede sleep. When one is

95

dozing after dinner or beside the fire, one is very aware of them, being still sufficiently conscious. Is there a great difference in intensity between these and the novelist's intuition, or artistic and poetic image, as you know it? Or rather is the difference simply that the images or hallucinations occurring on the verge of sleep are disconnected and involuntary?

You would do me a service, a great service, if, drawing on your own experience, you could reply to some or all of these questions. I am addressing similar ones to Doré, to a chess player who can make his moves without looking at the board, and to a mathematician who can make extended calculations in his head.

Several of Flaubert's replies are incorporated in *De l'intelligence*, where Taine refers to him as "the most lucid and most accurate of modern novelists."

◇◇◇◇◇

To Hippolyte Taine

Croisset, Tuesday night [late November 1866]

Let the blockheads talk away, cher ami—your style is neither "fatiguing" nor "unintelligible." The author of the brilliant passages which fill your last book has mastered the art of expressing his thoughts in prose.

Only, travel writing as a genre is *per se* almost impossible. To eliminate all repetitions you would have had to refrain from telling what you saw. This is not the case in books devoted to descriptions of discoveries, where the author's personality is the focus of interest. But in the present instance the attentive reader may well find that there are too many ideas and insufficient facts, or too many facts and not enough ideas. I'm the first to regret that you don't describe more landscapes, to counterbalance—for the sake of the total effect—your numerous descriptions of pictures. But I have very definite ideas about travel books, having written one myself.[1] We'll talk about that again. Now to answer your questions:

1. Yes, always. For me, the mental image of things is as true as their objective reality, and what has been supplied by reality very soon ceases, for me, to be distinguishable from the embellishments and modifications I have given it.

2. The characters I create drive me insane; they haunt me; or, rather, I haunt them: I live in their skin. When I was writing about Madame Bovary taking poison, I had such a distinct taste of arsenic in my mouth, was poisoned so effectively myself, that I had two attacks of indigestion, one after the other—two very real attacks, for I vomited my entire dinner.

There are many details that I do not write down. Thus, M. Homais as I see him is slightly pitted by smallpox. In the passage I am writing just now I *see* an entire set of furniture (including the stains on certain of the pieces): not a word will be said about all this.

The third question is more difficult to answer. I think that in general (no matter what has been said on the theme) memory idealizes—or, should I say, selects. But perhaps the eye, too, idealizes? Think of our surprise when confronted with a photographic print. *That* is something we have never seen!

In its evanescent character, artistic intuition actually resembles hypnagogic hallucination: it flits before your eyes; and that is when you must grasp it, avidly.

But often, too, the artistic image forms itself slowly, bit by bit, like the various components of a décor that is being assembled.

Incidentally, do not confuse the inner vision of the artist with that of a man suffering from actual hallucinations.[2] I know those two states perfectly: there is a gulf between them. In genuine hallucination there is always terror; you feel that your personality is slipping away from you; you think you're going to die. In poetic vision, on the contrary, there is joy. It is something that permeates you. Nevertheless, here too you lose your bearings.

That is all I can think of to tell you on the spur of the moment. If you find my answers unsatisfactory, let me know, and I'll try to explain myself better.

1. *Par les champs et par les grèves,* of which Flaubert wrote alternate chapters with Maxime DuCamp (see Volume I).

2. Here Flaubert is referring to the hallucinations he experienced in the epileptiform attacks that had played so great a role in his youth (see Volume I), and that seem now to occur very rarely if at all. Responding to a new request by Taine, he describes them in greater detail in the following letter.

To Hippolyte Taine

Croisset, December 1 [1866]

Mon cher ami

This is what I experienced whenever I had hallucinations.

1. First, an indeterminate anxiety, a vague malaise, a sensation of expectancy accompanied by distress, *the sort of thing that precedes poetic in spiration,* when one feels that "something is about to happen." (A state that can only be compared to the feeling, while fucking, that the sperm is coming and that discharge is about to take place. Do I make myself clear?)

2. Then, suddenly, like a thunderbolt, instantaneous invasion, or rather irruption, *by memory;* for hallucination, properly so-called, is

nothing other than that, at least for me. It is a spewing out of memory, an outpouring of what it has stored up. You feel images escaping from you like a hemorrhage. It is as though everything inside your head were exploding all at once, like the thousand fragments of a firework, and you have no time to observe these internal images which follow one another furiously. In other circumstances, the hallucination begins with a single image, which grows, expands, and ends by obscuring objective reality, like, for example, a spark that flits about and then becomes a great flaming fire. In the latter case, one may well be thinking of something else at the same time, and this is almost indistinguishable from the phenomenon called "black butterflies"—those small shining specks we see floating in the air when the sky is gray and our eyes are tired.

I believe that Will plays a great role in hallucinations. When I have tried to induce them, I have never succeeded; on the other hand, often, in fact usually, I have rid myself of them by force of will.

In my early youth I used to have a peculiar hallucination: when I was in a theatre I always saw skeletons, instead of the spectators; or at least I had that idea so strongly that it resembled a hallucination—where one begins and the other ends can be hard to determine.

I know the story of Nicolai.[1] I have had that experience: *seeing* things that are not there—knowing that they're an illusion, being convinced of it, and yet perceiving them as clearly as though they were real. But in sleep you experience something similar, when you know, while dreaming, that you are dreaming.

So indisputably, for me, does memory play a part in hallucination, that the only way to imitate someone perfectly (to reproduce his voice and portray his gestures) is by great concentration of memory.[2] To be a good mime, your memory must be of hallucinatory clarity—you must actually *see* those you imitate, be permeated by them. It is true that certain bodily organs, too, play their part—the muscles of the face and larynx.

You should ask composers if they actually hear the music they are going to write, the way we novelists see our characters.

In artistic hallucination, the picture is *not definitely circumscribed*, exact though it may be. Thus, I see *perfectly* a piece of furniture, a face, a bit of landscape. But it floats, as though suspended; I don't know where it is. It exists by itself, disembodied from the rest; whereas, in reality, when I look at an armchair or a tree, I see at the same time the rest of the furniture in my room, the other trees in the garden, or at least I perceive vaguely that they exist. Artistic hallucination cannot occupy a large space, cannot move within a very wide frame. If the space enlarges, you [automatically] fall into a reverie, and grow calm again. In fact, artistic hallucination always ends that way.

You ask whether, for me, it adapts itself to the surrounding reality.

No. The surrounding reality has disappeared. I no longer know what exists around me. I belong exclusively to that apparition.

By contrast, in hallucination pure and simple you can perfectly well see a false image with one eye and real objects with the other. Indeed, therein lies the anguish.

Adieu. Work well. All yours—

1. An eighteenth-century case history of hallucination, included by Taine in his *De l'intelligence*, I, 105–107.
2. Flaubert was, from childhood, an excellent mime.

To Ernest Feydeau

Croisset, Tuesday [early 1867]

Cher Vieux

I don't know whether you're still in existence, but since I'm writing to ask you a favor I hope you'll give a sign of life. This is the thing—it concerns my book:[1]

My hero Frédéric quite properly wants to have a little more money in his pocket, and he plays the market; he makes a little, then loses everything, fifty or sixty thousand francs. He's a young bourgeois, completely ignorant in such matters—even a three percent government bond is a mystery for him. This takes place in the summer of 1847.

So: from May to the end of August, what were the securities favored by speculators?

My story has three phases:

1. Frédéric goes to a broker with his money and follows the broker's advice. Is that how it's done?

2. He makes a profit. How? How much?

3. He loses everything. How? Why?

It would be very good of you to send me this information—the episode shouldn't take up more than six or seven lines in my book. But explain it all to me clearly and exactly.

Keep the date in mind—1847, the summer of the Praslin and Teste scandals.

And use the occasion to tell me a little about how you are and what you're up to.

1. *L'Éducation sentimentale*, Part II, Chapter 4. Feydeau was well acquainted with the Paris Bourse.

To Edmond and Jules de Goncourt

[Croisset,] Saturday night [January 12–13, 1867]

If it's a consolation for you to know I'm bored, so be it—for I'm none too jolly. I'm working very long hours and feeling fed up. When I say working, it's a figure of speech. I'm giving myself a lot of trouble, and perhaps that's all it amounts to. No matter—I think I've passed the emptiest stretch of my interminable novel. But I'll never again undertake anything of the kind. I'm growing old, and it's time for me to write something worthwhile that I myself enjoy.

I spend entire weeks without seeing a human being or exchanging a word with anyone congenial. Besides, I'm becoming unsociable, like Marat, who is fundamentally "my man." I'd even like to put his bust in my study, solely to shock the bourgeois, but he's too ugly. Alas—beautiful morally, but not plastically. With the result (the foregoing being a parenthesis) that at dinner at my niece's in Rouen the day before yesterday I took pleasure in abusing various local people who were present, and made myself thoroughly disagreeable. My balls ache—word of honor!—from my excessive chastity. For I have nothing at hand to empty them into. You'll protest that I do have it (my hand). But I no longer turn myself on . . . Which doesn't prevent Mme Sand from believing that every so often "some lovely lady comes to see me"—so little do women realize that we can live without them.[1] For company I have a regiment of rats that makes an infernal racket at night, overhead. We gave them poison—which killed my dog. Wind, rain, pitch dark, the river chafing against its banks, and the whistling of the leafless trees—that completes the picture. Here in my study, in the glow of my lamp, I shout out my sentences. I go to bed at four in the morning and get up at noon. Such is the existence of yours truly.

. . . I hope to see you in about a month, when I'll have finished my chapter. Then I'll be at the halfway point in this long book about a poor devil—being one myself, a rather sad one. Come—try to get it up again (your brain, I mean!), and don't be too depressed. Je vous embrasse.

1. Flaubert wrote to George Sand by the same post: "Whatever you may suppose, no 'belle dame' comes to see me. 'Belles dames' have greatly occupied my mind, but they have taken up very little of my time. To speak of me as an anchorite is perhaps a juster image than you think."

GEORGE SAND TO FLAUBERT

Nohant, January 15 [1867]

. . . Why do I love you more than most others, more even than some old and well-tried friends? . . .

The solitude you live in would seem delicious to me in good weather. In winter I think it stoical, and have to remind myself that you don't find regular exercise a necessity for your morale. I had supposed that you employed your strength in a different way during this claustration:

as it is, it may be very fine, but you mustn't prolong it indefinitely. If the novel must go on still longer you must interrupt it, or vary it with some distractions. Truly, dear friend, think of the life of the body, which grows stiff and resentful if too long neglected. When I was sick in Paris I saw a doctor who was quite crazy but very intelligent. He told me that I was "spiritualizing" myself to an alarming degree; and when I told him, thinking of you, that it was possible to abstract oneself from everything except work and have one's strength increase rather than the opposite, he replied that there was as great a danger in accumulation as in diminution—and, in this connection, many excellent things that I wish I knew how to tell you.

Of course you know all this, but you take no account of it. So the work you complain of is really your passion, and a grand passion. Then let me tell you what you tell me: for the love of all of us, and especially of your old troubadour, take a little care of yourself.

· · ·

To George Sand

[Croisset,] Wednesday night [January 23–24, 1867]

I have followed your advice, chère maître. I have taken some exercise. Am I a splendid fellow, or not? Sunday night at eleven o'clock the moonlight on the river and the snow was such that I was seized by the itch of locomotion. And I walked for two and a half hours—working myself into a state and pretending that I was traveling in Russia or Norway. When the tide came in and cracked the ice floes on the Seine and the thin ice covering the farm-courts—no joking: it was superb. I thought of you and missed you.[1]

I dislike eating alone. I have to associate someone or the idea of someone with the things that give me pleasure. But that someone is rare. I, too, ask myself why I love you. Is it because you are a great man, or a "charming human being"? I have no idea. What is certain is that for you I have a *particular* feeling, one I cannot define.

Apropos, do you believe (you who are a Master in psychology) that one can love two people in the same way? And that one ever has two identical feelings? I think not, since one's *self* keeps changing at every moment of its existence.

You write me beautifully about "disinterested affection." That is true. But so is the opposite, is it not? We always make God in our own image. At the heart of all our loves and all our admirations don't we discover—ourselves, or something approaching ourselves? What matter, if "ourselves" are good?

My *me* bores me to death at the moment. What a heavy burden that fellow is, at times! He writes too slowly! And he isn't striking the

101

slightest pose when he complains about his work. What a chore! And what an idea, to have picked such a subject! You should give me a recipe for working faster . . .

You know very well that you have never told me what your illness is. What is it? Is it serious? Are you going to spend the winter in the Midi? Don't stay too long, eh? I'd not like it if we weren't to see each other soon. I'll be in Paris in a month—and you?

I've had a little note from Sainte-Beuve that reassures me about his health, but is lugubrious nonetheless. He seems disconsolate at no longer being able to haunt the Cyprian groves! He is right, after all, or at least right according to his lights, which is the same thing. Perhaps I'll be like him when I reach his age? I think not, however. Not having had the same youth, I'll have a different old age. That reminds me that I once thought of writing a book about Sainte-Périne.[2] Champfleury treated that subject idiotically. For I see nothing comic there (either in the subject, or in Champfleury). I would have made it dreadful, lamentable. I believe the heart does not grow old. There are even people in whom it expands with age. I was drier, harsher, twenty years ago than I am today. I've been feminized and softened by wear and tear—which harden other people. That makes me indignant. I feel I'm becoming too impressionable. I'm emotional over nothing. Everything troubles and agitates me. Everything, to me, is like the north wind to the reed.[3]

Something you said came back to my mind and is making me reread *La Jolie Fille de Perth* just now. It's charming,[4] whatever they may say about it. That fellow had some imagination, decidedly.

So: adieu. Think of me. I send you my best affection.

1. The river Seine is tidal for forty miles or more above its mouth in the English channel—that is, beyond Rouen, of which Croisset is a down-river suburb. As for this particular "locomotion" of Flaubert's, Mme Sand wrote: "You, my dear, you go walking in the snow, at night. For someone unaccustomed to it, such a promenade is quite mad, and could make you ill, like me. It wasn't the moon, but the sun, I urged you to take advantage of—we're not owls, for heaven's sake."

2. That is, a book about old age, set in L'Institution de Sainte-Périne. This was an endowed residence for elderly persons, particularly retired civil servants or their widows, who could afford to pay modest sums for board. Founded in the very early 1800s, under the patronage of the Empress Josephine, it was originally in Chaillot, then transferred in 1862 to buildings in Auteuil. Most of these have now been demolished and are being replaced by modern hospital facilities. Champfleury published his novel *Les Amoureux de Sainte-Périne* in 1859.

3. An allusion to LaFontaine's fable *The Oak and the Reed*. The oak says to the reed: "To you everything is north wind, to me all seems zephyr." (A.J.)

4. Sir Walter Scott's novel *The Fair Maid of Perth*. Flaubert owned a thirty-two-volume set of Scott's novels in French translation. His adjective for the book is *coquet*: the translation "charming" could possibly be improved, if one could fathom his meaning here. *La Jolie Fille de Perth* was literally "in the air" in 1867: Georges Bizet's four-act opera, its libretto taken from the novel, would have its first performance at the Théâtre Lyrique in Paris on December 26.

To George Sand

[Croisset,] Wednesday [February 6, 1867]

First, let's talk about you. Anemia! I'm not surprised! You *must* take a tonic of iron, and walk and sleep—and go to the Midi, whatever it costs! Yes! Otherwise, made of oak though you may be, you'll crack. As for money, it can be found; as for time, just take it. You'll do nothing that I advise, naturally. Well, you're wrong. And it grieves me.

No, I do not have what are called money worries. My income is very limited, but secure. Only, since it's your friend's habit to anticipate said funds, he's occasionally a little short, and grumbles about it "within these four walls." But not elsewhere. Barring the unexpected, I'll always be able to keep myself in food and firewood to the end of my days. My heirs are, or will be, rich. (I'm the poor man of the family.) But enough of that.

As for earning money by my pen, it's something I've never envisaged, recognizing that I'm fundamentally incapable of it. Therefore one leads a modest country life on what one has. Not a supremely amusing existence. But there are so many other people, more deserving than I, who haven't a sou, that it would be wrong to complain. Besides, railing against Providence is such a common way of going on that one should abstain if only for good form.

One more word about lucre, which will be a secret between us. As soon as I get to Paris, about the twentieth or thirtieth of this month, I'll be able easily, with no strain whatever, to lend you a thousand francs in case you need it to go to Cannes. I propose this to you bluntly, as I would to Bouilhet or any other intimate. No fuss about it, please. Among conventional folk this would be thought improper, I know, but between troubadours much can be dispensed with.[1]

You are very kind, with your invitation to Nohant. I *will* come. Because I long to see your house. It bothers me not to know it, when I think of you. But I must postpone that pleasure until next summer. Just now I should stay in Paris for a while. Three months is not too long for all I want to do there.

I return herewith the page by the excellent Barbès.[2] Of his *true* biography I know very little. All I know about him is that he is honest and heroic. Give him a handclasp from me as my thanks for his words of appreciation. Is he, between you and me, as intelligent as he is good? I need, now, some men of that camp who will speak frankly with me. Because I'm about to study the revolution of '48.

You promised to look out for me, in your library at Nohant, (1) an article on faïence, (2) a novel by Father X——, a Jesuit, about the Virgin Mary.

But such severity toward old [Sainte-]Beuve, who is neither Jesuit nor

Virgin! He bewails, as you say, "what is least to be regretted, taken in the sense he intends." Why so? All depends on the *intensity* one puts into the thing. I find you fundamentally tainted (in this matter) with Catholicism, O chère maître. Men will always consider sexual pleasure the most important thing in their lives. Woman, for all of us, is the Ogive of the Infinite. This isn't noble, but such is the very core of the Male. There's an immense amount of joking about all this. Thank God there is—for the sake of Literature, and for individual Happiness, as well. No matter! Glory be to Venus!

. . .

Ah! I missed you greatly just now. The high tides are superb. The wind is moaning, the river is white and overflowing its banks. It makes one think of the ocean, and one feels the better for it.

Adieu, I embrace you the way I love you—very tenderly.

1. In reply to Flaubert's offer of a loan, Mme Sand wrote (February 8) that *she* had been thinking of offering *him* a thousand francs. "I kiss you for your kind thought," she said, "and do not accept. I would accept, I assure you, if I had no other resource. Let me say that if someone should lend me money, it's Seigneur Buloz [her publisher], who has bought châteaux and many acres with my novels. He has even offered to. So I'll accept from him if it becomes necessary. But I'm in no state to leave."

2. Armand Barbès (1809–1870), the republican revolutionary, was condemned to death in 1839, charged with murdering a lieutenant of the National Guard. He did not commit the crime, but was the leader of an insurrectionary group one member of which fired the fatal shot. His sentence was commuted to life imprisonment the day before the scheduled execution, when Victor Hugo sent a plea in verse to Louis-Philippe. After four years at Mont-Saint-Michel (at that time used as a prison), he was transferred to the milder climate of Nîmes because of ill health caused in part by maltreatment. Released in 1848 and playing a role in the revolutionary government, he was again imprisoned after the June Days, and in 1854 was once again released, almost against his will, by Napoleon III. At the time of this letter he was living in self-imposed exile in Holland. George Sand, who had been one of Barbès's political comrades, had sent Flaubert a portion of one of his letters to her, in which he praised *Madame Bovary*.

Writing on February 8, Mme Sand answered Flaubert's question about Barbès: "Barbès is intelligent, certainly. But single-minded . . . His character can only be compared with Garibaldi's. Incredible in his saintliness and perfection. Of immense value, but a value from which the France of the present moment is incapable of profiting. Born into the wrong milieu—a hero out of another age or another land." (See also pages 108–110 and 149–150.)

To George Sand

[Paris,] Saturday [April 13?, 1867]

Chère maître

Really, you should seek the sun somewhere. It doesn't make sense to be unwell all the time, so do get away and rest. Resignation is the worst of the virtues.

I need a quantity of them, to put up with the stupidities I keep hearing! You have no idea of the pass things have come to. France, which has had occasional attacks of St. Vitus's dance (as under Charles VI), now seems to me to be stricken with paralysis of the brain. Fear is making everybody idiotic: fear of Prussia, fear of strikes, fear concerning the Exposition, which "isn't going well," fear about everything. You have to go back to 1849 to find such a degree of cretinism. At the last Magny dinner the conversation was on such a servants'-hall level that I swore to myself never to set foot there again. Nothing was talked about except M. de Bismarck and Luxembourg. I'm still fed to the teeth with it all. All in all, I'm becoming difficult to live with. Instead of getting blunted, my sensibility grows ever more acute; all kinds of trivialities cause me pain. Forgive me this weakness, you who are so Strong and tolerant!

The novel isn't progressing at all. I'm deep in the newspapers of '48. I've had to look into things in various places—Sèvres, Creil, etc.—and have more of that kind of work to do.

Old Sainte-Beuve is preparing a speech on Free Thought which he will read in the Senate, concerning the law on the Press. He has been very stalwart, you know.[1]

. . .

1. At the urging of Princesse Mathilde and her brother, the Emperor had appointed Sainte-Beuve a Senator, with a salary of 30,000 francs a year. As will be seen, they were to regret it. His maiden speech, on March 29, 1867, was on the subject of freedom of thought. He was now preparing a second speech, on freedom of the press. (Flaubert's "Free Thought" is a bit of absentmindedness.) For Sainte-Beuve's second speech, see Flaubert's letter to Sainte-Beuve of June 27, 1867.

To George Sand

[Paris,] Friday morning [May 17, 1867]

. . .

Axiom: hatred of the Bourgeois is the beginning of virtue. As for me, I include in the word "bourgeois" the bourgeois in overalls as well as the bourgeois in frock coat. It's we, we alone—that is, the educated— who are the People, or, to put it better, the tradition of Humanity.

. . .

To George Sand

[Croisset,] Wednesday night, 2 [June 1867]

. . .

Early this week I spent 36 hours in Paris in order to attend the ball at the Tuileries.[1] No joking whatever: it was splendid. Indeed the whole trend in Paris now is toward the colossal. Everything is becoming crazy and out of proportion. Perhaps we're returning to the ancient East. I keep expecting idols to come out of the ground. There's the threat of a

Babylon. And why not? The *individual* has been so negated by Democracy that he'll be reduced to complete effacement, as under the great theocratic despotisms.

I deeply disliked the czar of Russia. He seemed a boor. Paralleling the noble Floquet, who with no risk to himself shouts "Long live Poland!," we have the chic people who sign the visitors' book at the Elysée.[2] What an era!

As for my novel, it goes *piano*. As I advance, new difficulties arise. It's like dragging a heavy cartload of stones. And you complain of something that takes you six months! I still have two years to go, at least. How the devil do you handle transitions of ideas? That's what's delaying me. Moreover, this book requires tedious research. On Monday, for example, I visited, one after the other, the Jockey Club, the Café Anglais, and an attorney.

.   .   .

A week ago I was enraptured by an encampment of gypsies who had stopped in Rouen. This is the third time I've seen them, each time with new pleasure. The wonderful thing is that they were arousing the *Hatred* of the Bourgeois, even though they were harmless as lambs. The crowd looked its great disapproval when I gave them a few sous. I heard some delightful remarks à la Prud'homme.[3] That hatred stems from something very deep and complex. It's to be found in all "champions of order." It's the hatred felt for the Bedouin, the Heretic, the philosopher, the hermit, the Poet. And there is fear in this hatred. I'm infuriated by it, being always on the side of minorities. It's true that many things infuriate me. The day I stop being indignant I'll fall flat on my face, like a doll when you take away its prop.

For example, the stake that held me upright last winter was my indignation against our great national historian M. Thiers, who has been elevated to the status of demigod; and the Trochu pamphlet, and the eternal Changarnier surfacing again.[4] Thank God, the delirium of the Exposition has delivered us momentarily from those buffoons.

.   .   .

1. Flaubert had written to Caroline a few days earlier: "Their Majesties wishing to take a look at me, as one of the most splendid curiosities of France, I am invited to spend the evening with them next Monday." After the ball he wrote to Princesse Mathilde: "The Tuileries ball stays in my memory as something from a fairy tale, a dream. The only thing lacking was an opportunity to have a closer view of you and speak with you. Don't I sound like Madame Bovary, dazzled by her first ball?"

2. The Palais de l'Elysée was being used during the Exhibition of 1867 to house distinguished official guests, the czar among them. Following the Russian repression of the Polish uprising of 1863, French sympathy for Poland was exploited by those in opposition to the imperial regime at home. During the czar's visit to the Sainte-Chapelle on June 4 someone shouted "Vive la Pologne, Monsieur!" Charles Floquet, a leading republican, was generally credited with the "outrage," but denied it, putting the responsibility on Gambetta. (A.J.)

3. For Prud'homme see page 31, note 7. *Le Nouvelliste de Rouen* reported on May 30 that "Forty-three individuals of the Zingaro type, come from Hindustan, fleeing the invasion of the Mongols," had arrived in the city two days before and set up their tents in the Cours la Reine. On June 8 the same newspaper announced that they had left on the sixth for Le Havre, where they would take ship for America. (A.J.)

4. Adolphe Thiers (for Flaubert as archetypal a bourgeois as Monnier's Prud'homme) had been officially dubbed "national historian" by Napoleon III. He was nevertheless in the opposition, and on March 14, 1867, had made a speech, lamenting France's loss of prestige because of misgovernment, which brought him much acclaim.

General Louis-Jules Trochu had recently published a pamphlet attacking the government for its plans to reorganize the French army. An article on the same subject had appeared in *La Revue des Deux Mondes* for April 15, written by the ex-General Nicolas-Anne-Théodule Changarnier, who had been arrested during the coup d'état of 1851, expelled from France, and given amnesty in 1859. He had until now been living obscurely in the provinces.

To Charles-Augustin Sainte-Beuve

[Croisset,] Thursday [June 27, 1867]

Mon cher maître

All those who aren't sunk in the crassest stupidity, all who love Art, all who think, all who write, owe you infinite gratitude. For you have pleaded their cause[1] and defended their God—our nameless God who is being outraged.

In such a place, it was the only thing to say. The moderation and precision of your language only throw into stronger relief the intemperance and vagueness of their ineptitude. They are decidedly not bright—no, not bright at all.

What a sad thing is mankind! Behold the foremost political assembly of the foremost nation on earth!

No matter: very politely, you have spat the truth at them. It will stick to them. My only regret is that you didn't give them more of it. You can't be very sick, if you're able to speak with such energy!

Ask M. Troubat to give me news of you.[2]

I wish my arms were thirty-four leagues long, that I might embrace you. That is what I count on doing a month from now.

Ever yours, cher maître.

1. On June 25, 1867, Sainte-Beuve delivered a second speech in the Senate, this one on freedom of the press. He spoke vigorously against the petition by "the taxpayers of the city of St. Etienne" that Voltaire's *Candide*, Rousseau's *Confessions*, the works of Michelet and Renan, and all novels by Balzac and George Sand be excluded from their public library. The speech was directed particularly against clerical interference in public matters, and aroused the indignation of Conservative senators.

On the twenty-sixth, immediately after learning of the speech, Flaubert had already sent Sainte-Beuve a short message written on a visiting card: "Thank you, mon cher maître, for us, for all of us. Damaged though it may be, your bladder can be their lantern!" (Flaubert's words are a somewhat convoluted reference to Sainte-Beuve's diseased bladder and to an ancient proverbial French description of someone who is particularly stupid: *Il prend des vessies pour des lanternes*—"He takes bladders for lanterns." A bilingual friend of the present translator suggested, on reading Flaubert's message, the free translation: "May your liver be their lights."

2. Jules Troubat, Sainte-Beuve's secretary.

◇-◇-◇-◇

About Sainte-Beuve's speech, Flaubert wrote to Princesse Mathilde: "What do you have to say about le père Sainte-Beuve? I thought him splendid. He defended the cohort valiantly, and in well-chosen words. His adversaries seem to me of a hopeless mediocrity. Why this hatred of literature? Is it envy, or stupidity? Both, no doubt, with a strong dose of hypocrisy into the bargain."

The princess's reply was apparently chilly (we shall see later a more pronounced example of her displeasure at a display of independence by her protégé), bringing from Flaubert the following, in a letter also expressing horror at the recent execution of the Emperor Maximilian in Mexico: "What you say to me about Sainte-Beuve is perhaps true. He perhaps did go too far (from a certain point of view, which I must add is not mine). But his adversaries had set him the example, and then the question of 'proper limits' is so difficult. Stay within them and you're a coward; go beyond them, and you're a firebrand. What to do?"

Flaubert wrote more forthrightly to George Sand late in July: "Speaking of stupidity, it seems that the official world is furious with Sainte-Beuve. Camille Doucet's distress touches on the sublime. From the point of view of future liberty, we must perhaps bless this religious hypocrisy of the worldly, which so revolts us. The later the question is settled, the better the settlement will be. *They* can only weaken, and we grow stronger."

IN SEPTEMBER, Flaubert consulted Mme Sand about another matter: "In my notes I find the following: '*National* of 1841. Maltreatment of Barbès. Kicked in the chest; dragged by beard and hair to be transferred to an *in pace* [oubliette]. Protest by a group of lawyers against these abominations, signed: E. Arago, Favre, Berryer.' Find out from him whether that is accurate, will you? I'll be much obliged." Barbès replied directly to Flaubert:

◇-◇-◇-◇

ARMAND BARBÈS TO FLAUBERT

The Hague, October 2, 1867

My dear compatriot,

Our illustrious friend, Mme Sand, has forwarded to me a question you sent her about an incident at Mont-Saint-Michel, and asks me to reply.

The story in the *National* is true.

We were at that time in the "loge-cells," situated at the very top of the building, where we had been transferred because double or triple grilles were being installed in our ordinary prison-quarters.

I don't have to tell you that this transfer was already in violation of all the customary rules of detention, and an act of sheer violence on the part of a jailer, the better to garrote his captives.

Returning one day to my cell after the usual short, obligatory walk in the former cloister, I saw that they had taken advantage of my absence to close an opening that had always existed in the door of each cell.

I realized that they were beginning with me, but that they intended to do likewise to all my comrades, and I refused to enter until things had been restored to their former state.

My good friend Martin Bernard and others made the same declaration, and all together we asked that the warden be sent for.

Instead of coming, he sent the chief of guards, with his entire squad; and it was then that there occurred that scene, the hideousness and horror of which naturally seem to you scarcely credible.

During the interval in which I had been left as it were master of the cell-corridor, the guards having all decamped to organize themselves under their chief's orders on a lower floor, I had opened the door of Martin Bernard's cell and that of another friend, Dessade, which had been merely bolted, not locked.

Seeing the three of us together, the guards (there were at least twenty of them, reinforced in the rear by a company of troops summoned for the occasion) fell on us—no warning being given—the only words uttered being "Seize them! Hit them!" shouted by their chief.

I was the most severely injured because I was the first they reached. Struck in the face and on all parts of the body, thrown to the floor, throttled with my tie, my beard torn out, dragged from those cells at the uppermost point of Mont-Saint-Michel to the "black hole" (the lowest level), down flights of stairs with my head striking every step: yes, all that took place.

Martin and Dessade were accorded identical treatment.

In the black hole they made us change into convict's garb—that is, castoffs that had been worn by nonpolitical prisoners and they wanted to strip me of my flannel undervest, a kind of garment I have worn all my life, to me like a second skin.

I was able to keep it only by threatening to throw myself on the bayonets and kill myself instantly, since without it I was certain to freeze to death in the glacial place to which they were taking us.

They could see that I was absolutely resolved to do as I said; and when the lieutenant in charge of the soldiers interceded on my behalf I was able to keep my "second skin."

Ah! People are trying today to rehabilitate the reign of Louis-Philippe. For my part, I no longer feel hatred for anyone. I even think I can truthfully say that I tend toward leniency precisely because I was harshly treated at that time.

But it was a sad reign and a sad period, I assure you. May Frenchmen not forget! Our beloved France has suffered so much! Violence was done her then; may she fend off the trickery threatening her now: were she to succumb again, the shame and cowardice would be the greater.

This letter is much longer than I intended. Forgive me, in the name of our common cult of George Sand. It was she who asked me to write you, and you perhaps know that for me she represents, or is, France. I love her as you love her, as we both love our country—humiliated today, but certain to rise again.

George Sand, at least, is always a shining light—ever more so.

In her name, then, forgive my writing at such length, and accept a cordial handshake from one of your admirers ever since *Madame Bovary*, and from one of your friends ever since I learned of the affection in which you are held at Nohant.

A. Barbès.

To Armand Barbès[1]

Croisset, October 8, 1867

I do not know, Monsieur, how to thank you for your letter, so amiable, so cordial, so noble. I have long respected you; now I love you.

The details you send me will be put (quite incidentally) into a book I am writing, in which the action extends from 1840 to 1852. Although my treatment is purely analytical, I sometimes touch on the events of the period. My foregrounds are invented, my backgrounds real.[2]

You know better than anyone many of the things that would be useful to me, and that I ought to hear. But there is no way for us to see each other, since you live where you do and I here. Without Mme Sand, I wouldn't even know how to send you my thanks. I was very touched by what you say of her. She is a religion you and I have in common—and share with others.

Allow me to clasp your hands very firmly, and to declare myself

All yours,
G^ve Flaubert

1. Flaubert sent this letter via Mme Sand, Barbès not having given him his address in The Hague. "Here are a few lines of thanks for Barbès, who wrote me a warm, fascinating letter. Since I have no 'patriotic' past whatever, and was bellowing sentences in my study while he was risking his life for liberty in the streets, I didn't think I should write him all the good things I thought about him. I'd have seemed like a kind of fawning courtier."

Mme Sand sent Barbès Flaubert's letters to him and to her, with a few words of her own: "I send you Flaubert's thanks, and also a note he has scribbled to me that contains some open-hearted talk of you. I thank you for giving him exact dates and information. He is a great artist, and one of the few who are *men.*" (A.J.)

2. In *L'Éducation sentimentale* (Part II, Chapter 4), the workingman Dussardier, the novel's most sympathetic character, angrily recalls, in 1847, earlier abuses by the authorities, among them the massacre of the working-class inhabitants of a house in the rue Transnonain in Paris in 1834 (immortalized in Daumier's lithograph); and the treatment of Barbès in 1841: "To transfer Barbès to a dungeon, they dragged him by the legs, by his hair! They kicked him in the stomach, and his head bounced against every step on the stairs!" Later (Part III, Chapter 4), Dussardier, uneasy about his own role in the June Days of 1848, is anguished by the reaction that soon followed: "The workers are no better than the bourgeois! . . . Some wretches are calling Barbès an aristocrat!"

To Jules Duplan

Croisset, Sunday [December 1867]

How I'd love to be with you: first because I'd be with you; second because I'd be in Egypt; third because I wouldn't be working; fourth because I'd be seeing the sun, etc.[1] You can't imagine the horrible weather here today. The sky is dirty gray, like a chamber pot long uncleaned, and even more stupid-looking than ugly.

At the moment I'm living alone, my mother being in Rouen.[2] Monseigneur comes to see me almost every Sunday, but today he's at home giving dinner to an upholsterer friend. He is now regaining his serenity, and I think is about to begin something, but his change of residence[3] completely unhinged him. The day before yesterday I had a letter from Maxime. He seems to be in very good form, fulminating against M. Thiers, who is now king of France.[4] That's the point we've reached— completely clericalized. Such is the fruit of democratic stupidity. If we had continued on the highroad of M. de Voltaire, instead of veering off via Jean-Jacques, neo-Catholicism, the Gothic, and Fraternity, we wouldn't be where we are. France is going to become a kind of Belgium, openly divided into two camps. So much the better! What a culprit is Isidore![5] But since one must always derive some private enjoyment from everything, I *rejoice* in the triumph of M. Thiers. It confirms my disgust with my country and the hatred I feel for that Prud'homme. Can one conceive of more idiotic, irresponsible talk about religion and philosophy! I intend, by the way, to "fix" him in my novel, when I come to the reaction that followed the June Days. In the second chapter of my Part Three I'll have a dinner where his book on property is praised to the skies.[6] I'm working like thirty thousand niggers, for I want to finish my Part Two by the end of January. In order to complete the whole thing by the spring of '69, so as to publish it two years from now, I don't have a week to spare: you see what I'm facing. There are days, like today, when I feel utterly fagged out. I can scarcely stand on my feet, and I have choking fits when I can scarcely breathe.

Last Thursday I was 46—occasion for philosophical reflection! Looking back, I don't see that I have wasted my life, and yet what have I accomplished, God help me? It's time to produce something worthwhile.

Don't forget to observe, for me, the rascally Oriental-Occidental types; store in your memory some anecdotes of the kind I'll need;[7] take notes with me in mind. Don't waste your time in the European cafés. Treat yourself to another visit to the dancing girls, and go to see the Pyramids. Who knows whether you'll ever be in Egypt again? Profit from the occasion: take the advice of an old friend who has had plenty of experience and who loves you. If you think of it, bring me (1) a flask of sandalwood oil; and (2) a trouser belt made of webbing—remember, your friend has a big belly.

. . . By way of reading, I've lately been devoting myself to a study of croup.[8] Never did anyone write in a more long-winded, empty style than physicians! Such windbags! And they despise lawyers! . . .

1. Duplan was in Egypt as secretary to Henri Cernuschi, politician and economist. (Cernuschi's collection of Oriental art, which he left to the city of Paris, is housed in his former residence, now the Musée Cernuschi, avenue Velasquez.)

2. Mme Flaubert spent the coldest months in a flat in Rouen.

3. Louis Bouilhet had recently been appointed director of the Municipal Library in Rouen, thanks in part to Flaubert's friendship with Princesse Mathilde.

4. "Flaubert goes a bit astray here," Mr. Jasper Ridley, author of *Napoleon III and Eugénie* (London: Constable, 1979) writes to the present translator. "Thiers was certainly not 'King of France' in 1867, nor was he a clerical supporter. As the spokesman for big business and the Conservative urban bourgeoisie, he was opposed on many issues to the Catholic Party, which derived its strength from the clergy, the Army, the old nobility, and above all from the great mass of the peasantry; but Thiers, who believed that 'the Reds' were the greatest threat to society, always supported the Catholics against the Radicals and the Socialists."

Thiers' political power was increasing. Following another speech on foreign policy, December 7, 1867 (this one—mistakenly, as it turned out—jeering at the government's warnings about Prussia's military strength), he had become chief of an oppositional "coalitional majority."

5. No one seems to know why Flaubert calls Napoleon III "Isidore."

6. Actually, in the third chapter. "They [the Dambreuses' dinner guests] especially praised M. Thiers for his volume against Socialism, in which he showed himself to be as great a thinker as a writer." The book is Thiers' *De la propriété* (1848).

7. Among Flaubert's never-realized projects was a novel to be called "Harel-Bey" and laid in the modern "Orient."

8. The nearly fatal croup of the Arnoux' young son is one of the determining events of the novel.

TO GEORGE SAND

[Croisset,] Wednesday night [December 18–19, 1867]
Chère maître, dear friend of Divine Providence,
"Parlons un peu de Dozenval!"[1] Let's do some roaring against M. Thiers!

Is it possible to find a more triumphant imbecile, a more abject ass, a more turd-like[2] bourgeois? No! Nothing can give an idea of the vomiting inspired in me by this old diplomatic idiot, rounding out his stupidity like a melon ripening on a manure pile—the manure pile of the bourgeoisie! Is it possible to treat philosophy, religion, peoples, liberty, the past and the future, history, natural history—everything and all the rest—with more naive, inept crudity? To me he seems as eternal as mediocrity itself! I'm flattened by the very thought of him.

But what is really splendid is our glorious National Guard, whom he threw into the clink in 1848, now once again beginning to cheer him! What infinite madness! Which goes to prove that temperament is everything. Prostitutes, like France, have a weakness for old humbugs.

I shall try, in the third part of my novel (when I reach the reaction that followed the June Days) to slip in a panegyric of said gentleman, apropos of his book on Property, and I hope he'll be pleased with me.

What is the best form in which to express one's opinion, occasionally, about affairs of this world without risking being taken later for a fool? It's a difficult problem. It seems to me that the best way is simply to depict the things that exasperate you. Dissection is revenge.

. . .

1. "Let's talk a bit about Dozenval." A complimentary copy of the present volume to the first reader convincingly identifying this quotation.

2. *Etroniforme*—term coined by Flaubert.

GEORGE SAND TO FLAUBERT

Nohant, December 21 [1867]

At last, someone who shares my opinion of that political cur! It could only be you, friend of my heart. *Etroniforme* is a sublime word to classify that vegetable species *Merdoïde.*[1] I have friends, perfectly nice fellows, who bow low before *any* symptom of opposition, whatever it may be and wherever it may come from, and for whom that empty-headed mountebank is a god. But they've been keeping their tails between their legs since the last speech with full orchestra. They begin to think he's going a bit far—and perhaps it's all to the good that in order to make himself king of parliament the idiot has shown the world the dead cats and other refuse that make up his entire bag of dirty tricks. That will reach some people. Yes, you'll do well to dissect that cardboard donkey, that cobweb talent. Unfortunately, when your book appears he'll perhaps be gone, and no longer much of a danger, for such men leave nothing behind them; on the other hand, he may be in power—we can expect anything: in that case, it will be a good lesson.[2]

. . .

1. Term coined by Mme Sand: "Of the shit family." A friend suggests a link with *ca-cafuego,* listed in the Oxford English Dictionary, which cites a 1696 usage: "A Spanish word signifying Shitefire, and it is used for a bragging, vaporing fellow."

2. In 1871 the "turd-like bourgeois" and "political cur" would of course be elected first president of the Third French Republic.

When Thiers died, in 1877, and received an immense state funeral, Flaubert wrote rather differently about him, to Mme Roger des Genettes: "Yes, I too watched old Thiers' funeral, and I assure you it was splendid. That truly *national* manifestation moved me. I didn't love that king of the Prud'hommes—no matter! Compared with those around him he was a giant; and then he had another rare virtue, patriotism. No one exemplified France as he did. Hence the immense effect of his death."

TO ALFRED BAUDRY[1]

[1867–1868]

My friend,

I am *not at all* of your opinion, being a born enemy of texts that explain drawings, and drawings that explain texts. My conviction about this is radical, and forms part of my aesthetic.

I *defy* you to cite me one example among the moderns, whose idiosyncrasy this is (the ancients abstained from such sacrilege), which speaks for the contrary. The explanation of one artistic form by another is a monstrosity. You won't find in all the museums of the world a good picture that needs a commentary. Look at exhibition catalogues. The longer the entry, the worse the painting.

.   .   .

1. Younger brother of the Frédéric Baudry who would play an important role in Flaubert's last years.

TO EDMOND AND JULES DE GONCOURT

[Croisset,] Wednesday [May 20, 1868]

.   .   .[1]

Returning to my apartment [in Paris] on Sunday night at half-past eleven, I go to bed promising myself a deep sleep, and blow out my candle. Three minutes later, a blaring of trombones and beating of drums! It was a wedding at Bonvalet's.[2] Said tavernkeeper's windows being wide open (because of the heat of the night), I didn't miss a single quadrille, a single shout. The orchestra (as I have the honor to repeat) was enhanced *by two drums!*

At six A.M., masons again. At seven, I betake myself to the Grand Hotel.

There, a forty-five-minute prowl before finding a room. Scarcely was I there (in the room), when hammering begins in the room adjoining. Another prowl in the same hotel in search of refuge. At nine, I give up and go to the Hotel du Helder, where I find a wretched closet, black as a tomb. But the peace of the grave was lacking: shouts of guests, rumbling of carriages in the street, clanking of tin pails in the court.

From one o'clock to three I pack my bags and leave the Boulevard du Temple.

From four to six, tried to sleep at DuCamp's, rue du Rocher. But I had reckoned without yet other masons, who are building a wall alongside his garden.

At six, I transport myself to a bath establishment, rue Saint-Lazare. There, children playing in the yard, plus a piano.

At eight, I return to the rue du Helder, where my man has laid out on my bed everything I required that night for the Tuileries ball. But I hadn't dined, and thinking that hunger was perhaps weakening my nerves, I go to the Café de l'Opéra.

I had scarcely entered, when a gentleman vomits beside me.

At nine, return to the Hotel du Helder. The idea of dressing exhausts me, like a bloodletting in both arms and both legs. I give up in disgust, and decide to return to the country as fast as I can. My man packs my bag.

That's not all. Final episode: my bag rolls off the top of the cab and crashes on my shoulder. I still have the bruises.

Voilà!

Yours—

1. The first page of the autograph has been lost.
2. A restaurant almost directly opposite Flaubert's flat at 24 boulevard du Temple. The confusion of tenses in this letter is perhaps a consequence of the adventures it describes.

◇◇◇◇◇

In May 1868 George Sand paid her third visit to Croisset, staying two days. She had a certain interest in phrenology—in her novel *Mauprat* she calls it "a system which has its good side"—and phrenology lies behind an entry she made in her journal—her only characterization of Caroline's husband: "Croisset, May 24, 1868. We dine with the others and Monsieur Commanville, whose forehead is *flat.*" In other words, Ernest did not have the pleasantly convex brow that among phrenologists was thought to denote a generous spirit. During Flaubert's later years, which were to be filled with difficulties stemming from the Commanvilles, Mme Sand's references to the niece she knew Flaubert loved would always be of the utmost politeness—"Your charming niece," etc. To Commanville she never refers again.

Mme Chevalley-Sabatier, in her book about Flaubert and Caroline (see Appendix I), says of Caroline's unpublished memoirs:

115

In the account she gives of [her meetings with George Sand], we find that she did not share the respectful affection displayed by her uncle for the Good Lady of Nohant. Was this a slight touch of jealousy, or resentment that her youth was given insufficient consideration? In any case, Caroline is not indulgent in her description of Mme Sand as 'a little old lady, certainly well past sixty, carelessly dressed, whose only coquetry seemed to be confined to an extraordinary coiffure, which combined black velvet ribbons, white daisies, and barrettes' . . . Mme Sand was very free-spoken, quite bold and crude in her language: that did not please Caroline. When the hour grew late, the latter would retire, and leave the two interlocutors to their seemingly endless dialogue, which sometimes lasted till dawn.

◇◇◇◇◇

To George Sand

Croisset, Sunday, July 5 [1868]

.　　.　　.

I've been slaving away madly for the past six weeks. The patriots won't forgive me this book, nor the reactionaries either! So much the worse: I write things as I feel them—that is, as I believe they exist. Is this foolish of me? But it seems that our unhappy condition is attributable exclusively to people of our own kind?[1] All the Christianity I find in Socialism appalls me! Here, for example, are two little notes now lying on my table:

"This system [Louis Blanc's own] is not a system of disorder. For it has its source in the Gospels. And from this divine source *there cannot flow* hatred, warfare, total conflict of interests. For the doctrine formulated from the Gospels is a doctine of peace, union, and love." (L. Blanc)

"I even make bold to assert that with the disappearance of respect for Sunday, the last spark of poetic fire has been extinguished in the souls of our rhymesters. As the saying has it: 'Without religion, no poetry.' " (Proudhon)

Apropos of the latter, I beg of you, chère maître, to read, at the end of his book on the celebration of Sunday, a love story entitled, I think, *Marie et Maxime*. One must know this to have an idea of the Style of our Thinkers. It should be placed with the excursion to Brittany in *Ça et là*, by the great Veuillot.[2] This doesn't prevent some of our friends from admiring these two gentlemen. Whereas they deride Voltaire.

In my old age I intend to write criticism: it will relieve me. For I often choke on suppressed opinions. No one understands better than I Boileau's outbursts against bad taste: "The stupidities I hear uttered at the Academy are hastening my end." There was a man for you!

Whenever I hear the steamers passing, one after another, I think of you: I remind myself that you liked the sound, and it irritates me less. What moonlight tonight on the river! . . .

1. By "patriots" Flaubert means the "radicals" or "socialists" defeated during the June Days of 1848; by "reactionaries" the triumphant, repressive bourgeois (Thiers was their great man); by "people of our own kind," intellectuals, scholars, Voltairean freethinkers. In *L'Éducation sentimentale*, Dussardier and Sénégal represent the first category; the Dambreuses and their friends the second. (A.J.)

2. Louis Veuillot (1813–1883), Catholic writer. Brittany was, and remains, strongly Catholic.

GEORGE SAND TO FLAUBERT

Nohant, July 31 [1868]

· · ·

You disturb me when you say that in your book you'll blame the patriots for all that went wrong [in 1848]. Is that really true? They—the vanquished! Surely it's enough to be defeated through your own fault, without having your nose rubbed in all your stupidities. Have pity! There were so many splendid souls even so. The Christian aspect was a fad. I confess that Christianity has always been seductive. When you see only its gentle side, it wins your heart. But you have to think of all the harm it has done. I'm not surprised that a generous heart like L. Blanc should have dreamed of seeing it purified and restored to its ideal. I too had that illusion, but as soon as you take a step back into the past you see that it cannot be revived, and I am sure that today L. Blanc is smiling at his dream. One must think of that, too. One must tell oneself that all who had some intelligence have come a very long way in the past twenty years, and that it would not be generous to reproach them for what they themselves probably regret. As for Proudhon, I never thought him sincere. He was an orator—of genius, so it is said. I don't understand him. He is a kind of perpetual antithesis, insoluble. I think of him as one of those sophists old Socrates made fun of.

I trust you to be *generous*. With a word more or a word less, with the hand wielding its strength gently, one can flick the whip without causing a wound. You are so good—you cannot be cruel.

· · ·

TO GEORGE SAND

Dieppe, Monday [August 10, 1868]

· · ·

I expressed myself badly if I told you that my book will "blame the patriots for all that went wrong." I don't recognize my right to blame anyone. I don't even believe that the novelist should express his opinion on matters of this world. He can communicate it, but I don't like

117

him to state it. (Such is part of my poetics.) Thus I confine myself to describing things as they appear to me, to expressing what seems to me to be true. Hang the consequences. Rich or poor, winners or losers—I take no account of all that. I want to have neither hate, nor pity, nor anger. As for sympathy, that's different. One can never have enough of it. The reactionaries, by the way, will be treated even less gently than the others. For they seem to me more criminal . . .

Now let me say that since I have absolute confidence in the greatness of your spirit, I will read my third part to you when it's done, and if there is something in my work that seems cruel to you I'll remove it. But I'm convinced in advance that you'll make no objection. As for allusions to individuals, there isn't a trace.

. . . .

To Jules Duplan

Croisset, Thursday night [late August or September 1868]

Cher Vieux

Here's the thing.

I tell—or rather, a cocotte in my book tells about her childhood.[1] She was the daughter of workers in Lyons. I need details about the homes of such people.

1. A few lines about the living quarters of Lyons workers.

2. The "canuts" (as I think the silk weavers are called) work in very low-ceilinged rooms, don't they?

3. In their own homes?

4. Their children work too?

I find the following in my notes: the weaver working at a Jacquard loom is continually struck in the stomach by the shaft of the roller on which the cloth is being wound as it is completed.

5. Is it the roller itself that strikes him? Clarify, please.

In short, I want to write a four-line description of a working-class domestic scene, to contrast it with another interior that comes later—the luxurious establishment in which our heroine is deflowered. Her tambourine is punctured by a Saint-Florent.[2] Unfortunately I have no room to expatiate on these people. If you know one of your compatriots whom you want to "stigmatize," send me his photograph. But all this is unimportant: what I need is my picture of "canuts" doing their work amidst their household paraphernalia.

It would be kind of you to send me this information right away. I need it.

. . . .

1. Rosanette reminisces with Frédéric in the forest of Fontainebleau. (*L'Éducation sentimentale*, Part Three, Chapter I). Jules Duplan was a Lyonnais.

2. A character in Sade's *Justine* and *La Nouvelle Justine*.

To JULES DUPLAN

[Croisset,] Wednesday, 5 o'clock [September 16, 1868]

Dear old chap,

Look what's happened.[1] After making the trip to Fontainebleau and back by train, I was struck by a doubt: and now I'm sure, alas! that in 1848 there was no railroad between Paris and Fontainebleau. This means I have to scrap two passages and begin afresh. I see in *Paris-Guide* (vol. I, p. 1660) that the line to Lyons began only in 1849. You can't imagine what a nuisance this is for me. So—I need to know: 1. how, in June 1848, one went from Paris to Fontainebleau; 2. perhaps *part* of the line was already in use? 3. what coaches did one take? 4. and what was their terminus in Paris? Here is the situation: Frédéric is at Fontainebleau with Rosanette; he hears that Dussardier has been wounded (this is June 25), and he leaves for Paris with Rosanette, who doesn't want to be left behind. But on the way she loses her courage and comes no farther. He arrives in Paris alone. Because of the Saint-Antoine barricades he has to make a long detour before reaching Dussardier, who lives at the far end of the faubourg Poissonnière.

Can you recall what the ambulances looked like? If you remember any details of the nights in Paris that week, send them to me.

My hero wanders through the streets the last night, June 25–26 (everything ended on the 26th).

Now you see the situation as clearly as I. Be a good chap: try to find me definite information.

My bugger of a novel is draining the very marrow of my bones. I'm dog-tired, and beginning to be depressed.

In 1848 the line between Corbeil and Paris was open. Remains to know how one got from Fontainebleau to Corbeil . . .

---

1. Flaubert is verifying details concerning events twenty years past—the end and aftermath of the June Days, 1848, his evocation of which is possibly the most powerful section of *L'Éducation sentimentale*. Over a year later he would still be cooking information, this time from Ernest Feydeau: "You'd be very kind if you could answer these two questions: (1) In June 1848, where were the posts of the National Guard in the Mouffetard, Saint Victor, and Latin quarters? (?) The night of 25–26 June (Sunday–Monday), was it the National Guard or the regular infantry that occupied the Left Bank in Paris? I've already asked these questions of several persons, and have had no answer. I'm stuck, with three pages remaining blank."

About his pages on Fontainebleau, he wrote to George Sand on September 9, 1868: "I'm working furiously. I've written a description of the forest of Fontainebleau that made me want to hang myself from one of its trees. I had interrupted myself for three weeks, and had great trouble getting back into my stride. I'm like a camel—you can't stop him when he's on the go, nor make him start when he's resting. I still have a year's work ahead. After that, no more bourgeois, definitely. Too difficult, and too ugly. It's time for me to do something good that I'll enjoy."

Saturday night [Croisset, September 29, 1868]

You are surprised, chère maître?[1] Not I! I told you, but you wouldn't believe me.

I feel for you. For it's sad to see people you love change. The substitution of one spirit for another, in a body that remains the same as before, is heartbreaking to witness. One feels *betrayed*. I have experienced that, and more than once.

Still, what is your conception of woman, then, oh you who are of the Third sex? Are they not, as Proudhon says, "the desolation of the Just"? Since when have they been able to dispense with chimeras? After love, Piety; that's the way it goes. Sylvanie has no more men; she takes up with God. That's all it amounts to.

Rare are those who have no need of the Supernatural. Philosophy will always be the portion of aristocrats. Fatten the human herd, bed them with straw up to their bellies, even gild their stable—to no avail: they will remain brutish, whatever anyone may say. The only progress to be hoped for is that the brutes may be made a little less vicious. But as for elevating the ideas of the masses, giving them a conception of God that is broader and therefore less Human, I am very dubious, very dubious.

I am just now reading a very respectable little book (by a friend of mine, a judge) about the Revolution in the department of the Eure. It is full of documents written by bourgeois of the period, ordinary small-town citizens. Well, I assure you there are few of that caliber nowadays. They were well-read, admirable people, full of good sense, ideas, and generosity. Neo-Catholicism on the one hand and Socialism on the other have made France less intelligent. Everything is either the Immaculate Conception or workers' lunches.

I told you that I don't flatter the Democrats in my book. But I assure you the Conservatives aren't spared, either. I'm now writing three pages on the abominations committed by the National Guard in June '48, which will make me highly popular with the bourgeois. I'm doing my best to rub their noses in their own turpitude.

You give me no details about *Cadio*.[2] Who are the actors? etc. I'm wary of your novel about the theatre. You are too fond of those people. Have you known many of them who love their art? So many actors are merely bourgeois gone astray![3]

So we'll see each other three weeks from now, at the latest. I'm very happy about that, and meanwhile send you a kiss.

G^ve Flaubert

What about the Censor? For your sake I hope he'll commit some howlers; indeed it would grieve me were he false to his traditional role . . .[4]

1. George Sand's friend the actress Mme Arnould Plessy ("Sylvanie") had been converted to Catholicism. She had been one of Prince Napoleon's many mistresses.

2. The play adapted by George Sand and her collaborator Paul Meurice from her novel of that name was in rehearsal. She was also in the midst of writing her novel about actors, *Pierre qui roule.*

3. Flaubert is perhaps speaking from intimate knowledge. He and Bouilhet had been having affairs with actresses, Flaubert notably with Béatrix Person.

4. In addition to speaking here as veteran of the *Madame Bovary* prosecution, Flaubert shows himself the former law student in his use of a legalistic phrase: *si elle manquait à ses us.*

To His Cousin Louis Bonenfant

Croisset, Thursday [1868?]

Mon cher ami

I haven't thanked you enough. Your account is excellent in every way, and will supply me with some good details. You have done me a real service in sending it. I'm grateful to my little cousin Émilie, too, for her list of Nogent expressions; and I repay her kindness with the blackest ingratitude, because:

I cannot do as she would like, which is to change the name of the hero of my novel. You must remember, cher ami, that four years ago I asked you whether there were still in Nogent people named Moreau? You replied that there were none, and you supplied me with several local names that I could feel free to use. On the strength of your information I went blithely ahead. It's too late to change. A proper name is extremely important in a novel—*crucial.* It is no more possible to change a character's name than his skin; it's like wanting to bleach a Negro.

So much the worse for the Moreaus now living in Nogent!

Not that they'll have any cause for complaint: my M. Moreau is a very elegant young man.

◇ ◇ ◇ ◇ ◇

Charles Baudelaire had died on August 31, 1867. Now, over a year later, Mme Jacques Aupick, his twice-widowed mother, probably thinking of his friendship with Flaubert and the prosecution they had both suffered—for *Madame Bovary* and *Les Fleurs du mal*—saw to it that Flaubert received a copy of her son's posthumously published *Oeuvres complètes.* Of Flaubert's letter to Mme Aupick, written on [December 31, 1868], there is available only the single sentence quoted in an autograph dealer's catalog of 1968, offering the letter for sale:

"I am very touched by your sending me the works of your son, whom I greatly loved and whose talent I appreciated more than anyone." In the remaining part of the letter (so says the catalog), Flaubert recalls his 1851 visit to General and Mme Aupick in Constantinople, where the general, Baudelaire's none too sympathetic stepfather, had been French "minister plenipotentiary." The present whereabouts of the letter have not been disclosed by the dealer.

◇◇◇◇◇

To George Sand

[Croisset, January 1, 1869]
New Year's Eve, 1 o'clock

Why shouldn't I begin the year 1869 with the wish that for you and yours it may be "good, and happy, and followed by many more"? Rather rococo, but I like it.

Now let's chat. I am not "working myself to death," for I have never been better. In Paris I was told I was "fresh-faced as a girl," and people ignorant of my biography attributed that healthy look to the country air.[1] Such are ready-made ideas. Each has his own hygiene. I, when I'm not hungry, can eat only dry bread. And the most indigestible foods, like unripe cider-apples, and bacon, are my cures for stomach ache. And so on. A man who has no common sense mustn't live according to common-sense rules.

As to my mania for work, I'll compare it to a rash. I keep scratching myself and yelling as I scratch. It's pleasure and torture combined. And nothing that I write is what I want to write. For one doesn't choose one's subjects: they impose themselves. Will I ever find mine? Will there ever drop down on me from heaven an idea in perfect harmony with my temperament? Will I be able to write a book into which I put my entire self? It seems to me, in my moments of vanity, that I am beginning to glimpse something that will be what a novel should be. But I still have three or four to write before that one (which is as yet very vague); and at the rate I go it will be all I can do to write those three or four. I am like M. Prud'homme, who thought the most beautiful church of all would have the spire of Strasbourg, the colonnade of St. Peter's, the portico of the Parthenon, etc. I have contradictory ideals. Hence, confusion, stoppage, impotence!

As for the cloistered life to which I condemn myself being a "delicious existence"—no! But what to do! To get drunk on ink is better than to get drunk on brandy. The Muse, crabbed though she may be, is the source of less grief than Woman! I cannot accommodate the two. One has to choose. My choice was made long ago. There remains the question of the senses. Mine have always been my servants. Even in the days of my greenest youth I did with them exactly as I pleased. I am now almost fifty, and their ardor is the least of my worries. This regime is not very merry, I agree. There are moments of emptiness, of hideous boredom. But these grow rarer as one grows older. To be truthful, *living* strikes me as a trade I wasn't cut out for! And yet! . . .

I was in Paris for three days, which I spent doing research and errands for my book. I was so exhausted last Friday that I went to bed at seven o'clock. Such are my wild orgies in the capital.

I found the Goncourts in a state of frantic (sic) admiration for a book called *Histoire de ma vie*, by G. Sand—which goes to show that they are stronger in good taste than in erudition.[2] They even wanted to write you to express their admiration. On the other hand I found our friend Harrisse[3] stupid. He compares Feydeau to Chateaubriand, greatly admires *Le Lépreux de la Cité d'Aoste*, considers *Don Quixote* tedious, etc.

Are you struck by how rare the literary sense is? A knowledge of languages, archaeology, history, etc.—all that should help. But not at all! So-called enlightened people are becoming more and more inept as regards art. Even what art *is* escapes them. Glosses are more important for them than the text. They value crutches more highly than legs.

.   .   .

I shan't budge from here before Easter. I count on finishing by the end of May. You'll see me at Nohant this summer, even though bombs should fall.

And your work? What are you doing now, chère maître?

When shall we see each other? Will you be coming to Paris in the spring?

Je vous embrasse.

G^{ve} Flaubert

1. A number of phrases in this letter refer to advice that Mme Sand has been giving him, or to comments she has made, about working himself to death, staying holed up in his library and not getting enough fresh air, really finding his cloistered life (about which he constantly complains) a delicious existence, and so on. The tone of her letters is increasingly maternal.

2. Flaubert means that since the last volume of *Histoire de ma vie* had been published in 1855, the Goncourts should have read it before now.

3. Henry Harrisse (1829–1910), born in Paris of American parents, was a lawyer, bibliophile, and historian, author of books on the Abbé Prévost and his *Manon Lescaut*.

GEORGE SAND TO FLAUBERT

[Nohant,] January 1, [18]69

It's one in the morning. I have just kissed my children. I'm tired from making a complete costume for a big doll for Aurore, but I don't want to go to bed without kissing you too, my dear friend, my great precious child. May '69 be good to you and see the end of your novel, may you keep well and be always *you*. I can imagine nothing better, and I love you.

G. Sand[1]

1. Flaubert replied, in a letter dated January 14: "You know, chère maître, it's very nice about the two of us—writing to each other simultaneously on New Year's Eve. There is certainly some strong link between us."

To Princesse Mathilde

[Croisset,] Thursday [January 7, 1869]

Your letter of yesterday distressed me, Princesse, and I'd have answered it immediately had it not been for the wedding of Mlle Leroy, the Prefect's daughter. A great debauch for me—to Rouen, for an evening party!

Since you are upset,[1] so am I. But let me say it seems to me you're giving a rather inflated importance to the reason. It's never the flag that's to be considered, but what it flies over; *where* one writes is of little importance: the main thing is *what* one writes.

I am not at all defending *Le Temps*, which I profoundly dislike, as for that matter I dislike all newspapers. I hate that paltry way of publishing one's thoughts, and I express my hatred by abstaining completely, despite the money I could earn.

The press is dangerous only because of the exaggerated importance given to it; on this score, friends and enemies are all of one mind, unfortunately! Ah! If only the skeptic might be allowed free rein!

To return to Sainte-Beuve. His greatest offense, to my mind, lies in his doing something that displeases you; and from the moment you asked him not to write for that newspaper he should have complied. Such are my political opinions.

On the other hand, I perfectly understand his fury if they refused an article. One has to be a man of letters to know how wounding such things can be. I brought suit against the *Revue de Paris* when it took upon itself to cut three or four lines of mine.[2] My maxim is that in this regard one must be obdurate.

Therefore I excuse his resentment. But what I would not excuse would be a break with a government that has so greatly honored him. Surely this is not possible! Despite all you tell me, I still doubt it.

I am rereading your letter as I write, and it brings tears to my eyes, for I sense that this affair has hurt you to the quick, and that you are suffering from it as from a betrayal.

It would be good of you if you would explain the matter to me more fully; I long to learn that you have been mistaken. Because, in the end, if he writes only purely literary criticism for *Le Temps*, the harm done is slight. But, once again, what I dislike and what I do not forgive him, is that he should distress you. You, you, Princesse!, who have been, for him especially, more than good, *devoted*. No: really, from the moment you urged him . . .

Despite my virtuous resolution not to return to Paris before the end of March, I'm promising myself a little visit to you next month.

Ever at your feet, Princesse, I kiss your hands, and am

Entirely yours,
G^{ve} Flaubert

1. Sainte-Beuve had broken with the semi-official *Moniteur Universel* over their insistence that he delete, from one of his weekly articles, an unfavorable reference to Mgr. Le Courtier, bishop of Montpellier. He had gone over to *Le Temps*, the mouthpiece of the liberal opposition, despite Princesse Mathilde's request that he not do so. In her displeasure the princess revealed the spirit of her benefactions to Sainte-Beuve by saying that his acceptance of a senatorship had made him "a vassal of the Empire." (André Billy, *Sainte-Beuve: Sa vie et son temps*, 2 vols., Paris: Flammarion, 1952.)

2. Not quite accurate. For Flaubert's quarrel with the *Revue de Paris* over cuts in its serialization of *Madame Bovary*, see Volume I.

To George Sand

Croisset, Tuesday, February 2 [1869]

Ma chère maître:

Your old troubadour is the very picture of exhaustion. I spent a week in Paris verifying boring details (seven to nine hours of cabs a day, a fine way to get rich with Literature! Well . . .) I have just read over my outline. The amount I still have to write overwhelms me, or rather it makes me almost vomit from discouragement. It's always so when I get back to work. It's then that I'm bored, bored, bored! But this time it's worse than ever. That's why I so dread any interruption of the grind. I had no choice, however. I had myself carted to undertakers' establishments, to Père-Lachaise, to the valley of Montmorency, past stores selling religious articles, etc.[1]

In short, I still have four or five months' work ahead of me. What a sigh of relief I'll give when it's done! And what a long day it will be before I tackle the bourgeois again. It's time I enjoyed myself.

I have seen both Sainte-Beuve and the Princess. And I know everything about their break, which seems to me irrevocable. Sainte-Beuve was indignant with Dalloz,[2] and went over to *Le Temps*. The Princess begged him not to. He wouldn't listen to her. That's the whole story. My opinion, if you care to have it, is this: the first offense was committed by the Princess, who was intemperate; but the second and more serious offender is Sainte-Beuve, who acted ungallantly. When you have so accommodating a friend, and when this friend has provided you with an income of thirty thousand francs a year, you owe her some consideration. It seems to me that in Sainte-Beuve's place I'd have said: "Since it displeases you, let's say no more about it." He was bad-mannered, inelegant. What disgusted me a little, just between us, was the

125

way he praised the Emperor to me. Yes: to me! Praise of Badinguet! And we were alone.

The Princess took the thing too seriously from the start. I wrote her, siding with Sainte-Beuve; whereas he, I'm sure, found me cold. It was at that point, to justify himself in my eyes, that he protested his love for Isidore, which humiliated me a little. For it amounted to taking me for an utter imbecile.

I think he's preparing himself for a funeral like Béranger's, and that old Hugo's ability to speak the language of the people makes him jealous. Why write for newspapers when you can write books and aren't starving to death?

He's far from being a sage, that man; he's not like you! Your Strength charms me and amazes me. I mean the Strength of your entire person, not only your brain.

You spoke of criticism in your last letter, saying it will soon disappear. I think the contrary, that it's barely at its dawn. Its trend is the opposite of what it used to be, that's all. (In the days of La Harpe critics were grammarians; in the days of Sainte-Beuve and Taine they're historians.) When will they be *artists,* nothing but artists, *real* artists? Where have you seen a piece of criticism that is concerned, intensely concerned, with the work in itself? The milieu in which it was produced and the circumstances that occasioned it are very closely analyzed. But the *unconscious* poetics which brought it into being? Its composition? Its style? The author's point of view? *Never.*

Such criticism as that would require great imagination and great goodwill. I mean an ever-ready faculty of enthusiasm. And then *taste—* a quality rare even among the best, to such a point that it is no longer even mentioned.

What infuriates me every day is to see a masterpiece and a turpitude put on the same level. The insignificant are exalted and the great disparaged. Nothing could be more stupid or more immoral.[3]

⋅ ⋅ ⋅

In Père-Lachaise I was overcome by a deep and painful disgust for mankind. You cannot imagine the fetishism of the tombs. The true Parisian is more idolatrous than a black. It made me want to lie down in one of the graves.

⋅ ⋅ ⋅

1. Flaubert's surviving notebooks testify to his indefatigable investigations in these—and many more—places and establishments.

2. Paul Dalloz, the owner and director of *Le Moniteur Universel.*

3. In a letter written this same February 2, to Turgenev, who had recently visited Croisset and "charmed everyone," Flaubert repeats his strictures on La Harpe, Sainte-Beuve, and Taine as critics, adding: "I am eager to see your literary criticism, for yours will be that of a practitioner . . . With your kind of feeling, so original and so intense, your criticism will equal your creations, I'm sure."

GEORGE SAND
portrait drawing by
Thomas Couture

"I prefer the drawing by Couture. For me, old
Romantic that I am, it is the 'portrait of the
author' that so often set me dreaming
in my youth."
(Flaubert to George Sand)

FLAUBERT
portrait drawing by E. Liphart

ERNEST COMMANVILLE
"His forehead is *flat.*" (George Sand)

CAROLINE COMMANVILLE
"l'altière Vasthi"

FLAUBERT
caricature by E. Giraud

27. avril 1880.

SAINT POLYCARPE

◊ EDUCATION SENTIMENTALE ◊

MADAM. OVARY

SALAMMBÔ

LA TENTATION DE Sᵗ ANTOINE

M. Gustave Flaubert.

MENU

Potage velouté à la Bovary
Saumon, sauce Mathô
Poulet Homais
Filet. Education Sentimentale
Jambon Sᵗ Antoine
Salade au Cœur Simple
Haricots verts, Hamilcar
Glace Salammbô
Fromage (aux mangeurs de choses
          immondes.)
Dessert
café. vins Sᵗ Julien.(legende.) champagne &

THE LAST SAINT POLYCARP DINNER
"The Saint Polycarp celebration left me speechless!
. . . The menu [was] composed of dishes all named
for my books."

Nohant, February 11, [18]69

.   .   .

As for our friend, he is ungrateful, whereas our other friend is too demanding. As you say, both are wrong, and neither is to blame. It's the mechanism of society that makes it so. The kind of gratitude—that is, submission—that she demands, stems from a tradition that the present generation still turns to account (therein lies the trouble), but which it doesn't accept as a duty. The ideas of the person "under obligation" have changed; those of the one doing the "obliging" should change also. *She* should tell herself that one doesn't purchase another's moral liberty by performing a good office; and as for him, he should have foreseen that he would be considered as being bound. The simplest would have been not to require 30,000 francs a year. It's so easy to do without it! Let them work it out for themselves. They won't get us mixed up in it—we're not that stupid. You say some very good things about criticism. But to practice it in your sense would require artists, and the artist is too busy with his own work to forget himself in fathoming that of others.

.   .   .

TO GEORGE SAND
[Croisset,] Tuesday night [February 23–24, 1869]

What do I have to say about it, chère maître? Whether sensitivity in children should be fostered or repressed?[1] It seems to me that in this matter one should not have preconceived ideas. It's according to whether they tend toward having too much or too little. Moreover you can't alter basic character. There are affectionate natures and cold natures—there's no remedy for that. Furthermore, the same sight, the same lesson, can produce contrasting effects. Nothing should have hardened me more than being brought up in a hospital and playing as a small child in a dissecting room. And yet no one is more easily moved than I by the sight of physical suffering. It's true that I'm the son of a man who was extremely humane, sensitive in the good meaning of the word. The sight of a dog in pain brought tears to his eyes. Yet this in no way impaired his efficiency when performing operations. And he invented some terrible ones.

"Show children only the sweet and good side of life, up to the time when reason can help them accept or combat evil," [you say]. Such is not my opinion. For then something terrible is bound to take place in their hearts, an infinite disillusionment; and besides, how can reason develop if it doesn't apply itself (or isn't applied daily) to distinguishing

127

right from wrong? Life is perforce an incessant education. Everything has to be learned, from Talking to Dying.

You say some very true things about the unconscious of children.[2] He who could see clearly into their little brains would discover the roots of human genius, the origin of the Gods, the sap that determines subsequent actions, etc. A black speaking to his idol and a child to its doll seem to me very close.

The child and the barbarian (the primitive) do not distinguish reality from fantasy. I remember very clearly that when I was five or six I wanted to "send my heart" to a little girl I was in love with. (I meant my *physical* heart.) I pictured it lying on a bed of straw in a basket—an oyster basket!

But no one has gone as far as you in these analyses. Your *Histoire de ma vie* has pages on the subject that are extraordinarily profound. What I say is true, since minds remote from yours have found them amazing—witness the Goncourts.

Have you read their *Madame Gervaisais?* You should.

Your poor daughter-in-law must be very distressed. And Maurice, in consequence? And you too? I'm sorry for all of you. I saw M. Calamatta twice: once at Mme Colet's, and the second time at your house, rue Racine, the first time I called on you. Tell me what news there is of him.

Winter is approaching its end. I have seldom passed a better, despite an abominable grippe that has kept me coughing and streaming for three weeks. In about ten days I hope to begin my next-to-last chapter. When it is well under way (half done), I'll install myself in Paris—toward Easter, not before. I *count* on a reunion with you there. Because, like an animal—or, rather, like a man who prizes things of the mind—I miss you.

Our good Turgenev should be in Paris by the end of March.[3] It would be nice if the three of us could dine together.

I have been thinking more about Sainte-Beuve. To be sure, one can "do without 30,000 francs a year." But there is something simpler yet: having such an income, not to spout every week in those bum-wipers called newspapers. Why doesn't he write books, since he's rich and talented?

I am just now rereading *Don Quixote.* What a giant of a book! Is there anything more splendid?

Soon it will be four o'clock. Time to climb between the sheets.

Adieu. I kiss you on both cheeks—you're like fresh bread—and Mlle Aurore too, with all the affection of your troubadour.

1. George Sand's son, Maurice, and his wife, Lina, had gone to Milan, where Lina's father, the artist Louis Calamatta, was fatally ill. (He was to die on March 9.) Mme Sand, remaining at Nohant with the couple's three-year-old daughter, Aurore, had asked Flaubert for his thoughts about very young children: "You who have raised a niece who is

charming and intelligent." Mme Sand was not on good terms with her own daughter, Solange, whose marriage to the sculptor Jean-Baptiste Clésinger had failed and whose two daughters by him had died in infancy (as had the first-born, a son, of Lina and Maurice).

2. "L'inscience des enfants."

3. He was, and Flaubert saw him. "I dined with Turgenev yesterday and the day before," he wrote Mme Sand to Nohant (March 31, 1869). "That man paints such powerful pictures, even in conversation, that he *showed* me G. Sand, leaning on a parapet of Mme Viardot's château at Rosay. Below the turret was a moat; in the moat, a boat. And Turgenev, sitting in that boat, was looking up at you. The setting sun was falling on your black hair."

Pauline Viardot-Garcia (1821–1910), "a great lyric actress and singer" (*Grove's Dictionary of Music and Musicians*, 1935), was a mezzo-soprano, the younger sister of the contralto Marie Malibran—both of them daughters of the Spanish tenor and teacher Manuel Garcia and his wife, Joaquina Sitchez, an actress. In 1841 she married Louis Viardot, writer, critic, and at that time director of the Théâtre Italien in Paris. George Sand, her close friend, depicted her in the novel *Consuelo* and dedicated the book to her. When not in Russia, Turgenev usually lived with the Viardots. Madame Viardot was the love of his life.

◇-◇-◇-◇-◇

As we have seen, Flaubert had thought from the beginning to give his new novel the title he had already used for one of his early, unpublished works; but it was not until it was almost done that he announced to George Sand—on April 3, 1869—that he had definitely decided to call it *L'Éducation sentimentale*, "all other ideas having failed." He now added a subtitle: *Histoire d'un jeune homme* (The Story of a Young Man)—which is printed in all French editions although not in all translations. "I don't say that the title is good," he told Mme Sand, "but so far it's the one that best renders what I had in mind. This difficulty in finding a good title makes me think that the *idea* of the work (or rather its concept) isn't clear. I'd very much like to read you the end." He did not tell her—at least in any surviving letter—of its being the same title he had long ago given his youthful work. Perhaps Mme Sand, like all but a handful of his old friends, remained ignorant of the existence of that early novel, which would be published only posthumously.

◇-◇-◇-◇-◇

To Jules Duplan (?)
    [Paris,] Sunday morning, May 6, 1869. 1 minutes before 5

Fini! mon vieux! Yes, my book is finished! This calls for your stopping work and coming to embrace me.

I've been at my desk since 8 o'clock yesterday morning. My head is bursting. No matter—there's a tremendous weight off my stomach!

              A toi—

◇◇◇◇◇

At this time George Sand was in Paris for a month or more making arrangements concerning her new play, *L'Autre*; Flaubert saw her frequently, and on two occasions read her parts of his novel.[1] "C'est de la belle peinture," she wrote in her diary after the first session; and after the second, "The end is excellent." Following that, she read him, in turn, from *L'Autre*, which made him, she wrote Maurice, "cry like a calf."

There were also readings from *L'Éducation sentimentale* in the rue de Courcelles. "Princesse Mathilde twice asked me to read parts of my novel to her," he wrote to Caroline. "At the third request I gave in, and yesterday I read her the first three chapters. Whereupon, enthusiasm from the Areopagus impossible to describe, and I *have* to go on and read her the whole thing—which means (amid my other occupations) four sessions of four hours each." Two weeks later: "My last reading to the Princess attained the supreme limits of enthusiasm. (Literally.) A good part of the success must have been due to the way I read. I don't know what got into me that day, but I delivered the last chapter in such a way that I was dazzled myself."

It is understandable that the reading of the last chapters of *L'Éducation sentimentale*, especially the scene of Frédéric Moreau's reunion with the now white-haired Madame Arnoux, whom he had long romantically loved, should have inspired Flaubert to eloquent delivery. That "session" must have been charged not only with pride and relief in having completed the work at last, but particularly with thoughts of Elise Schlesinger, the young mother he had met as an adolescent on the beach in Trouville more than thirty years before. He had always romantically cherished the memory of that meeting and of subsequent visits to the Schlesingers' house in Paris during the otherwise dreary winters of his law studies. He had drawn the heroine of his novel in Elise Schlesinger's image; and he knew her now to be ill and unhappy, living with her feckless husband in Baden.

It is also curious to think of his reading to the princess the scenes, near the novel's end, in which he describes the armed repression marking the December 2, 1852, coup d'état of her cousin Louis-Napoleon, the present Emperor. That act of caesarism had led, along with its many other consequences, to her enjoying her present importance—the importance which, in turn, brought her Flaubert's friendship and now the private readings. "The memory of those five afternoons I spent with you reading my long novel," Flaubert wrote her, "will be with me eternally, as one of the best things in my life."

THE NEXT STEP, after having the manuscript recopied and before sending it to the printer, would be to go over it—as he had gone over both *Ma-*

dame Bovary and *Salammbô*—with Louis Bouilhet, with whom he had been constantly in touch since the novel's inception. But Bouilhet was ill, and had gone to Vichy in hope of relief. "By the end of next week, Monseigneur will be back in Paris," Flaubert wrote Caroline on June 24, "and we shall set about correcting *L'Éducation sentimentale* sentence by sentence. It will take us at least a fortnight."

But that was not to be.

1. He had read her three hundred pages of it in May 1868, during one of her visits to Croisset.

❖-❖-❖-❖-❖

To Maxime DuCamp

Croisset, July 23, 1869

Dear old Max, I feel the need of writing you a long letter; I don't know whether I'll have the strength, but I'll try.

Since his return to Rouen our poor Bouilhet was convinced he would never leave the place alive. Everybody, I along with the rest, teased him about his pessimism. He was no longer the man you knew; he was *completely* changed—except for his literary intelligence, which remained the same. In short, when I returned from Paris early in June, I found him in a lamentable state. A trip he made to Paris about *Aïssé,*[1] when Chilly asked him to make changes in the second act, so exhausted him that he could barely drag himself from the train to the Odéon. When I went to see him the last Sunday in June, I found Dr. Péan from Paris, another brute from Rouen named Leroy, Dr. Morel the alienist, and a pharmacist, a good man and a friend, named Dupré. Bouilhet didn't *dare* consult Achille,[2] suspecting himself to be very ill and fearing to be told the truth. Péan sent him to Vichy, whence Willemin quickly dispatched him back to Rouen. On arriving in Rouen, he finally called in Achille. His case was hopeless, as indeed Willemin had written me.

During that last fortnight my mother was at Verneuil, visiting the Vasse ladies, and letters from Caroline were taking three weeks;[3] you can imagine the anguish I went through. I saw Bouilhet every other day, and *found him improving.* His appetite was excellent, as were his spirits, and the swelling in his legs was subsiding. His sisters came from Cany to make scenes about religion, and were so disgusting that they shocked a decent canon from the cathedral. Our poor friend was *superb;* he sent them packing, telling them in so many words to go fuck themselves. When I left him for the last time, on Saturday, he had a volume of La Mettrie on his bed-table; it reminded me of poor Alfred reading Spinoza.[4] No priest set foot in his house.

His anger against his sisters was still sustaining him on Saturday, and I left for Paris hoping he might still live a long time.

At five o'clock on Sunday he became delirious and began to compose aloud the plot of a medieval drama on the Inquisition. He kept calling for me, to show it to me, and was enthusiastic about it. Then he was seized with trembling, stammered "Adieu! Adieu!," burying his head in Léonie's breast, and died very peacefully.

On Monday morning at nine my porter woke me with a telegram informing me of the event in telegraphic style. I was alone; I sent the news to you; I went to tell it to Duplan, who was in the midst of business; then I tramped the streets near the station until one o'clock—it was very hot.

From Paris to Rouen, in a crowded car, I had opposite me a cocotte who smoked cigarettes, put her feet up on the seat, and sang. When I saw the cathedral towers of Mantes[5] I thought I'd lose my mind, and am sure I wasn't far from doing so. Seeing me so pale, the cocotte offered me eau de Cologne. That revived me, but what a thirst! Ours in the desert of Kosseïr was nothing to it.

Finally I reached the rue Bihorel: here I spare you details. I have never known anyone better-hearted than young Philippe; he and Léonie, that good, kind woman, gave Bouilhet *admirable* care. They behaved in a manner I consider exemplary: to reassure him, to persuade him that he was not dangerously ill, Léonie refused to marry him; and her son encouraged her in this resistance. Bouilhet had so fully intended to marry her that he had obtained all the necessary documents. On the part of the young man, especially, I find such behavior *assez gentleman.*

D'Osmoy and I took charge of the funeral. There was a large crowd at the cemetery, at least two thousand people! The Prefect, the Attorney General, etc.—every Tom, Dick, and Harry. Will you believe that as I followed his coffin I relished most keenly the grotesque aspect of the ceremony? I kept hearing remarks he was making to me about it. Inside me, somewhere, he was speaking to me. It seemed to me that he was there, beside me, and that together we were attending the funeral of someone else. The heat was terrible; there was a storm in the offing. I was drenched with sweat, and the climb to the cemetery finished me.

His friend [Gabriel] Caudron (Mayor Verdrel's former clerk) had chosen a plot very close to my father's. I leaned on the railing to catch my breath. The coffin was resting on poles, over the grave. The speeches were about to begin (there were three). At that point I gave up. My brother and someone I didn't know took me away.

The next day I went to fetch my mother at Serquigny. Yesterday I went to Rouen to get *all* his papers. Today I have been reading the letters people have written me . . . Ah, it's a bitter blow!

By his will he leaves thirty thousand francs and something more to Léonie. All his books and papers go to Philippe, whom he directs to consult with four friends as to what should be done with his unpublished works: me, d'Osmoy, you, and Caudron; he leaves an excellent volume of poems, four prose plays, and *Aïssé*. Chilly dislikes the second act; I don't know what he will do. This winter you'll have to come here with d'Osmoy and we'll decide together what should be published.

. . . My head is aching too badly for me to go on. Besides, what could I say? . . . Now there is only you, only you! . . . *All* the letters I have received contain the phrase "Close ranks!" A gentleman *I don't know* sent me his card with these two words: *Sunt Lacrymae!*

1. Bouilhet's drama in verse, *Mademoiselle Aïssé*, which Flaubert would succeed in having produced in 1872. Charles-Marie de Chilly was the manager of the Théâtre de l'Odéon.

2. Flaubert's brother, Dr. Achille Flaubert, codirector of the Rouen hospital.

3. Caroline was in Scandinavia with her husband, Ernest Commanville, in connection with his lumber business.

4. See Volume I, page 95.

5. Where Flaubert had spent nights with Louise Colet and where he had often visited Bouilhet when the latter was librarian there.

To Frédéric Fovard[1]

[Croisset,] Thursday night [July 22, 1869]

He died of albuminuria, discovered too late to be cured.

His end was hastened by his two sisters, who came to the house and made scenes about religion (and came again yesterday wanting to take away the furniture). He received them like an antique Roman. But the reaction doubtless caused his edema to mount to his chest and his brain. He became delirious at five o'clock on Sunday and died about ten, unaware of what was happening.

For me it is an irreparable loss. What I buried two days ago was my literary conscience, my judgment, my compass—not to count the rest.

. . . . .

1. Flaubert's notary in Paris.

◇◇◇◇◇

"I have just buried a part of myself," Flaubert wrote to Princesse Mathilde; and to Jules Duplan: "I tell myself, 'What's the use of writing, now that he's no longer there?' It's finished—the good talk, our common enthusiasms, our dreaming together about our future work." Flaubert would never cease to mourn Louis Bouilhet, as he mourned Alfred Le Poittevin.

He accepted Maxime DuCamp's offer to substitute himself as reader and "corrector" of the manuscript of L'Éducation sentimentale, the purpose being—as he had told the princess of his own final rereading—to "eliminate mistakes in French and deprive malevolent critics of as many pretexts as possible. They won't spare me anyway, but as to that I'm quite indifferent." DuCamp had forfeited much of Flaubert's literary confidence by behaving as he had when serializing Madame Bovary in the Revue de Paris, and by the superficiality of much of his own subsequent writing; and now Flaubert wrote to Jules Duplan: "I haven't had the strength to read over my novel, especially since Maxime's comments and suggestions irritate me, justified though they may be. I'm afraid of accepting them all, or of scrapping his entire list." Eventually, of DuCamp's 251 written objections, most of them on points of grammar, he accepted about two-thirds, rejecting the rest on the authority of Littré's dictionary.[1] The manuscript went off; Lévy paid 16,-000 francs for the rights for ten years; and Flaubert, once again putting aside his old Temptation of Saint Anthony, devoted himself to negotiating for the production of Mademoiselle Aïssé and the printing of a volume of Bouilhet's last poems, for which he would write an introduction.

Then came another loss. "Sainte-Beuve died today, exactly at half-past one," he wrote DuCamp on October 13, 1869. "I arrived at his house by chance at 1:35. Another gone! The little band diminishes! One by one the rare survivors of the raft of the Méduse[2] disappear. With whom can one talk of literature now? He loved it, and although he wasn't precisely a friend, his death grieves me profoundly. Everyone in France who wields a pen has suffered an irreparable loss." And to Caroline: "I had written L'Éducation sentimentale in part for Sainte-Beuve, and he died without knowing a line of it! Bouilhet never heard the last two chapters. So much for our plans! The year 1869 will be marked as a hard one for me—I continue to haunt the cemeteries. Let's talk about something else."

L'Éducation sentimentale was published on November 17, 1869—"the day," as Flaubert noted in a letter to Caroline, "of the opening of the Suez Canal."

1. Maxime DuCamp says, in a passage in his Souvenirs Littéraires (which should be read with caution, like all his remarks about Flaubert): "I had a discussion with Flaubert that lasted three weeks. I would lunch with him, he would dine with me, and we would sometimes battle for fourteen or fifteen hours at a stretch. There were times when I was exhausted. I laugh as I remember those struggles, during which, like Vadius and Trissotin [characters in Molière's Les Femmes Savantes], we would hurl blunt truths at each other's heads, without ever causing a wound . . . [Flaubert] claimed, he always claimed, that a writer is free, according to the demands of his style, to accept or reject the grammatical rules which govern the French language, and that the only laws he must observe are the laws of harmony . . . He said that style and grammar are two different things: he would quote the greatest writers, who were almost all incorrect, and point out that no

grammarian ever knew how to write. On these points we were on agreement, for his opinions were based on irrefutable examples."

2. See page 29, note 2.

◇-◇-◇-◇-◇

GEORGE SAND TO FLAUBERT

[Nohant,] Tuesday, November 30, 1869

Dear friend of my heart,

I wanted to reread your book, and my daughter-in-law has read it too, and several of my young friends, all of them sincere and spontaneous, and not at all stupid. We are all of the same opinion, that it is a splendid book, with the strength of the best of Balzac and more real— that is, more faithful to the truth from beginning to end. It takes the great art, the exquisite form, and the austerity of your work to make us willing to forgo the flowers of fantasy. Nevertheless you do fill your painting with poetry, whether or not your characters are aware of it. Rosanette at Fontainebleau doesn't know what plants she's treading on, but she is poetic all the same. It is all the work of a master—so live as calmly as you can in order to last long and produce much.

I have seen two scraps of articles that don't seem to begrudge you your success, but I know little of what goes on except that the papers seem given over to politics. Keep me informed. If they didn't do you justice, I'd be angry and say what I think. That's my right.

.   .   .

TO GEORGE SAND

[Paris, December 3, 1869]

Chère bon maître,

Your old troubadour is being greatly berated in the press. Read last Monday's *Constitutionnel* and this morning's *Gaulois*—they mince no words. They treat me like a cretin and a scoundrel. Barbey d'Aurevilly's piece in the *Constitutionnel* is a model of this genre, and the one by our friend Sarcey, though less violent, is no less uncomplimentary. These gentlemen protest in the name of morality and the ideal! I have also been flayed in the *Figaro* and in *Paris*, by Cesena and Duranty.

I don't care in the least, but it does surprise me that there should be so much hatred and dishonesty.

The *Tribune*,[1] the *Pays*, and the *Opinion Nationale*, on the other hand, have praised me to the skies.

As for my friends—people who received copies adorned with my signature—they are afraid of compromising themselves, and speak to me about everything except the book. Instances of courage are rare.

135

Nevertheless, the book is selling very well despite the political situation, and Lévy seems satisfied.

I know that the Rouen bourgeois are furious with me because of old Roque and the cellar of the Tuileries.[2] Their opinion is that "the publication of such books should be forbidden" (I quote verbatim), that I favor the Reds, that I am guilty of fanning revolutionary passions, etc. etc.

In short, I have gathered very few laurels so far, and have been wounded by no folded rose petal.[3]

.   .   .

All the papers adduce as proof of my baseness the episode of la Turque[4]—which they garble, of course; and Sarcey compares me to the marquis de Sade, whom he admits he hasn't read!

None of this destroys my composure. But I keep asking myself: Why publish?

1. The article in the *Tribune* was by the twenty-nine-year-old Emile Zola, of whom more anon.

2. Calling "Here you are!" the bourgeois Roque, a member of the National Guard on duty at the Tuileries, shoots between the bars of a basement window into a group of prisoners calling for bread.

3. An allusion to one of the "histories" of the Roman Aelianus (d. A.D. 140) in which the Sybarite Smindyrides complains of spending a sleepless night because one of the rose petals strewn on his bed was folded in two.

4. The much discussed last scene in the book, when Moreau and Deslauriers recall the fiasco of their adolescent approach to a brothel as having been "the best moment of their lives."

To George Sand

4, rue Murillo, parc Monceau,[1] Tuesday, 4 o'clock
[Paris, December 7, 1869]

Chère maître,

The way they're all jumping on your old troubadour is unheard of. People who have received a copy of my novel from me are afraid to talk to me about it,[2] for fear of compromising themselves or out of pity for me. The most indulgent are of the opinion that what I have written is merely a series of scenes, and that composition and pattern are completely lacking. Saint-Victor, who extols the books of Arsène Houssaye, won't write about mine, finding it too bad. Voilà. Théo is away,[3] and no one (absolutely no one) is coming to my defense.

Therefore (you can guess what's coming), if you would care to take on that role you'd oblige me. If it embarrasses you, do nothing. No mere indulgence between us two.

.   .   .

Sarcey has published a second article against me. Barbey d'Aurevilly claims that I pollute a stream by washing myself in it. (*Sic.*) All that upsets me not the slightest. But God! how stupid people are!

When are you coming to Paris?

Je vous embrasse.

1. Flaubert had recently left his old apartment at 42, boulevard du Temple.

2. Of the hundred and fifty or so people to whom he had sent copies of *L'Éducation sentimentale*, Flaubert wrote Jules Duplan on December 9, thirty at most had replied.

3. Théophile Gautier was in Egypt, sent by the *Journal Officiel* to cover the festivities celebrating the opening of the Suez Canal.

◇◇◇◇◇

George Sand noted in her diary on December 8, 1869: "Letter from Flaubert. Article immediately . . . I go upstairs early to finish my article." By the following night at 2 A.M. she could write to Flaubert:

Mon camarade, it's done. The article will go off tomorrow. I send it to—whom? Reply by telegram. I'd like to send it to Girardin.[1] But you may have a better idea. I'm not too familiar with the importance or repute of the various newspapers. Send me a name and an address by telegram. I have Girardin's address.

I'm not entirely satisfied with my prose. I've had fever and a sprain of some kind for the last two days; but we must act quickly.

Je t'embrasse.

Flaubert responded immediately, on December 10, by telegram: "To Girardin."[2] In his letter of thanks, sent the same day as the telegram, he told her of still more attacks on his novel.

1. Emile Girardin (1806–1881), formerly owner and director of the newspaper *La Presse*, and now of *La Liberté.*

2. George Sand's review of *L'Éducation sentimentale* would be printed in *La Liberté* for Wednesday, December 22, 1869, the day before Flaubert's arrival at Nohant.

◇◇◇◇◇

GEORGE SAND TO FLAUBERT

[Nohant, December 10–11, 1869]

You seem surprised by the ill will. You are too naif. You don't know how original your book is. You don't realize how it *must* vex people by its very strength. You think you write things that will go as smoothly as a letter in the mail. That's what you *think!*

In my article I emphasize the *structure* of your book. That is what people understand the least, and it's the book's strongest feature. I have tried to make simple readers understand how they should read it, for it's the simple readers who make a book a success. Clever, malicious

137

folk don't want others to succeed. I haven't concerned myself with them—it would do them too much honor.

GEORGE SAND TO FLAUBERT

[Nohant,] December 14 [1869]

. . .

We're making preparations for our family Christmas celebration beside the fire. We're expecting Plauchut,[1] and I've told him to try to bring you along. If you can't come with him, at least come for Christmas Eve and escape New Year's in Paris. It's so dreary! Lina charges me to tell you that you need never wear anything but dressing-gown and slippers. There will be no ladies and no outsiders. You'll make us very happy, and you've been promising so long to come . . .

1. Edmond Plauchut (1814–1909), world traveler and devoted admirer of Mme Sand, was one of the habitués of Nohant. He is buried in the family cemetery there.

GEORGE SAND TO FLAUBERT

Sunday, Nohant, December 19, 1869

. . .

Here's the program for the 24th. We'll dine at 6 sharp, trim the Christmas tree, and have the marionettes for the children, so that they can get to bed by 9. Afterwards we'll chat, and have supper at midnight . . . You must stay with us a very long time, a very long time; there'll be more merriment for New Year's Eve. This is a crazy, happy house, and it's time for some recreation after our work. Tonight I'm finishing my task for the year.[1] Seeing you, dearly beloved old friend, will be my reward: don't refuse me.

1. Her novel *Malgrétout*.

◇◇◇◇◇
Flaubert replied on December 20: "Agreed, chère maître! I'll leave for Nohant Thursday by the 9 A.M. train." George Sand's diary describes Flaubert's stay at the "crazy, happy house":

Thursday, December 23: . . . Flaubert and Plauchut arrive at 5:30. Much embracing, dinner, talk, playing the python,[1] Arab songs. Flaubert tells stories. To bed at one o'clock.

Friday, December 24: Rain and snow all day. Everyone gay. I come down for lunch with the others at eleven o'clock. Flaubert gives Christmas presents to the little girls, who are enchanted. Lolo [Aurore] carries her doll all day . . . After dinner, marionettes, tombola, fairy-like decorations. Flaubert enjoys himself like a child. Christmas tree on the stage. Presents for all ... Splendid Christmas Eve. I go upstairs at three o'clock.

Saturday, December 25: Lunch at noon ... Flaubert reads us his great *féérie*[2] from three to half-past six. Delightful, but not destined for success [on the Paris stage]. We greatly enjoy it—much talk about it. Everybody very gay tonight. Flaubert has us dying with laughter at *The Prodigal Son.*[3]

Sunday, December 26: Sunny and cold. We walk in the garden, even Flaubert, who wants to see the farm. We go all over it, show him the ram we've named "Gustave" ... At three o'clock Maurice and Edme[4] improvise a marionette show ... Flaubert splits his sides laughing; he appreciates the marionettes ... Upstairs at two.

Monday, December 27: Steady snow. Fadet [the dog] refuses to set foot outdoors. Lunch at noon. Lolo dances all her dances. Flaubert puts on woman's clothes and dances the cachucha with Plauchut. It's grotesque—we all behave like lunatics. Visit from M. and Mme Duvernet sobers us ... Quiet evening of talk. Flaubert makes his farewells.

1. So she calls the "serpent," or "serpent horn," a now obsolete musical instrument, usually made of wood, consisting of a serpentine tube about eight feet long—"the natural bass of the ancient cornet family." (*Grove's Dictionary of Music and Musicians*, 1935.)

2. *Le Château des coeurs* (see page 73).

3. Unidentified. Perhaps one of Flaubert's "turns" as a mime.

Thirty years before, in the early 1840s, it had been Chopin who mimed at Nohant, jumping up from the piano to give "an extraordinary imitation of the Emperor of Austria or an old Polish Jew," and so on. (André Maurois, *Lélia.*) Chopin invented the Nohant theatricals. At first they were pantomimes and more or less improvised short pieces; then Maurice Sand added marionettes, which became the house specialty. Maurice's theatre and his marionettes (many of their costumes made by George Sand) may still be seen at Nohant.

4. Edme Simonnet, one of Mme Sand's adolescent great-nephews—grandsons of her older (illegitimate) half-brother, Hippolyte Chatiron, who was her father's son by a maidservant. Edme was George Sand's favorite among the many young relatives and friends who were such frequent guests at Nohant as to be members of the household. (There was now a new infant granddaughter, Aurore's younger sister, Gabrielle, born March 11, 1868.)

✥✥✥✥✥

To George Sand

Monday morning [Paris, January 3, 1870]

Chère maître,

I wrote last Tuesday to tell you that I had a very good trip back. The letter will probably have been delayed, what with New Year's and the weather ...

I didn't tell you nearly emphatically enough how charming I found the hospitality at Nohant. Those were the best moments of 1869, a year that wasn't kind to me.

... I've begun to read again for *Saint Anthony* ... Kiss Lolo for me, and don't forget anyone in giving my remembrance and affection, not even Fadet!

Tout à vous, chère maître.

GEORGE SAND TO FLAUBERT

Nohant, January 9, [18]70

· · ·

Your book is still being attacked. That doesn't keep it from being a beautiful and good book. Justice will be done later; justice is always done. It hasn't come at the proper time, apparently; or, rather, the time is *too* right. It confirms the present confused state of people's minds all too strongly. It rubs the raw wound. People recognize themselves too clearly in it.

Everyone adores you here, and our consciences are too clear for us to be offended by the truth: we speak of you every day. Yesterday Lina was telling me that she greatly admired everything you do, but that she preferred *Salammbô* to your depictions of modern life. If you had been concealed somewhere nearby, this is what you would have heard coming from her, from me, and from the others:

He is taller, larger, than the average person. His mind is like him, out-size. In this he has at least as much of Victor Hugo as of Balzac, but he has the taste and discernment that Hugo lacks, and he is an artist, which Balzac was not.—Does that mean he is greater than both of them?—*Chi lo sa?* He hasn't yet spoken with his full voice. The immense capacity of his brain confounds him. He doesn't know whether to be a poet or a realist, and since he's both, that troubles him.—He must learn to cope with his own great radiations. He sees everything, and wants to grapple with everything at once.—In that he is unlike the public, which wants to take its nourishment in small mouthfuls, and chokes on anything big. Nevertheless the public will make its way to him, when it understands him.—It will even reach him quite soon if the author will deign to *want* to be understood.—For that, he will perhaps have to make some concessions to the laziness of its intelligence.—But we must think carefully before daring to offer him that advice.

Such is the résumé of what we have all been saying. It isn't without value to know the opinions of good people and young people. The youngest say that *L'Éducation sentimentale* made them sad. They didn't recognize themselves in it, they who haven't yet lived. But they have illusions, and they say: Why does this man, so good, so lovable, so gay, so simple, so sympathetic, want to discourage us from living? It isn't properly thought out, what they say, but since it's instinctive, it should perhaps be taken into account.

. . .

❖❖❖❖❖

As Flaubert himself had written a few weeks before to Mlle Leroyer de Chantepie, the author of one of the few favorable reviews: "It will be, I hope, with *L'Éducation sentimentale* as it has been with *Bovary*. In the end, people will understand its morality and find it 'quite simple.'"

VI

Interlude:
Early 1870

B ACK FROM NOHANT, Flaubert plunged into further reading for
the perennial *Saint Anthony*, both at home and in Paris libraries, and
began to prepare his preface to Louis Bouilhet's last poems. He was still
depressed, and in a low state of energy. And soon he had to mourn another death, that of the faithful Jules Duplan on March 1, 1870. In mid-
March came an episode of a kind which almost every writer of fiction
encounters in one form or another.

◇◇◇◇◇

TO GEORGE SAND

[Paris,] Thursday, March 17 [1870]

Chère Maître,

Last evening I received a telegram from Mme Cornu[1] reading as follows: "Please come. Important." So I called on her today. And this is
the story:

The Empress claims that you have made very unfavorable allusions
to her in the last number of the *Revue* [*des Deux Mondes*].[2]

"How could she! With everybody attacking me now! I wouldn't have
believed it! And I wanted to have her elected to the Academy! What
have I done to her? Etc." In short, she is very unhappy, and the Emperor
as well. He was not indignant, but "prostrated" (*sic*).

Mme Cornu vainly insisted that she was mistaken, that you had
made no allusion to her whatever, and tried to explain to her how
novels are written.

"Well then, have her write to the newspapers that she had no intention of offending me."

"That she won't do, I'm sure."

"Then you write to her, and ask her to tell you so."

"I wouldn't presume to take such a step."

"But I want to know the truth! Do you know someone who . . ."

143

At that point Mme Cornu named me.

"Oh, don't say that I spoke to you about this."

Such is the dialogue that Mme Cornu reported to me. She would like you to write me a letter saying that the Empress was not your model. I am to send your letter to Mme Cornu, who will pass it on to the Empress. That's all.

I find the whole thing idiotic. Those people are certainly sensitive! You and I have to put up with a good deal more than that!

Now, chère Maître du bon Dieu, you must do exactly as you please.

The Empress has always been very pleasant with me, and I wouldn't mind doing her a kindness. I have read the passage in question, and find nothing offensive in it. But women's brains are so peculiar!

I am very tired of my own (my brain, I mean), or rather it's at a decidedly low ebb for the moment. Try as I may, I don't get ahead with my work. Things aren't going well at all. Everything irritates and wounds me; and after controlling myself in the presence of others I'm occasionally seized by fits of weeping during which I think my end has come. In short, I'm experiencing something quite new: the onset of old age. The shadow is engulfing me, as old Hugo would say.

Mme Cornu spoke to me enthusiastically about a letter you wrote her concerning a method of teaching. I'm going to see L'Autre with my niece next Saturday.

I'm waiting with double impatience for you to return to Paris. Because as soon as you leave it again I'll return to Croisset. Paris is beginning to get a little too much on my nerves.

Did I tell you that I'm taking cod liver oil, like a baby? Pathetic, no?

I embrace you with all my heart.

Your crusty old troubadour.

1. Mme Sébastien Cornu (born Hortense Lacroix) was namesake and goddaughter of the Emperor's mother, Queen Hortense, and was what the French call his *soeur de lait* ("milk-sister"): that is, they had shared the same wet-nurse. She had grown up with him, and was now a confidante of the Empress.

2. The reader will decide for himself whether the beautiful, Spanish-born Eugénie, known for her ambition when she was Mlle de Montijo, had reason to think herself alluded to in the following passage, spoken by a Spanish beauty, Mlle d'Ortosa, in the second installment of George Sand's novel, *Malgrétout,* in the *Revue des Deux Mondes* for March 15, 1870:

"I know about all the eminent men, all the powerful women, of the past and the present. I have taken the exact measure of them all, and I fear none of them. The day will come when I will be as useful to a sovereign as I can be today to a woman who asks me for advice on how to dress. I give the impression of attaching great importance to trivialities; no one suspects the serious preoccupations that engross me; this will become known later, when I am queen, czarina, grand duchess . . ."

Nohant, March 19 [1870]

I know, my friend, that you are very devoted to her. I know that *She* is very good to the unfortunate who are brought to her attention: that is all I know about her private life. I have never had either a revelation or a document concerning her, *not a word, not a fact*, that would have enabled me to depict her. Therefore I merely traced a figure of fancy, I swear it: and those who would claim to recognize her in a satirical context would certainly be bad servants and bad friends.

As for me, I never write satire. I do not know what it is. Nor do I paint *portraits;* that is not my profession: I *invent.* The public, ignorant of what invention is, always claims to find models. This is a mistake, and demeans art.

Such is my *sincere* reply. I have just time to put it in the mail.

G. Sand

To GEORGE SAND

[Paris, March 20, 1870]

I have just sent your letter (for which I thank you), to Mme Cornu, enclosing it in an epistle by your troubadour in which I permit myself to say *tartly* what I think. The two documents will be submitted to the gaze of the lady, and will give her a little lesson in aesthetics.

To MADAME HORTENSE CORNU

[Paris,] Sunday night [March 20, 1870]

Your devotion caused you to take false alarm, chère Madame. I was sure of it. Here is the reply: it reaches me by return mail.

People in society, I tell you again, see allusions where there are none. When I wrote *Madame Bovary* I was often asked "Was it Mme So and so you had in mind?" And I received letters from people completely unknown to me, among them one from a gentleman in Rheims who congratulated me for having "avenged" him! (His wife had been unfaithful.)

All the pharmacists of the Seine-Inférieure recognized themselves in Homais and wanted to come and give me a whipping; but best of all (I learned of it five years later), in Africa there was an army doctor's wife named Mme Bovaries, who resembled "Madame Bovary"—a name I had invented by changing the name "Bouvaret."[1]

The first thing our friend Maury said in speaking about *L'Éducation sentimentale* was: "Did you know X——, an Italian, professor of mathematics? Your Sénécal is his living likeness, physically and morally. It

145

has everything, even his haircut!" Others claim that in Arnoux I intended to depict Bernard Latte (the former publisher), whom I never saw, etc.

All this is to tell you, chère Madame, that the public is mistaken in attributing to us intentions we do not have.

I was very sure that Mme Sand had no intention of painting a portrait: first because of her high-mindedness, her taste, and her respect for Art, and second because of her character, her sense of decorum and fairness.

I even think, between you and me, that this accusation has hurt her a little. The newspapers bespatter us with filth every day, and we don't answer, even though it's our profession to wield the pen; and people think that in order to make an effect, to win some applause, we set out to lampoon this person or that. No, I assure you! We are not such poor things! Our ambition is higher, and our probity greater. When one respects one's mind, one doesn't go in for the kind of thing required to please the rabble. You understand me, don't you?

But enough. I'll come to see you one of these mornings. Looking forward to that pleasure, chère Madame, I kiss your hands and am all yours.

1. Readers of Volume I may recall that "Bouvaret" was the name of a hotel-keeper in Cairo, at the time of Flaubert's visit in 1849–1850.

To George Sand

[Paris,] Monday morning, 11 o'clock [April 4, 1870]

. . .

The lovely lady in question has sent me very proper excuses concerning you, assuring me that she had "never intended any insult to genius."

. . .

To George Sand

[Croisset,] Saturday night [May 21–22, 1870]

No, chère maître, I'm not sick, but I've been busy with my move from Paris and settling in again at Croisset. Furthermore, my mother was not at all well: now she is herself again. And then I've had to sort out the papers left behind by my poor Bouilhet, and have begun my piece about him. This week I've written almost six pages—quite an accomplishment for me; the task is a painful one for all kinds of reasons. The difficulty is to know what not to say. I'll relieve my feelings a little by spouting two or three dogmatic opinions on the art of writing. It's an opportunity to express what I think: an agreeable occupation, which I have always denied myself.

You write me very beautifully and with great goodness, wanting to restore my courage. I have none, but I proceed as though I had, which perhaps amounts to the same thing.

I no longer feel the *need* to write, because I wrote especially for one sole being who is no more. That is the truth. And yet I will continue to write. But the taste for it is gone, the enthusiasm has vanished. There are so few people who love what I love, who are concerned with the things that are my chief care. Do you know, in all the vastness of Paris, a single house where the talk is about Literature? And when it is alluded to incidentally, it is always in connection with its minor, external aspects—the question of success, morality, utility, timeliness, etc. I feel I'm becoming a fossil, a being unconnected with the life around me.

I should like nothing better than to find comfort in some new attachment. But how? Almost all my old friends are married, set in their ways, thinking all year round of their little concerns, with shooting during their holidays and whist after dinner. I don't know a single one who is capable of spending an afternoon with me reading a poet. They have their worldly involvements: I have none. Note that I am in the same position as regards company as when I was eighteen years old. My niece, whom I love as though she were my daughter, does not live with me, and my poor old mother is growing so old that any conversation with her (except about her health) is impossible. All that scarcely makes for a madcap existence.

As for ladies, there are none available hereabouts, and even if there were! . . . I have never been able to accommodate Venus with Apollo. For me it has always been the one or the other—being, as I am, a creature of excess, given over entirely to whatever I'm engaged in.

I keep repeating to myself Goethe's words: "Forward! Beyond the tombs!" and I hope to grow accustomed to this new emptiness around me. But no more than that.

The more I know you, the more I admire you. How strong you are!

But you are too good to have written once again to the child of Israel.[1] Let him keep his gold!!! The rascal has no idea of what a fine specimen he is. He thought himself perhaps very generous in proposing to lend me money without interest, but on the condition that I bind myself to him with a new contract. I bear him no grudge whatever, for he hasn't hurt me—he hasn't touched any sensitive spot.

Except for a little Spinoza and Plutarch, I have read nothing since my return, being fully occupied with my present task. This will take me to the end of July. I'm eager to be rid of it, so that I can plunge back into the extravagances of good old Saint Anthony, though I'm afraid of not being able to wind myself up to the proper pitch . . .

1. Mme Sand had interceded with Flaubert's publisher, Michel Lévy, in an attempt to make him more open-handed. Finding him intractable, she offered Flaubert a loan from her savings. He declined, claiming he had discovered a forgotten nest-egg of his own.

◇◇◇◇◇

The warm welcome at Nohant raised Flaubert's spirits briefly; but continued efforts by George Sand to counter his depression with encouraging letters were defeated by events—and, one must now recognize, by what had become, for Flaubert, habitual melancholy and lamentation.

◇◇◇◇◇

TO HIS NIECE CAROLINE

Croisset, Tuesday, midnight [June 28-29, 1870]

A week ago I made a sad trip to Paris. What a funeral.[1] I have rarely seen anything so moving. What a state poor Edmond de Goncourt was in! Théo, whom people accuse of being heartless, wept buckets. Nor was I very stoical myself: the ceremony plus the great heat was too much for me, and for several days I was inconceivably tired. Since yesterday I have felt better—thanks, I believe, to bathing in the Seine.

From the seven we were at the beginning of the Magny dinners, we are now only three: I, Théo, and Edmond de Goncourt. In the past eighteen months there have disappeared Gavarni, Bouilhet, Jules de Goncourt, and that's not all. But there's no point in distressing you with my sorrows . . .

1. Jules de Goncourt had died on June 20.

TO EDMOND DE GONCOURT

[Croisset,] Sunday night [June 26, 1870]

How I pity you, my poor friend! Your letter, this morning, broke my heart. Apart from the private detail you confide to me (and which I shall keep to myself, you may be sure),[1] it told me nothing new, or at least I had suspected all you tell me. For I think of you every day and many times every day. The thought of my friends who have died inevitably leads to thoughts of you. A pretty list, during the past year! . . . Your brother, Bouilhet, Sainte-Beuve, Duplan . . . Such are the ideas, like so many tombs, I live with these days.

But with you I dare not complain. For your sorrow must be beyond anything one can feel—or imagine.

You ask me to tell you about myself, my dear Edmond? Well, I am giving myself over to a heart-rending task: I am writing the preface to a volume of Bouilhet's poems. I have scanted the biographical part as much as possible, and will give most of my space to an examination of the work, and still more to his (or *our*) literary doctrines.

I've been re-reading everything he wrote. I've been going over our old letters, stirring up a series of memories, some of them dating back thirty-seven years! Not very gay, as you see! Besides, here at Croisset I'm pursued by his ghost; I find it lurking behind every bush in the garden, on the sofa in my study—even in my clothes, in my dressing gowns that he sometimes wore.

I hope to dwell less on such things when this abominable task is done; that is, in about six weeks. After which I'll try to take up my *Saint Anthony* again. But I have little heart for it. You well know that one always writes with someone in mind. Now, with that someone no longer here, my courage fails me.

So I live alone with my mother, who grows older every day, and more feeble, and complaining. A conversation of any serious kind has become impossible with her, and I have no one to talk to.

I hope to go to Paris in August, and to see you then. But where will you be? Let me have news of you sometime, my poor Edmond! No one pities you more than I.

Je vous embrasse très fortement.

1. Perhaps the fact that Jules de Goncourt had been destroyed by syphilis.

To George Sand

[Croisset,] Saturday night, July 2 [1870]

Chère bon maître

The death of Barbès[1] has greatly saddened me, for your sake. We are both of us in mourning. What a procession of deaths during the past year! It leaves me dazed, as though I'd been hit over the head. What distresses me (for we always refer everything back to ourselves) is the terrible solitude I live in. I no longer have anyone—no one at all—to talk with.

"Qui s'occupe aujourd'hui de faconde et de style?"[2] Apart from you and Turgenev, I don't know a single mortal with whom I can share the things closest to my heart, and you live far away from me, both of you.

I continue working, however. I have [now] resolved to take up my *Saint Anthony* tomorrow or the next day. But to begin[3] a long and exact-

149

ing work one must feel a certain liveliness that I lack. Still, I hope the extravagance of this work will take hold of me. Oh, how I'd love to be able to stop thinking about my poor *me*, about my miserable carcass! Actually, the carcass is in very good shape. I sleep tremendously. "I'm holding my own," as the bourgeois say.

... Lately I've been reading some deadly theological works, interspersing them with a little Plutarch and Spinoza ...

Poor Edmond de Goncourt is in Champagne with his relatives. He has promised to come here at the end of the month. I don't think that the hope of being reunited with his brother in a better world is consoling him for having lost him in this. One is the dupe of empty words in this question of immortality. For the question is to know whether the *self* persists. The affirmative seems to me a presumption of our self-pride, a protest by our weakness against the eternal order! Death has perhaps no more secrets to reveal to us than life.

What an accursed year! I feel as though I were lost in the desert. Nonetheless I assure you, chère maître, that I'm keeping a stout heart. And making prodigious efforts to be stoical. But the poor brain is weak at times. I need only one thing (and that isn't to be had for the asking): to feel some sort of enthusiasm.

Your letter of two days ago was very sad. You too, you heroic being: you too feel weary! What's to become of us?

· · ·

I have just read the *Conversations of Goethe and Eckermann.* There was a man, that Goethe! But he had everything: everything was in his favor!

1. On June 26, Mme Sand had announced it to Flaubert: "I am weeping for Barbès, one of my religions, one of those beings who reconcile us to mankind." Later, writing to Flaubert in 1871 about her own revolutionary past, she would mention Barbès again: "I have lived through revolutions, and I have seen their leading protagonists at close hand; I have seen the depths of their souls, and I must tell you that their secret is this: *no principles.* Also, no real intelligence, no strength, no consistency: nothing but a personal goal and the means of attaining it. One, only one, had principles—not all of them good, but all sincere, and to him far outweighing personal considerations: Barbès."

2. "Who cares these days for eloquence and style?" Unidentified. See offer, p. 113.

3. This would be the third "beginning" of *The Temptation of Saint Anthony,* or rather the beginning of the third, and final, version. Flaubert had first begun the work in 1848, before setting out for Egypt; then again in 1857, during the prosecution of *Madame Bovary* (see Volume I). Both those versions had been put aside. The "deadly theological works" mentioned in this letter are part of what would be the interminable research for this third version.

Flaubert had just completed his preface for the volume of Louis Bouilhet's last poems, which was to appear only in 1872.

◇◇◇◇◇

And then it was as though the private troubles had been accumulating only to explode in national disaster.

The burgeoning power of Prussia under the leadership of Bismarck had been alarming France, particularly since the Prussian victory over Austria at Sadowa in 1866. Greatly increased tensions in 1870 brought the two countries to the brink; and in July, in a deceitfully insolent message known to history as "the Ems telegram," Bismarck tricked France into becoming the "aggressor." On Bastille Day, July 14, inflamed Paris mobs chanted "On to Berlin!" and that night, with special authorization by the Emperor, the singer Marie Sasse, draped in the tricolor, sang *La Marseillaise* at the Opéra, to the cheers of the audience. On July 19, France, though hopelessly unprepared, declared war. (A.J.)

◇-◇-◇-◇-◇

To George Sand

Croisset, Friday night [July 22, 1870]

What has become of you, chère maître—you and yours?

As for me, I am nauseated, heartbroken, by the stupidity of my compatriots. The incorrigible barbarism of mankind fills me with blackest gloom. This enthusiasm [for war], unmotivated by any idea, makes me long to die, that I might witness it no longer.

The good Frenchman wants to fight (1) because he is jealous of Prussia; (2) because man's natural condition is savagery; (3) because in war there is an inherent mystical element that enraptures the crowd.

Have we reverted to the wars of the races? I fear so. The frightful butchery now being prepared for lacks even a pretext. It's a craving to fight for the sake of fighting.

I lament the destruction of bridges, the blowing-up of tunnels, the waste of so much human work, such fundamental *negation*.

Peace conferences are anathema for the moment. Civilization seems to me a far-distant thing. Hobbes was right: *Homo homini lupus.*[1]

Here the bourgeois is at the end of his patience. He considers that Prussia was too insolent, and wants to "avenge himself." Did you see that a gentleman in the Chamber [of Deputies] has proposed the sacking of the Duchy of Baden?[2] Ah, why can't I go live with the Bedouins!

I have begun *Saint Anthony*. And it might go well if I could stop thinking about the war . . .

1. "Man is wolf to man." Originally what seems to be a proverb, in Plautus, *Asinaria: Lupus est homo homini, non homo, cum qualis sit non novit.*
2. It was the Comte de Kératry, deputy from Finisterre and later prefect of police, who made the proposal. It has been suggested that Flaubert may have been particularly agitated (he will deplore the proposal again in a subsequent letter) because the now elderly Mme Schlesinger, idol of his youth and his inspiration for Mme Arnoux in *l'Éducation sentimentale*, was living in Baden. (A.J.)

VII

The War
and the Commune
1870–1871

WRITING of the international tensions of the 1860s in his *Souvenirs littéraires*, Maxime DuCamp describes Flaubert's attitude at that period:

> One single man, among my friends, was unaffected by the vague anxiety that preyed on us all: Gustave Flaubert, who was exasperated whenever anyone raised this question on which our very existence might well depend. Flaubert belonged to a group of thinkers, writers, politicians, all of them eminent in their respective fields, who met twice a month, always around the same table, for conversation. These deipnosophists lacked an Athenaeus.[1] One day Flaubert arrived at my house furious and vociferous. He told me he had just walked out of one of those dinners with his friends because they had been talking politics—an indecency among intellectuals. "What are Prussia and Austria to us?" he said. "Those men claim to be philosophers, and they spend their time wondering whether the Blues have beaten the Whites; they're nothing but bourgeois, and I find it pitiable to see X and Y discussing annexations, border realignments, dislocations, reconstitutions, as though they had nothing better to do, as though there were no longer any great poetry to recite, any sonorous prose to be written." I tried to calm him, without success. "They're nothing but bourgeois," he repeated. "We are neither French nor Algonquins; we are artists; Art is our country; a curse on those who have any other." Hot-headed words, which implied no lack of patriotism, for Flaubert would suffer to the point of tears when France surrendered to Germany.

That was in 1866, during the Austro-Prussian War. In 1869, according to DuCamp, Flaubert, paradoxical as always, disapproved the French government's inauguration of a policy of increased liberalism:

> The wave of political renovation which seized the country at that time was not at all to his taste. It sometimes exasperated him, and he considered that freedom of the press merely encouraged the

diffusion of bad writing. He said that everything that excites public opinion is detrimental to literature, which is made secondary to matters of ephemeral concern. The publication of a poem or a novel, the first performance of a play, was to him more important than any political action. He would have been glad to see legislative discussions replaced by lectures on Goethe, Michelangelo, and Ronsard. Outside literature and art, he saw nothing:[2] that is what sets him apart among his contemporaries and lends him a kind of greatness, restricted but powerful. As to his preferred form of government, I have heard him express two opinions, which, though diverse, were directed to the same purpose. He favored a kind of *mandarinat:* the running of the country would be entrusted to men who, after study, examinations, and competition, were recognized as the most intelligent. In this way, he was sure (he was, of course, wrong), writers and artists would become the masters of the nation's destiny, and this would result in an intellectual flowering beneficial to mankind. When the practical difficulties of such a system were pointed out to him, he would cry: "Give me a tyrant of genius who will protect arts and letters and lead us out of the mediocrity we're wallowing in!" I don't know whether this was actually his own opinion or whether he had taken it from Théophile Gautier, who all his life called for the reign of a Medici or a François Premier.

Such, according to DuCamp, were Flaubert's expressed political opinions—if political they can be called—at the outbreak of the Franco-Prussian War. Readers of the letters will have noticed that only when he undertook to document the background of *L'Éducation sentimentale* did he begin to discuss political matters to any extent with his correspondents. From then on we have seen him comment on French politics of the '40s, '50s, and '60s, led to do so by his research and by his realization of the fatal continuity of those decades. His hardening opinions were to lead him into conflict—increasing, but always affectionate—with George Sand. Her reply to his letter of July 20, 1870, found them still close to agreement.

1. "A grammarian of Naucratis, in Egypt, who composed an elegant and miscellaneous work, called *Deipnosophistae*, 'Dons at Dinner,' replete with very curious and interesting remarks and anecdotes of the ancients." (Lemprière, *Classical Dictionary*.) The Goncourt brothers, in their *Journal*, parts of which DuCamp probably saw later, are a kind of Athenaeus of the Magny dinners. The "Blues" and the "Whites," a few lines below, were rival teams of Roman charioteers.

2. Here again, as during their youthful trip together to Egypt, there is a notable contrast between DuCamp the journalist, expert in "current affairs," and Flaubert the novelist, sensitive to the human condition. Throughout his adult life, Flaubert—who truly "saw nothing" of the ingrown daily world of politicians—was prophetic on the theme of impending world war and the dehumanizing implications of new technology.

◇-◇-◇-◇-◇

GEORGE SAND TO FLAUBERT

Nohant, July 26 [1870]

I think this war is infamous; this authorized *Marseillaise* a sacrilege. Men are ferocious and conceited brutes. We are in Pascal's "half as far"; when will come the "farther ahead than ever"?[1]

It is between 40 and 45 degrees *in the shade* here. There are many forest fires—another barbarous stupidity! The wolves come and prowl in our farmyard, and at night we chase them away, Maurice with a revolver and I with a lantern. The trees are losing their leaves and perhaps their lives. Soon there will be no water for drinking. The harvests are almost nothing: but we have war—what luck! Crops are dying, famine threatens, poverty is lurking, waiting to transform itself into a Jacquerie:[2] but we'll fight the Prussians. *Malbrough s'en va-t-en guerre!*

You said rightly that in order to work one needs a degree of cheerfulness. Where is it to be found in these accursed times? Happily, we have no one ill at our house. When I see Maurice and Lina busy, Aurore and Gabrielle playing, I dare not complain, for fear of losing everything.

I love you, my dear old friend, we all love you.

Your troubadour,

G. Sand

1. An allusion to one of Pascal's *Pensées*, which George Sand had copied and kept on her desk. "Nature progresses *itus et réditus*. It advances and retreats, goes on farther, then half as far, and then farther than ever. Such are the tides of the sea; the sun too seems to move in this way." One understands its double appeal to George Sand, given her love of nature and belief in eventual "progress."

2. A fourteenth-century revolution of French peasants, which gave its name to subsequent rural uprisings. (Originally from "Jacques Bonhomme," a name derisively given to peasants by the nobility.)

TO GEORGE SAND

Croisset, Wednesday [August 3, 1870]

What, chère maître? You too? demoralized, sad? What's to become of weak souls, then?

As for me, my heart is oppressed in a way that astonishes me. And I wallow in a bottomless melancholy, despite work, despite our friend Saint Anthony, who ought to distract me. Is it the result of my repeated griefs? Perhaps. But the war has much to do with it. I feel we are entering black darkness.

Behold "natural man"! Make theories! Extol Progress, enlightenment, the good sense of the Masses, and the sweetness of the French people! I assure you that anyone who ventured to preach Peace here would get himself murdered.

Whatever happens, we're in for a long setback.

Perhaps the wars between the races are to begin again? Before a century passes we'll see several million men kill one another at one go? All the East against all Europe, the old world against the new! Why not? Great international enterprises like the Suez Canal are perhaps, in some other form, outlines and preparations for monstrous conflicts we can only guess at?

And Prussia is perhaps to be given a great drubbing, as part of the schemes of Providence for reestablishing European balance of power? That country was tending to be hypertrophied, like France under Louis XIV and Napoleon. The other organs are unfavorably affected by it. Hence universal disorder. Might tremendous bloodlettings be salutary?

Ah, we intellectuals! Mankind is far from our ideal! And our immense error, our fatal error, is to imagine it is like us, and to want to treat it accordingly.

The reverence, the fetishism, for universal suffrage revolts me more than the infallibility of the Pope (which has just nicely misfired, by the way, poor old chap!)[1] Do you think that if France, instead of being governed, in effect, by the crowd, were ruled by the Mandarins, we'd be where we are now? If instead of wanting to enlighten the lower classes we had busied ourselves educating the upper, we wouldn't have M. de Kératry proposing the sack of the duchy of Baden—a measure the public finds very proper.

Have you been watching Prud'homme[2] these days? He's marvelous! He admires Musset's *Rhin* and asks whether Musset has written anything else. Musset, accepted as the national poet, ousting Béranger! What an immense buffoonery everything is! But a buffoonery far from merry.

Poverty begins to be very evident. Everybody is hard up, starting with me! But perhaps we were too accustomed to comfort and tranquillity. Perhaps we were sinking into materialism. We must return to the great tradition: hold no longer to Life, to Happiness, to money, to anything; but be what our grandfathers were—light, airy beings.

In former times men passed their entire lives in a state of starvation. Now that same prospect looms on the horizon. What you tell me about poor Nohant is terrible. The countryside here has suffered less than yours.

.   .   .

1. The doctrine of papal infallibility had been promulgated on July 18. It was followed almost immediately by the loss of the papal states to the kingdom of Italy. Flaubert seems to be making the common mistake of thinking that the infallibility claimed by the doctrine was total: actually, it is "restricted" to matters of dogma and morality.

2. For Prud'homme see page 31, note 3.

"Le Rhin Allemand" [The German Rhine, 1840], a short patriotic poem by Alfred de Musset, one of George Sand's former lovers, was a rejoinder to a provocative German

"Rhine song," "Sie sollen ihn nicht haben" [You shall not have it], of the same year, by Nikolaus Becker (1809–1845). Musset's words had been set to music and were enjoying new popularity at that moment. Lamartine had also answered Becker, in a poem called "La Marseillaise de la paix" (1841). (J.B.)

◇◇◇◇◇

As news from the battlefronts rapidly grew alarming, as military disaster loomed and public panic spread, Flaubert's patriotism flared despite his hatred of "Isidore." "Well, we're in a pretty pickle!" he wrote to Caroline's husband, Ernest Commanville, in Dieppe. "The Empire is now only a question of days, but we must defend it to the end!" In a letter to Caroline he foretold the siege of Paris, only to change his mind later; and writing to Mme Roger des Genettes he foresaw what total defeat would bring: "To think we're only in the first act! Because, when peace is made (in one way or another) we'll find ourselves in a revolution."

◇◇◇◇◇

George Sand to Flaubert

[Nohant,] August 15 [1870], evening

I don't feel very valiant. There is still a woman under the skin of the old troubadour. This human butchery tears my poor heart to shreds. And I tremble for my children and my friends, who may be slaughtered.

And yet in the midst of all this my soul rises up in great bursts of faith. These dreadful lessons we must learn so as to understand our imbecility must be of some use to us. Perhaps we are reverting for the last time to the mistakes of the old world. There are sharp, clear principles for all of us today, which must emerge from this torment. Nothing is useless in the material system of the universe. The moral order cannot escape the law. Evil engenders good. I repeat that we are in Pascal's "two steps back," in order to arrive at the "farther ahead than ever."

I have finished a novel in the midst of this torment, hurrying lest I break down before the end. I'm as tired as though I were fighting along with our good soldiers.

Je t'embrasse. Tell me where you are and what you are thinking.

We all love you.

To George Sand

Croisset, Wednesday [August 17, 1870]

I arrived in Paris on Monday and left on Wednesday. Now I know what the Parisian is really like! And in my heart I forgive the most

157

ferocious politicians of 1793. Now I understand them. For I saw such stupidity! Such cowardice! Such ignorance! Such presumption! My compatriots make me want to vomit. They're worthy of being put in the same bag as Isidore! This country *deserves* to be punished, and I fear it will be.

It is impossible for me to read anything whatever: still more, to write. I spend my time like everybody else, waiting for news. Ah! If it weren't for my mother I'd certainly have joined up by now.

Not knowing how to keep busy, I've volunteered as a nurse at the Hôtel-Dieu in Rouen, where my services may be of use, as my brother has no more students.[1] My inaction stifles me to the point of explosion.

If the Germans besiege Paris, I'll go and fight. My rifle is ready. But until then I'll remain at Croisset because I must. I'll tell you why.

The examples of ignominy I saw in the capital are enough to add years to a man's life.

And we're only in the first act, because soon we'll be moving into *"la Sociale."*[2] Which will be followed by a vigorous and long reaction!

This is what we've been brought to by Universal Suffrage, the new God I consider as stupid as the old. No matter. Do you think it will be abashed, good old Universal Suffrage? Not at all! After Isidore we'll have Pignouf I![3]

What makes me wretched about this war is that the Prussians are right. Their turn next! Then Russia's. Ah! how I wish I were dead, not to have to think about all this!

At Nohant you must be less tormented than we by the question of money. In a few days all the workers in the Seine-Inférieure are going to ask for relief. My nephew Commanville is very active and keeps his workmen busy despite everything.[4] My brother has abandoned his patients and devotes himself to public affairs.[5] Rouen is arming and maintaining, at its own expense, its entire *garde mobile*—an idea not yet adopted by any other municipality.

Poor literature! Utterly forsaken, chère maître. *Saint Anthony* is only at page fourteen. Impossible to keep going . . .

1. They had probably been called up.
2. Current slang for "Socialist Republic."
3. That is, "After Napoleon the Third, Boor the First." This would be Thiers.
4. Since the end of July the blockade of the Normandy coast had closed factories, causing unemployment and poverty. But Commanville had obtained a government order for his lumber mill. (A.J.)
5. On August 10 Dr. Achille Flaubert had been elected to the Rouen Municipal Council. (A.J.)

◇◇◇◇◇

George Sand may have replied directly to Flaubert's tirade against universal suffrage. (Letters from her to him dated, according to her diary, August 22 and September 7, are lost.) In any case, she answered it publicly, with no mention of him, in a few sentences contained in her "Letter to a Friend" in *Le Temps* for September 5, 1870:

> France, always in the forefront of action, possesses an arm which the Teutons will not snatch from her, and which is the supreme weapon in battles of will: universal suffrage. Recently I have heard it much execrated, even by serious-minded men, this redoubtable missile that has so often been turned against us by our own hands. But so it is with all weapons one doesn't know how to use. This one is the universal safety of the future. This is the machine gun that must resolve, peacefully, all the questions awaiting their answer in days of tumult and terror—let us not forget it! The day it begins to function properly, errors of Power, whatever they may be, will become impossible.

Thinking to escape a German advance, relatives from Nogent-sur-Seine took refuge at Croisset, crowding the house.

◇◇◇◇◇

TO HIS NIECE CAROLINE

Croisset, Wednesday, 5 o'clock [August 31, 1870]

My dear Caro

The Bonenfants seem very happy to be far from "the theatre of war." Their girls are no trouble, but poor Bonenfant with his perpetual spitting! Would you believe it, from my bed I hear him spitting in the garden. That's what wakes me in the morning, along with your grandmother arguing with [her maid] Hyacinthe. I swear I can't go on like this, Carolo. If such a life were to continue, I'd go mad or collapse into idiocy. I have stomach cramps and a permanent headache. And no one, you realize, *absolutely no one*, even to talk with! Your grandmother complains endlessly about the weakness of her legs and her deafness. It's all dreadful . . .

◇◇◇◇◇

The next day, September 1, saw the annihilating Prussian victory at Sedan in the Ardennes: 82,000 French troops, and the Emperor himself, surrendered to the enemy and became prisoners of war. French killed and wounded numbered about nine thousand. On September 4 the Third Republic was proclaimed in Paris, its "Government of National Defense" resolving to continue the fight. On the fifth George Sand

159

wrote in her diary: "Maurice wakes me, telling me that the republic is proclaimed in Paris without a shot being fired! An immense fact, unique in human history! . . . May God protect France! Once again she has become worthy of His regard."

❖❖❖❖❖

To George Sand

[Croisset,] Saturday [September 10, 1870]

Chère maître,

Here we are, "at the bottom of the abyss"; a shameful peace will perhaps not be accepted.[1] The Prussians want to destroy Paris—such is their dream. Our only rational hope is in *chemistry*. Who knows? Perhaps methods of defense have been found, new ones?[2]

I don't believe that the siege of Paris is imminent. But to force its surrender they will (1) intimidate it by a display of cannon, and (2) ravage the surrounding countryside.

At Rouen, we're expecting the visit of those gentlemen. Since Sunday I've been lieutenant of my company.[3] I drill my men and go to Rouen to take lessons in military art.

The deplorable thing is that opinion is divided; some are for defense to the death and others for peace at any price.

I am dying of grief.

What a house this is! Fourteen people, all groaning, all driving me crazy.

I curse women: they are the cause of all our woes.[4]

I expect Paris to suffer the fate of Warsaw.[5]

And you distress me with your enthusiasm for the Republic. At this moment, when we're being defeated by Positivism at its purest, how can you still believe in Phantoms? Whatever happens, those now in Power will be sacrificed. And the Republic will suffer the same fate. Please note that I defend it, the poor Republic. But I have no faith in it.

Yesterday I saw Dumas at Dieppe, where I went especially to talk with him, to quash an idiotic calumny about the Princess, who has been accused of stealing 51 million *in gold*. In fact she left France with clean hands. But the same cannot be said of her brother, who since the beginning of the war has had the trees at the Château de Meudon cut down and sold for his profit. Splendid, no? Badinguet is (has become?) an imbecile, an idiot. He keeps repeating, like a machine, "No arms! No supplies!" The Prince Imperial is dying. These last details were given me (indirectly) by Mme Trochu.[6]

That's all I have to tell you now. I have many other things in my head, but can't collect them—I feel I'm drowning in sorrow—in cascades, rivers, oceans, of it. It is impossible to suffer more than this: at

160

times I fear I'm going insane. The sight of my mother's face, when I turn my eyes toward her, drains me of all energy. And I dare not tell you what I sometimes wish for.

This is where our crazy refusal to recognize the truth has led us, our passion for humbug and everything meretricious. We'll become another Poland, then another Spain. Then it will be Prussia's turn—she'll be devoured by Russia.

As for me, I consider myself *finished*. My brain will never recover. One cannot write when one has lost one's self-esteem. I ask but one thing—to die, so as to be at peace.

Adieu, chère maître. And above all, don't try to comfort me!

I embrace you with as much tenderness as is left in me. I feel my heart is withered and dry. I'm becoming stupid and nasty. Once again, all affection.

1. Jules Favre, Minister of Foreign Affairs in the "Government of National Defense," had published, on September 6, a "manifesto to the Powers," declaring that France would not surrender "a single stone of her fortresses, not one inch of her territory." (A.J.)

2. Flaubert is probably thinking of the "Scientific Committee for Defense," instituted on September 2. It was presided over by his fellow member of the Magny dinners, the chemist Marcelin Berthelot, and concerned itself chiefly with the manufacture of nitro-glycerine and dynamite. (A.J.)

3. The Croisset company of the National Guard.

4. Perhaps a reference to the Empress, who had fled to England on September 7. She was blamed for having encouraged her husband to listen to pro-war advisers; or, more popularly, was hated as the wife of the man who had brought the country to defeat. Crowds were calling for her head when she left Paris. Readers of earlier letters will recall numerous mysogynistic pronouncements by Flaubert; and most of the Nogent refugees were women. But the remark seems particularly offensive in a letter to George Sand.

5. The scene of savage Russian repression following the Polish insurrection of 1863.

6. Princesse Mathilde had left Paris on September 4 and taken shelter with Alexandre Dumas the younger at Puys, near Dieppe. Her baggage had already been put aboard a steamer for England when a rumor arose that it included the crown jewels and pictures from the Louvre. The captain ordered it opened, to convince the crowd of onlookers that it contained only personal effects, and the princess was allowed to depart. The story about Prince Napoleon's trees may also belong to the realm of wartime rumor. Similarly, the Emperor had not lost his mind, nor was the Prince Imperial (the fourteen-year-old son of the Emperor and Empress) dying: after serving in the army he too had gone to England. He would be killed in Zululand in 1879, a volunteer in an English army expedition. Mme Trochu was the wife of General Louis Jules Trochu, recently appointed military governor of Paris. (A.J.)

To GEORGE SAND

[Croisset,] Wednesday [September 28, 1870]

I have stopped being sad. Yesterday I took up my *Saint Anthony*—I had to. We must resign ourselves—accustom ourselves to man's natural condition: that is, to evil.

The Greeks in the time of Pericles devoted themselves to Art without knowing where their next day's bread would come from. Let us be Greek! I confess, however, chère maître, that I feel more like a savage. Scholar though I am, the blood of my forefathers, the Natchez or the Hurons,[1] is seething in my veins, and I have a grim, stupid, animal *desire to fight*. Explain that if you can! The idea of signing a peace now infuriates me, and I'd rather see Paris burned, like Moscow, than occupied by the Prussians. But we haven't yet reached that point, and I think the tide is turning.

. . . I have read several letters from soldiers. They are exemplary: a country in which such things are written can't be swallowed up. France is a resourceful jade, and will rise again.

Whatever happens, another world is in the making, and I feel too old to adjust myself to new ways.

My nephew Commanville is making a thousand biscuit-boxes a day for the army, not to mention huts. As you see, we're not asleep in these parts. Paris is overflowing with troops and provisions. In those respects, all is secure.

How I miss you! How I long to see you!

I kiss you all.

Your old troubadour,
G^{ve} Fl.

Here we are resolved to march on Paris should the compatriots of Hegel besiege it. Try to put some guts into your neighbors in Berry.[2] Tell them to help you prevent the enemy from eating and drinking in a country that doesn't belong to them.

The war will (I trust) deal a heavy blow to the "Authorities." Will the individual, rejected and trampled on by the modern world, come into his own again? Let's hope so.

1. Flaubert believed, or pretended to believe, the family legend that an ancestor had married a Canadian Indian.
2. In one of her lost letters from Nohant (in the old province of Berry), Mme Sand had apparently written of lethargy or fatalism among her rural neighbors.

◇◇◇◇◇

Recalling this abrupt resurgence of Flaubert's spirits even as the Germans began to fan out over France, Maxime DuCamp quotes Bossuet: "The greatest disorder of the mind is wishful thinking." For a time, euphoria persisted. "Today I began my night patrols," Flaubert wrote Caroline on September 27, 1870. "I have just made a fatherly speech to my men, informing them that I would run a sword into the belly of the first to falter, and ordering them to shoot me should they see me run away. Your old uncle achieved a truly epic tone. What a weird thing brains are, especially mine! Would you believe it, I now feel almost gay. I began to work again yesterday, and my appetite has returned. Everything wears itself out—anguish included."

It could not last. The first erosion was caused by the decamping of Caroline herself: she took ship at Dieppe for England (see Appendix I). The visitors from Nogent left Croisset, only to be briefly replaced by French troops. The gate-bell began to be rung by refugees from occupied areas and factory-hands thrown out of work. "Are you still alive?" Flaubert wrote to George Sand on October 11. "Where are you, you, Maurice and the others? . . . What wretchedness here! Today I have had 271 poor people at the gate. We gave them all something. What will it be like this winter? The Prussians are now twelve leagues from Rouen, and we have no orders, no one in command, no discipline, nothing, nothing!"

◇◇◇◇◇

GEORGE SAND TO FLAUBERT

[La Châtre, October 14, 1870]

We are alive, at Le Châtre. Nohant is ravaged by smallpox with complications, horrible. We had to take our little ones away . . .

To speak of all the peril and trouble involved in establishing the Republic in the depths of our provinces would be quite useless . . . Don't let's say it's impossible; don't let's think it. Don't let's despair over France. She is expiating her madness, and will be reborn whatever happens. We, perhaps, shall no longer be here. To die of pneumonia or of a bullet is—equally—to die. Let's die without cursing our race!

We love you always and we all embrace you.

. . .

◇◇◇◇◇

On her return to Nohant Mme Sand would learn that one of two balloons that the Republican government had sent out from Paris early in October for Tours, carrying delegates to encourage resistance in the provinces, was named the "George Sand." The other, which had carried Gambetta, was the "Armand Barbès."

The Germans had now encircled Paris, beginning the famous siege; no foodstuffs could enter, and there was an occasional bombardment. To escape that fate, Rouen declared itself an open city. Some sort of postal service continued to function; and alone at Croisset with his mother, Flaubert wrote anguished letters to Caroline in England, to Princesse Mathilde, who was now in Brussels, and to George Sand.

◇◇◇◇◇

TO GEORGE SAND

[Croisset,] Sunday night [November 27, 1870]

I'm still alive, chère maître, but scarcely the better for being so, such is my sorrow. My reason for not writing earlier is that I was awaiting your news. I didn't know where you were.[1]

For six weeks we have been expecting the arrival of the Prussians from one day to the next. We keep listening, thinking we hear the sound of cannon in the distance. They now surround the Seine-Inférieure, at a radius of fourteen to twenty leagues. They are even closer, since they occupy the Vexin, and have completely devastated it. What horrors! It makes one blush to be a man.

If we have a victory on the Loire, their coming will be delayed. But will we have that victory? When I feel hope I try to suppress it. And yet, deep within me, despite everything, I can't help hoping a little, just a little.

I think that in all France there is no sadder man than I. (Everything depends on one's sensitivity.) I am dying of grief. That is the truth. And anything said in consolation irritates me. What breaks my heart is (1) human ferocity; (2) the conviction that we are about to enter an era of stupidity. We'll be utilitarian, militaristic, American, and Catholic. Very Catholic! You'll see! This war with Prussia concludes and destroys the French Revolution.

"But what if we're victorious?" you'll ask. That hypothesis goes against all historical precedent. Where have you ever seen the south defeat the north, Catholics prevail over Protestants? The Latin race is in its death throes. France will follow Spain and Italy; the Age of the Boor is upon us.

What a collapse! What a fall! What wretchedness! What abominations! Is it possible to believe in progress and civilization in the face of all that's happening now? What good is science, since that nation, full of scientists, is committing abominations worthy of the Huns! And worse, because they are systematic, cold-blooded, deliberate, without the excuse of passion or hunger.

Why do they execrate us so? Don't you feel yourself crushed by the hatred of 40 million men? The thought of such an immense, hellish abyss makes my senses reel.

There's no lack of ready-made slogans. "France will rise again!" "Do not despair!" "It's a salutary punishment!" "We were really too immoral!" Etc. Oh, eternal nonsense! No! One does not recover from such a blow.

I feel myself stricken to the core. Were I twenty years younger, I might not think all this; were I twenty years older, I would resign myself to it.

Poor Paris! I find it heroic. But if we see it again it will no longer be

164

our Paris. All the friends I had there are dead or dispersed. I no longer have a center. Literature seems to me a vain and useless thing. Will I ever be capable of writing again?

I find it impossible to occupy myself with anything. I spend my days in gloomy, devouring idleness. My niece Caroline is in London. My mother grows older by the hour. Every Monday we go to Rouen and stay there till Thursday, to escape from the solitude of the country. Then we return here.

Oh! if I could flee to a country where one doesn't see uniforms and hear the sound of drums! Where there's no talk of massacres, where one doesn't have to be a *citizen!* But the earth is no longer habitable for us poor Mandarins!

Adieu, chère maître. Think of me and write to me. I feel that I would be stronger were you nearby. Kiss all your family for me; and to you, affection a hundred thousand times over from your

old troubadour
G^{ve}

◇◇◇◇◇

With Paris isolated and close to starvation, the Germans were in no hurry to extend their conquest. Very slowly, one of their armies approached Rouen.

After the war—DuCamp relates in his memoirs—Flaubert described to him "at least twenty times" his "émotion poignante" on the day in December 1870 when he first saw "the spike of a Prussian helmet glittering in the sun on the tow-path at Croisset." Billeting of the invaders was almost immediate.

◇◇◇◇◇

To His Niece Caroline

Rouen, Sunday, December 18, 1870

My dear Caro,

How you must be worrying about us! Be reassured—we are all alive; we have passed through a time of terrible emotion, and are still plunged in indescribable difficulties. God be thanked that you've been out of it. At times I thought I'd go mad. The night before we left Croisset was horrible. Your grandmother slept at the Hôtel Dieu every night for a week; I spent one night there. At present we are on the quay,[1] with two [Prussian] soldiers quartered on us. At Croisset there are seven, plus three officers and six horses. So far we have had no reason to complain about these gentlemen. But what humiliation, poor Caro! What ruin! What sadness! What wretchedness! Don't expect me to write you an account: it would be too long, and besides I wouldn't be up to it. For a fortnight it has been impossible for us to receive a letter from any-where, or a newspaper, or to communicate with the outside; from the English papers you must know more about it all than we do. We've been unable to send a letter to your husband, and he has been unable to write to us. Let's hope that when the Prussians are completely en-trenched in Normandy they will let us move about. The English consul in Rouen tells me that the Newhaven boat is out of service. As soon as it resumes, as soon as the road from Dieppe to Rouen is clear, come back to us, dear Caro! Your grandmother is growing so old! She longs for you so, needs you so! What months I have spent with her since your departure! My sufferings have been so atrocious that I wish them on no one, not even on those who caused them. When we are not doing er-rands for the Prussians (yesterday I was on my feet three hours getting them hay and straw) we are asking each other for news or sit weeping in a corner. I was not born yesterday, and during my life I have suffered many blows; but all was as nothing, compared with what I am enduring now. Nothing, nothing! How can we stand it? I marvel that it is possible.

And we don't know when it will end. Poor Paris is still holding out! But eventually it will give in. And meanwhile France will be completely sacked, ruined. And what will happen then? What a future lies ahead! There will be no lack of sophists to prove that we'll be the better for it, and that "misfortune purifies." No! Misfortune makes us selfish and vicious and stupid. This disaster was inevitable; it is in accordance with the laws of history. But what a mockery are the words "humanity," "progress," "civilization." Oh, poor dear child, if you could know what it means to hear them drag their swords on the sidewalk, to have their horses whinny in your face! What a disgrace! What a disgrace!

My poor head aches so that I have to make a great effort to write. How will this letter reach you? I have no idea. I was given hope this eve-ning that I could send it to you by a roundabout way. Your uncle Achille Flaubert has had and is still having great difficulty in the munic-ipal council—it held a session while workingmen were firing rifles out-side the windows. I am constantly on the verge of vomiting; your grandmother never leaves the house, and when she walks in her room she has to support herself against the furniture and the wall. When you can safely return, do so. I think it your *duty* to be near her. Your poor husband was very sad because of your long absence, and he must feel worse after the past fortnight. The Prussians are said to have been in Dieppe twice, but not to have stayed. The first time, they were in search of tobacco: people who have it hide it, and it grows steadily scarcer. But we have no definite news at all, for we are cut off as in a besieged city. This uncertainty comes on top of all our other anguish. When I think of the past it seems to me a dream. The Boulevard du Temple—what a paradise! Do you realize that at Croisset they occupy *all* the rooms?

166

There would be no place for us if we wanted to return. It is eleven at night, the wind is blowing, the rain is lashing the windows. I am writing you in your old bedroom, and can hear the snores of the two soldiers sleeping in your dressing-room. I toss and plunge in my sorrow like a boat foundering at sea. I never thought my heart could hold so much suffering and remain alive.

I embrace you with all my strength. When shall I see you?

Your old uncle, who can stand no more.

1. In Mme Flaubert's usual winter apartment in Rouen, on the Quai du Havre.

To His Niece Caroline

[Rouen,] Monday night, [January] 16 [1871]

. . . Your husband suggested taking us to Dieppe, but (1) your grand-mother would have no company (here she has visitors every day); (2) she would worry about your Uncle Achille; (3) the trip would be very uncomfortable. Besides, I don't want to be too far from my manservant, who is alone at Croisset, coping as best he can in the midst of the Prus-sians. How will I find my study, my books, my manuscripts? All I was able to put in a safe place were my papers relating to *Saint Anthony*. Émile [the servant] has the key to the study, but they keep asking for it, and go in and take books, which they leave lying around their bed-rooms . . .

[Rouen,] Monday, [January] 23 [1871]

. . . We are now expecting Mecklenburg's troops, which are to re-place Manteuffel's. The men now occupying Croisset will be replaced by others, who may be worse: these have done no damage and have re-spected my study. But Croisset has lost all its attraction for me, and I wouldn't set foot there now. If you knew what it's like to see Prussian helmets on your bed! What fury! What misery! This frightful war shows no sign of ending! . . .

Rouen, Saturday, [January] 28 [1871]

. . . I went to Croisset this morning—an ordeal . . . Poor Émile is at the end of his tether. In forty-five days they have burned 420 francs worth of wood . . . The cold has intensified again . . . I hear sabers rattling on the sidewalks . . .

◇◇◇◇◇

Amid details about the invaders (for a brief time forty Prussians were crowded into the house at Croisset), about the feeble health of his seventy-seven-year-old mother, and about his own desperation, and along with appeals to Caroline to return,[1] Flaubert repeatedly expressed pity for the besieged Parisians. And well he might have. A few words from Maxime DuCamp's account of their plight (his report is one of many describing that terrible time) must suffice here: "Paris is without meat: Parisians are eating rats, cats, dogs ... They are cutting down trees, breaking up the wooden benches along the sidewalks, burning their furniture ... In January [1871] 19,233 hearses took the road to the cemeteries." (Four times the normal death rate.) The starving city capitulated on January 28. Ten days before, in the palace at Versailles, the King of Prussia had been proclaimed Emperor of Germany.

1. Flaubert wrote also to Commanville: "Make Caro come back! . . . Her grandmother absolutely needs her. She is dying of grief and aging hour by hour." And: "What a wretched idea, her fleeing to England! . . . I repeat: her prolonged absence is killing her grandmother. That's all. Simply that."

❖❖❖❖❖

To His Niece Caroline

[Rouen,] February 1 [1871]

Dear Caro,

Your husband wrote me yesterday that he would urge you to come back as soon as the boat from Newhaven resumes service. Does this mean that the blockade has been lifted? I think not. He adds that he expects to see you within a week. I'm afraid the week will go by without your return. That will be a great disappointment to your grandmother, who is at the end of her strength and her patience. There is always the road from Saint-Valéry, but is it safe?[1]

The capitulation of Paris, even though expected, has plunged me into an indescribable state. One could hang oneself out of fury. I regret that Paris wasn't burned to the last house, leaving only a great black void. France has fallen so low, is so dishonored, so debased, that I wish she might disappear completely. But I hope that civil war will kill a lot of people for us. Would that I might be included in the number! In preparation for that event, there is to be an election of deputies. What bitter irony! Needless to say, I shall abstain from voting. I no longer wear my Legion of Honor ribbon, for the word "honor" is French no longer; and so strongly do I feel myself no longer French that I intend to ask Turgenev (as soon as I'm able to write him) what one has to do to become a Russian.

Your uncle Achille Flaubert threatened to jump off one of the bridges, and Raoul Duval[2] seemed for a time to have gone raving mad. No matter how much you have read in the newspapers, or how vividly you have pictured to yourself what the invasion might be like, *you have no idea of it,* I assure you. Every soul with the slightest claim to pride has been mortally stricken, and like Rachel "refuses to be comforted."

Since last Sunday morning, we no longer have any Prussians at Croisset (though many are returning to Rouen). As soon as things have been cleaned up a little, I'll go and take another look at the old house—which I no longer love, and dread to enter, for I can't throw everything those gentlemen handled into the river. If the house belonged to me, I would certainly have it demolished.

Oh! Such hatred! Such hatred! It stifles me. I, who was born oversensitive —I'm choking on gall . . .

1. That is, since the main road from Dieppe (where Caroline would be arriving from England) to Rouen might well be blocked by the Prussians, she should inquire about conditions on the other, secondary road. Caroline returned from England early in February.

2. Lawyer and politician, later deputy from the Seine-Inférieure. He would play an important role in Flaubert's later life.

◇◇◇◇◇

The Germans outside Paris waited a month, giving the National Assembly time to declare the end of the Empire and the Bonapartist succession, and to accept the peace terms proposed. On March 1 they celebrated their victory by entering the city and parading down the Champs-Elysées. On the fourth, from Dieppe, Flaubert wrote to Princesse Mathilde: "Well, we have swallowed our shame. But not digested it. How I thought of you on Wednesday, and how I suffered! All day I *saw* the bayonets of the Prussians flashing in the sun on the Champs-Elysées, and heard their bands, their hateful bands, playing under the Arc de Triomphe! The man who sleeps in the Invalides must have turned in his tomb with rage."

After occupying Paris for forty-eight hours, the Germans withdrew: they knew what they were doing—that they could leave the city to its own divided inhabitants. On March 18, 1871, the "Commune de Paris" was declared, a revolutionary, collectivist state within the regular state, setting off the civil war that Flaubert had hoped would "kill a lot of people." His wish was granted. For six weeks, under the eyes of the Germans encamped on surrounding heights, the city was again besieged this time by the "Versaillais," the troops of the regular, national government, which was sitting at Versailles. Executions by the Communards, their burning of public buildings, indeed their very existence *as* Communards, made them the target of savage reprisals by the victorious Versaillais when they entered the city in the last week of May. During that week, *la Semaine Sanglante* (Bloody Week), thousands of Parisians (some historians say as many as 20,000) were killed by

French soldiers. The story of the Commune and its aftermath remains one of the most dramatic and tragic chapters in the history of France, along with that of the macabre years of the later German occupation, Vichy government, and deportations of 1940–1945.

Shortly before the proclamation of the Commune in Paris, the city of Rouen staged a demonstration of a different kind. Prince Frederik Karl of Prussia was to arrive there on Sunday, March 12, to review the occupying troops; on Friday the tenth the Rouennais hung black flags from their houses, shops, and public buildings; and shop windows displayed signs saying "Closed because of national mourning." It was on the eleventh that Flaubert, perhaps inspired by unaccustomed pride in his native city, wrote in a letter to George Sand his most celebrated lines about the Prussians—many of whom, billeted on Rouen families, had behaved brutally, in contrast to Flaubert's restrained, though loathed, "guests" at Croisset.

◇–◇–◇–◇

To George Sand

Dieppe, March 11 [1871]

Chère maître,

When shall we see each other again? Paris doesn't sound very gay. Ah! What kind of a world are we going to inhabit? Paganism, Christianism, Boorism: such are the three great evolutions of mankind. It's sad to find oneself at the beginning of the third.

I'll not tell you everything I have suffered since September. How have I stayed alive? That's what surprises me! No one has been more *desperate* than I. Why? I have had bad times in my life, I have suffered great losses, I have often wept, endured much anguish. Well, all those griefs put together are nothing—nothing at all—compared with these. And I don't get used to it. I find no consolation. I have no hope.

I didn't consider myself a believer in progress or a humanitarian. No matter! I did have illusions! What barbarism! What retrogression! I resent my contemporaries for having inspired me with the feelings of a brute of the twelfth century. I am choking on gall. These officers who smash your mirrors with white-gloved hands, who know Sanskrit and fling themselves on your champagne, who steal your watch and then send you their visiting-card, this war for money,[1] these savages for all their civilization—they horrify me more than Cannibals.[2] And everybody is going to emulate them, turn military. Russia now has four million troops. All Europe will be in uniform. If we take our revenge, it will be ultra-savage. And you can be sure that we'll be thinking of nothing but that, of avenging ourselves on Germany. The government, whatever it may be, will be able to maintain itself only by harping on that

170

passion. Murder on a grand scale is going to be the goal of all our efforts, France's ideal!

I cherish the dream of going to live in the sun, in some tranquil land.

We must expect new hypocrisies: declamations about virtue, diatribes about corruption, austerity in dress, etc. Officiousness to the last degree.

At this moment I have *forty* Prussians at Croisset. As soon as my poor house (which I now hold in horror) is emptied and cleaned, I'll return to it; then I'll probably go to Paris, despite the unhealthiness of the place. But as to that I don't give a damn . . .

1. The Germans levied taxes on each occupied city, increasing them at the least sign of resistance. In addition, heavy "reparations" were part of the peace terms. In 1914, at the outbreak of the First World War, France was still paying "reparations" to Germany for the war of 1870–1871.

2. As future letters will show, Flaubert retained a hatred of Germany for the rest of his life.

◇◇◇◇◇

Of the Paris Commune, Flaubert had no direct experience, but much to say.

On March 17, 1871, the day before the Commune was proclaimed, leaving his mother with Caroline at Neuville, he traveled from Paris by train with Alexandre Dumas the younger to spend four days on a visit of friendship and sympathy to Princesse Mathilde in Brussels. Before returning to France he visited London, writing Caroline that he had promised Juliet Herbert to do so. Back in Neuville he found a letter from George Sand, written from Nohant the day of his departure. She expressed fears of violence and vengeance among Frenchmen, and added: "I don't know whether you agree with me, that full and complete liberty [*la liberté pleine et entière*] would save us from such disasters and put us back on the road of possible progress. Abuses of liberty don't frighten me in themselves; but those whom they do frighten always incline toward abuses of power." Those words, and the disorders that had erupted in Paris, gave Flaubert an opening he did not fail to take.

To GEORGE SAND

Neuville, near Dieppe, Friday, March 31 [1871]
In reply to yours of March 17.

Chère maître,

Tomorrow, at last, I resign myself to returning to Croisset. It will be hard, but I must do it. I'll try to take up my poor *Saint Anthony* again, and forget France.

My mother will stay here with her granddaughter until it's possible to know where to go without fear of the Prussians or of rioting.

Some days ago I left here with Dumas for Brussels, thinking to return directly to Paris. But "the new Athens" seems to me to surpass Dahomey in ferocity and imbecility.

Have we reached the end of the swindle? Are we done with the hollow metaphysics and the clichés? All the evil stems from our colossal ignorance. What ought to be pondered, is simply believed, without discussion. Instead of considering, people *tell* you.

The French Revolution must cease to be a dogma, and become an object of scientific inquiry, like everything else that's human. If people had known more, they wouldn't have believed that a mystical formula is capable of creating armies, or that the word "Republic" suffices to defeat a million well-disciplined men. They would have left Badinguet on the throne *expressly* to make peace, ready to send him to the galleys afterward. If they had known more, they would have understood what the volunteers of '92 were, and the retreat of [the duke of] Brunswick, bribed by Danton and Westermann.[1] But no! always the same old story! Always nonsense! Now we have the Paris Commune, reviving sheer medievalism. They're frank enough about it! The business about controlling rents is particularly splendid. Now the government interferes in Natural Right, intervening in contracts between individuals. The Commune asserts that we do not owe what we owe, and that one service is not to be paid for by another. It's an enormity of ineptitude and injustice.

Many conservatives who wanted to preserve the Republic out of love of order are going to miss Badinguet and in their hearts call back the Prussians. The people in the Hôtel de Ville[2] have *deflected our hatred.* That's why I resent them. It seems to me that we have never been lower.

We're being tossed back and forth between the Society of Saint Vincent de Paul and the International. But the latter is committing too many idiocies to last long. If it should defeat the Versaillais and overthrow the government, the Prussians will enter Paris and "order will prevail"—as it did in Warsaw. If, on the contrary, it is beaten, the reaction will be fierce and all liberty strangled.

What can one say of socialists who imitate the methods of Badinguet and Wilhelm: requisitions, suppressions of newspapers, executions without trial, etc.? Ah! What a vile beast the crowd is! And how humiliating to be a man!

Je vous embrasse bien fort.

Your old troubadour

G[ve]

1. In 1792 the army of the First French Republic repulsed the German invaders in the Battle of Valmy, arousing great popular enthusiasm in France. Considerable surprise was

expressed, however, that the German commander, the Duke of Brunswick, should immediately withdraw his troops instead of continuing the campaign, and there were rumors that he had accepted French bribes.

Flaubert is saying that, just as in 1792—when victory was won not, as patriotic tradition would have it, by the "spirit of the Republic," but by bribery of the enemy—so in 1870 the mystical idea of "proclaiming the Republic" would not win the war. (J.B.)

2. The government of the Commune, whose headquarters were in the Hôtel de Ville (the Paris City Hall).

To His Niece Caroline

Croisset, Wednesday, 2 o'clock [April 4, 1871]

My dear Caro,

Contrary to my expectations, I find myself *very well off* at Croisset, and I think no more about the Prussians than if they had never come here! It was a very sweet feeling, to be back in my study and see all my little belongings once again. My mattresses have been attended to, and I sleep like a log. On Saturday night I began to work again, and if nothing interrupts me I'll have finished my Heresies by the end of this month. So, my poor darling, the only thing I lack is the presence of those I love; a small group, with you in the front row, my lovely lady.

When we were reunited at the beginning of February, I had lost my bearings completely; but thanks to you, your sweet company and your nice house, I gradually recovered, and now I'm looking forward to the day when you'll come here (for a month, I hope). The garden is going to be very beautiful, the buds are opening, primroses everywhere. Such peace and quiet! I'm quite dazed by it.

On Sunday I spent the day in a delicious stupor. I relived the days when my poor Bouilhet would arrive on Sunday morning with his notebook of poems, when père Parain would wander about the house with his newspaper sticking out of his back pocket, and you, poor baby, would be running on the lawn in your white apron. I'm becoming too much of a sheik,[1] burying myself in the past! Let's speak of the present.

Your husband must be relieved: "our brothers"[2] have just been given a good drubbing. I'd be very surprised if the Commune were to last beyond next week. I was moved by the murder of Pasquier.[3] I knew him very well: he was an intimate friend of Florimont, a chum of your uncle Achille, a pupil of père Cloquet, and Mme Lepic's first cousin.

·　·　·

1. See page 66, note 1.
2. The Communards.
3. A military surgeon shot by the Communards.

Nohant, April 28 [1871]

I haven't managed to be alone a single moment since this ugly adventure began without falling into bitter despair. I make great efforts to resist, I don't want to be discouraged, I don't want to forswear the past and dread the future! But my will and my reason struggle against a profound depression that is so far insurmountable. That is why I didn't want to write you before feeling better; not because I'm ashamed of having these fits of despondency, but because I wouldn't want to increase your already deep sadness by adding the weight of mine.

For me, the ignoble experiment that Paris is attempting or undergoing does nothing to disprove the laws of the eternal progression of men and of things; and if my mind has acquired certain principles, good or bad, they are neither shaken nor changed by it. I have long accepted patience as one accepts the weather, the length of the winter, old age, lack of success in all its forms. But I think that the members of the various parties (those who are sincere) must change their formulas—or perhaps perceive the emptiness of every a priori formula.

That is not what saddens me. When a tree dies you must plant two others. My grief comes from pure weakness of heart, which I don't know how to overcome. I cannot close my eyes to the suffering and even the ignominy of others. I pity those who do the evil; even though I recognize their unworthiness, their moral condition distresses me. We pity a fledgling that falls from the nest: how not pity a vast number of human consciences fallen into the mire? One suffered less during the siege by the Prussians. One loved Paris when it was unhappy through no fault of its own. One pities it all the more today when one can love it no longer. Those who have no love for anything are indulging themselves by hating it mortally. What reply should we make? None, perhaps. Scorn—to be scorned by France—is perhaps the required punishment for the arrant cowardice with which the Parisians submitted to riot and to the desperados who led it. It's a sequel to the acceptance of the desperados of the Empire. Different felons, same cowardice.

But I didn't want to talk to you about this: you roar enough about it as it is! . . .

You haven't told me in what state you found your charming nest at Croisset. The Prussians occupied it: did they soil it, loot it, ruin it? Your books and bibelots—did you find them all? They respected your name, your study? If you *can* resume work there, your mind will be at peace. I must wait for mine to recover, and I know I must assist in my own cure by a certain faith: this is often shaken, but I'm making a duty of it.

Tell me whether the tulip tree escaped freezing last winter, and if the peonies are lovely now. I often travel in my mind: I see your garden and its surroundings. How far away all that is; how much has happened! One is tempted to think oneself a hundred years old . . .

We embrace you and we love you.

◇◇◇◇◇

Flaubert wrote Princesse Mathilde on May 3: "Mme Sand has written me a desperate letter. She sees that her old idol was hollow, and her republican faith seems to me completely extinguished! That's a disaster that won't befall me."

◇◇◇◇◇

TO GEORGE SAND

Croisset, April 30 [1871]

Chère maître,

Let me answer at once your questions insofar as they concern me personally. No, the Prussians did not loot my house. They made off with a few trifles—a dressing case, a box, some pipes; but on the whole they did no damage. My study they respected. I had buried a large box full of letters, and hidden my voluminous notes for *Saint Anthony.* All that, I found intact.

The worst effect of the invasion *for me* is that it has aged my poor mother by ten years. What a change! She can no longer walk alone, and her frailty is heartrending. How sad it is to watch the slow deterioration of those you love! . . .

To stop thinking about public miseries and my own, I have plunged furiously back into *Saint Anthony,* and if I can continue at this pace without interruption it will be finished next winter. I long to read you the sixty pages that are done. When railway journeys become possible again, come and see me. Your old troubadour has been waiting a long time for you. Your letter that came this morning touched me. What a fine fellow you are, and what a great heart you have!

I am unlike the many people I hear lamenting the [civil] war in Paris. I find it more tolerable than the invasion, because after the invasion any further despair is impossible—another proof of the depths to which we have sunk. "Ah, thank God the Prussians are there!" is the universal cry of the bourgeois. I put Messieurs the workers into the same bag, and I'd like to throw the whole lot of them into the river. That's where they're headed anyway—and then things will quiet down. We'll become a big, dreary, industrial country—a kind of Belgium. The disappearance of Paris (as the seat of the government)[1] will make France dull and stagnant. She will have no heart, no center—and, I think, no mind?

As for the Commune, which is in its death throes, it is the latest manifestation of the Middle Ages. Will it be the last? Let's hope so!

I hate democracy (at least as it is understood in France), because it is based on "the morality of the Gospels," which is immorality itself, whatever anyone may say: that is, the exaltation of Mercy at the expense of Justice, the negation of Right—the very opposite of social order.

The Commune is rehabilitating assassins,[2] just as Jesus forgave thieves; and they are looting the homes of the rich because they have learned to curse Lazarus—who was not a *bad* rich man, but simply a rich man.[3] The slogan "The republic is above all argument" is on a par with the dogma that "The pope is infallible." Always formulas! Always gods!

The God-before-last—universal suffrage—has just played a terrible joke on his faithful by electing "the assassins of Versailles."[4] What are we to believe in, then? Nothing! Such is the beginning of Wisdom. It is time to rid ourselves of "Principles" and to espouse Science, objective inquiry. The only rational thing (I keep coming back to it) is a government of Mandarins, provided the Mandarins know something—in fact, a great many things. The *people* never come of age, and they will always be at the bottom rung of the social scale because they represent number, mass, the limitless. It is of little importance that many peasants should be able to read and no longer listen to their priests; but it is infinitely important that many men like Renan or Littré be able to live *and be listened to.* Our only salvation now lies in a *legitimate aristocracy*, by which I mean a majority composed of something more than mere numbers.

·　　·　　·

1. On March 10, 1871, the National Assembly had transferred itself from Paris to Versailles, where it would remain (rebaptized the Chamber of Deputies in 1875) until 1879.

2. Doubtless an allusion to the assassination, more or less approved by the Commune, of generals Lecomte and Thomas. (A.J.)

3. Flaubert misremembered his Luke (16:19–31). Lazarus was the poor man. (A.J.)

4. After the first encounters, on April 2, the Versaillais had shot several prisoners; thenceforth the Commune called the members of the Assembly and the Versailles government "assassins." (A.J.)

◇◇◇◇◇

The week that followed the writing of that letter was the Semaine Sanglante. Very shortly thereafter, as soon as entry into the city was possible, Flaubert was given permission to consult books in the Bibliothèque Impériale, still officially closed because of the disorders. (He had known it as the Bibliothèque Royale before 1848, and now it would soon reopen as the Bibliothèque Nationale, as it is called today.) The odor of decaying corpses still hung over the city. Many public buildings

were burnt-out shells and would have to be demolished, most prominent among them the Palais des Tuileries, where he had attended Imperial balls, and the Hôtel de Ville (later reconstructed). "You'll see some
mighty ruins," he wrote Caroline. "It's sinister and weird. I haven't seen
nearly everything, nor shall I. One should really walk about the city
taking notes for a fortnight."

◇◇◇◇◇

To George Sand

Croisset, Sunday night [June 11, 1871]

Chère maître,

Never did I have a greater desire or greater need to see you than now.
I have just come from Paris, and I don't know whom to talk to. I'm
choking—crushed, or, rather, disheartened. The odor of the corpses
disgusted me less than the miasmas of egotism exhaled from every
mouth. The sight of the ruins is as nothing compared with the immense
Parisian stupidity. With very rare exceptions it seemed to me that
everybody ought to be tied up. Half the population wants to strangle the
other half, and vice versa. This can be seen plainly in the eyes of the
people in the streets. And the Prussians no longer exist! People excuse
them, *admire* them!!! "Reasonable" people want to be naturalized German. I assure you, it's enough to make one despair of the human race.

I was in Versailles on Thursday. The excesses of the Right are fright-
ening. The vote on the Orleans[1] is a concession made to it, to appease it
and gain time to prepare against it.

Did you know that Troubat[2] had written articles urging the murder
of the hostages? Even so he was not arrested. And he confessed to me
that he had been "imprudent": charming word.

From the general madness I except Renan, who on the contrary
seemed to me very philosophical. Our nice Soulié charged me with a
thousand affectionate messages for you. Princesse Mathilde several
times asked for news of you. She is losing her wits. She wants to return
to Saint-Gratien "despite everything."[3] I've collected a mass of horrible
unpublished details, all of which I spare you.

My short stay in Paris has upset me extremely, and I'm going to have
a hard time getting back to work.

What do you think of my friend Maury, who kept the tricolor flying
over the Archives throughout the Commune? I think few men capable
of such pluck.[4]

. . .

Have you read the outline of a novel by Isidore that was among the
documents found in the Tuileries last September? What a scenario![5]

. . .

I wrote you a very long letter about a month ago.

1. The abrogation of the 1848 law exiling members of the French royal houses.

2. Jules Troubat, formerly Sainte-Beuve's secretary, had been secretary to Félix Pyat, publisher of pro-Commune newspapers, but no article by him of the kind mentioned by Flaubert has been found. (A.J.)

3. Part of her property there was occupied by German troops; besides, the local population might be hostile to her as a Bonaparte. She had returned to France a few days earlier. She soon succeeded in obtaining government permission to reopen her château, and was given German protection there until the end of the occupation. Flaubert found this undignified. "She returned because she's a spoiled child, unable to school her passions," he wrote to George Sand. "That's the entire psychology of the thing. And I made a considerable concession (of which she was quite unaware) in going to see her at Saint-Gratien in the midst of Prussians! There were two sentries at the door. Though I haven't the blood of an emperor in my veins, I blushed to the roots of my hair as I passed them in their boxes. I quite did without my house as long as the Prussians were in it. I think she might have done the same."

4. Other public buildings in Paris flew the red flag of the Commune. In a letter to Mme Roger des Genettes, Flaubert added, in a tribute to Maury: "Which didn't keep him from continuing to write his little articles on the Etruscans. So there are still a few philosophers. I'm not one of them."

5. The present whereabouts of this outline are not known. It was entitled *L'Odyssée de M. Benoît*, and is said to have been "probably political, intended to demonstrate the benefits of the imperial regime." (A.J. and J.B.)

GEORGE SAND TO FLAUBERT

[Nohant, June 14, 1871]

You want and need to see me, and you don't come! That's not nice; for I too, and all of us here, long for you. We parted so gaily eighteen months ago, and so many terrible things have happened in the meantime! To see each other would be the consolation that is our *due*. For my part, I can't stir; I haven't a sou, and have to work like a black. And then, I haven't seen a single Prussian, and want to keep my eyes unsoiled. Ah, my friend, what years we are going through! We cannot revert to what we used to be, for the hope we had then has disappeared, along with the rest.

What sort of reaction may we expect to follow this infamous Commune? Isidore, or Henri V,[1] or the kingdom of the *pétroleuses*[2] restored by anarchy? I, who have had such patience with my species, and have looked so long on the bright side, now see nothing but darkness. I judged others by myself. I had achieved relative mastery over my inborn character, having rid myself of useless and dangerous enthusiasms; I had sown grass and flowers on my volcanos and they were flourishing; and I imagined that all the world could become enlightened, could correct itself, or restrain itself; that the years I had passed with my fellows could not be lost to reason and experience: and now I wake from a dream to find a generation divided between idiocy and delirium tremens! Anything is possible at present.

178

However, it is wrong to despair. I'll make a great effort, and perhaps I'll become equable and patient once more. But at present it's beyond me. I'm as disturbed as you are, and I don't dare talk, think, or write, I'm so afraid of reopening the gaping wounds in every soul.

I did indeed receive your other letter, and I was summoning the courage to answer it; I'd like to do only good to those I love, especially to you, who feel so keenly. At the present moment I'm up to nothing. Indignation devours me; disgust is killing me.

All I know is that I love you. My children say the same. Embrace your dear mother for me.

G. Sand

1. Henri, comte de Chambord, the Bourbon pretender, who was about to return to France from exile and assert his claim to the throne.

2. "The name given to women who, during the Commune, are said to have poured kerosene on certain buildings to quicken the fires" (*Grand Larousse Encyclopédique*). Their existence is questioned by many historians, but in the hysteria of the reprisals a number of women were executed on the charge.

❖-❖-❖-❖

George Sand has been criticized for basing some of her opinions concerning the Commune, at this time, on false news printed in the Versaillais (anti-Commune) press. Flaubert, wishing to believe that she was abandoning her old attitudes, wrote about her to Princesse Mathilde on September 6: "Have you read an article by Mme Sand (published [yesterday] in *Le Temps*) on the workers? She is very gradually coming to see the most difficult thing of all: the truth. For the first time in her life she calls the rabble by its name."

❖-❖-❖-❖

GEORGE SAND TO FLAUBERT

Nohant, September 6 [1871]

Where are you, my dear old troubadour? I don't write you: I'm perturbed to the depths of my soul. This will pass, I hope, but I am infected with the sickness of my people and my generation. I cannot isolate myself, cannot take refuge in my rationality and my innocence. I feel that great ties have been loosened, almost broken. It seems to me that we're setting out for some unknown destination. Do you have more courage than I? Give me a little of it.

I send you the pretty faces of our little girls. They remember you, and tell me I must send you their portraits . . .

To George Sand

Ah! how sweet they are! What darlings! What good little faces, so serious and charming! My mother was greatly touched, and so was I. That is what I call a delicate attention, chère maître, and I thank you greatly for it. I envy Maurice! His existence is not arid, like mine.

Our two letters crossed again. That doubtless proves, does it not? that we are affected by the same things, at the same time, and in the same degree.

Why are you so sad? Mankind is displaying nothing new. Its irremediable wretchedness has embittered me ever since my youth. So I am not disillusioned now. I believe that the crowd, the mass, the herd, will always be detestable. Nothing is important save a small group of minds, ever the same, which pass on the torch. As long as no deference is paid to the Mandarins, as long as the Academy of Sciences doesn't take the place of the Pope, all Politics, and Society down to its very roots, will be nothing but an assortment of distressing humbugs. We are floundering in the afterbirth of the Revolution, which was a miscarriage, a failure, a gross blunder, no matter what may be said about it. And the reason is that it had its origin in the spirit of the Middle Ages and Christianity, an antisocial religion. The idea of equality (which is all that modern democracy is) is an essentially Christian idea and opposed to that of justice. Observe how *Mercy* predominates now. Sentiment is everything, the law nothing. There is no longer even any public indignation against murderers. And the people who set fire to Paris are punished less than the slanderer of M. Favre.[1]

If France is to rise again, she must pass from Inspiration to Science, she must abandon all metaphysics in favor of objective inquiry—that is, the examination of reality.

Posterity will consider us very stupid, I'm sure. The words "Republic" and "Monarchy" will make them laugh, just as we laugh at "Realism" and "Nominalism." For I defy anyone to show me one essential difference between those two terms. A modern republic and a constitutional monarchy are identical. No matter: there's great squabbling over it anyway—shouting, fighting!

As for the good "People," "free and compulsory" education will be the end of them. When everybody is able to read the *Petit Journal* and the *Figaro*, they won't read anything else, since those are the only things read by the bourgeois, the rich gentleman. The press is a school that serves to turn men into brutes, because it relieves them from thinking. Say that! It will be courageous of you, and if you prevail you'll have performed a noble service.

The first remedy would be to abolish universal suffrage, that insult to human intelligence. As it is constituted, one single element prevails, to the detriment of all the rest: *Number* dominates over mind, education, race, and even over money, which is preferable to Number.

But perhaps a Catholic society (which always needs a beneficent God, a Savior) isn't capable of self-preservation. The conservative party hasn't even the instinct of the Brute (for the brute at least knows how to fight for its lair and its food). It will be absorbed by the Internationals, those Jesuits of the future. But the Jesuits of the past, who had neither Country nor Justice, did not succeed. And the International, too, will founder, because like theirs, its principles are false: no ideas, nothing but greed!

Ah! chère bon maître, if you could only hate! That is what you lack: Hate. Despite your great sphinx eyes, you have seen the world through a golden haze. That comes from the sun in your heart. But so many shadows have loomed that you no longer discern things. Come, now! Cry out! Thunder! Take your great lyre and touch the brazen string. The Monsters will flee. Sprinkle us with the blood of the wounded Themis.[2]

Why do you feel that "great ties have been broken"? What is broken? *Your* ties are indissoluble, for your affinity can only be for Eternal things.

Our ignorance of history makes us slander our own times. Mankind has always been like this. A few years of quiet fooled us. That's all. I too used to believe in the progressive "civilizing" of the human race. We must expunge that mistake and think no better of ourselves than people did in the age of Pericles or Shakespeare, dreadful periods in which great things were accomplished.

Tell me you're in better spirits. And think sometimes of your old troubadour, who loves you.

1. Jules Favre, Minister of Foreign Affairs, had recently been the successful plaintiff in a libel suit. Even though Favre admitted to being guilty of peculation, his accuser was sentenced to a year in prison and a fine of a thousand francs. (A.J.)
2. In Greek mythology, the deity representing divine justice.

◇◇◇◇◇

Mme Sand's response to Flaubert's summons to "cry out" was immediate, but hardly what he desired.

That her distress over the turn of events was exacerbated by his recent letters—harsh and deliberately insensitive toward her and what he well knew her feelings to be—has been apparent not only in her replies themselves but in their unwonted infrequency. Now she found his call for "hatred" intolerable. She started to write him, and her letter took another form, to become one of the most impassioned of all her writings. Her "Reply to a Friend," which appeared in *Le Temps* on October 3, 1871, is translated as Appendix II in the present volume.

She wrote to Flaubert, advising him of her action.

◇-◇-◇-◇-◇

GEORGE SAND TO FLAUBERT

Nohant, September 16, 1871

Cher vieux,

I was answering you the day before yesterday, and my letter took on such dimensions that I have sent it as an article to *Le Temps*—I promised to give them two a month.[1] This letter "to a friend" makes no mention of you even by an initial: I don't want to argue with you in public. In it I give you my reasons for suffering and for continuing to look ahead. I'll send it to you, and it will be like talking with you again. You'll see that my grief is part of me and that I have no right to believe that progress is a dream. Without that hope no one amounts to anything.

.　.　.

Come, let me suffer! That is better than "to look on injustice with a serene countenance," as Shakespeare says.[2] When I have drained my cup of bitterness I shall feel better. I am a woman, I feel affection, pity, and anger. I shall never be a sage or a scholar.

.　.　.

I'm glad you enjoyed the faces of the children. You are so good: I knew you would love them. I embrace you tenderly. Mandarin though you may be, I don't find you Chinese at all, and I love you with all my heart.

1. This was her second in the series. The first had been the "article on the workers" mentioned by Flaubert to Princesse Mathilde, which had in part inspired his letter of September 8.

2. Mme Sand's words, *voir l'injustice avec un visage serein*, paraphrase a French translation (by Guizot and A. Pichot, 1821) of a passage from *Julius Caesar*, II, i: "such suffering souls that welcome wrongs." The translation reads: *ces âmes patientes de qui l'injustice reçoit un accueil serein.* (A.J.)

TO GEORGE SAND

[Croisset,] Saturday [October 7, 1871]

Chère maître,

I received your article yesterday, and would answer it at length were I not preparing to leave for Paris. I'm going to try to finish up with *Aïssé.*[1]

The middle section of your piece made me "shed a tear"—without convincing me, of course. I was moved, that was all, but not persuaded.

I comb your article for a certain word and find it nowhere: "Justice."[2]

All our affliction comes from forgetting utterly that first premise of morality, which to my mind embraces *all* morality. Mercy, humanitarianism, sentiment, the ideal, have played us sufficiently false to make us try Righteousness and Science.

If France does not soon enter a period of self-appraisal, I think she will be irrevocably lost. Free compulsory education will do nothing but swell the number of imbeciles. Renan has said that superbly, in the preface to his *Questions contemporaines.* What we need most of all is a *natural,* that is to say, a legitimate, aristocracy. Nothing can be done without a brain; and universal suffrage as it now exists is more foolish than divine right. You will see some extraordinary things if it is retained! Masses, numbers, are invariably idiotic. I have few convictions, but I have that one, and strongly. Nevertheless the masses must be respected, however inept they may be, because they contain seeds of incalculable fertility. Give them liberty, but not power.

I believe no more than you do in class distinctions. Castes belong to archaeology. But I believe that the Poor hate the Rich, and that the Rich are afraid of the Poor. It will be ever thus. It is as futile to preach love to the one as to the other. The most urgent thing is to educate the Rich, who after all are the stronger. Enlighten the bourgeois first! For he knows nothing, absolutely nothing. The entire dream of democracy is to raise the proletariat to the level of bourgeois stupidity. That dream is partly realized! They read the same newspapers and share the same passions.

The three levels of education have shown within the past year what they can accomplish: (1) higher education caused Prussia to win; (2) secondary education, bourgeois, produced the men of the fourth of September;[3] (3) primary education gave us the Commune. Its Minister of Public Education was the great Vallès,[4] who boasted that he despised Homer.

Suppose that three years from now *all* Frenchmen know how to read. Do you think we'll be the better for it? Imagine, on the other hand, that in each community there was *one* bourgeois, one only, who had read Bastiat,[5] and that that bourgeois was respected: things would change!

I learn today that the mass of Parisians is sorry to have lost Badinguet. A plebiscite would declare for him, I'm sure. So fine a thing is universal suffrage!

However, unlike you I am not discouraged, and I like the present government, because it has no principle, no metaphysics, no humbug.

I'm expressing myself very badly. You deserve a different answer, but I'm very hurried—which doesn't prevent me from kissing you heartily.

Your old troubadour,
G^{ve} Flaubert

Not such a troubadour as all that, however! For the silhouette of the "friend," as glimpsed by the reader of your article, is that of a not very amiable blockhead and selfish beast.

1. Flaubert was trying to secure a production of Bouilhet's play.
2. It is there—the word itself as well as the implication.
3. Date of the proclamation of the Third Republic, in 1870.
4. Jules Vallès (1832–1885), who took refuge in England after the end of the Commune. Later, following the amnesty, he would revive his radical Paris newspaper, *Le Cri du peuple.*
5. Frédéric Bastiat (1801–1850), liberal economist and politician, a strong opponent of socialism in 1848.

GEORGE SAND TO FLAUBERT

Nohant, October 10 [1871]

I reply to your *post scriptum.* If [in "Reply to a Friend"] I had answered *Flaubert,* I wouldn't have—*answered;* for I well know that with you, heart doesn't always agree with mind—a disagreement that all of us, for that matter, are ever compelled to. What I answered was part of a letter from some friend whom nobody knows nor can recognize, since I address myself to a segment of your reasoning that is not the whole *you.*

You are a troubadour all the same, and if I had to write to you *publicly* the character would be all it should be. But our true discussions must remain between ourselves, like caresses between lovers—and sweeter than those, since friendship also has its mysteries, without the storms of personality.

The letter you wrote me in haste is full of well-expressed truths against which I do not protest. But the link and agreement between your truths of reason and my truths of feeling must be found. France, alas! is neither on your side nor on mine. She is on the side of blindness, ignorance, and folly. Oh! *That* I do not deny—and it is exactly what I deplore.

. . .

◇◇◇◇◇

Mme Sand then changes the subject, and speaks of Bouilhet's *Aïssé* and the present state of the Paris stage. We have seen how she and Flaubert had recognized their fundamental differences from the beginning; and her tact now helped Flaubert to realize that he had perhaps fulminated enough. Not that he could stop abruptly. "In my opinion the entire Commune should have been sentenced to hard labor. The bloodthirsty fools should have been chained by the neck like common criminals and made to clean up the ruins of Paris." And, more generally Flaubertian, a sentiment that he might have expressed at any time in his life: "I'd like to drown my contemporaries in their latrines, or at least rain torrents of abuse, cataracts of invective, on their heads. Why is this? I ask myself." To those remarks Mme Sand replied obliquely; and, with only a brief faltering, their affection continued as before.

AMONG FLAUBERT'S expressions of grief and indignation over events related to the war and the Commune, one was directed close to home—to his friend Charles Lapierre, owner-editor of the local newspaper *Le Nouvelliste de Rouen.* Victor Hugo, returning from exile on Guernsey after the fall of the Empire, had (as Enid Starkie puts it)[1] "turned toward the Left as the revolutionary he liked to think he was," and had written a pamphlet which "gave the impression that he supported and admired the Commune." An article in the *Nouvelliste* for May 27, 1871, contained the following paragraph:

> A man whom France for a time believed she could count among her supreme geniuses, and who had the talent to earn an income of many thousand francs by his sonorous phrases and fantastic antitheses, a wretched poet, supporter of the Monarchy, of Bonapartism, and of Republicanism in that order—you will have guessed we refer to Victor Hugo—has just given his opinion on the appalling tragedy we are witnessing. This product of a brain that is utterly softened or deranged is entitled *Paris et la France.*

1. In *Flaubert the Master* (see Works of Related Interest).

◇◇◇◇◇

TO CHARLES LAPIERRE

[Croisset,] May 27 [1871]

Confidential

My dear Lapierre,

It is to you alone that I'm writing; therefore, I'm going to unburden my heart to you without constraint.

Your paper seems to me to be "on a slippery slope," and it is sliding down so swiftly that your issue of this morning scandalized me.

The paragraph on Hugo outdoes everything. "France believed she could count [him] among her supreme geniuses": that "believed" is sublime! It means, "Formerly we had no taste, but revolutions have enlightened us in the matter of art," and it's become abundantly clear that he's only a "wretched poet," "who had the talent to earn an income"— are you now attacking money?—"with sonorous phrases and fantastic antitheses"! Try to imitate him, my good fellow! I find you all very droll, there in the rue Saint-Étienne-des-Tonneliers!

Proudhon[1] has already said "It takes more genius to be a boatman on the Rhine than to compose *Les Orientales.*" And Augustine Brohan,[2]

185

during the winter of 1853, proved in the *Figaro* that the said Hugo had never possessed the slightest talent. Don't imitate those two—clown and whore. In the interest of public order and the return to moral standards, the first thing to try to do is to talk about what one knows. Let's choose our arms! Don't let's put our enemies in the right; and, when you want to attack the personality of a great poet, don't attack him as a poet: otherwise those who know something about poetry will shun you.

.   .   .

I'm talking too much literature: forgive me. But as an old Romantic I was exasperated by your paper this morning. Old Hugo's foolishness pains me too much as it is, without his being insulted in his genius. When our masters demean themselves, we must do as the sons of Noah did, and cover their shame. Let us at least retain our respect for what was great. Don't let's add to our ruins . . .

1. The socialist writer Pierre Joseph Proudhon (1809–1865), author of the famous definition: *La propriété c'est le vol* ("Property is theft").
2. (1807–1887), an actress at the Comédie Française.

◇◇◇◇◇

As Enid Starkie points out, Flaubert's letter to Lapierre was written during the Semaine Sanglante, when in Paris Frenchmen were killing Frenchmen by the thousand. After listening at length to Flaubert, the master of self-contradiction, on the subjects of war and politics, it is good to hear him again as artist and champion of art.

Armed with the results of his latest researches—some of them, as we have seen, undertaken in devastated Paris immediately after that bloody week—and writing at last what would prove to be the definitive version of *The Temptation of Saint Anthony*, Flaubert found relief for his spirits in grappling with the mysteries of eastern religions. In response to a letter from his friend Frédéric Baudry couched in the style of those writings, he replied in kind.

◇◇◇◇◇

To Frédéric Baudry[1]

[Croisset,] Saturday night [June 24–25 (?), 1871]

O Bodhisattva! O youth of gentle birth! O perfect Buddha!

Like an old stork, I am sorrowful and dejected in spirit; like an old elephant fallen into the mire, I lack strength.

I need, O youth of gentle birth, the fourth of the medicinal plants that induce well-being in any situation, whatsoever it may be.

186

I have read the Lalitavistara, O Bodhisattva, I have read *The Lotus of the Wonderful Law*,[2] O youth of gentle birth!

But I would spend innumerable (hundreds) of myriads of Kotis of Kalpas,[3] without understanding, O holy name of God, in what Buddha consists.

I search within myself, to see whether I may not possess the thirty-two qualities of the imbecile.[4]

In short, I'm going to send to you at the end of next week for the Barthélémy-Saint-Hilaire.[5] Thank you for the legend of the deer, but what I especially lack is the theology of Buddhism, the very doctrines of Buddha.

You will probably see me toward the end of July or the beginning of August.

If you see Renan, give him my warm thanks for his book.[6]

It seems to me that politics are calming down. Ah, if people could accustom themselves to living without "principles," i.e. without dogmas—what progress!

Here are two lines from *The Lotus of the Wonderful Law* that drive me crazy! They concern a house haunted by demons: "Seizing the dogs by their feet, they overturn them onto their backs; and growling they squeeze them by their throats and take pleasure in choking them to death." What a picture! How one sees it! Doesn't it make you want to do the same?

Adieu, old Richi.[7] O, the Law! O, the Assembly!

Your disciple,

G^{ve} Flaubert

1. A philologist. A Rouennais, he had been a friend of Flaubert's since childhood. He will be heard of again, in subsequent pages.
2. One of the canonical books of Buddhism, in prose and verse, probably dating from the third century A.D. There is an English translation (from the Chinese version) by W. E. Soothill (Oxford: Clarendon Press, 1930).
3. Billions of years, a metaphor from *The Lotus*.
4. The allusion is to the thirty-two qualities of goodness that distinguish the sage.
5. Jules Barthélémy-Saint-Hilaire (1805–1895) wrote *Du bouddhisme* (1855) and *Le Bouddha et sa religion* (1862).
6. *La Réforme intellectuelle et morale* (1871).
7. A being of perfect saintliness.

◇◇◇◇◇

"Ouf! I've just finished my section on the Gods!" Flaubert wrote George Sand on November 14. "That is, the mythological part of my *Saint Anthony*, which I've been on since the beginning of June. How I long to read it to you, chère maître du bon Dieu!"

The year ended with his receiving a new book by a thirty-one-year-old novelist who had proclaimed himself his disciple, and whose earlier book, *Thérèse Raquin*, he had praised even while complaining that it was "not preoccupied above all else with what is for me the goal of art, namely, Beauty."

◇◇◇◇◇

TO ÉMILE ZOLA

[Paris] 4 rue Murillo, Friday night [December 1, 1871]

I have just finished your dreadful and splendid book [*La Fortune des Rougon*]. I'm still giddy after reading it. It's strong! Very strong!

I find fault only with the preface. In my opinion, it spoils your book, which is so impartial and so lofty. You give away your secret: that is carrying candor too far; and you express your opinion, something which in my poetics a novelist hasn't the right to do.

Those are my *only* reservations.

But you have a noble talent and you are a valuable man.

Send me a line to say when I can come to see you, to talk at length about your book.

I shake your hand most cordially, and am your

G^{ve} Flaubert

VIII

The Temptation of Saint Anthony. The Beginning of Bouvard and Pécuchet. Le Candidat. Three Tales 1872–1877

I WANT to embrace you at the beginning of the new year," George Sand wrote Flaubert from Nohant on January 4, 1872, "and to tell you that I love my old troubadour now and always . . . Here we invoked you at the stroke of midnight on Christmas Eve. We shouted your name three times. Did you hear it at all? We are all well. The little girls are growing up. We speak of you often. My children embrace you, too. May our affection bring you happiness!"

But during this year—which was to see the death of his mother—and for some time to come, Flaubert's letters to Nohant would often strain even George Sand's great faith in the power of affection over grief. With Madame Flaubert's disappearance he became the oldest survivor (apart from the servant Julie, who was to inspire one of his *Three Tales*) in his immediate world of Croisset; and, having long since taken to calling himself "old"—an "old" Romantic, an "old" troubadour, a "fossile"—he now entered, quite willfully, at fifty, into premature old age.

There were other factors: the approaching death of Théophile Gautier, which symbolized for Flaubert the end of Romanticism; the public's incomprehension of *L'Éducation sentimentale*; and, not least of all, the terms of his mother's will and the characters and misfortunes of his niece and her husband.

However, his mother's death was the dominating event. Four years later, when his spirits had somewhat revived, he would recognize this, and write to Caroline: "Shall I tell you my opinion? I think that (without knowing it) I was deeply and secretly sick after the death of our poor old lady. If I'm wrong, how does it happen that for some time now my mind has been functioning more clearly? It's as though a fog were lifting. Physically I feel rejuvenated."

Flaubert's loyalty to Louis Bouilhet's memory never wavered. He celebrated and defended him in his preface to the posthumously published volume of his verse; he wrote and published a scathing "Letter to the Municipal Council of Rouen" after that provincial body, by a vote of thirteen to eleven, had declined his committee's offer to pay for the erection of a monument to the poet;[1] and he exhausted himself securing and supervising a production of Bouilhet's play, *Mademoiselle Aïssé*, at the Théâtre de l'Odéon, only to see it be blasted by critics and close after three performances.

There was some consolation in the increasing admiration he received from writers of a younger generation who sent him their works.

1. The monument—a bust of Bouilhet and a fountain—was eventually executed. It stands against the façade of the present Rouen Municipal Library, successor to the building that Bouilhet knew.

◇◇◇◇◇

To Alphonse Daudet

[Paris,] Tuesday morning [March 1872]

It's purely and simply a *masterpiece!* That's the word that springs to my lips, and I'll not take it back.

I began *Tartarin*[1] Sunday at midnight, and finished it at 2:30! Everything, absolutely everything, kept me entertained, and I burst out laughing several times.

The camel is a marvelous invention, well developed, and providing "the crowning touch."

Tartarin on the minaret, fulminating against the Orient, is sublime!

In short, your little book seems to me of the very highest quality. Such is my opinion.

I plan to return to my house in the country in a little under two weeks. Between now and then I'm entirely taken up. But I'd like to see you. How shall we do it? I'll be at home on Sunday afternoon.

And you? When are you free?

Where can I find your brother, whom I haven't yet thanked for his book?

Until soon, I hope, and all greetings.

The hunters, the caps! Barbassou, the negroes eating sticking plaster, the Prince, etc.! Very fine, very fine!

1. By 1872, Alphonse Daudet (1840–1897) had already published his *Lettres de mon moulin* and *Le Petit Chose*. Chapters from the immensely popular *Tartarin de Tarascon* would become familiar to generations of secondary-school students of French in England and the United States, but today its coy, racial humor is difficult to swallow. Indeed all of Alphonse Daudet's work is at present in eclipse. The title of one of his plays, *L'Arlésienne*, is known today chiefly as the name of the suite of music composed for it by Georges Bizet.

Ernest Daudet, elder brother of Alphonse, was a respected novelist and historian. The book for which Flaubert had not yet thanked him was perhaps his novel *Thérèse*.

Alphonse Daudet was the father of Léon Daudet, cofounder, with Charles Maurras, of the ultranationalist newspaper, *L'Action Française*.

Mme Flaubert died on April 6, 1872. Of the replies to the terse announcements that Flaubert sent to friends, two, written five days apart, are from George Sand, who was ill at Nohant.

> I am with you all day, all night, at every instant, my poor dear friend. I keep thinking of all the heartbreaking things that are taking place around you. I long to be near you. Resentment at being pinned down here makes me feel even more ill than I am ... All I can do is to open a maternal heart to you: it can be no substitute, but it is suffering together with yours ...

> ... If you should feel like doing some traveling, and lack the wherewithal, I have just earned a few sous, which are at your disposal. Have no more hesitation than I would with you, dear child. *Le Temps* will be paying me for my novel in five or six days ...

To George Sand

[Croisset,] Tuesday, [April] 16 [1872]

Chère bon maître

I should have answered your first letter at once, it was so sweet. But I was exhausted, I lacked the physical strength. Today I'm at last beginning to hear the birdsong and see the fresh green of the leaves. I've stopped resenting the sunshine! That's a good sign. If only I could feel like working again I'd be saved.

Your second letter (that of yesterday) moved me to tears. How good you are! What a wonderful being! I have no need of money at the moment. Thank you. But if I should feel the need, it is certainly you I would turn to.

My mother has left Croisset to Caroline, with the condition that I retain my quarters here. So until things are finally settled I'll stay on. Before deciding about the future, I must know what I'll have to live on. After that we'll see. Will I have the fortitude to live absolutely alone here, in solitude? I doubt it. Caroline cannot live here now. She already has two places of her own. And the Croisset house is expensive to maintain.

I think I'll give up my apartment in Paris. All my friends are dead. And the last of them, poor Théo, isn't long for this world. Ah! It's hard to grow a new skin at fifty!

I have realized for a fortnight now that my poor dear mother was the being I loved most. I feel as though part of my entrails had been torn out.

I need to see you so badly! So badly! As soon as things are cleared up I'll visit you. If you go to Paris, let me know, and I'll come running to embrace you.

Mme Viardot, Turgenev, and I have a plan—to visit you at Nohant in July. Will this little dream be realized?

I give you a great hug.

Your old troubadour
G^{ve} Flaubert

◇-◇-◇-◇-◇

To Caroline he wrote a fortnight later: "You can't imagine how lovely and how quiet *your* Croisset is. Everything is suffused with an infinite sweetness, and there is a kind of assuagement in the silence. The memory of my poor old lady never leaves me: it hovers around me like a mist—I'm as though enclosed in it."

And to George Sand: "Whatever happens, I'll keep my rooms at Croisset. They will be my refuge, and perhaps my only habitation."

That June he did "come running" to Paris to see Mme Sand—it was their first meeting in over two years, her first view of the city since the ravages of the war and the Commune. (She found the "stupor" of the Parisians even sadder than the ruins.) And then, after working obsessively to finish *Saint Anthony* by the end of the month, Flaubert spent several weeks with Caroline at Bagnères-de-Luchon, a watering place in the Pyrenees. (It was during this stay, after her grandmother's death, that she first spoke openly to Flaubert about her unsatisfactory marriage: see Appendix I.) He did not, after all, accompany Mme Viardot and Turgenev when they visited George Sand at Nohant in September: instead, saying that he had lately been too much of a "vagabond," and now had to stay at home,[1] he plunged into reading for his next novel.

This would be the book about the two "troglodytes" whose outline he had put aside in 1864 in favor of *L'Éducation sentimentale*. In a letter of August 1872 to Mme Roger des Genettes, with whom he had apparently discussed the new work, he now speaks of it as "the farcical story of those two characters who copy a kind of critical encyclopedia. I think I gave you some idea of it. I'm going to have to study many things I'm ignorant of—chemistry, medicine, agriculture. I'm now into medicine. One has to be insane—wildly mad—to undertake such a book!" And to his friend Mme Brainne:[2] "All this for the sole purpose of spitting out on my contemporaries the disgust they inspire in me. I'm finally going to proclaim my way of thinking, exhale my resentment, vomit my hate, expectorate my bile, ejaculate my anger, purge myself of indignation—and I shall dedicate my book to the shade of St. Polycarp."

He had already decided to call it *Bouvard and Pécuchet.*[3]

Bouvard and Pécuchet, the story of two uneducated, retired copy-clerks and their disillusioning quest for knowledge, will be referred to throughout the remaining pages of the present work. In the form in which it is generally known, the novel is a single volume of ten chapters. Most editions include also Flaubert's outline for an eleventh chapter, unwritten at his death in 1880. Those eleven chapters would have made up the first volume of a planned two-volume work. Flaubert once spoke of a possible subtitle: "Encyclopedia of Human Stupidity."

For a summary of *Bouvard and Pécuchet*, never a widely read novel, one cannot do better than quote Jean Bruneau and Jean A. Ducourneau's remarks in their *Album Flaubert* (Gallimard, 1972):

> Flaubert's idea is to show, with the aid of his two characters, the dangers of "lack of method in the sciences." After failing in all their experiments, Bouvard and Pécuchet devote themselves to copying a *sottisier*—an encyclopedia of stupid statements and opinions expressed over the years by all mankind, not excepting Flaubert himself. Flaubert imagines a very restricted fictional "situation," as in *The Temptation of Saint Anthony*: Bouvard and Pécuchet meet by chance on a bench on the boulevard Bourdon in Paris, buy a house in the country, experiment with one science after another, participate in their own way in the events of 1848, undertake a biography of the duc d'Angoulême, dabble in religion, love, the education of boys and girls, and after repeated failure in all these fields they join Flaubert in his judgment of the society of his day. "Then their minds developed a deplorable capacity—that of perceiving stupidity and finding it insufferable." They have become Flaubert—just as Flaubert himself, he said, had become them.

What the second volume would have been is not precisely known; but from Flaubert's letters and notes it seems that it would have consisted almost entirely of the *sottisier*—a collection of howlers copied by the baffled and disillusioned clerks from the very books they had hoped would offer them wisdom. Most of that material, as left by Flaubert, is an inchoate mass. It has been tentatively organized and published in French in several versions, but only one section has appeared in English—*The Dictionary of Accepted Ideas*, translated by Jacques Barzun (see Works of Related Interest).

Readers of the first volume of the present work may recall that in the very earliest of the letters the nine-year-old Flaubert already spoke of writing down the "stupid things" said by "a lady who comes to see papa." Apparently he never stopped recording such utterances. He mentioned a projected "dictionary" of them to Louis Bouilhet in a letter of 1850, and quoted a few items from it to Louise Colet in 1852. His notes also include a "Catalogue of chic opinions" and an "Album of the Marquise." It was apparently a story by Barthélemy Maurice, "Les Deux Greffiers" [The Two Clerks], first published in 1841, that suggested the framework which would allow him to present his collected stupidities as the work of a pair of copyists.

READERS OF the previous volume may also recall his adolescent infatuation with a young married woman, Elise (Mme Maurice) Schlesinger, on the beach at Trouville. He saw something of the Schlesingers in Paris while he was a law student, he celebrated Mme Schlesinger in his youthful *Mémoires d'un fou* (published only posthumously), and corresponded with her husband after the Schlesingers left France to live in Baden-Baden, where Elise suffered from depression and spent some time in a mental hospital. "I had only one true passion," he wrote about her to Louise Colet in 1846. "I was barely fifteen, and it lasted until I was eighteen." Then, almost twenty years later, calling on his memories of Elise Schlesinger, he invented the character of Mme Arnoux in the definitive *L'Éducation sentimentale.*

In 1871, learning of her husband's death, he wrote her twice, in a tone more openly affectionate than he would have used before her widowhood: "For me, the sand on Trouville beach still holds your footprints." Now, in 1872, he wrote her again.

1. Actually, "staying at home" included a secret few days in Paris with Juliet Herbert, Caroline's former governess, who came from England to be with him. The episode is obscure, as is the entire relation with Miss Herbert, with whom he apparently corresponded and whom he apparently saw each year. (See Hermia Oliver, *Flaubert and an English Governess*, in Works of Related Interest.) The multiple presence, during the summer of 1872, of women for whom Flaubert felt affection—Mme Sand, Caroline, Juliet Herbert, and (as we shall see) Mme Schlesinger, not to mention Mme Roger des Genettes and his "three angels" (see below)—led Hermia Oliver to head her chapter covering these months with a quotation from a letter Flaubert wrote to Caroline on September 24: "My heart is large enough to contain all kinds of affection: the one doesn't exclude the other, nor the others."

2. Mme Charles Brainne (née Rivoire), an attractive widow, who is said to have "granted her favors" to Flaubert, and to whom at all events he often wrote quite freely, was a sister of the equally attractive Mme Charles Lapierre, wife of the owner-editor of *Le Nouvelliste de Rouen.* Flaubert sometimes called these ladies, and their friend the actress Madame Pasca (Mme Alice Séon-Pasquier), his "three angels." It was the custom of the trio to give him an annual dinner in honor of St. Polycarp, one of the Apostolic fathers, whom Flaubert had chosen as his patron out of sympathy with the saint's reputed lament: "Oh God, oh God, in what a century hast Thou made me live!"

Flaubert was sometimes oppressed by the limitations of these charming bourgeoises. "My 'angels' are pretty silly," he confided to Caroline after spending an evening at the Lapierres'. "I think they love the man in me, but as for the mind I'm aware that I often shock them or seem mad."

3. It may seem strange that for the name of one of his two copy-clerks Flaubert should choose something so similar to "Bovary"; but variations on the name of his Cairo host (see page 146, note 1) apparently fascinated him. There is also the association, in this case, of the French word *buvard* ("blotter" or "writing pad"). There was an "actual" Pécuchet—a Rouen banker involved in Commanville's business affairs (see page 248, note 2).

❖❖❖❖❖

To Madame Maurice Schlesinger

Croisset, Saturday [October 5, 1872]

Ma vieille Amie, ma vieille Tendresse,

I can never see your handwriting without being shaken. So this morning I eagerly tore open the envelope of your letter.

I thought it would announce your visit. Alas! no. That will be for when? For next year? I should so love to welcome you here, to have you sleep in my mother's bedroom!

It wasn't for my own health that I was at Luchon, but for my niece's, her husband being kept at Dieppe by his business. I returned early in August, and spent all September in Paris, where I'm going again in December to commission a bust of my mother. Then I'll come back here for as long as possible. I'm happiest in solitude. Paris is no longer Paris; all my friends are dead; those who remain count for little, or are so changed that I no longer recognize them. Here, at least, nothing irritates me, nothing distresses me directly.

The spirit of the public so disgusts me that I keep myself detached from it. I continue to write, but no longer want to publish, at least not until better times. I have been given a dog.[1] I take him for walks, watch the effect of the sun on the yellowing leaves, and like an old man dream of the past—for I *am* an old man. For me the future no longer holds dreams, but the days of the past seem as though bathed in a golden mist. Against that background of light, beloved phantoms reach out to me: and the face that stands out most splendidly is—yours.—Yes, yours. Oh, poor dear Trouville!

In the division of my mother's estate, Deauville[2] came to me. But I must sell it and invest the money, to have an income.

How is your son? Is he happy?[3] Do let us write to each other from time to time, if only a word, to show that we are still alive.

Adieu, and ever yours—

1. A greyhound, given to him by his friend Edmond Laporte, of whom more will be heard. A younger man, Laporte was an *avocat-général* (defined in legal dictionaries as "deputy director of public prosecutions at a court of appeals"—in this case at Rouen), a *conseiller-général* (member of the local council) in the Rouen suburb of Grand-Couronne (across the river from Croisset), and manager of a lace factory there. Flaubert baptized the dog "Julio"—"for a number of mystic reasons," he told Laporte: possibly in honor of Juliet Herbert. He quickly developed a particular affection for Julio.

2. A farm there, which we shall see Flaubert selling not "to have an income," but to pay some of Commanville's debts. One suspects that advice to sell was already being given by Commanville, who was thinking of how he, as Flaubert's "investment counsel," might profit from what the farm would bring.

3. A few months earlier, Mme Schlesinger had come to Paris for her son's wedding: Flaubert had attended, and, overcome by memories (mixed, no doubt, with thoughts of his novel), he wept—as he wrote Caroline—"like an idiot."

◇◇◇◇◇

That is the last known letter from Flaubert to his "vieille Tendresse": with it, mentions of the Schlesinger family disappear from the correspondence. Mme Schlesinger was to die in 1888, in Baden-Baden, where she had again entered a mental hospital.

THÉOPHILE GAUTIER was not one of Flaubert's frequent correspondents. But for the young Flaubert he had been a star in the constellation, the "band," of Romantics. To have had the poet become his friend and admirer counted for a great deal with the mature Flaubert. They first met on the eve of Flaubert's departure for Egypt with Maxime DuCamp, in 1849; it was in Gautier's magazine, L'Artiste, early in 1857, that the "second" Temptation of Saint Anthony had appeared (the first of the versions to be printed); Flaubert had rejoiced in Gautier's praise of Salammbô and been proud to have Gautier's novel, Le Roman de la momie, as companion-target in the attack on Salammbô by Guillaume Froehner. Gautier died on October 22, 1872.

◇◇◇◇◇

TO HIS NIECE CAROLINE

[Croisset,] Friday, 2 o'clock [October 25, 1872]

Loulou,

You are right! The death of my poor old Théo, expected though it was, has laid me low, and yesterday I spent a day that I'll remember. I received the news in a telegram enclosed in a letter, with the result that at the moment I learned of my old friend's death he was being buried.

Having previously made appointments with Caudron and with Mme Lapierre and her sister, I went to Rouen to keep them, so as not to be thought of as a "sensitive plant." On the boat from La Bouille, conversation with Emangard. Caudron was on the dock, and we decided certain things concerning Bouilhet.[1] He went with me to the Hôtel-Dieu, where I asked after Pouchet's father. Your brilliant aunt talked about nothing but the hot weather and her own vapors and the quality of the steaks her butcher sent her. After which I crossed the city on foot, meeting three or four Rouennais. The spectacle of their vulgarity, their overcoats, their hats, what they said and the sound of their voices, made me want to vomit and weep at the same time. Never, since I have been in this world, have I been so choked with disgust for my fellow men. I thought continually of the love my old Théo had for art, and felt as though I were being submerged in a tide of filth. For he died, I am sure, of prolonged asphyxiation caused by the stupidity of the modern world.

I was in no mood, as you can imagine, for the jollifications of the Saint-Romain fair.[2] The "angels" of the rue de la Ferme sensed that, and I went to the cemetery, to see the graves of those I loved. My two friends very kindly went with me; they and Lapierre waited for me at the gate. Such delicacy touched me to the heart. Lapierre was dining out, so I spent the evening alone with the two ladies, and the sight of their kind and lovely faces did me good. I am grateful to them.

When I returned here that night, my poor Julio was all over me with caresses. I don't know why I tell you all this, but you'll gather my state of mind from the details . . .

1. There was regular steamer service on the river, with a stop at Croisset. Gabriel Caudron was treasurer of the committee for the Bouilhet monument. Otherwise unidentified, "Emangard" is referred to in a later letter as a Rouen bourgeois who on one occasion began a conversation with Flaubert in a way the latter enjoyed: "Now you're a man who does nothing . . ."

2. The "foire Saint-Romain," named for a seventh-century bishop of Rouen whose feast day, October 23, is celebrated in Rouen churches, including the cathedral, on the third Sunday in October. The fair (a tradition of eight centuries) begins on the Saturday closest to October 23 and continues for four weeks. On the Friday immediately preceding its opening there is a one-day horse fair.

Flaubert frequented the fair from boyhood, and is said to have owed his first acquaintance with the story of St. Anthony to a marionette show presented each year in one of the booths. Tormented by devils, who made off with his celebrated pig, the saint cried out in supplication: "Messieurs les démons, laissez-moi donc! Messieurs les démons, laissez-moi donc!" Schoolboys and students in the audience were wont to add their voices to the saint's plea. Flaubert inscribed it on the title page of the manuscript of his first version of the work, and it has since been reproduced in printed editions of that version.

GEORGE SAND TO FLAUBERT

Nohant, October 26, [18]72

Here is another sorrow for you, this one foreseen but none the less painful for that. Poor Théo, I pity him profoundly—not for dying, but for not having lived for the past twenty years. And if he had consented to live, to exist, to act, to forget his intellectual *personality* a little in order to conserve his actual *person*,[1] he could have lived on for a long time and refreshed his resources, which he had allowed to become too sterile a treasure. They say he suffered great hardship. I understand that he might have done, during the siege, but afterwards? Why, and how?

I'm concerned at having no news of you for a long time. Are you at Croisset? You must have been in Paris for our poor friend's funeral. What cruel, repeated severances! I'm angry with you, though, for becoming such a savage, so at odds with life. It seems to me that you're too inclined to regard happiness as something attainable, and that you're overly angered and astonished by its absence, which is our chronic state. You flee your friends; you plunge into work; and you regard the time you would spend in loving or being loved as time lost. Why didn't you come to us with Mme Viardot and Turgenev? You like them, you admire them, you know you are adored here—and you run off to be alone.

Why shouldn't you marry? Being alone is odious, it's deadly, and it's cruel also for those who love you. All your letters are disconsolate, and they wring my heart. Isn't there some woman you love, and who would find joy in loving you? Take her to live with you. Isn't there a small boy somewhere whom you could think of as your son? Bring him up, make yourself his slave, forget yourself in him.

Living within your *self* is bad. There is no intellectual pleasure like re-entering that self after being outside it for a long time. But to live continually inside that *me*—the most tyrannical, the most demanding, the most capricious of companions: no, that you must not do.

I beg you: listen to me! You are sequestering an exuberant nature in a prison. You are trying to turn a tender and indulgent heart into a deliberate misanthrope, and you will not succeed. I'm worried about you. Perhaps I'm talking nonsense, but we are living in cruel times, and we must not give in to them and excoriate them, but transcend and pity them. There: I love you. Write to me.

1. Gautier's unhygienic habits were legendary.

To George Sand

[Croisset,] Monday night [October 28–29, 1872]

Chère maître,

You guessed aright that there had been a redoubling of my grief, and your letter is sweet and kind. Thank you. And I embrace you even more warmly than usual.

Even though it was expected, poor Théo's death leaves me heartbroken. With him, the last of my intimate friends is gone. The list is now closed. Whom shall I see now, when I go to Paris? Who is there to talk with about what interests me? I know thinkers (or at least people who call themselves such), but an *artist*—where is there one?

Believe me, he died of disgust with the "putrefaction of the modern world." That was his expression, and he repeated it to me several times last winter. "I'm dying of the Commune," etc. The fourth of September inaugurated an order of things in which people like him had no place. You can't demand apples from orange trees. Deluxe artisans are useless in a society dominated by the plebs. How I miss him! He and Bouilhet have left a great void in my life, and nothing can replace them. Besides, he was so good, and, whatever they say, so *simple!* He will be recognized later (if anyone ever again cares about literature) as a great poet. Meanwhile he is an absolutely unknown writer. But then, so is Pierre Corneille.

He had two hatreds. In his youth, hatred of Philistines. That gave him his talent. In his maturity, hatred of the rabble. That killed him. He died of repressed rage, of fury at being unable to speak his mind. He was *stifled* by Girardin, by Turgan, Fould, Dalloz.[1] And by the present Republic. I tell you this because I have seen some abominable things, and because I was perhaps the only man in whom he confided fully. He lacked the quality that is most important in life—for oneself as well as for others: *character*. His failure to be elected to the Academy was a real source of grief to him. What weakness! What lack of self-esteem! To seek an honor, no matter what, seems to me an act of incomprehensible humility!

That I missed the funeral was due to Catulle Mendès,[2] who sent me a telegram too late. There was a great crowd. A lot of idiots and rascals came to show off, as usual; and today being Monday, the day for theatre news in the papers, there will certainly be articles. He will make "good copy."

To sum up, I don't pity him: *I envy him.* For, frankly, life is not much fun.

No, I do not think of happiness as being attainable—but tranquillity, yes. That's why I keep away from what irritates me. I am unsociable; therefore I flee Society, and find myself the better for doing so. A trip to Paris is a great undertaking for me, these days. As soon as I shake the bottle, the dregs rise and spoil everything. The slightest discussion with anyone at all exasperates me, because I find everybody idiotic. My sense of justice is continually outraged. All talk is of politics—and *such* talk! Where is there the least sign of an idea? What is there to hold on to? What cause is there to be passionate about?

Still, I don't consider myself a monster of egoism. My *me* is so dispersed in my books that I spend whole days unaware of it. I have had bad moments, it's true. But I pull myself together by reminding myself that at least nobody is bothering me—and soon I'm back on my feet. All in all, it seems to me that I'm following my natural path. Doesn't that mean I'm doing the right thing?

As for living with a woman, marrying, as you advise, it's a prospect I find fantastic. Why? *I have no idea.* But that's how it is. Perhaps you can explain. The feminine being has never fitted in with my existence. And then I'm not rich enough. And then, and then . . . Besides, I'm too old. And also too decent to inflict my person on another in perpetuity. Deep down, there is something of the priest in me that no one senses. We'll go into all this much better in conversation than in a letter.

I'll see you in Paris in December. But in Paris one is constantly disturbed by "the Others." I wish you 300 performances of *Mademoiselle de Quintanie.* But you'll have a lot of trouble with the Odéon. It's an odious place: I suffered horribly there last winter. Every time I've undertaken to lead an active life I've been burned. So—enough is enough! "Conceal your life," says Epictetus. My entire ambition now is to avoid trouble. And by doing so I'm certain to avoid causing any to others, which is saying much.

I'm working like a madman, reading about medicine, metaphysics, politics, everything. For I'm undertaking a work of enormous scope, which will require a very long time—a prospect I like.

For the past month I've been expecting Turgenev from one week to the next. But gout constantly prevents him from coming. Adieu, chère bon maître. Continue to love me.[3]

1. Girardin, Dalloz, and Turgan were editors of newspapers for which Gautier wrote art and theatre criticism. Achille Fould, Finance Minister under Napoleon III, was responsible for literary pensions. Gautier was granted one (three thousand francs a year) only when decrepit, a year before his death.

2. The poet and dramatist, husband of Gautier's daughter Judith.

3. That same day, or the next, Flaubert wrote to Princesse Mathilde: "Today I received, from Mme Sand, a letter about Théo that is very kind and contains much advice concerning myself. I'll confess to you, just between us, that her perpetual pious optimism—her peculiar brand of logic, if you will—sometimes sets my teeth on edge. I'm going to answer her with some invectives against democracy: that will relieve me."

Gautier had been a devoted member of the princess's salon. She had helped him financially by appointing him her "librarian," at six thousand francs a year.

To Ivan Turgenev

Croisset, Wednesday, [November] 13 [1872]

Your last letter touched me deeply, my dear Turgenev. Thank you for your exhortations. But alas! My ailment is incurable, I fear. Besides my personal reasons for grief (the death during the last three years of almost everyone I loved), I am appalled by the state of society. Yes, such is the case. Stupid, perhaps, but there it is. The stupidity of the public overwhelms me. Since 1870 I've become a patriot. Watching my country die, I feel that I loved her. Prussia may lay down her arms: we can destroy ourselves perfectly well without her help.

The bourgeoisie is so bewildered that it has lost all instinct to defend itself; and what will succeed it will be worse. I'm filled with the sadness that afflicted the Roman patricians of the fourth century: I feel irredeemable barbarism rising from the bowels of the earth. I hope to be gone before it carries everything away. But meanwhile it's not very gay. Never have things of the spirit counted for so little. Never has hatred for everything great been so manifest—disdain for Beauty, execration of literature.

I have always tried to live in an ivory tower, but a tide of shit is beating at its walls, threatening to undermine it. It's not a question of politics, but of the *mental state* of France. Have you seen Simon's circular, with its plan for the reform of public education? The paragraph about physical training is longer than the one about French literature. There's a significant little symptom![1]

In short, my dear friend, if *you* weren't living in Paris I'd promptly surrender my flat to my landlord. The hope of seeing you there occasionally is my only reason for keeping it on.

I can no longer talk with anyone at all without becoming furious, and everything I read by my contemporaries makes me quiver with indignation. A fine state to be in! Not that it's preventing me from preparing a book in which I'll try to spew out my bile. I'd like to talk with you about it. So, as you see, I'm not letting myself be disheartened. If I didn't work, my only course would be to jump in the river with a stone around my neck. 1870 drove many people insane, made imbeciles of others, and left others in a permanent state of rage. I'm in that last category. It's the *right* one.

Mme Sand, admirable woman that she is, is probably weary of my bad humor. I hear nothing from her or about her. When is her play to appear? Isn't it for the beginning of December? That is when I hope to pay you a visit.

Meanwhile, take care of your gout, my poor friend, and know full well that I love you.

1. Jules Simon (1814–1896) was Minister of Public Instruction under Thiers.

Flaubert's forebodings, in this as in other matters, were amply justified: the ratio of sports "coverage" to literary matter in any modern newspaper speaks for itself.

◇◇◇◇◇

Toward the end of this year there arose a situation that was to be chronic during the rest of Flaubert's life: he had to beg Caroline several times to have her husband send him money for household expenses—money of Flaubert's own, which he had unwisely given Commanville to "manage" for him, and money from Caroline for the upkeep of the house, which was now hers. Here we find Caroline, owner of Croisset for less than a year, already making her fond uncle's heart rebel by reproaching him for careless housekeeping. See Appendix I: one begins now to feel the hand of Caroline's husband and to sense the preaching of "wifely duty" by her Dominican counselor. Commanville, who was beginning to have financial difficulties, must have chafed against Mme Flaubert's testamentary provision that Croisset ("expensive to maintain," as Flaubert, probably echoing the Commanvilles, had written to George Sand) not be sold as long as Flaubert wanted to live there.

◇◇◇◇◇

To His Niece Caroline

[Croisset,] Tuesday, 4 o'clock [November 19, 1872]

... As to your financial letter, what was its purpose? You were right in thinking it would depress me. There is no reason to call my attention to my poverty: I think about it quite enough.

Do you expect your remarks to change my temperament? Do you think I can "keep an eye on what my cook spends"! Suicide is sweet compared with such a prospect—there is nothing to do but sigh and resign oneself.

I still have my flat in Paris, for two and a half years. After that, I'll give it up, perforce—and that will be that. My life is abominably arid, devoid alike of pleasure and of any opportunity to open my heart. But I'm not going to carry my asceticism to the point of worrying about the cooking. Things are dreary enough as it is. Bonsoir! Let's say no more about it ...

◇-◇-◇-◇-◇

By the following Easter Flaubert was finally willing to take time from planning *Bouvard and Pécuchet* to make his second visit to Nohant. He stayed for a week, Turgenev joining the company for the last few days. Again, George Sand's diary describes the visit.

Saturday, April 12, [1873]: Flaubert arrives during dinner ... We play dominoes. Flaubert plays well, but shows impatience. He prefers to talk, always in an emphatic manner.

Sunday, April 13 (Easter): ... [After dinner,] dancing. Flaubert puts on a skirt and tries the fandango. He is very funny, but after five minutes he is out of breath. Really, he is older than I! Always mentally exacerbated, to the detriment of his body.

Monday, April 14: Flaubert reads us his *Saint Anthony* from three to six and from nine to midnight. It is splendid.

Thursday, April 17: ... The young people come for dinner. Turkey with truffles ... Afterwards, dancing, singing, shouting—a headache for Flaubert, who keeps wanting everything to stop so that we can talk literature.

Friday, April 18: Flaubert talks with animation and humor, but all to do with himself. Turgenev, who is much more interesting, can hardly get a word in. They leave tomorrow.

Saturday, April 19: One lives with people's characters more than with their intelligence or greatness. I am tired, *worn out*, by my dear Flaubert. I love him very much, however, and he is admirable; but his personality is too obstreperous. He exhausts us ... We miss

Turgenev, whom we know less well, for whom we have less affection, but who is graced with real simplicity and charming goodness of heart.

Although on his return to Paris Flaubert sent Mme Sand a letter of thanks as warm and affectionate as those he had written in 1869, his behavior this time amid the young people, the noise, and the gaiety, is eloquent of what had become one of his chief difficulties—adaptation to the habits of others. And he was aware of what was now, following the disappearances of the last few years, the short supply of another quality. He wrote to Mme Regnier: "Mme Sand is now, with Turgenev, my only literary friend. Those two are worth a crowd of others, it is true, but something nearer the heart would not be unwelcome."

That companionship he was beginning to find in someone much younger than himself.

Guy de Maupassant, last heard of, in the present volume, in his mother's letter to Flaubert about *Salammbô*, had visited both Flaubert and Bouilhet in 1868–1869, when he had been a boarder in his first year at the Rouen lycée. The men had talked with the boy about literature and read some of his early verse, for Maupassant's dream was to become a poet. Now he was twenty-one and recently demobilized from the quartermaster corps after a period of wartime service in the infantry. He had reluctantly obtained a clerical post in the Naval Ministry in Paris, where his father had friends. He and Flaubert saw something of each other, and Flaubert spoke of him in his answer to a letter from the young man's mother:

❦ ❦ ❦ ❦ ❦

TO LAURE DE MAUPASSANT

Croisset, October 30, 1872

My dear Laure,

. . .

Your son is right to love me, because I feel a true friendship for him. He is witty, well read, charming—and then he is your son, my poor Alfred's nephew.

The next work I send to the printer will carry your brother's name, for I have always thought of *The Temptation of Saint Anthony* as dedicated "to Alfred LePoittevin." I spoke to him about this book six months before his death, and I have at last finished it, after working on it intermittently for twenty-five years. Since he is no longer here, I'd have liked to read it to you in his stead, my dear Laure. I don't know when I'll publish it: the times aren't at all propitious . . .

LAURE DE MAUPASSANT TO FLAUBERT

Etretat [February 1873]

I hear of you so often that I'm impelled to write and thank you with all my heart and soul. Guy is so happy to see you every Sunday, to be allowed to stay for hours, to be treated with such flattering familiarity, that all his letters tell and retell the same thing. The dear boy writes me about what he does each day, about our friends whom he meets in Paris, about his distractions; and then invariably the chapter ends: "but the house I like best, the place where I enjoy going more than anywhere else, is Monsieur Flaubert's." I assure you that I do not find his words monotonous! On the contrary, I cannot describe my joy in knowing that my son is so welcomed by the best of my old friends. For don't I count for something in your graciousness to him? The nephew resembles the uncle, so you told me in Rouen; and I see, not without a mother's pride, that more intimate observation has not entirely destroyed the illusion.

If you want to please me, take a few minutes and tell me, yourself, some of your news. And talk to me of my son; tell me whether he has read you some of his poems, and if you think they show anything beyond mere facility. You know what confidence I have in you; I will believe what you believe, I will follow your advice. If you say yes, we'll encourage the boy in his chosen path. But if you say no, we'll have him learn wig-making or some such trade. So speak frankly to your old friend.

TO LAURE DE MAUPASSANT

Paris, February 23, 1873

You have got ahead of me, my dear Laure, because for the past month I have been meaning to write you, to send you a declaration of my affection for your son. I can't tell you how charming I find him, how intelligent, good, sensible, and witty—in short (to use a modish term), *sympathique*. Despite the difference in our ages I consider him a friend; and then he reminds me so much of our poor Alfred! Sometimes I'm really startled by the likeness, especially when he lowers his head as he has a way of doing when he recites poetry. What a man Alfred was! He remains in my memory as without peer. Not a day passes that I don't think of him. For that matter, the past, the dead (*my* dead), obsess me. Is this a sign of old age? I think so.

When shall we see each other? When can we talk about "le Garçon"? Won't you come with your two sons and spend a few days at Croisset? I have plenty of room for you here now; and I envy the serenity you

204

seem to enjoy, my dear Laure, for I am becoming very somber. The age we live in, and existence itself, weigh heavy on my shoulders. I am so disgusted with everything, and particularly with polemical literature, that I have renounced publishing. Life is no longer good for people of taste.

Even so, we must encourage your son in his predilection for poetry, because it is a noble passion, because literature can be a consolation in times of misfortune, and because he may have some talent—who knows? So far, he hasn't produced enough to make it possible for me to cast his poetic horoscope; and anyway, where is the man who can determine another's future?

I think our boy is something of an idler, not too fond of work. I should like to see him undertake something long and exacting, execrable though it might turn out to be. What he has shown me is certainly as good as anything published by the "Parnassians" . . . With time he will acquire an originality, an individual manner of seeing and feeling (which is everything). As to the result, as to his possible "success," what difference does it make? The principal thing in this world is to keep one's soul aloft, high above the bourgeois and democratic sloughs. The cult of Art gives one pride; no one can have enough of it. Such is my morality . . .

◇◇◇◇◇

Flaubert's renunciation of publishing was short-lived. As of January 1873, Michel Lévy's rights to *Madame Bovary* and *Salammbô* terminated. Angered by Lévy's neglect of Bouilhet's posthumous volume of verse, Flaubert sold the rights to the two novels to a new, young publisher, Georges Charpentier, who had been recommended to him by Turgenev. In December he sold him *Saint Anthony* as well, to appear in 1874.

Meanwhile he interrupted the planning of *Bouvard and Pécuchet* to prepare the staging of another of Louis Bouilhet's unfinished plays, *Le Sexe faible*. This was never produced. However, stimulated by working in the dramatic form, Flaubert composed a satirical comedy of his own, *Le Candidat*, the story of a wealthy provincial who, bored by everything except the prospect of power, sacrifices all—his wife, his daughter, and his "honor"—to ensure his election to the Chamber of Deputies. "Between you and me," Flaubert wrote to Mme Roger des Genettes, "I don't attach great importance to this work. I think it's 'all right,' but no more than that, and I have only two reasons for wishing it success: (1) to earn a few thousand francs, and (2) to irritate a few imbeciles."

And he added: "I'm now reading the aesthetics of the noble Lévesque,[1] professor at the Collège de France. What a cretin! A good fellow, and full of the best intentions. But how odd they are, the professors, as soon as they start meddling with Art!"

Léon Carvalho, director of the Théâtre du Vaudeville, was enthusiastic about *Le Candidat*. It went into rehearsal, and after several disquieting postponements finally opened on the night of March 11, 1874. It met the reception all too often reserved for the work of the novelist who has been drawn from his desk by "the lure of the footlights."

Mme Sand had been kept away from the première by the illness of her grandchildren at Nohant.

1. Presumably Pierre-Charles Lévesque (1736–1812), a hellenist and historian.

◇◇◇◇◇

To George Sand

[Paris,] Thursday, 10 o'clock [March 12, 1874]

Chère maître,

If ever there was a flop! People wanting to flatter me insist that the play will catch on with the general public, but I don't believe it for a second.

I know the defects of my play better than anyone. If Carvalho hadn't driven me crazy for a month making one foolish "correction" after another (I scrubbed them all), I'd have done some retouching and changing myself that might have altered the final result. But as it was, I grew so disgusted with the whole business that I wouldn't have changed a line for a million francs. In a word, I was sunk.

Besides, it has to be said that the audience was detestable, all fops and stockbrokers who had no understanding of what words *mean*. Anything poetic they took as a joke. A poet says: "I'm a man of the 1830s, you know: I learned to read from *Hernani* and I wanted to be Lara."[1] That brought a roar of ironic laughter. And more of the same.

And then the public was misled by the title. They were expecting another *Rabagas*.[2] The conservatives were annoyed because I didn't attack the republicans, and the communards would have liked me to throw a few insults at the legitimists.

My actors played superbly, Saint-Germain among the rest. Delannoy, who carries the entire play, is much distressed, and I don't know how to console him. As for Cruchard,[3] he is calm, very calm. He dined very well before the performance, and after it supped even better. Menu: two dozen Ostend oysters, a bottle of iced champagne, three slices of roatsbeaf [sic], truffle salad, coffee, liqueur.

. . . I confess I'd have liked to make some money. But since my fiasco has nothing to do with art or any deep concern, I really don't give a damn. I tell myself, "At last it's over," and feel much relieved.

The worst of all was the scandal about tickets. Note that I was given twelve orchestra seats and one box (the *Figaro* had eighteen orchestra seats and three boxes). I never even *saw* the chef de claque. It's almost as though the management of the Vaudeville set things up for a failure.[4] Their dream came true.

I didn't have a quarter of the seats I'd have liked to dispose of. And I bought a number—for people who then proceeded to knife me during the intervals. The "bravos" of a few supporters were quickly drowned in a sea of "Shhhs." At the mention of my name after the final curtain there was some applause (for the man, not the play), together with two rounds of booing from the top gallery. Such is the truth.

This morning's minor newspapers are polite. I can't ask more of them than that.

Adieu, chère bon maître. Don't pity me. Because I don't feel myself pitiable.

.   .   .

My man said something nice as he handed me your letter this morning. Recognizing your handwriting, he sighed, and said: "Ah, the best lady wasn't there, last night."

Which is my sentiment precisely.

1. The unworldly Flaubert is surprised that a boulevard (corresponding to "Broadway" or "West End") theatre audience should laugh at references to Romantic poetry by Hugo and Byron in the midst of a satirical comedy.

2. A comedy by the popular Victorien Sardou, produced in 1872.

3. Early in his acquaintance with George Sand, in reply to a burlesque letter from her, Flaubert had composed for her a six-page farcical "Life and Works of the Reverend Father Cruchard, by the Reverend Father Cerpet of the Society of Jesus, dedicated to the Baronne Dudevant." Father Cruchard, invented to embody some of Flaubert's characteristics, was a fashionable ecclesiastic who enjoyed hearing the confessions of beautiful society women. (A.J.)

4. In a note to Alphonse Daudet (March 17), Flaubert says: "Huegel, one of the administrators of the [Théâtre du] Vaudeville, *booed* me, I am assured by Peragallo [a theatrical agent]." If true, it perhaps means that some of those connected with the Vaudeville were partisans of a play by someone else, which was awaiting its turn to be produced.

GEORGE SAND TO FLAUBERT

[Nohant,] Saturday [March 14, 1874]

I have passed through that ordeal about twenty-five times, and the worst is the feeling of disgust that you mention. One doesn't see one's play, one doesn't hear it, one doesn't recognize it, one doesn't care about it. Hence the philosophy with which authors who happen also to be artists accept the verdict, whatever it may be.

I already had news of the performance. The audience wasn't a good one. The subject was too close to home to be enjoyable. People don't like to see themselves as they are. There is no longer any middle ground, in the theatre, between the ideal and *dirt*. There is an audience for each of those extremes. Any study of how men and women really live and behave is offensive to people who have no principles; and since there is perhaps no other species nowadays, anything disagreeable is called boring. Well—you're not upset about it, and that's the way one has to be until the moment of requital.

I know nothing of your play, except that it is full of superior talent. (Saint-Germain[1] told me so in a letter, recently, but said he feared it might not appeal to the taste of the day.) You'll send it to me when it's printed, and I'll tell you whether it's Cruchard or the public that's mistaken. Watch the second and third nights, and see whether the different types of audience have differing reactions. That might be helpful to you.

As for tickets being given to everyone except the author, it has always been that way for me. We are too easy-going. And as for friends stabbing you in the back, it has been that way always, with everybody.[2]

I kiss you and I love you. Now be quick and take your revenge. I'm not worried about the future.

1. Gilles de Saint-Germain, the actor who played the role of the opposing candidate, was an old friend of Mme Sand's.
2. Something of this can be found in Edmond de Goncourt's *Journal* for March 12. After recording with obvious satisfaction the failure of *Le Candidat*, the behavior of the audience, and Flaubert's pitiful attempt, afterward, on the deserted stage, to make a show of indifference, Goncourt adds: "This morning, the newspapers vie with one another in trying to cushion Flaubert's fall. I thought that if it had been I who had written that play, had it been I who had that experience last night, what insults and vilification I would have been treated to in the press. And why? I lead the same exigent life as Flaubert, I have the same devotion to art . . ."

To GEORGE SAND

[Paris,] Sunday [March 15, 1874]

Since there would have had to be a fight, and since Cruchard detests the idea of a struggle, I have withdrawn my play, even though there was five thousand francs' worth of advance sales. Too bad, but I won't have my actors hissed and booed. The second night, when I saw Delannoy come off the stage with tears in his eyes, I felt like a criminal and decided that was enough. (I'm touched by the distress of three people— Delannoy, Turgenev, and my manservant.) So it's over. I'm having the play printed; you'll receive it by the end of the week.

I'm being flayed by all parties—the *Figaro* and the *Rappel*. It's unanimous. People for whom I procured tickets either by plaguing the management or by paying for them myself are treating me like a cretin—for instance Monselet, who *asked* his paper to print an article against me.

All of which leaves me untouched. Never have I been less upset. I'm astonished by my own stoicism (or pride). And when I seek the reason for this I wonder whether you, chère maître, aren't partly responsible. I remember the first night of *Villemer*, which was a triumph, and the first night of *Don Juan du Village*, which was a defeat. You don't know how much I admired you on those two occasions. The nobility of your character (a thing rarer even than genius) uplifted me! And I said a prayer: "Oh! May I be like her under such circumstances!" Who knows? Was I perhaps sustained by your example? Forgive the comparison.

Well, I don't give a damn, and that's the truth.

But I regret the several thousand francs I might have earned. My little money-box is broken. I had wanted some new furniture for Croisset. Nothing doing!

My dress rehearsal was deadly. The entire Parisian press! They took everything as a joke. In your copy I'll underline the passages they pounced on.

Yesterday and the day before, those passages no longer bothered anybody. Perhaps Cruchard's pride carried him away.[1]

And they wrote articles about my house, about my slippers, and about my dog![2] They described my apartment, where they saw "pictures and bronzes on the walls." In fact there is nothing at all on my walls. I know that one critic was indignant with me for not paying him a call: this morning an intermediary came to tell me that, and asked, "What answer shall I give him?"—"Shit."—"But Dumas and Sardou and even Victor Hugo aren't like you."—"Oh, I'm quite aware of that!"—"Well, then, don't be surprised if . . ." Etc.

Adieu, chère bon maître. Greetings to all, kisses to the little girls, and to you all my affection.

1. In the opinion of some professionals, *Le Candidat* might have succeeded had Flaubert not impulsively withdrawn it. But, as mentioned above, there were apparently those at the Vaudeville itself who were against the play, and whom Flaubert would have had to "fight."

2. One of the reporters wrote of "the hermitage of Croisset," where Flaubert worked "shut away for weeks on end, writing at night, sleeping on a rug during the day, with his big dog Salambô [*sic*] for company." (A.J.)

◇◇◇◇◇

The letter Mme Sand wrote Flaubert after reading the printed text of *Le Candidat* was long, detailed, affectionate, and professional. She analyzed the difficulties and pitfalls of writing for the stage (as illustrated by what she felt were the defects of his play), she described aspects of the theatrical world of which Flaubert appeared ignorant, and she encouraged him to try another play at once instead of continuing with *Bouvard and Pécuchet*. She was dubious about that novel:

I am afraid, from what you have told me about the subject, that it may be too true, too well observed, too well rendered. You have those qualities in the highest degree; and you have others—faculties of intuition, broad vision, true power, which are superior in other ways . . . You have two publics, one for *Madame Bovary*, and one for *Salammbô*. So bring them together in a theatre and make them both happy.

Flaubert took her words in good part. "One of the most comical things of our day," he wrote in reply, "is the theatrical arcana. It would seem that the art of the theatre exceeds the limits of human intelligence, and that it is a mystery reserved for those who write like cab drivers. Instant success counts for more than anything else. It's a training in demoralization."

Despite Mme Sand's urging that he persist, *Le Candidat* and his work on Bouilhet's never-produced *Sexe faible* were Flaubert's last writings for the theatre, although to the end of his life he continued to peddle his early effort, *Le Château des coeurs*, the "féérie" he had written with Bouilhet and d'Osmoy in 1863, before beginning *L'Éducation sentimentale*. (It too was never produced. In 1879–1880 its text was serialized in a magazine, accompanied by another supposed interview with Flaubert and illustrated with drawings, some of them by Caroline.)

However, although Flaubert never wrote another play, Mme Sand's wish that he might have a theatrical "revenge" was fulfilled—belatedly and in another country. In 1980, 126 years after its Paris premiere, *Le Candidat*, revived in translation as *Candidato al Parlamento*, was produced in Italy by the late actor-director Tino Buazelli. Flaubert would have tasted recompense in the good notices of his play and the recognition of its timeliness—or timelessness—printed in the newspapers and magazines of Rome, Milan, and Naples. One might wish to have heard comment from him on the easy acceptance by Italian reviewers of his scathing picture of political corruption. Whatever the technical faults of his dramatic satire, Italians of 1980—less hypocritical perhaps than the French of 1874—enjoyed its amusing realism.[1]

The Temptation of Saint Anthony was published by Charpentier on March 31, 1874. This third and definitive version (the only one commonly known) is one-third the length of the original composition which Flaubert had read aloud (for thirty-two hours, according to DuCamp) to Louis Bouilhet and Maxime DuCamp before setting out for Egypt in 1849. Most of that version had remained in manuscript following its condemnation by Flaubert's two friends. The definitive version of twenty-five years later incorporates, with some changes, the portions published in Théophile Gautier's magazine *L'Artiste* in 1857.[2]

Sales began well: the first edition of two thousand copies was gone in three weeks—"Charpentier," Flaubert wrote, "is rubbing his hands." But soon a political crisis involving President MacMahon distracted public attention; the book trade suffered; and meanwhile the journalistic critics were giving *Saint Anthony* their usual kind attention.

1. Two other revivals of *Le Candidat* are mentioned in the *Enciclopedia dello Spettacolo:* by Antoine, for a single night, April 20, 1910, at the Odéon in Paris; and a German "adaptation" in 1914. The latter was by Karl Sternheim, who, according to the same encyclopedia, after writing a farce called *J. P. Morgan,* produced in 1931 the "first, pallid satire of nazism," *Aut Caesar aut nihil,* and soon thereafter was lucky enough to leave his country alive.

2. For the story of the reading of the first *Saint Anthony* to Bouilhet and DuCamp, see Volume I, pages 100–101, and the present translator's *Flaubert and Madame Bovary.* To say that *Saint Anthony* was of capital importance to Flaubert is an understatement: he called it "the work of my entire life," and the correspondence contains innumerable references to its prolonged composition. However, the publication and reception of the final version are but briefly referred to in the letters. Readers interested in the peculiar complexity of its content are referred to the recent translation and study by Kitty Mrosovsky listed in Works of Related Interest.

Literary scholars have always been fascinated by the several versions of *Saint Anthony,* and articles about it abound in international literary journals. One of the early articles on Flaubert to appear in a language other than French was that by George Saintsbury, in *The Fortnightly Review* (London) for 1 April 1878, in which *Saint Anthony* is praised as "the highest expression of dream literature." Flaubert was very pleased by the trans-Channel attention. To Mme Roger des Genettes, on September 1, 1878, he wrote: "In *The Fortnightly Review* for last May 1 [*sic*] I read an article by a son of Albion which was really marvelous." And he quoted a line (of verse?): "C'est du nord aujourd'hui que nous vient la lumière." Or, as a contemporary son of Albion put it: "But westward, look, the land is bright!" (For the French quotation, the offer made on page 113 of this volume is repeated here.)

In his letters Flaubert had always displayed a particular relish for his work on *Saint Anthony,* both in the research and the writing—a double refuge, as *Salammbô* had been, from the modern world, which had grown even grimmer of late. After resurrecting the manuscript from its wartime grave in 1871, he had written about it to Princesse Mathilde: "In order not to think about [the condition of France], I've gone back to work furiously. I'm happy to be home again, and I continue, as before, to turn sentences. It's just as innocent and useful as turning napkin rings"—a reference to Binet at his lathe in *Madame Bovary.* His total reading in preparation for *Saint Anthony* was probably even more extensive than that for *Salammbô.* The final manuscript was almost indecipherable, so dense was the rewriting. "The faces of the copyists had to be seen to be believed, such was their bewilderment and exhaustion," he wrote Caroline. "They told me the job made them physically sick and that it was 'too much for them.'" And later, to Mme Sand: "I won't hide from you that I had a very sad quarter of an hour when the final proofs began to arrive. It's painful to take leave of an old companion!"

❖─❖─❖─❖─❖

To Madame Roger des Genettes

Paris, May 1, 1874

. . . The symphony is complete. Not one of the newspapers fails in its mission . . . My God, are they stupid! What asses! Underneath it all I

211

sense personal hatred. Why? And to whom have I done wrong? It can all be explained by one word: I *annoy;* and I annoy even less by my pen than by my character; my isolation (which is both natural and deliberate) being taken as a sign of disdain . . .

To George Sand

[Paris,] Friday night, May 1, 1874

Chère maître,

"All goes well!" The insults are piling up! It's a concerto, a symphony, with all the instruments playing full blast. I've been torn to pieces by everything from the *Figaro* to the *Revue des Deux Mondes,* including the *Gazette de France* and the *Constitutionnel.* And it's not over yet. Barbey d'Aurevilly insulted me personally, and the generous René Saint-Taillandier, saying I'm "unreadable," ascribes to me ridiculous expressions I have never used. So much for what's in print. What's being said is more of the same. Saint-Victor tore into me at the Brébant dinner (out of servility to Michel Lévy, perhaps?), as did Charles-Edmond, etc., etc. On the other hand, I'm admired by the professors of the faculty of theology at Strasbourg, by Renan, by Père Didon, and by the cashier at my butcher's. Not to mention a few others. Such is the truth.

What comes as a surprise is the hatred underlying much of this criticism—hatred for me, for my person—deliberate denigration; and I keep looking for the reason. I don't feel hurt. But this avalanche of abuse does depress me. One would rather inspire good feelings than bad. However, I no longer think about *Saint Anthony*—it's over and done with.

This summer I'm going to set to work on another book of the same brand, after which I'll go back to novels pure and simple. I have two or three in my head that I'd very much like to write before I die.[1] Just now I'm spending my days in the Bibliothèque [Nationale], making quantities of notes. In a fortnight I'll return to my house in the country. In July I'm going to decongest myself on a Swiss mountaintop, following the advice of Dr. Hardy, who calls me "a hysterical woman"—an observation I find profound.

Turgenev leaves next week for Russia. The trip will interrupt his picture-buying mania: our friend now spends all his time in the auction rooms. He is a man of passions: so much the better for him. I greatly missed you chez Mme Viardot, two weeks ago. She sang arias from *Iphigenia in Aulis.* I can't tell you how beautiful it was—soul-stirring, utterly sublime. What an artist that woman is! What an artist! Such emotions console one for existing . . .

1. *Saint Anthony* and *Bouvard and Pécuchet* are books "of the same brand" in that in each of them Flaubert uses a series of "situations" as a vehicle for the exposition of

ideas—chiefly religious in the one, chiefly scientific in the other, and, in both, social and philosophical as well. In this those two books differ from the "straight novels," *Madame Bovary* and *L'Éducation sentimentale.*

From Flaubert's correspondence and notebooks we know some of the books he had "in his head" and never wrote: *Under Napoleon III* (or, *A Parisian Household,* as he later decided to call it), *Harel-Bey* (about the Near East), and *Thermopylae.*

◇◇◇◇◇

Among the "others" who admired *The Temptation of Saint Anthony* was Victor Hugo, who wrote Flaubert on April 5:

> A philosopher who is a charmer: that is what you are. Your book is dense as a forest. I love this darkness and this clarity. Sublime thought and great prose are the two things dear to me; I find them in you. I am reading you and shall reread you. Until soon: I shall come to see you.
>
> Your friend,
Victor Hugo

Flaubert's letters in these later years mention a number of meetings with Hugo, the hero of his youth whom he still immensely admired "except when he talks politics to a gallery." "The men in my profession are so little of my profession!" Flaubert wrote to George Sand on December 2, 1874. "There is scarcely anyone except Victor Hugo with whom I can talk about what interests me. Two days ago he quoted to me by heart from Boileau and Tacitus. It was as if I had been given a present, the thing is so rare. On the days when there are no politicians with him he is an adorable man."

There was also a letter from Taine, characteristically if legitimately pedantic (Flaubert had given the gods Roman names rather than Greek, whereas the historic St. Anthony, although living in Roman times, spoke only Greek, and so on), but his verdict was in general favorable. He was cautiously impressed by Flaubert's Queen of Sheba: "Very titillating . . . I am sure that for her moral and physical type, and for her costume, you have authorities, or at least documents, things to go by?"

◇◇◇◇◇

To Ivan Turgenev

Kaltbad, Rigi, Switzerland, Thursday, July 2, 1874

I am hot, too,[1] and my condition is superior, or inferior, to yours in that I'm colossally bored. I came here as an act of obedience, having been told that the pure mountain air would un-redden my face and calm my nerves. So be it. But so far, I'm aware only of immense boredom, due to solitude and idleness; besides, I'm no man of Nature—her "wonders" move me less than those of Art.[2] She overwhelms me, without inspiring me with any "great thoughts." I feel like telling her: "All right, all right, I just left you, I'll be back with you in a few minutes; leave me alone, I need other kinds of amusement."

Besides, the Alps are out of scale with our little selves. They're too big to be useful to us. This is the third time they have had a disagreeable effect on me; I hope it may be the last. And then my fellow vacationers—the honorable foreigners living in this hotel! All Germans or English, equipped with walking sticks and field glasses. Yesterday I was tempted to kiss three calves that I met in a meadow, out of sheer humanity and a need to be demonstrative. My trip got off to a bad start— at Lucerne I had a tooth extracted by one of the local artists. A week before leaving for Switzerland I made a tour in the Orne and Calvados, where I finally found the place to settle my two characters. I'm impatient to get started on this book, which terrifies me cruelly in advance.

You mention *Saint Anthony,* saying it hasn't found favor with the general public. I knew in advance that this would be so, but I expected to be more widely understood by the elite. Had it not been for Drumont and Pelletan, I shouldn't have had a single favorable review. As yet I've seen none from Germany. But we're in God's hands; what's done is done, and as long as *you* like the book I'm amply rewarded. Popular success has deserted me since *Salammbô.* What I cannot reconcile myself to is the failure of *L'Éducation sentimentale;* the utter lack of understanding that greeted it astonishes me.

Last Thursday I saw Zola, who gave me your news (your letter of the seventeenth arrived the next day). Apart from you and me, no one has spoken to him about *La Conquête de Plassans,* and he hasn't had a single review, either for or against. The times are hard for the Muses . . .

1. Turgenev had written him from "Spasskoié, Gov't. d'Orel, ville de Mtensk, June 17 (June 5 Russian calendar)," that the temperature was 16 degrees (Réaumur: about 75 Fahrenheit).

2. "I'd give all the glaciers for the Vatican Museum," he wrote to George Sand a day or two later.

◇◇◇◇◇

On July 12 Turgenev, still in Russia, wrote to him about *Bouvard and Pécuchet,* which they had discussed earlier: "The more I consider it, the more I think it's a subject to treat *presto,* à la Swift or à la Voltaire. You know that was always my opinion. As you described it to me, your plot seemed charming and funny. But if you overdo it, or fill it with too much learning . . . ?"

◇◇◇◇◇

To Ivan Turgenev

Dieppe, Wednesday, July 25 [really July 29, 1874]

My dear Turgenev

I shall be back at Croisset on Friday, the day after tomorrow, and on Saturday, August 1, I'll at last begin *Bouvard and Pécuchet*. I have made the vow. There's no more turning back. But such terror as I feel! Such dread! It seems as though I'm embarking on an immensely long journey toward unknown shores, and that I'll not return.

Despite the immense respect I have for your critical sense (for in your case the Judge is on the same level as the Creator—which is saying not a little), I am not at all of your opinion as to the way of handling this subject. If it were to be treated briefly, made concise and light, it would be a fantasy—more or less witty, but without weight or plausibility; whereas if I give it detail and development I'll seem to be believing my own story, and it can be made into something serious and even formidable. The great danger is monotony and boredom. That is what frightens me—and yet, there will always be time to compress and cut. Besides, I can never write anything short. I'm unable to expound an idea without pursuing it to the end.

.   .   .

Politics is becoming incomprehensible in its stupidity. I don't expect the dissolution of the Chamber. Speaking of politics, in Geneva I saw something very curious: the restaurant run by old Gaillard, the shoemaker and ex-general of the Commune. I'll describe it to you when I see you. It's a world in itself, the world democracy dreams of and that I'll never see, thank God. The things that will hold the center of the stage during the next two or three hundred years are enough to make a man of taste vomit. It's time to disappear . . .

To His Niece Caroline

Thursday, 3 o'clock [August 6, 1874]

It was in obedience to your command, dear Loulou, that I sent you the first sentence of *Bouvard and Pécuchet*. But since you refer to it, or rather exalt it, as a "holy relic," and since one mustn't adore relics that are false, please be informed that the one you possess is no longer authentic. Here is the real one: "*Comme il faisait une chaleur de 33 degrés, le boulevard Bourdon se trouvait absolument désert.*"[1]

So much for that, and you won't know a word more for a long time to come. I'm floundering, scratching out, feeling generally desperate. Last night it all gave me a violent stomach upset.[2] But it will go ahead now: it *must*. Yet this book is fearsome in its difficulties. It may well be the end of me. The important thing is that it will keep me busy for years. As long as one is working, one doesn't think about one's wretched self.

There's nothing more to tell you. I live in solitude, like a quiet little old hermit, with Julio my only company. And speaking of quiet, Fortin[3] is of the opinion that I seem calmer and in better shape. That's possible, but I think Switzerland had the effect of making me a bit stupid: the first step toward becoming a right-thinking member of society.

. . .

In your last letter you wrote me something sublime: "I never let anyone touch my beloved volumes of the ancients." Since you were referring to Seneca, it made me think of Montaigne saying "An insult to Seneca is an insult to myself."

. . .

1. "Because the heat had reached 33 degrees, the Boulevard Bourdon was absolutely deserted." The revised, authentic "holy relic" remains the opening sentence of the novel. Thirty-three degrees (Celsius) is 91.4 degrees Fahrenheit.

2. Writers, especially those beginning novels, will recognize the symptoms. A month later, Flaubert would again be suffering: "Since Thursday morning I've been prey to an abominable colic—I can hardly stand on my feet. I do nothing but go upstairs and down again. If I'm not better by Monday I'll employ some energetic methods. This indisposition is so wearing that yesterday I slept for fourteen hours, and last night for twelve." Anything to stay away from the desk—which remains, nevertheless, the only place one wants to be.

3. According to his obituary in *La Chronique Médicale* (a bimonthly medical review) for February 1, 1903, [Edouard] Fortin (1831–1902) had served as doctor with the French navy and lived for a time in Peru, before taking up residence at Croisset. Flaubert refers to him (see page 270) as "a simple health officer." (An *officier de santé* was a licensed medical man without an M.D. degree, who could practice within certain legal limitations. The category was abolished in 1892.) The obituary, in which he is given the title "Doctor," states: "Although a simple *médecin de campagne*, Fortin was, we are told, an excellent clinician, of sure judgment and great good sense."

To Monsieur X ——

Croisset, near Rouen, March 17, 1875

I cannot possibly grant your request. On several previous occasions I have already refused to allow *Madame Bovary* to be turned into a play. I think the idea a poor one. *Madame Bovary* is not a subject for the stage.[1]
With all my regrets, believe me
Cordially yours,

1. The various dramatizations that have been made of *Madame Bovary*, for both cinema and stage, are all interesting—in showing how right Flaubert was. It has also been given on television.

To Madame Roger des Genettes

Paris, Thursday [April 1875]

. . .

My health is deteriorating. As to what's wrong with me, I have no idea, nor has anybody else—the term "neurosis" expressing both a

number of different phenomena, and ignorance on the part of physicians. They advise me to rest. But why rest? To relax, to avoid solitude,
etc., a lot of unattainable goals. I know of only one remedy: time! And
besides, I'm bored thinking about myself. If after one month at Croisset
I don't feel in better form I'll use Charles XII's remedy and take to my
bed for six.

Judging from the way I sleep—ten to twelve hours a night—I have
probably done some damage to my brain. Is it beginning to soften, do
you suppose? Bouvard and Pécuchet occupy me to such a point that I
have become them. Their stupidity is mine, and I'm dying of it. Perhaps
that's the explanation.

One has to be under a curse to think up such a book! I've finally finished the first chapter and prepared the second, which will include
Chemistry, Medicine, and Geology—all that in no more than thirty
pages! and with some secondary characters, for there must be a pre-
tense at action, a kind of continuous story so that the thing doesn't
seem like a philosophical dissertation. What makes me desperate is
that I no longer believe in my book. The prospect of its difficulties depresses me in advance. It has become a chore for me.

.   .   .

◇-◇-◇-◇-◇

Readers by now familiar with Flaubert's modes of expression in the
correspondence will scarcely have to be told that those lines constitute
an announcement that the book was progressing.

And then it was harshly interrupted. For that spring there came the
crisis in Ernest Commanville's business affairs described in Appendix I.
The correspondence for the following months, both before and after
Flaubert's imprudent sale of his property at Deauville for the Commanvilles' benefit, contains one agonized letter after another to Caroline. Flaubert finally confided his circumstances to a few friends. Turgenev, back from Russia and staying with his friends the Viardots
near Paris, had written, suggesting that he pay a long-deferred visit to
Croisset.

◊ ◊ ◊ ◊ ◊

TO IVAN TURGENEV

[Croisset, Friday,] July 30 [1875]

My last letter was "lugubrious," you say, my dear friend. But I have
cause to be lugubrious, for I must tell you the truth: my nephew Commanville is *absolutely ruined!* And I myself am going to be very badly affected as a result.

217

What makes me desperate is the situation of my poor niece. My (paternal) heart suffers for her. Sad days are beginning: lack of money, humiliation, lives upset. *Everything* is bad, and my brain no longer functions. I feel that from now on I'll be capable of nothing whatever. I'll not recover from this, my dear friend. I'm stricken to the core.

Such days as we're passing through! I don't want you to share in them, so we must postpone the visit you suggest in your letter of yesterday. We cannot have you here just now. And yet God knows that an embrace from my old Turgenev would lighten my heart!

I don't yet know whether I'll go to Concarneau.[1] In any case, it won't be for a month or six weeks yet.

For a very long time now I haven't written to Mme Sand. Tell her I think of her more than ever. But I haven't the strength to write her.

We'll have to gather our wreckage together. It will be a long business. What shall we be left with? Not much. That's what is clearest of all. Nevertheless, I hope to be able to keep Croisset. But the good days are gone, and my only prospect is a lamentable old age. The best thing that could happen to me would be to die.

Such is my selfishness that I haven't said a word about you. I am aware of it. Why don't I have your troubles?[2] I don't wish mine on anyone.

Give me your news, and always love your

Gustave Flaubert

1. Flaubert had planned to go—and in mid-September he would go—to rest at Concarneau in Brittany, where his friend Dr. Georges Pouchet (1833–1894) was director of the Laboratory of Marine Biology, a branch of the Museum of Natural History in Paris. In 1879 Pouchet would be named professor of comparative anatomy at the Museum. His father, Dr. Félix-Archimède Pouchet, also a naturalist, held theories of spontaneous generation which brought him into celebrated conflict with Pasteur.
2. This is probably a reference to Turgenev's gout, which on several occasions kept him from visiting Croisset.

IVAN TURGENEV TO GEORGE SAND

Bougival, near Paris, Friday, August 13, [18]75

Dear Madame Sand

. . .

All goes well here, but there is another friend who finds himself just now in a cruel situation—Flaubert, whose letter I enclose. I reproach myself all the more for not having written you for so long when you see that he never stops thinking of you ... A letter from you would be a great boon to him. And when I think that I have kept his letter for ten days, ah! truly, I am furious with myself for my indolence and selfishness. I well know that in everything Flaubert says there is the involuntary exaggeration of an impressionable and nervous man, accustomed to an easy, unfettered life; still, I feel that he has indeed been stricken, perhaps even more deeply than he realizes. He has tenacity without energy, just as he has self-esteem without vanity. Misfortune enters into his soul as into so much butter. I have twice asked him to let me visit him at Croisset, and he has refused. In a more recent letter to me he speaks [again] of the mortal wound he has suffered.

.   .   .

To Agénor Bardoux

Croisset, near Rouen, August 29 [1875]

Mon cher ami,

I cannot tell you how deeply moved I was by what Raoul Duval told me—by what you and he propose.[1] No one could have better friends than the two of you. That you should take the initiative in offering such help makes it doubly precious. But, my dear friend, I ask you to be the judge: were you in my place you would not accept it.

The disaster that has overtaken me is of no concern to the public. It was up to me to manage my affairs better, and I don't think I should be fed from public funds. Remember: such a pension would be published, printed, and perhaps attacked in the press and in the Assembly. What could I—we—reply? Others enjoy this favor, it's true; but what is permitted to others is forbidden to me. Besides, God be thanked, I haven't yet reached *that* point! However, since my life is going to be restricted, if you can find me a post worth three or four thousand francs in a library, along with lodging (such as exists at the Mazarine or the Arsenal), I think that would be good for me. We might think about it and keep our eyes open . . .

For the past four months my poor niece and I have been living in hell. I think that bankruptcy will be avoided. Honor will be safe. But nothing more than that. So, my dear friend: it is understood: do not ask for a pension for me. Because, frankly, *I cannot accept it.* But if you were to find an advantageous sinecure, it would be different. Thank you again for what you have done for me.

1. Flaubert's friends Agénor Bardoux and Raoul Duval were deputies in the National Assembly, the latter from Flaubert's *département*, the Seine-Intérieure. Learning of Flaubert's financial difficulties, they had proposed asking the proper ministry that he be granted a government pension. (Duval had already consented, along with Edmond Laporte, to be a guarantor of sums pledged to Commanville's creditors by Caroline. See Appendix I.) The pension was a form of aid frequently extended to needy men of distinction in various fields: in the case of a man of letters, the grantor would be the Ministry of Education. Flaubert expresses his preference for a government *post:* even a sinecure seems to him more respectable than a dole. The question was to arise again a few years later.

To His Niece Caroline

Concarneau, Saturday, 3 o'clock [September 25, 1875]

Am I going to have a letter from my poor little girl today?

Watch as I may the fish in the aquarium, and stare as I may at the sea, with a walk and a swim every day, I never stop worrying about the future. What a nightmare! Ah! Your poor husband wasn't born to make me happy. But no more of that: what's the use? I assure you I'm being very reasonable. I have even tried to begin something short: I've written (in three days!) half a page of the outline of *The Legend of Saint Julian the Hospitaler*. If you want to know about it, look at Langlois' treatise on stained glass. I'm calmer than I was—on the surface, at least; deeper down everything is quite black.

Here life is pleasantly dull. In bed before ten, up at eight or nine. I do nothing, and my idleness no longer weighs on me. Quite often I manage to think about nothing. Those are the best moments.

My windows look out on a square, with the harbor beyond. In the background are the fortifications of old Concarneau (a crenellated wall with two towers and a drawbridge). I can see the entire length of the quai, with the small boats that go sardine fishing. I have just spent an hour watching them come in, and then had a little nap. Waking up is never cheerful: what a twinge when reality takes over!

Pennetier left us two days ago, and now I'm alone with Pouchet. Such a good fellow, and so self-assured! I envy him that: *I* feel uprooted, like a mass of dead seaweed tossed here and there in the waves.[1]

. . .

Here he is, come to get me for our swim—it's our usual time. But the weather seems to be chillier, and the tide is too low. I think I may renege.

6:30

I did renege. It was too chilly. But I enjoyed a splendid sunset. A real Claude Lorrain. Why weren't you here, poor girl, you who love nature so! I was thinking how nice it would be to have you beside me there on the beach, with your easel, hurrying to paint the clouds while they were at their best . . .

1. When next writing to Caroline, Flaubert would use another image taken from his stay at Concarneau with the naturalist Pouchet: "Despite your advice, I can't succeed in 'hardening myself,' dear child. My sensitivities are all aquiver—my nerves and my brain are sick, very sick; I feel them to be so. But there I go, complaining again, and I don't want to distress you. I'll confine myself to your mention of a 'rock.' Know, then, that very old granite sometimes turns into layers of clay. I have seen some examples of it here, which Pouchet has pointed out to me . . ."

One of the things Caroline had urged him to "harden himself" to was the sale, for the Commanvilles' benefit, of his last remaining property, a large farm at Deauville called "La Cour Bénouville"—land forming part of the present race course—which he had inherited from his mother. It brought 200,000 francs. "Yes, the two days at Deauville were hard," he wrote Caroline on September 18 from Concarneau, "but I stood them well: I had the strength not to show what I was feeling." Of this sacrifice Jacques Suffel has written (*Gustave Flaubert*, Paris: Éditions A.-G. Nizet, 1979): "The gesture was generous, but absurd, because he ruined himself, whereas nothing forced him to do this, and his sacrifice did not put Commanville in the clear. The 200,000 francs brought by the farm covered only a part of the liabilities." In other words, it would have been more practical had Flaubert let Commanville go into bankruptcy, and helped Caroline with his own income. But it was a question of "honor."

◇◇◇◇◇

The mention of *Saint Julian* to Caroline is the first reference to what would become Flaubert's next book—*Trois Contes* [Three Tales], of which *The Legend of Saint Julian the Hospitaler* would be one. The other two would be *Un Coeur Simple* [A Simple Heart] and *Hérodias*. The trio would refute his remark in a recent letter to Turgenev that he could never write anything short.

E.-H. Langlois, who had been Flaubert's teacher of drawing at the Rouen lycée, wrote his treatise on stained glass in 1832. René Descharmes, in his edition of Flaubert's works, notes: "The reader will recall the last sentence in *The Legend of Saint Julian the Hospitaler:* 'And that is the story of St. Julian the Hospitaler, more or less as it is depicted in a stained-glass window in a church in my part of the world.' The window is in the Rouen cathedral, on the left of the choir, between the left transept and the apse. Langlois' book describes it in detail, with two illustrations by Mlle Espérance Langlois."

The Saint Julian window is still in place—or, rather, back in place following its removal before World War II and the subsequent repair of the heavily damaged cathedral. Flaubert had had the story of St. Julian in mind for many years. His preparatory reading was, as usual, very wide; and the episodes of the saint's life as he recounts them in his story differ considerably from the iconography of the window[1]—a fact that, as we shall see, was later to give him a peculiar pleasure.

ON RECEIVING Turgenev's letter, George Sand had written to Flaubert at once, urging him to take heart; and she wrote also, without telling Flaubert and without immediate result, to a friend highly placed in the government, asking—as Flaubert himself had asked Bardoux—whether some sinecure might be found. Several letters passed between Flaubert and Mme Sand during these months: in one dated October 3 he told her of abandoning *Bouvard and Pécuchet*, of beginning *Saint Julian*, and of his fear of losing Croisset.

1. Benjamin F. Bart and Robert Francis Cook discuss the subject in detail in *The Legendary Sources of Flaubert's "Saint Julian"* (see Works of Related Interest).

◇◇◇◇◇

Nohant, October 8, [18]75

Come, come! your health is returning in spite of yourself, since you sleep such long hours. The sea air is forcing you to live, and you have made progress: you have renounced a project that would never have been a success. Write something more down to earth that everybody can enjoy.

Tell me: how much would Croisset bring if your niece were forced to sell it? Is it just the house and garden, or is there a farm, some land? If it's not beyond my means I might buy it, and you could spend the rest of your life there. I have no money, but I'd try to shift a little capital. Do answer me seriously: if I can do it, it will be done.

To George Sand

Monday [Concarneau, October 11, 1875]

Ah, chère maître! What a great heart you have! Your letter touched me to tears. You are adorable, simply adorable. How can I thank you? What I long to do is give you a great hug.

Well, this is how things stand. My nephew has devoured half my fortune, and with the remainder I indemnified one of his creditors who wanted to put him into receivership. Once the liquidation is completed, I hope to recover approximately the amount I have risked. From now until then, we can keep going.

Croisset belongs to my niece. We have definitely decided not to sell it except in the last extremity. It is worth a hundred thousand francs (which would bring an annual yield of five thousand), and it brings in no income, as the upkeep is expensive. Any possible income from the stables, gardens, etc. is counterbalanced by the gardener's wages and the maintenance of the buildings.

My niece's marriage contract contained a dowry stipulation, and therefore she cannot sell a piece of land unless she immediately reinvests the proceeds in real estate or securities. Thus, as things stand, she cannot give Croisset to me.

To help her husband, she has pledged her entire income—the only resource she has.

As you see, the situation is complicated. To live, I need six or seven thousand francs a year (at least), *and* Croisset.

I may perhaps recoup the six or seven thousand francs at the end of the winter.[1] As for Croisset, we'll decide about it later. Such is the present state of affairs. It will be a great grief to me if I have to leave this old house, so full of tender memories. And your goodwill would be powerless, I fear. Since there is no urgency at the moment, I prefer not to think about it. Like a coward, I dismiss, or rather would like to dismiss, from my mind all thoughts of the future and of "business." Am I fed up with it! And have been for five months—good God!

I continue to work a little, and take walks. But now it is growing cold and rainy. Still, I won't return to Paris before the eighth or tenth of November.

You approve of my abandoning my bitch of a novel. It was too much for me, I realize. And that discovery is another blow. Despite all I can do to harden myself against fate, I feel very feeble.

Thank you again, chère bon maître. I love you: you know that.

Your old

     Cruchard,

                more than ever a stupid old wreck.

1. As usual, Flaubert is vague when writing about finances. He probably means that he may recover some income-producing capital if the liquidation of Commanville's assets, the sawmill and adjoining land, brings enough.

◇◇◇◇◇

It was after his return from Concarneau that Flaubert's Paris Sunday afternoons became the events one reads of in literary chronicles of the period. As we have seen, they had begun in a small way in the boulevard du Temple and continued in the rue Murillo; now his visitors came to the unfashionable end of the rue du Faubourg Saint-Honoré, where his reduced circumstances had brought him. Here, a few Sundays a year, he took concentrated "revenge" on the long solitudes at Croisset. Despite his lament to George Sand that the death of Gautier had left him with no artist to talk to, and despite his dissatisfaction with "realists" and "naturalists"—indeed with almost everybody—Flaubert enjoyed his Paris Sundays: for one thing, they made him forget, for a while, the financial cares the Commanvilles had heaped on him.

"Externally my life [in Paris] has scarcely changed," he wrote to George Sand on December 16, 1876. "I see the same people, have the same visitors. My Sunday regulars are, first, the great Turgenev, who is nicer than ever, Zola, Alphonse Daudet, and Goncourt. You have never spoken to me about Zola and Daudet. What do you think of their books? . . . I read nothing at all, except Shakespeare, whom I'm going through again from first to last. How he reinvigorates one, puts air into the lungs as though one were atop a high mountain! Everything seems mediocre beside this prodigy . . ."

There were many other guests at Flaubert's sometimes crowded Sundays, among them Guy de Maupassant, as yet unpublished and still a clerk in the Naval Ministry. Later, Maupassant chronicled Flaubert's "receptions":

He received his friends on Sunday from one to seven, in a very simple fifth-floor bachelor apartment. The walls were bare and the furniture modest, for he detested artistic fripperies. As soon as a peal of the bell announced the first visitor he covered the papers on his work table with a piece of red silk, thus concealing his tools, sacred for him as objects of worship for a priest. Then, his servant always being free on Sunday, he opened the door himself.

The first to arrive was often Ivan Turgenev, whom he embraced like a brother. Taller even than Flaubert, the Russian novelist loved the French novelist with rare and deep affection. He would sink into an armchair and talk in a slow, pleasant voice, a trifle low and hesitant, but giving great charm and interest to his words. Flaubert listened religiously. Their conversation rarely touched on current affairs, but kept close to matters of literature and literary history. Often Turgenev brought foreign books, and translated aloud poems by Goethe, Pushkin, or Swinburne.

Others gradually arrived. Monsieur Taine, with his timid air, his eyes hidden by spectacles, brought with him historical documents, unknown facts, an aroma of ransacked archives. Here come Frédéric Baudry, Georges Pouchet, Claudius Popelin, Philippe Burty. Then Alphonse Daudet, bringing an air of Paris at its gayest, its most lively and bustling. In a few words he sketches amusing silhouettes and touches everyone and everything with his charming irony, so southern and personal; the delicacy of his wit is enhanced by the charm of his face and gestures, by the polished perfection of his anecdotes. Emile Zola comes in, breathless from the long stairs . . . He flings himself into a chair and looks about him, seeking to gauge from the guests' faces their states of mind and the tone and trend of the conversation. Then still others: the publisher Charpentier, the charming poet Catulle Mendès with his face of a sensual and seductive Christ, Emile Bergerat, his brother-in-law, who married Théophile Gautier's other daughter; José-Maria de Heredia, the marvelous maker of sonnets who will always remain one of the most exquisite poets of the age; Huysmans, Hennique, Céard, Léon Cladel the obscure and refined stylist, Gustave Toudouze. And finally, almost always the last, a tall, slender gentleman with an air of high breeding, Edmond de Goncourt.

Yet another occasional visitor was the young Henry James, climbing to Flaubert's "small perch"—as he characteristically called it—"far aloft, at the distant, the then almost suburban, end of the Faubourg Saint-Honoré." James told his friend William Dean Howells that he didn't "like the wares" of most of the French writers present; and later he wrote rather primly of their conversation:[1]

What was discussed in that little smoke-clouded room was chiefly questions of taste, questions of art and form, and the speakers, for the most part, were in aesthetic matter, radicals of the deepest dye. It would have been late in the day to propose among them any discussion of the relation of art to morality, any question as to the degree in which a novel might or might not concern itself with the teaching of a lesson. They had settled these preliminaries long ago, and it would have been primitive and incongruous to recur to them. The conviction that held them together was the conviction that art and morality are two perfectly different things, and that the former has no more to do with the latter than it has with astronomy or embryology. The only duty of a novel was to be well written; that merit included every other of which it was capable.

In his letter to Mme Sand about his Sunday "regulars" and about reading Shakespeare, Flaubert had said also that he was seeking a new subject for a novel, not being sure that he would ever resume *Bouvard and Pécuchet*.

1. In his introduction to W. Blaydes' translation of *Madame Bovary*, published in London in 1902 by Heineman as volume 9 in the series "A Century of French Romance." (A bowdlerized version of this translation of *Madame Bovary* was published in the United States in December of the same year by D. Appleton & Co., as volume 10 in the same series.) James reprinted that introduction as an essay in his volume *Notes on Novelists and Some Other Notes* (New York: Scribner's, 1914); and it was later reprinted by Leon Edel in the United States in *The Future of the Novel* (New York: Vintage, 1956), and in England in *The House of Fiction* (London: Rupert Hart-Davis, 1957). Another essay by James on Flaubert is included in James's *French Poets and Novelists*, the most recent edition of which, with an introduction by Leon Edel, was published by Grosset and Dunlap (New York) in 1964. Both essays are expected to be reprinted shortly in a new collection edited by Mr. Edel.

◇◇◇◇◇

GEORGE SAND TO FLAUBERT

[Nohant,] December 18 and 19, 1875

At last I find my old troubadour again! He was a source of grief and serious worry to me. Here you are, back on your feet, hoping for natural luck in the realm of external events and rediscovering in yourself the strength to conjure it—whatever it may turn out to be—by work . . .

What shall we do next? You, of course, will go in for *desolation*, and I for *consolation*. What our destinies depend on is unknown to me. You watch them pass, you criticize them, you abstain from any literary appraisal of them. You restrict yourself to depicting them, carefully and systematically concealing your personal feelings. Still, your writings make very clear what these are, and you depress your readers. Whereas I want to make mine less unhappy. I cannot forget that my personal victory over despair was the work of my will, and of a new way of understanding—quite the opposite of that which I had formerly.

I know that you are opposed to the intervention of personal doctrine in literature. Are you right? Isn't this a lack of conviction, rather than a

225

principle of aesthetics? If one has a philosophy in one's soul it is bound to manifest itself. I have no literary advice to give you, I pass no judgment on the writer friends you speak of. I told the Goncourts myself everything I thought. As for the others, I fully believe they are better educated and more talented than I. Only I think that they, and you especially, lack a well-defined and large view of life. Art is not merely painting. Besides, true painting is full of the soul of whoever wields the brush. Art is not only criticism and satire. Criticism and satire paint only one face of the truth. I want to see man as he is. He is not good or bad. He is good *and* bad. But he is something more—nuance: nuance, which is for me the goal of art. Being good and bad, he possesses an internal force that makes him either very bad and slightly good, or very good and slightly bad.

It seems to me that your school is not concerned with fundamentals—that is, it stops too close to the surface. But expending its strength in the search for form, it neglects matter. It addresses itself to the well educated. But we are none of us "well educated," properly speaking. We are human beings, first and foremost. At the heart of every story, of every fact, we seek the man. That was what was lacking in *L'Éducation sentimentale*, about which I have so often reflected, wondering why there was such dislike of a work so well done and so solid. This lack was the failure of the characters to develop: they submitted to events and never seized control of them. Well, I think the principal interest of a story is what you neglected to put into this one. For the time being you are again feeding on Shakespeare, and you are quite right. He shows men grappling with events: and please note that by his men, whether for better or worse, events are always conquered. They crush them, or crush themselves along with them.

·   ·   ·

All the dear ones around me embrace you and rejoice to learn that you are better.

To George Sand

[Paris, about December 31, 1875]

Chère maître,

I have given a great deal of thought to your good letter of the eighteenth, so affectionate and motherly. I have read it at least ten times, and confess I'm not sure that I understand it. Just what do you think I should do? Be more specific.

I constantly do all I can to broaden my mind, and I write according to the dictates of my heart. The rest is beyond my control.

I don't "go in for desolation" wantonly: please believe me! But I cannot change my eyes. As for my "lack of convictions," alas! I am only too full of convictions. I'm constantly bursting with suppressed anger and indignation. But my ideal of Art demands that the artist reveal none of this, and that he appear in his work no more than God in nature. The man is nothing, the work everything! This discipline, which may be based on a false premise, is not easy to observe. And for me, at least, it is a kind of perpetual sacrifice that I burn on the altar of good taste. It would be very agreeable for me to say what I think, and relieve M. Gustave Flaubert's feelings by means of such utterances; but of what importance is the aforesaid gentleman?

I think as you do, mon maître, that Art is not merely criticism and satire. That is why I have never deliberately tried to write either one or the other. I have always endeavored to penetrate into the essence of things and to emphasize the most general truths; and I have purposely avoided the fortuitous and the dramatic. No monsters, no heroes![1]

You say: "I have no literary advice to give you. I pass no judgment on your writer friends, etc." But why not? I *want* your advice; I long to hear your opinions. Who should give advice and express opinions if not you?

Speaking of my friends, you call them my "school." But I wreck my health trying *not* to have a school. A priori, I reject all schools. Those writers whom I often see and whom you mention admire everything that I despise, and worry very little about the things that torment me. Technical detail, factual data, historical truth, and accuracy of portrayal I regard as distinctly secondary. I aim at *beauty* above all else, whereas my companions give themselves little trouble over it. Where I am devastated by admiration or horror, they are unmoved; sentences that make me swoon seem very ordinary to them. Goncourt, for example, is very happy when he has picked up in the street some word that he can stick into a book; I am very satisfied when I have written a page without assonances or repetitions. I would willingly exchange all Gavarni's captions for a few such marvels as Victor Hugo's "l'ombre était nuptiale, auguste et solennelle," or Montesquieu's "Les vices d'Alexandre étaient extrêmes comme ses vertus. Il était terrible dans sa colère. Elle le rendait cruel."[2]

In short, I try to think well *in order* to write well. But my aim is to write well—I don't conceal that.

I lack a "well-defined and large view of life." You are a thousand times right! But I ask you: how can it be otherwise? You won't illuminate my darkness—mine or anyone else's—with metaphysics. The words Religion or Catholicism on the one hand, Progress, Fraternity, Democracy on the other, no longer satisfy the spiritual demands of our time. The brand-new dogma of Equality, preached by Radicalism, is given the lie by experimental Psychology and by History. I don't see how it is possible today to establish a new Principle, or to respect the old ones. Hence I keep seeking—without ever finding—that Idea from which all the rest must proceed.

Meanwhile I repeat to myself what Littré once said to me: "Ah, my friend, man is an unstable compound, and the earth a very inferior planet."

Nothing comforts me more than the hope of leaving it soon and not moving to another, which might be worse. "I should prefer not to die," Marat said. Ah, no! Enough of toil and trouble!

What I am now writing is a little something of no consequence, which mothers can safely recommend to their daughters. The whole thing will run to only thirty pages. It will take me another two months. Such is my verve! I will send it to you as soon as it appears—not the verve, the story . . . May 1876 be good to you all . . .

1. This, from the author of *Salammbô*.
2. "The darkness was nuptial, august and solemn"; and "Alexander's vices were extreme as his virtues. His anger was terrible. It made him cruel."

George Sand to Flaubert

Nohant, January 12, 1876

Every day, I have wanted to write to you, and there has been absolutely no time. Here at last is a free moment: we're buried under snow. This is weather of a kind I adore: the whiteness is like a general purification, and makes the diversions inside the house all the sweeter and cosier. Can anyone hate winter in the country? The snow is one of the most beautiful sights of the year.

.   .   .

L'Éducation sentimentale has been a misunderstood book, as I have told you repeatedly—but you have not listened to me. There should have been a short preface, or, here and there, an expression of judgment, even if only a well-chosen adjective to condemn a wrong, to characterize a defect, to emphasize an aspiration. All the characters in this book are weak and come to nothing except those with evil instincts; that is what you are reproached with, because people didn't understand that you wanted to depict precisely a deplorable society, which encourages those bad instincts and destroys noble aspirations. When people don't understand our work, it is always our fault. What the reader wants, above all, is to penetrate our thought, and that is what you arrogantly deny him. He thinks you scorn him and want to mock him. *I* understood you, because I knew you. If I'd been given your book without your name on it, I'd have thought it splendid, but strange, and I'd have asked myself whether you were immoral, skeptical, indifferent, or heartbroken. You say that that's how it should be, and that M. Flaubert would violate the rules of good taste if he were to reveal his opinions and the aim of his book. That is false—utterly false. When M. Flaubert writes well and seriously, one sympathizes with him and is ready to sink or swim with him. If he leaves you in doubt, you lose interest in his work, you skim over it, or put it down.

I have already challenged your favorite heresy, which is that one writes for twenty intelligent people and doesn't care a fig for the rest. That is not true, since you yourself are irritated and troubled by lack of success. Moreover, there haven't been even twenty reviews favorable to this book which was so well written and so important. So one mustn't write for twenty persons any more than for three, or for a hundred thousand. One must write for all those who have a thirst to read and can profit from good reading. Then the writer must exhibit his own highest moral principles, and not make a mystery of the moral and beneficent meaning of his book. In *Madame Bovary*, people perceived what that was. If one part of the public cried scandal, the healthier and more numerous part saw in it a severe lesson given to a woman without conscience or faith—a striking lesson to vanity, to ambition, to irrationality. They pitied her: art required that; but the lesson was clear, and it would have been more so, it would have been so for *everybody*, if you had wished it to be, if you had shown more clearly the opinion that you held, and that the public should have held, about the heroine, her husband, and her lovers.

This wish to portray things as they are, the adventures of life as they present themselves to the eye, is not well thought out, in my opinion. It's all the same to me whether one depicts inert things as a realist or as a poet; but when one touches on the emotions of the human heart, it's a different matter. You cannot detach yourself from this consideration; for you are a human being, and your readers are mankind. Your story is inevitably a conversation between you and the reader. If you show him evil coldly, without ever showing him good, he's angry. He wonders whether he is the villain, or you. What you wanted to do, however, was to rouse him and maintain his interest; and you will never succeed if you are not roused yourself, or if you conceal your emotion so effectively that he thinks you indifferent. He's right: supreme impartiality is antihuman, and a novel must above all be human. If it isn't, the public cares nothing for its being well written, well composed and well observed in every detail. The essential quality—interest—is lacking.

The reader also turns away from a book in which all the characters are good, without nuance and without weakness; he sees clearly that this, too, is not human. I believe that art, this special art of narration, is effective only through the opposition of characters; but, in their struggle, I want to see right prevail. Events may overwhelm a good man: I accept that; but let him not be soiled or diminished by them, and let him go to the stake feeling that he is happier than his executioners.

January 15, 1876

I wrote those pages three days ago, and every day I've been on the point of throwing them into the fire; for they are long and diffuse and probably useless. Natures opposed on certain points understand one another only with difficulty, and I fear you won't understand me any better today than last time. However, I send this scrawl so that you can see I'm concerned about you—almost as much as about myself.

You *must* have a success, after the bad luck that has so depressed you. What I tell you will assure that success. Retain your cult for form, but pay more attention to matter. Don't hold true virtue to be a cliché in literature. Give it its representatives; portray the honest man and the strong, along with the maniacs and dolts you so love to ridicule. Show what is substantial, what endures despite these intellectual miscarriages. In short, abandon the conventions of the realists and turn to true reality, which is a mixture of beautiful and ugly, dull and brilliant, but in which the desire for good nevertheless finds its place and its role.

I embrace you for all of us.

To George Sand

[Paris,] Sunday night [February 6, 1876]

And now, chère maître—and this is in reply to your last letter—here, I think, is the essential difference between us. You, always, in whatever you do, begin with a great leap toward heaven, and then you return to earth. You start from the *a priori*, from theory, from the ideal. Hence your forbearing attitude toward life, your serenity, your—to use the only word for it—your greatness. I, poor wretch, remain glued to the earth, as though the soles of my shoes were made of lead: everything moves me, everything lacerates and ravages me, and I make every effort to soar. If I tried to assume your way of looking at the world as a whole, I'd become a mere laughingstock. For no matter what you preach to me, I can have no temperament other than my own. Nor any aesthetic other than the one that proceeds from it. You accuse me of "not letting myself go" naturally. But what about discipline? What about excellence? What do we do with those? I admire Monsieur de Buffon for putting on lace cuffs before sitting down to write. That bit of elegance is a symbol. And, lastly, I try, naively, to have the widest possible sympathies. What more can be asked of anyone?

As for revealing my private opinion of the people I bring on stage, no, no! a thousand times no! I do not recognize my *right* to do so. If the reader doesn't draw from a book the moral it implies, either the reader is an imbecile or the book is false because it lacks exactitude. For the moment a thing is True, it is good. Even obscene books are immoral only if they lack truth . . .

And please note that I execrate what is commonly called "realism," even though I'm regarded as one of its high priests.

Make what you can of all that.

. . .

To try to please readers seems to me absolutely chimerical. I defy anyone to tell me how one "pleases." Success is a result; it must not be a goal. I have never sought it (though I desire it), and I seek it less and less.

. . .

I'm touched by the length of your last letter. You do love me . . .

To George Sand

[Paris,] Friday night [March 10, 1876]

. . .

You make me a little sad, chère maître, when you ascribe to me aesthetic opinions that are not mine.[1] I think that rounding out a sentence is nothing. But that *to write well* is everything. Because: "Good writing implies strong feeling, accurate thinking, and effective expression." (Buffon.)

The last term is thus dependent on the two others, since it is necessary to feel strongly in order to think, and to think in order to express. Every bourgeois can have heart and delicacy, be full of the best feelings and the greatest virtues, without for that reason becoming an artist. And finally, I believe Form and Matter to be two abstractions, two entities, neither of which ever exists without the other.

The concern for external Beauty you reproach in me is for me a *method*. When I come upon a bad assonance or a repetition in one of my sentences, I'm sure I'm floundering in the False. By dint of searching, I find the proper expression, which was always the *only* one, and which is, at the same time, harmonious. The word is never lacking when one possesses the idea.

. . .

I am writing to Zola to send you his book [*Son Excellence Eugène Rougon*]. I'll also tell Daudet to send you his *Jack*. I'm most curious to have your opinion of these two books, which are quite different in workmanship and temperament, but both very remarkable.[2]

1. "You no longer look for anything but the well-turned sentence," Mme Sand had written him on March 9. "That is something, but only something—it isn't the whole of art, it isn't even half of it; it's a quarter at most, and when the three other quarters are fine one does without the one that is not."

231

2. "Testiculos habes, et magnos," were among the words of praise Flaubert had sent to Daudet about *Jack.*

◇-◇-◇-◇-◇

"I have a great deal to say about M. Zola's novels," George Sand wrote on March 25, "but it will be better for me to say it in an article than in a letter, because it raises a general question that should be explored when one's mind is calm and in repose."

And she goes on to speak from what seems, under the circumstances, a mind extraordinarily "calm and in repose":

"How are you? Turgenev tells me that your latest piece of writing is very remarkable.[1] So you're not 'done for,' as you claim? Your niece continues to improve, does she not? I am better, too, after stomach cramps that were enough to turn one blue, and appallingly persistent. Physical suffering is a good lesson when it leaves your mind free. You learn to endure and conquer it. Of course you have moments of discouragement, when you fling yourself on your bed; but I always think of what my old curé said to me when he had the gout: 'Either it will pass away or I shall.' And he laughed, enjoying his *bon mot.*"

Mme Sand's "stomach cramps" were caused by the cancer (yet undiagnosed) that would very soon be fatal. Her letters continued to be spirited, and full of appreciation of others: "I am enthusiastic about *Jack,* and I beg you to convey my thanks to M. Daudet. Ah, yes! He has talent and heart. How well it is all done and *seen!* I am sending you a volume of old things of mine that have just been put together."[2]

1. *St. Julian the Hospitaler,* which Flaubert had finished on February 17. On March 15 he wrote the first page of *A Simple Heart.*

2. Alphonse Jacobs thinks that this is probably *La Coupe, Lupo Liverani, Le Toast, Garnier, Le Contrebandier,* which had been published by Calmann-Lévy on March 18. There is an inscribed copy in what remains of Flaubert's library.

◇-◇-◇-◇-◇

To George Sand

[Paris,] Monday night [April 3, 1876]

Chère maître

I received your volume this morning. I have two or three other books here that various people lent me some time ago; I'll make haste to finish them, and will read yours at the end of the week, during a little two-day trip I have to make to Pont l'Evêque and Honfleur for my *Story of a Simple Heart*—a trifle at present "in the works," as M. Prud'homme would say.

I'm glad you liked *Jack.* It's a charming book, don't you think? If you knew the author, you would like him even more than his work. I have

232

told him to send you *Risler* and *Tartarin*. You'll thank me after reading them, I'm sure of it.

. . . I share neither Turgenev's severity concerning *Jack* nor the "immensity" of his admiration for *Rougon*. One has charm and the other strength. But neither is concerned *above all* with what is for me the goal of Art, namely Beauty! I remember how my heart throbbed, and what violent pleasure I experienced, when I looked at one of the walls of the Acropolis, a wall that is completely bare (the one to the left as you climb the Propylaea). Well, I wonder whether a book, quite apart from what it says, cannot produce the same effect. In the precise fitting of its parts, the rarity of its elements, the polish of its surface, the harmony of the whole, is there not an intrinsic Virtue, a kind of divine force, something eternal, like a principle? (I speak as a Platonist.) If this were not so, why should there be a relation between the right word and the musical word? Or why should great compression of thought always result in a line of poetry? Does it follow that the law of Numbers governs feelings and images, and that what seems to be outward form is actually essence? If I were to keep going very long on this track I'd find myself in a hopeless predicament. Because on the other hand Art must be humane; or rather, Art is only what we can make it. We are not free. Each of us follows his own path, willy-nilly. In short, your Cruchard no longer has a sound idea in his head.

But how hard it is to understand one another! Here are two men whom I greatly like and whom I consider true artists, Turgenev and Zola. For all that, they have no admiration whatever for the prose of Chateaubriand, and even less for Gautier's. Sentences that enrapture me seem to them hollow. Who is wrong? And how please the public, when those closest to you are so remote? All this greatly saddens me. Don't laugh . . .

◇-◇-◇-◇-◇

In the last letters they exchanged, both friends spoke of literature:
◇-◇-◇-◇-◇

GEORGE SAND TO FLAUBERT

Nohant, April 5, [18]76

. . . I have read *Fromont et Risler*. Please thank M. Daudet. Tell him I spent the night reading him, and I don't know which I prefer, *Jack* or *Risler*. *Risler* is very winning—I could almost say *riveting*.

I kiss you and I love you. When will you let me read some Flaubert?

233

To George Sand

Monday night [Paris, May 29, 1876]

.   .   .

I've been hard at work lately. How I'd love to see you and read you my medieval trifle! I have begun another tale, called *Story of a Simple Heart*. But I have interrupted it to do some research on the period of John the Baptist: I want to write about Herodias' feast.

. . . You will see from my *Story of a Simple Heart* (in which you will recognize your own direct influence) that I am not as stubborn as you believe. I think you will like the moral tendency, or rather the underlying humanity, of this little work.[1]

Adieu, chère bon maître. My greetings to all.

I embrace you most tenderly.

---

1. "My *Story of a Simple Heart* advances very slowly," he had written Mme Roger des Genettes a few weeks before. "I've done ten pages—no more. To document it I made a little trip to Pont l'Evêque and Honfleur. This excursion plunged me into melancholy, for inevitably it was a bath of memories. How old I am, mon Dieu! How old!"

The touching story, inspired in part by the example of his—and his parents'—servant Julie, who was still alive, was set in parts of Normandy he had known as a child. In writing it, he seems to have taken to heart Mme Sand's urging of the previous October: "Write something more down to earth that everybody can enjoy." Millions have enjoyed the tale of the servant Félicité, her life of labor, and her parrot—probably Flaubert's best-known work after *Madame Bovary*.

◇◇◇◇◇

George Sand died at Nohant on June 8, 1876.

◇◇◇◇◇

To Mademoiselle Leroyer de Chantepie

Croisset, June 17, 1876

My dear Correspondent,

No! I had not forgotten you, because I never forget those I love. But I was surprised by your long silence, and wondered about it.

You want to know the truth about Mme Sand's last moments. It is this: she did not have any priest attend her. But as soon as she was dead, her daughter, Mme Clésinger, asked the bishop of Bourges to authorize a Catholic burial, and no one in the house (except perhaps her daughter-in-law, Mme Maurice) stood up for our poor friend's ideas. Maurice was so prostrated that he had no energy left, and then there were outside influences, miserable considerations inspired by certain bourgeois. I know no more than that. The ceremony was immensely moving: everyone was in tears, I along with the rest.

.   .   .

Poor Mme Sand often spoke of you to me, or rather we often spoke of you together; you interested her very much. One had to know her as I did to realize how much femininity there was in that great man, and the vast tenderness in that genius. Her name will live with a unique glory as one of the great figures of France.

.　　.　　.

◇-◇-◇-◇-◇

Another unbeliever recently given Catholic burial at family insistence was Louise Colet, Flaubert's mistress of the 1840s and 1850s, who had died on March 8, 1876.

"You understood very well all my feelings on the death of my poor Muse," Flaubert wrote Mme Roger des Genettes. "This revival of her memory made me review the course of my life. But your friend has become more stoical during the past year. I have trampled on so many things, in order to stay alive! In short, after an afternoon given over to days gone by I *willed* myself to think of them no longer, and went back to work. One more thing concluded!

"The family, which is Catholic, took her to Verneuil in order to avoid civil burial, and there was no scandal. The newspapers made little mention of any of it. Do you remember the little apartment in the rue de Sèvres, and all the rest? Ah! God have mercy on us!"

"My heart is becoming a necropolis," Flaubert wrote to Princesse Mathilde after the deaths of the two women who had played such large parts in his life.

◇-◇-◇-◇-◇

To Ivan Turgenev

Croisset, Sunday evening, June 25 [1876]

.　　.　　.

The death of our poor Mme Sand grieved me immensely. I wept like a calf at her funeral, twice: the first time, when I kissed her granddaughter Aurore (whose eyes, that day, were so like hers as to be a kind of resurrection); and the second, when I saw her coffin carried past me.

There were some fine goings-on. In order not to offend "public opinion"—the everlasting and execrable "they"—her body was taken to the church. I will give you the details of this disgraceful business when I see you. I felt a tightening around my heart, I can tell you, and a positive desire to kill Monsieur Adrien Marx.[1] The very sight of him took away my appetite that evening at Châteauroux. Oh! The tyranny of the *Figaro!* What a public nuisance! I choke with fury when I think of those cocos . . .

You are right to mourn our friend, for she loved you dearly, and never spoke of you without calling you "le bon Turgenev." But why pity her? She had everything life had to offer, and will remain a very great figure.

The good country people wept copiously around the grave. We were up to our ankles in mud in the little village cemetery, and a gentle rain was falling. Her funeral was like a chapter in one of her books.

· · ·

1. A reporter for *Le Figaro.*

◇◇◇◇◇

Three Tales now advanced. "If I have been able to get back to work," Flaubert wrote Maurice Sand on October 31, 1876, "I owe it in part to your mother's good advice. She found the way to reestablish my self-esteem."

◇◇◇◇◇

To Edmond de Goncourt

[Croisset, Sunday, December 31, 1876]

Dear old chap,

May 1877 treat you gently! and among other wishes, may *La Fille Elisa* bring you joy! . . .

Turgenev, too, has lost a good deal of money. Fate seems to be giving our little company[1] a drubbing. Poor us!

The thought that you might have to leave your pretty house in Auteuil made me tremble, for at our age habits are tyrannical: to change them is disastrous. How will you get along this year, with your income uncertain? You and I are so incapable of earning our living! It's a sign of a lofty nature, but it's not always gay.

As for my affairs, they show no improvement: they're in the doldrums. I shall be very hard up for another four years,[2] unless my nephew finds some money. But the main thing is that whatever happens I shall not be leaving Croisset, where more and more I love to be. If necessary, I'd rather give up my Paris apartment, but we've not yet reached that point. Besides, during the past year I have learned (not without effort) to stop worrying about the future. Let whatever befalls, befall: each day is sufficient unto itself.

I'm working excessively hard, though my pages fill up slowly.

Hérodias is now at midpoint. All my efforts go into trying not to make it resemble *Salammbô*. What *will* it be? I have no idea.

I have just read Balzac's *Correspondence*. It shows him to have been a splendid man: one would have loved him. But what a concern for money, and so little love of Art! Have you noticed that he doesn't speak of it a single time? What he sought was Fame, not Beauty. And he was Catholic, legitimist, a landowner, dreaming of the Chamber of Deputies and the Academy; above all, an ignoramus, and provincial to the marrow of his bones: luxury dazzled him. His greatest literary admiration was for Walter Scott. All in all, for me a tremendous figure, but not of the very first rank. His end was lamentable! To die on the very threshold of happiness! Reading his letters was edifying, but I prefer Voltaire's correspondence: the compass spreads a bit wider there.

What more shall I tell you? I'm sturdy as an oak. Yesterday I walked in the woods for three hours. (I never take the air except when I begin to feel stifled.) And last night the moon was so beautiful that I went for a walk again, in my garden, "à la lueur poétique de l'astre des nuits."[3]

Last September I had dizzy spells like yours that alarmed me. They're of no consequence: don't worry about them. Mine came, I think, from wanting to act the young man again during my last stay in Paris. (What's more, I pulled it off.)[4]

Lately I've felt really frustrated at having nobody to talk to about the Germiny case.[5] Poor fellow—I've grown fond of him. And I think France should give him an official compensation: he has kept us all entertained, and every entertainer is a benefactor. That jerking-off of one gentleman by another in a public urinal has entranced the Capital of the Civilized World for a fortnight. Neither the most beautiful works of art nor the greatest scientific discoveries ever generated such excitement when they burst upon the world. The Far Eastern situation is completely overshadowed by this worthy citizen's discharge; and the masturbation with the jeweler (a pearl!) is of greater import than the diplomatic conference at Constantinople. Every Frenchman feels himself haunted by the skin of that man's balls. We feel ourselves entangled in his hair. We're asphyxiated by the effluvia of his urine!

What can we do to rival that fellow? I might apply for a professorship in a Catholic university—but they wouldn't have me. But then I've long been a washout. What an elegy one could make of that [scene in the urinal]! "By the murmuring stream in a sheltered nook . . ."

Adieu, I embrace you tenderly—

Your Old Reliable

1. The "little company" probably refers to "les diners des auteurs sifflés"—dinners to which were admitted only a small group of literary men, all of them friends, whose plays had been booed. "Flaubert was included because of the failure of *Le Candidat*," Daudet

wrote in his memoirs, "Zola for *Le Bouton de Rose*, Goncourt for *Henriette Maréchal*, and I for my *Arlésienne* . . . As for Turgenev, he swore that he had been booed in Russia, and since that was so far away we didn't bother to go and check."

2. The reference is to the future liquidation of Commanville's assets, the sawmill and adjoining property, on which Flaubert continued to pin his hopes. This had for some reason been postponed. As we shall see, the sale would take place not in "four years," but in 1879.

3. "In the poetic radiance of the star of the night." (The offer made on page 113 is repeated here.)

4. In the self-congratulations which sometimes appear in the correspondence following Flaubert's meetings with Juliet Herbert, no hint is ever given as to the identity of his partner.

5. "Eugène Lebègue, comte de Germiny, a prominent Catholic layman, son of the former governor of the Banque de France, born in Paris, July 11, 1841. Appointed in 1875 secretary of the Conseil général de la Seine. He was surprised in a scandalous attitude with a jeweler's apprentice named Chouard in a urinoir in the Champs Elysées [one of those with a 'murmuring stream']. When he was arrested he struck one of the policemen." (Note in Conard edition of Flaubert's *Correspondance*, VII, 370.)

◇◇◇◇◇

That winter Flaubert reveled in the grandeur of Renan's "Prayer on the Acropolis": "Incomparable," he wrote Turgenev, "in its originality and moral stature." (His Rouen friends the Lapierres, he noted, hadn't even cut the pages of the December issue of the *Revue des Deux Mondes* in which it was printed; Princesse Mathilde "didn't understand a word of it," and even Caroline failed to appreciate it and had to be told that it "summarized intellectual man of the nineteenth century.")

In a letter to Caroline written the previous June he had revealed, more or less incidentally, his opinion of Stéphane Mallarmé's *L'Après-midi d'un faune*: "I have received another present, a book from the FAUN, and this book is charming, for it's not by him. It's an oriental tale called *Vathek*, written in French at the end of the last century by an English *milord*. Mallarmé has reprinted it with a preface in which your uncle is praised."

To *Hérodias*[1] (known especially for its description of Salomé's dance before she asks for the head of John the Baptist) Flaubert devoted historical and archaeological research as painstaking as that for *Salammbô*. It was the last of the three tales to be finished. On February 14, 1877— "at three in the morning," as he wrote Madame Roger des Genettes—it was finally recopied.

During April the three stories were printed separately in newspapers. This was the first time since the incriminating and botched serialization of *Madame Bovary* in the *Revue de Paris* and the unsatisfactory appearance of parts of *Saint Anthony* in Gautier's magazine *L'Artiste* that Flaubert had allowed journals to print any of his fiction. Even now he was reluctant, but he needed the several thousand francs. Charpentier published the volume on April 24. (Flaubert had the manuscript bound, and gave it to Edmond Laporte, whom he had been seeing more and more frequently and who had accompanied him on his excursion to find suitable backgrounds for *A Simple Heart.*) A few of the reviews were hostile, but in general even the journalistic reception was more favorable than usual: for the first time Flaubert found himself praised in *Le Figaro,* and to his astonishment the book was recommended in the catalogue of a Catholic bookshop.

It has often been remarked that the three tales reproduce the tonalities of three of the earlier books: that *A Simple Heart* is painted in the Norman colors of *Madame Bovary,* that *Saint Julian* joins *Saint Anthony* in Flaubert's hagiology, and that *Hérodias* is no less exotic than *Salammbô.* When Henri Brunetière, in *La Revue des Deux Mondes,* claimed to find in this aspect of the volume an indication that Flaubert's "invention was flagging," he was quickly taken up by the young Jules Lemaître,[2] writing in *La Revue Bleue.* It was certainly true, Lemaître said, that "apple trees tend to produce apples, and that from a rose bush more roses can be expected."

Both Maurice and Lina Sand wrote to thank Flaubert for their copy of *Three Tales*—Lina, a lover of *Salammbô,* said she had been so entranced while reading *Hérodias* that "she didn't know where she was"—and on August 28, 1877, in reply to another letter from Maurice, Flaubert wrote: "You speak of your beloved and illustrious mother. After yourself, I think there can be no one who thinks of her more than I. How I miss her! How I need her! I began *A Simple Heart* exclusively for her, solely to please her. She died when I was in the middle of my work. So it is with all our dreams."

Three months later he wrote to Mme Roger des Genettes about some of these dreams:

> If I were younger and had the money, I'd return to the Orient—to study the modern Orient, the Orient of the Isthmus of Suez. A big book about that is one of my old dreams. I'd like to show a civilized man who turns barbarian, and a barbarian who becomes a civilized man—to develop that contrast between two worlds that end up by merging. But it's too late. It's the same with my *Battle of Thermopylae.* And *Monsieur le Préfet!* and many others! It's always good to hope, says Martin [in *Candide*]. Desire keeps one alive.

By now he was back at *Bouvard and Pécuchet.*

1. Flavius Josephus and the Gospels were Flaubert's chief sources for *Hérodias.* But again the Rouen cathedral provided inspiration: the sculpture over the left door of the façade, showing Salomé dancing on her hands—as Flaubert, twenty-seven years before, had seen a Nubian girl dancing on her hands at Assuan. At that time, after his Egyptian

and Near Eastern travels, in Perugia with his mother, he had made a note of Perugino's fresco of scenes from the life of John the Baptist.

2. Lemaître, who would distinguish himself as a critic, was then a twenty-four-year-old professor in the lycée of Le Havre, making his first appearances in literary magazines. He and Flaubert met, and Flaubert greatly enjoyed his company. "Jules Lemaître (from Le Havre) is coming to see me on Wednesday," he wrote Caroline on February 6, 1880. "For three days I'll be 'talking literature'—supreme joy! That will soothe me."

IX

The Last Years.
Bouvard and Pécuchet
1877–1880

D URING THE short time now left to him, melancholy and labor
would continue to dominate Flaubert's existence. The melancholy, general though it had long since become, would be constantly
exacerbated by events, especially by those pertaining to the Commanvilles; the present labor—the composition of *Bouvard and Pécuchet*—was
in part a product of misanthropy, and also nourished it. Yet, from letters written in the last weeks of his life, one senses that Flaubert's spirit
was finally eased. The reasons for this, and the constant interplay, at the
time, between principle and circumstance, give a particular tone to the
last scenes of the story.

IN 1864, when he had finished *Salammbô* and was uncertain as to
whether his next novel should be a "book of passion" or the book
about two copy-clerks, one of Flaubert's reasons for postponing the
latter was the "frightful difficulties" he foresaw in "varying the monotony of the effect." There is much comedy in *Bouvard and Pécuchet,* but
readers often do find the book intolerably monotonous; and one suspects that many of them either close it fairly quickly or skim through it.
As a concentration of Flaubert's obsession with human stupidity, *Bouvard and Pécuchet* has been a mine for savants and "explicators." Many
an opinion has been expressed as to whether his two "troglodytes"—
Flaubert sometimes called them his two "wood-lice"—are buffoons
symbolic of mankind, or sympathetic truth-seekers, or a subtle combi
nation of both. Flaubert himself, who in 1875 had written to Mme
Roger des Genettes "Their stupidity is mine, and I'm dying of it," wrote
later to Mme Brainne: "My (secret) aim is to disconcert the reader to
such a point that he goes crazy." Connoisseurs of the absurd are among
the greatest admirers of *Bouvard and Pécuchet.*
  The letters that follow were written during Flaubert's struggle,
against heavy odds, to complete this formidable book—which Turgenev had urged him to make "light," and which George Sand had

congratulated him on abandoning because it "would never have been a success."

ON APRIL 16, 1877, in the Restaurant Trapp near the Gare St. Lazare, a dinner was given by the group of young writers who for publicity's sake had baptized themselves "Naturalists"—Joris-Karl Huysmans, Henri Céard, Léon Hennique, Guy de Maupassant, Paul Alexis, and Octave Mirbeau. The guests of honor were their admired elders—Edmond de Goncourt, Flaubert, and Zola; and the menu (at least as reported in the newspapers) included "Potage purée Bovary," "Truite saumonée à la Fille Élisa," "Poularde truffée à la Saint Antoine," "Artichaut au coeur simple," and so on. Flaubert enjoyed himself that evening as he enjoyed having his young admirers attend his Sunday afternoons. But he had no respect for literary "schools" or for the titles conferred on them. He wrote to Turgenev later that year:

> It's not just a question of seeing. One must order and combine one's perceptions. Reality, according to me, should be only a *springboard*. Our friends are convinced that in itself it constitutes all of Art. Their materialism makes me indignant, and almost every Monday I'm irritated when I read our good Zola's article [in the newspaper *Le Voltaire*]. After the Realists we have the Naturalists and the Impressionists. Such progress! A bunch of jokesters, trying to delude themselves and us into believing that they discovered the Mediterranean.

And to Mme Roger des Genettes:

> My friend Zola is becoming absurd. He wants to "found a school," being jealous of old Hugo's fame. Success has gone to his head, so much more difficult is it to cope with good fortune than bad. Zola's self-confidence as a critic is explained by his inconceivable ignorance. I think that there is no longer any love of Art, Art in itself. Where is there anyone who relishes a good sentence? That aristocratic pleasure is in the realm of archaeology.

His favorite among the young writers—and the only one who was an intimate friend—was causing him concern. He wrote to Turgenev in July:

> I have received a pitiful letter from my disciple, Guy de Maupassant. He is worried about his mother's health and feels ill himself. He finds the Naval Ministry, where he works, so tiresome and deadening that he can no longer write, and the "ladies" are incapable of cheering him up. Besides, since our "ladies"—even more than our institutions—are the envy of all Europe,[1] they are at present in such demand that it's impossible to come near them. After the Exposition there will be twenty thousand of them dead from overwork.

242

1. Flaubert refers to the influx of foreign visitors to the Exposition of 1878 and their enjoyment of the pleasures of "Paree."

◇◇◇◇◇

To Guy de Maupassant

Croisset, August 1878

Bouvard and Pécuchet keeps trotting along. Now I'm preparing the chapter on politics. I've made almost all my notes—I've been doing nothing else for the past month—and I hope to begin writing in about a fortnight. What a book! As for expecting that the public will read a work like this—what madness!

.   .   .

Now let's talk about you. You complain about fucking being "monotonous." There's a very simple remedy: stop doing it. "The news in the papers is always the same," you say. That is a Realist's complaint, and besides, what do you know about it? You should scrutinize things more closely. Have you ever believed in the existence of things? Isn't everything an illusion? Only so-called relations—that is, our ways of perceiving objects—are true. "The vices are trivial," you say; but everything is trivial! "There are not enough different ways to compose a sentence." Seek and ye shall find.

Come now, my dear friend: you seem badly troubled, and that distresses me, for you could spend your time more agreeably. You *must*—do you hear me, young man?—you *must* work more than you do. I've come to suspect you of being something of a loafer. Too many whores! Too much rowing! Too much exercise! Yes, sir: civilized man doesn't need as much locomotion as the doctors pretend. You were born to write poetry: write it![1] *All the rest is futile*—beginning with your fun and your health: get that into your head. Besides, your health will be the better for your following your calling. That remark is philosophically, or, rather, hygienically, profound.

You are living in an inferno of shit, I know, and I pity you from the bottom of my heart. But from five in the evening to ten in the morning all your time can be devoted to the muse, who is still the best bitch of all. Come, my dear fellow, chin up. What's the use of constantly probing your melancholy? You must set yourself up as a strong man in your own eyes: that's the way to become one. A little more pride, damn it! ... What you lack are "principles." Say what you will, one has to have them; it remains to find out which ones. For an artist there is only one: sacrifice everything to Art. Life must be considered by the artist as a means, nothing more, and the first person he shouldn't give a hang about is himself.

... Let me sum up, my dear Guy: beware of melancholy. It's a vice. You take pleasure in affliction, and then, when affliction has passed, you find yourself dazed and deadened, for you have used up precious strength. And then you have regrets, but it's too late. Have faith in the experience of a sheik to whom no folly is unknown! Je vous embrasse tendrement . . .

1. It is not clear whether, at this time, Flaubert really thought Maupassant's gift was for poetry, or whether he encouraged him to write verse chiefly as a means to improve his prose. Maupassant had already had two stories printed in obscure publications.

Very soon after writing the present letter to Maupassant (in which he sometimes sounds like George Sand writing to *him*), Flaubert would succeed in having the young man transferred from his office in the Naval Ministry to a more agreeable post under his friend Agénor Bardoux, now Minister of Education. In his letter of recommendation to Bardoux (May 2, 1878), Flaubert had said he thought Maupassant was destined for "a very great literary future."

To Madame Charles Brainne

Croisset, Thursday, August [1878]

There are moments when I feel *crushed* by this frightful book. I am now studying Politics. What a mine of imbecility! My scorn for those who devote themselves to it grows stronger every day. It ought to be the science of sciences, and instead it's given over to special interests and passions. Moreover, people were stupider in 1848 than today. There's no difference between the Socialists and the Bourgeois; or rather there are nothing but Bourgeois.

Yesterday I was in Rouen, to return books to the library, and it quite undid me—I have never sweated so much in my life. I collapsed in a café (the Café Dubiez), and ordered a beer—abject! abject! Then—horror of horrors—what did I read, while downing that wretched drink, but the *Figaro!* To such a point of degradation am I reduced by a few hours in my native city.

I have written to young Guy to "raise his morale." No answer so far. I think my friend may be slightly lazy. If he worked more, he would be less bored. Life is so abominable that to be swallowed it has to be disguised. If it isn't sweetened with some fabulous drug, one is disheartened. Why so? There are days when happiness seems easy of attainment. And yet, haven't you noticed that without the Concept of Happiness existence would be more bearable? We demand more from it than it can give. There are days like today when I'm sunk in black melancholy. Besides, my penury is getting on my nerves. Money matters are not improving.

Let me end with a pleasant picture. I imagine (since you are taking the waters), I imagine a great room at the baths, vaulted in Moorish style, with a pool in the center. You appear, wearing a long chemise of yellow silk—and with the tips of your bare toes you test the water. *Crac!*

Off with the chemise, and we swim side by side—not for very long, because in the corner there's a lovely divan whereon my dear Beauty re-
clines—and to the sound of the fountain your Polycarp and his lady
friend spend a delicious quarter of an hour. Oh, why don't those things
happen, God damn it? Why? Because there are obstacles to everything . . .

To His Niece Caroline
                [Paris,] Tuesday morning [September 10, 1878]

I have put aside, to show to you, an abominable (but just) article that
appeared in yesterday's L'Evènement against Maxime DuCamp. It inspired me with "philosophical reflections," and I felt like having a
Thanksgiving Mass said, to thank heaven for having given me the taste
for pure Art. By messing about in so-called serious things, one ends in
crime. For Maxime DuCamp's history of the Commune has just caused
a man to be sentenced to penal servitude. A horrible story. Rather it
should be on his conscience than on mine. I felt sick about it all day
yesterday. My old friend now has a sad reputation: this is a real stigma.
If he had loved *style*, instead of loving publicity, he wouldn't be in the
present pass . . .[1]

1. Pierre Ludovic Matillon, chief accountant in the Naval Ministry in Paris, had been
arrested in June 1871 and charged with setting fire to houses in the Rue Royale during
the Commune. After being held for five months he was discharged for lack of evidence
and went to live abroad—some sources say in Antwerp, some in Trieste. His case was
reopened in Paris in 1872, and when he failed to appear he was condemned to death *in
absentia*. In 1876 he proposed returning to France to proclaim his innocence and demand
trial, but was dissuaded. In 1878, when DuCamp publicized his story in his history of the
Commune ("Les Convulsions de Paris," then being serialized in *La Revue des Deux
Mondes*), Matillon did return, and on September 4 was sentenced to penal servitude for
life. His appeal was rejected, but he was released the next year. (Most survivors among
those sentenced for activities during the Commune were amnestied on July 11, 1880.)
DuCamp was castigated in *L'Evènement* and other radical newspapers for his role in the
Matillon affair. In *pièces justificatives* printed in volume III of *Les Convulsions de Paris*, he says
that when Matillon wrote him after reading the installment in the *Revue des Deux Mondes*,
declaring his intention of returning to Paris, he did everything he could to dissuade him.

To Madame Charles Brainne
                [Croisset,] Tuesday night [December 10-11, 1878]

It was out of affection for you, my dear Beauty, that I didn't write. I
didn't want to burden you with the minutiae of my troubles, or rather
my penury. You can do nothing about it, and besides it hurts me to talk
about it. The news is that we are now at the bottom of the abyss, and
things are hopeless. Commanville's sawmill is going to be sold under

deplorable conditions—and then what? God knows what will become of us. Perhaps I'm overly apprehensive. Commanville will earn some money in one way or another. No matter: whatever happens, things won't be gay. My heart is heavy, I assure you. And it isn't the lack of money, and the consequent privations, and the complete absence of freedom I'm condemned to, that madden me. No, it's not those things. I feel spiritually *soiled* by all these sordid concerns, by all this commercial talk. I feel I'm being turned into a shopkeeper. Imagine a virtuous woman made to prostitute herself in a brothel, or a fastidious person being dragged about in a garbage cart, and you have my situation. There's great irony in it, and Providence is being hard on me at the moment. No success whatever, no luck. I wanted to earn a few sous with my *féérie* (a work that I consider remarkable, whatever anyone may say). Dalloz didn't even deign to answer, and had his secretary tell me that it "wasn't suitable for the magazine" but that they would be "glad to have something else of mine."

.   .   .

As for a job, a post, my dear friend, never! never! I refused one offered me by my friend Bardoux. Similarly with the officer's cross of the Légion d'Honneur, which he also wanted to give me. If the worst happens, it's possible to live in a country inn on fifteen hundred francs a year. That's what I'll do rather than take one centime of the government's money. Don't you know this maxim (coined by me): "Honors dishonor; titles degrade; bureaucracy benumbs"? Besides—am I capable of filling any sort of position? After a single day I'd be kicked out for insolence and insubordination. Misfortune doesn't make me more compliant—quite the contrary! More than ever I'm a wild idealist, resolved to die of hunger and fury rather than make the least concession.

I was quite low for several days, but my spirits are improving and I'm working. That's the important thing, after all.

I was touched by your kind thought of me, my poor precious Beauty, but put it out of your mind, I beg you. However, I thank you for the idea, as for a gift . . .

◇◇◇◇◇

Occasionally, in response to Caroline's continued exhortations to economize, he allowed himself a small irony, as in a letter of early January 1879, in which he wrote: "The weather is mild, and Monsieur is burning less wood . . ."

THE COMMANVILLES gave up their Paris apartment, and crowded their furniture into Flaubert's.[1] "If I don't come to Paris," he wrote Guy de Maupassant,[2] "it's because I haven't a sou. That's the entire mystery.

246

Besides, I have no place to stay, since I've turned my apartment over to my niece until her husband's affairs are fully settled—and until we know what's to become of us and what he'll be doing."

Both Commanvilles, it would seem, were now in the habit, in certain situations, of drafting letters for Flaubert to copy, sign, and send—to M. de Fiennes, their Paris landlord; and to Edmond Laporte, who preferred not to be put in closer touch with the Rouen bankers to whom he had given his guarantee.

1. Mme Chevalley-Sabatier, in her book about her aunt mentioned in Appendix I, suggests that this may have been done in part as a precaution against possible seizure of the Commanvilles' "goods and chattels" by creditors following the sale of the sawmill and other property that was now looming.

2. Maupassant had written: "I saw Zola last night, and he told me you wouldn't be coming this winter! This news so surprised and saddened me that I beg you to write me at once whether it's true. To spend the winter without seeing you seems impossible to me. My greatest pleasure of the year was to talk with you every Sunday for three or four hours, and I can't believe the summer can come without my having seen you."

◇◇◇◇◇

To His Niece Caroline

[Croisset, January 18, 1879]

My poor girl

I have just written a letter to de Fiennes following the model you sent me.[1] One more little cup of bitterness! It wouldn't have been difficult to spare me this one. The situation was easily foreseen: a simple visit would have sufficed. But no—your poor husband doesn't seem to me to have a clear sense of justice. De Fiennes is perfectly within his rights, he has been courteous with us, and as thanks we not only don't pay him, but are rude to him.

What I find superb is that Ernest should be indignant with Laporte because he doesn't want to visit Faucon![2] And he accuses him of "turning against him"—a very clever phrase, which would have put us on bad terms with him but which I removed, fortunately. Here I stop. Because I'd have too much to say. No matter. It's odd to think that others always have obligations toward us, whereas we ourselves have only rights.

1. Flaubert had written to Caroline on December 4: "I think that de Fiennes resents [Ernest's] not paying the rent the day it was due. This was certainly improper, and you know I was annoyed, and, to tell the truth, humiliated. When one wants to be respected as a Louis XIV, one doesn't behave like a Louis XI. (Between you and me, this little remissness is inexcusable, because I had just handed over to Ernest the 1400 francs from Delehante [the buyer of the Deauville farm]—that is, the very last remains of my capital. He could have used it to pay *my* debts.) Your fine husband does himself harm in people's eyes by many small turns of behavior he is unaware of."

◇◇◇◇◇

Living and working alone at Croisset, under a roof that needed repair, Flaubert added to his January 18 letter to Caroline: "I satisfy my need for affection by calling in Julie for a talk after dinner and looking at the old black-and-white checked dress Maman used to wear. In the midst of my sadness I continue reading metaphysics for my book—Kant, Hegel, Leibnitz. Not much fun . . ."

The sale of the Commanville assets was postponed, prolonging the uncertainty.

◇◇◇◇◇

To His Niece Caroline

[Croisset,] Tuesday, 2 o'clock [January 21, 1879]

My darling

I was expecting this disappointment. So it didn't surprise me. Yet another delay! "It won't be very long," you tell me. But on whom does it depend? When will we be finished, mon Dieu! When will we have some peace? . . . I long to put it all out of my thoughts, and I am making great efforts of will to do so. But that's impossible. It's becoming an obsession with me.

On Friday and Saturday my mental and nervous state frightened me. I keep mulling over the same recriminations, and constantly wallowing in grief. Then I go back to my books and try to write my chapter. My imagination is aroused; but instead of working on fictitious beings it sets to work on myself, and everything begins all over again.

There's no point in complaining! But there's still less in living! What is my future, now? Who is there to talk to, even? I live alone like an outcast, and the end of my solitude doesn't seem very near; for I'll have to spend two months in Paris this year if I want to finish *Bouvard and Pécuchet,* and during that time you'll be here—so that perhaps I'll not see my poor child till mid-May. As for all three of us living in the little flat in Paris, that is physically impossible—there isn't even a room for the cook. Here at least there's nothing to irritate me; that wouldn't be the case in Paris. Speaking of cooking—what do you do about food?

Today is your birthday, my poor Caro! You were born amid tears—that has brought you bad luck. But I'd better say goodbye now—I'm growing too sentimental. I'm weary of *trying,* though—of straining, of forcing my will: and for what? To what avail? Who is benefiting from all this?

I kiss you tenderly.

Your old uncle

◇◇◇◇◇

Financial strain and mental torment were not all Flaubert had to bear that winter. One night in January, walking along the riverbank in the moonlight, he slipped on a patch of thin ice and fell, breaking a bone in his leg.

◇◇◇◇◇

EDMOND LAPORTE (AND FLAUBERT) TO ÉMILE ZOLA

Croisset, January 30, 1879

Monsieur,

M. Gustave Flaubert asks me to give you his news.

He is suffering from a very bad sprain, complicated by a crack at the base of the fibula. The inflammation is disappearing, but he has been ordered to rest for three weeks. There is no cause for alarm.

"I'm stuck in bed, smoking a pipe and enjoying three consolations:

"(1) The annoyance the success of *L'Assommoir* is causing your fellow writers;

"(2) the story of the curé of Le Vésinet;[1]

"(3) the fact that our Savior will probably soon be gone.[2]

"My greetings to your wife.

"Share this bulletin with Maurice Roux and Hennique."

(Dictated by Flaubert.)

Your faithful servant,

F Laporte

1. The curé of Le Vésinet remains unidentified, but one can imagine the general nature of the "story." Flaubert rejoiced in the turpitudes of worthies, as in the case of the unfortunate Germiny.

2. The imminent forced resignation of the ultraconservative President MacMahon.

TO CLAUDIUS POPELIN[1]

Croisset, February 11 [1879]

... The accident was more serious than was first thought. The fracture of the fibula was nothing, but articulation was appallingly disrupted my foot looked like a pumpkin wrapped in red parchment! It was kept in ice packs for ten days. Fortunately the blood was reabsorbed, and the danger is over. Today I'm at last able to get up, thanks to a dextrin boot.[2]

My spirits have remained excellent—I profited from the occasion to give my poor brain a rest. I'll even tell you that this "misfortune" (as various people have called it) has seemed very slight to me compared with all the others! For during the past three years I have swallowed many a deep and bitter draught. This has even taken my mind off things, and calmed my nerves . . . Don't forget me when speaking with the Princess. Tell her, from me, all the best things you can think of.

1. (1825–1892), painter, enamelist, writer; at this time lover of Princesse Mathilde.

2. "To answer your question about my 'boot,'" Flaubert wrote to Caroline a day or two later, "the leg is wrapped in cotton wool and then in several layers of bandage, and onto this is applied a coat of dextrin (which is a resinous substance made from wheat, I believe). As it dries, this delightful preparation turns as hard as iron, and the leg is guaranteed immovable. I couldn't stand this shackle, and thought I'd die of the pain. Fortin slit it from top to bottom and held it together with strips of bandage, so that my foot and leg are now in a kind of cradle. I've had no pain for twenty-four hours, and am back in my study, making notes on spiritualism and religion."

◇-◇-◇-◇-◇

Flaubert was for a time almost completely immobilized, and for several months his activity would be much curtailed. "My distraction," he wrote to Princesse Mathilde, "consists in watching my dog, who sleeps before my fire, and the boats that pass on the river. I read as much as I can (and not very amusing things—metaphysics and spiritualism); I daydream about my past, like an old man, and then I have much longer thoughts about you, my dear Princess."

Edmond Laporte made himself errand boy, secretary, and nurse, often spending the night at Croisset, and earning from Flaubert the title of "Sister of Charity," or "Little Sister of the Poor."

◇-◇-◇-◇-◇

To His Niece Caroline

. . . Would you believe the following about the Sister? On Monday he left me by the eleven o'clock boat and was to return by the one at six-thirty. As the river road at Couronne was under water, he took off his trousers and waded to the ferry. The Seine was raging. Saint-Martin[1] had been refusing passengers. There's a true friend—who risks drowning, or at least pneumonia, in order not to miss an appointment—which after all could have been dispensed with . . .

1. The ferryman between Croisset and Couronne. In the summer, Flaubert sometimes swam from Saint-Martin's boat.

To Georges Charpentier

Croisset, Sunday [February 16, 1879]

My dear Friend,

I am not "unjust," for I am not "angry" at you and have never been so. Only, I thought that you should have told me at once, straight out, that the proposition didn't suit you.[1] In that case I'd have gone elsewhere. Let's not mention it again, and continue good friends.

At the end of *Saint Julian* I wanted to reproduce the stained-glass window from the Rouen cathedral. It was merely a matter of coloring the plate in Langlois' book. And I'd have liked the illustration *precisely because* it is not an illustration, but a historical *document*. Comparing the picture with the text, the reader would have been puzzled, and would have wondered how I derived the one from the other.

I dislike all illustrations, especially where my own works are concerned, and as long as I am alive there shall be none. *Dixi*. I am just as stubborn about my photograph, and almost broke with Lemerre[2] about it. I'm sorry, but I have principles. *Potius mori quam foedari.*[3]

I'm fed up with *Bovary*. The constant mention of that book gets on my nerves. Everything I wrote after it doesn't exist. I assure you that if I weren't in need of money I'd take steps to see that it was never reprinted. But necessity compels me to do otherwise. So—print away! As for the money, there's no need to send it here. Give it to me when I come to Paris. One observation: you mention a thousand francs for two thousand copies, which means ten sous a copy. It seems to me that you used to give me twelve or even thirteen per copy, but I may be mistaken.

Now something else. Next August 10 my contract with Lévy will expire. The rights to *L'Éducation sentimentale* will revert to me. I'd very much like to get something out of it . . .

I am not unaware of everything my friends have been doing for me lately. I send great thanks to Mme Charpentier, and as many again to you, my dear friend . . .[4]

1. Flaubert had suggested that Charpentier print a deluxe edition of *Saint Julian* for the holiday trade, and he had understood that Charpentier agreed. Instead, the special Charpentier book for the 1878-1879 holidays had been Sarah Bernhardt's *Dans les nuages* [In the Clouds], her account of a balloon ascension she had made with the painter Georges Clairin, who illustrated the book.
2. Under an arrangement with Charpentier, the publisher Lemerre issued inexpensive editions of *Madame Bovary* and *Salammbô*.
3. "Rather death than dishonor."
4. The reason for Flaubert's thanks will be found in the following letter.

To His Niece Caroline

Saturday, 2 o'clock [February 22, 1879]

My Loulou

Here's the real truth. I wanted to keep the story from you, to spare you pain, or at least indignation. The upshot is that I was once again wrong in following the advice of others and mistrusting my own judgment. But I'm incorrigible; I always put my trust in outside opinions, and then find myself in trouble. Here goes:

Early in January, Taine wrote me to say that M. de Sacy was at death's door and that Bardoux wanted to give me his post: 3,000 francs and living quarters.[1] Though I was tempted by the apartment (which is splendid), I replied that the post didn't suit me, because I should be poorer having to live in Paris with a salary of 3,000 francs than I am now at Croisset, and that I should prefer to spend only two or three months in Paris. Moreover, the Princess and Mme Brainne told me that my friends were trying to get me a position "worthy" of me.

Act Two, Monday. The moment you and Ernest were gone, Turgenev put on a solemn face and said: "Gambetta[2] asks whether you want M. de Sacy's post: 8,000 francs and living quarters. You must give me your answer at once." Using eloquence and affection (the latter word is not too strong), and seconded by Laporte, he overcame my distaste for the idea of becoming a civil servant. The thought that I should be less of a burden to the two of you was what really made me decide. After a sleepless night, I told him to go ahead. Everything was to be done quietly, and you were not to be told until all was settled.

Twenty-four hours later I had a letter from Turgenev telling me that he had been mistaken, that the post paid only 6,000, but that he felt he should continue his efforts.

Now Gambetta had promised nothing at all. Goncourt had asked him for a sinecure for me, as had the Charpentiers, who had been quite active about it. They had written to Mme Adam,[3] who was all on my side.

Then came another letter from Turgenev, to say that the post paid not 6,000, but 4,000!

At this point I received a visit from Cordier.[4] He was very helpful and spoke about me to Paul Bert,[5] who said he would do everything for me, and to Père Hugo, who then and there wrote a warm letter recommending me to Ferry.[6]

Then came the article in the *Figaro*[7] and Turgenev's departure for Russia. Shortly before that, I had been warned that Maître Senard,[8] one of the mainstays of the cabinet, was demanding the post for his son-in-law Baudry, who he insisted had first claim.

Last Monday came a letter from Baudry, asking (finally!) how I was and announcing his daughter's marriage. This letter is a model: in it the false friend gives himself away completely. He told me that he himself was taking steps to get M. de Sacy's post, and made no mention of those being taken on my behalf. Taine had spoken to him about it, but (said Baudry) the place wouldn't suit me at all. He also shed some tears over my misfortunes and criticized Bardoux for not giving me the post recently bestowed on Troubat: 3,000 francs and obligatory residence at Compiègne! (Charming thought!) Baudry is an *ass*. If he had written me frankly, and asked me, as a favor to him, to do nothing, my gentlemanly instincts would have obliged me to withdraw from the field. I asked Laporte to answer him that I was too unwell to write, and that I would explain the situation to him when I could once again hold a pen. With a Norman, one has to be a Norman and a half!

That is how things stand now. But I'm sure that Baudry will be appointed,[9] and that I'll look like a fool. I'll be regarded as a blundering schemer: that will be my sole achievement. Furthermore, the article in the *Figaro* will turn Madame Adam against me;[10] and it is already bringing me letters—there was one yesterday from Mme Achille—asking for explanations and requiring answers. A ghastly nuisance. Turgenev has written me from Berlin to apologize. He has no idea of the authorship of that elucubration, which contains some truths and some untruths.

I confess it has all made we weep tears of blood. To have my penury publicized, and to be pitied by those wretches, who talk about my "goodness"! It's cruel, cruel! I've done nothing to deserve it! I curse the day when I had the fatal idea of putting my name on a book! Had it not been for my mother and Bouilhet I would never have published. How I regret it now! I only want to be forgotten, left in peace, never spoken of again. I'm becoming odious to myself. Why can't I die, so that I can be left alone? You asked me to tell you the truth, my dear girl: well, now you have it! My heart is bursting with fury; these insults are too much for me.

It's not enough to have to write to de Fiennes and Faucon and ask them for favors: the *Figaro* has to drag me through the mud for its own political reasons. Well, I had it coming to me. I was a coward. I was false to my principles (for I too have principles), and I'm being punished for it. I mustn't complain, but I'm suffering, and cruelly. This is not a pose. The dignity of my entire life is lost. I consider myself disgraced. Oh, Other People! Always Other People! And all this happened because I wanted not to appear stubborn and proud, because I was afraid of seeming to strike a pose.

. . .

N.B. Popelin will probably be coming to see me next week. He'll have lunch or dinner here, and perhaps spend the night. So send me *the key to the cellar*, immediately. Otherwise I'll have only execrable wine to offer him [11]

1. Silvestre de Sacy (1801–1879), journalist and essayist, had been since 1836 librarian of the Bibliothèque Mazarine, one of the public libraries of Paris, housing special collections and occupying splendid quarters in the building of the Institut de France. The correct figure for Sacy's salary, as the letter eventually specifies, was 4000 francs.

2. Léon Gambetta (1838–1882), leader of the then dominant Republican party, had recently been appointed President of the Chamber of Deputies.

3. Mme Juliette Adam, née Lambert (1836–1936), novelist and essayist, had been a friend of George Sand, through whom she came to admire Flaubert. Her salon was frequented by Gambetta and other leading Republicans. She was the founder of *La Nouvelle*

Revue (1879–1926) and a strong propagandist for "La Révanche" (revenge against Germany for the defeat of 1870). This she lived to see in 1918. Later came the German counter-revenge of 1940 and the requital of 1945.

4. Alphonse Cordier (1820–1897), a life senator from Normandy (département de la Seine Inférieure.)

5. Paul Bert (1833–1886), physiologist and deputy, later Minister of Education.

6. Jules Ferry (1832–1893), who had just replaced Flaubert's friend Agénor Bardoux as Minister of Education.

7. The February 17 issue of the anti-Republican *Figaro* had carried, on its front page, a somewhat garbled gossip item, criticizing the government, and especially Gambetta, for not appointing the needy Flaubert to de Sacy's post.

8. Jules Senard (1800–1885), powerful in the legal profession and as a Republican deputy, had been Flaubert's defense attorney in the *Madame Bovary* trial. We have also met his son-in-law, Frédéric Baudry, the philologist, Flaubert's schoolmate and old friend. Baudry had been a librarian at the Bibliothèque de l'Arsenal from 1859 to 1874, and had then become Sacy's assistant at the Mazarine, at 3000 francs a year.

9. Flaubert did not yet know that on February 17 Baudry had already been appointed. It is generally considered appropriate that he should have been given the promotion.

10. Not at all. Mme Adam remained cordial, sent Flaubert her books, and begged him to give *Bouvard and Pécuchet* to her magazine for serialization. It did appear there, severely pruned, after Flaubert's death.

11. Presumably the wine that Flaubert habitually drank, while Caroline retained the key to his locked cellar.

◇-◇-◇-◇-◇
A few days earlier, Zola had written to Flaubert as spokesman for his disappointed—and apologetic—friends:
◇-◇-◇-◇-◇

ÉMILE ZOLA TO FLAUBERT

Paris, February 17, 1879

I wanted to write you, my friend, to tell you that all of us here have been clumsy in this business concerning you. I beg you: look on these things with the eye of a philosopher, an observer, an analyst. Our greatest mistake was to be overhasty—to remind Gambetta of his promise at a moment when he had been besieged with petitions all week. Since Mme Charpentier was sick in bed, we had to employ Turgenev, who was to leave for Russia the next day and had to act precipitately. The occasion was unfortunate: all kinds of unfavorable circumstances arose. I'll tell you about it in detail later. In a word, I think it required a woman to carry off the business promptly and conclusively. You bear no responsibility for any of it: nothing is lost as far as you are concerned; and if you are willing, all can be put right tomorrow.

As for the article in the *Figaro*, I don't know how they learned about the affair, but I shall find out. The paper acted with its usual indiscretion and brutality, as it has acted toward all of us since its inception. I beg you just to look the other way. In what the *Figaro* said, there is nothing that isn't highly honorable in your regard, and I assure you it will make no trouble for you with anyone. Everybody knows the *Figaro*, and is well aware that you have nothing whatever to do with its editing. We must ignore the press. We must let it lie about us, slander us, compromise us, without letting it trouble us, without even wasting a second of our time in reading what it says. We must pay that price for our peace of mind. I beg you: treat all this with that noble scorn of yours; don't be upset; remind yourself of what you so often say—that there is nothing important in life outside our work.

Reassure us that you remain strong and above it all. None of it matters. A good page written by you is more important than any of it. Your friends were not as clever as the occasion demanded; well, they beg your pardon, and will go no further. If you will allow them to, they will succeed another time. Light your pipe with the *Figaro* article, and wait until you are recovered before resuming work. All the rest is nothing.

I had thought for a moment of coming to see you and telling you all this in person, but I was terribly busy and moreover was afraid of tiring you. All of us here love you—you know that—and it would make us happy to prove it to you at this time. The worst thing is the way you are kept confined to Croisset by your wretched fall. I think you would look at things more coolly if you were among us. Let's hope you'll be able to walk soon and come back to us. And if recovery is delayed, please let us visit you for an hour when you're stronger.

I beg you once again: don't be sad. Rather, be proud. You are the best of us all. You are our teacher and our father. We do not want you to grieve in solitude. I swear to you that today you are as great a man as you were yesterday.

As for your life, I know you are somewhat harassed at this moment, but a solution will be found, you can be sure. Get better quickly, and you'll see that everything will be all right. Je vous embrasse.

To Émile Zola

[Croisset,] Tuesday, 2 o'clock [February 18, 1879]

Mon cher ami

Nobody could be a better chap than you. Thank you for your letter. It put some balm into my blood, as the saying goes.

As soon as I can get down to my dining room, you must come to lunch.

N.B. One word only. What do you mean when you say, ". . . if you are willing, all can be put right tomorrow"?

Je vous embrasse.

◇◇◇◇◇

On March 4, 1879, Commanville's sawmill was sold disastrously. The 200,000 francs it brought (a third of its estimated value) permitted the payment of some obligations; but neither then, nor even after March 24, when land adjoining the mill was sold for 30,000 francs more than expected, could debts be paid completely, and there would be nothing whatever for Flaubert—a mystery he never fathomed. Amid the murky commercial and legal details, a few seem partially decipherable: not only had Flaubert irrevocably lost all he had advanced in his attempt to save the Commanvilles, but for some of the remaining debts he bore a certain degree of responsibility; and payment had been guaranteed by his friends Raoul Duval and Edmond Laporte. Flaubert's letters to Caroline during the next few weeks showed constant concern for his guarantors:

> As for Raoul Duval and Laporte, *what shall we do?* That's what torments me. Answer me on this.

> . . . I'll be heartbroken if Laporte, next May, is obliged to pay Faucon twelve thousand francs or take out a mortgage on his house.[1] He's putting on a brave front, like the gentleman he is. But I see *perfectly well* that the idea of such a mortgage is infinitely galling to him, less because of the cost of getting it and the interest to be paid, than because of "what people will say." He fears it would have an adverse effect on his political position. (That last is conjecture on my part, but I'm convinced of it.) Do you see some way of avoiding this?

> How is it that with these last thirty thousand francs a way can't be found to clear things up completely with Raoul Duval and Laporte? Especially Laporte.

Following the news of this culminating financial disaster, Flaubert learned from Guy de Maupassant, who had been persistent in the Ministry of Education, the answer to the question with which he himself had ended his letter to Zola.

1. It sounds as though Caroline had fallen behind in her annual payments to Faucon, for which Raoul Duval and Laporte stood guarantors, and as though she foresaw incapacity to make them in the future. Raoul Duval was comfortably off, but Laporte was not, and at this moment was in particularly bad financial straits (see Appendix III).

◇◇◇◇◇

[March 7 or 8, 1879]

Mon cher Maître,

I have just been speaking with M. Charmes,[1] and we are in agreement. Everybody, *everybody*, considers the offer of a pension by the Minister to a man of letters a token of esteem. Princes have always given such things to their great men: why shouldn't our government do the same? And has anything changed, to make what was always considered an honor, painful and humiliating in your eyes?

Besides, the Minister wants to do something that will express his interest in you; and since you don't care about an honorific title, he can give you a pension that nobody will know about. That's the way it's usually done. He will sign an order that will be sent directly to the records office. No announcement will be made; it will be communicated to no newspaper. Only four people will know about it—the Minister, his Chef de Cabinet, Charmes and I: plus the despatch clerk and the recording officer of the Ministry.

I inquired about the various libraries. Unfortunately there is none, now, of the kind you want. Pensions for men of letters are taking the place of that kind of sinecure; and librarians are now required to be residents of Paris and to be in their offices every other day. You can see that that wouldn't suit you. Regular attendance is required at Sèvres, at the Beaux Arts, etc.—in all the small libraries, which for that reason are better paid than the large ones.

In short, I think you would be better off with a pension than with any kind of post. A pension is a token of esteem, it causes no trouble, it upsets nobody, makes nobody angry; and you can be sure that no newspaper will protest, so natural will it seem to all.

By accepting a post, you ... enter a hierarchy, you become official. You report to a Director, who in turn reports to the Minister. Nothing of that kind with a pension: it imposes no restriction, it leaves you completely free, and in no way detracts from your dignity. It is a decoration in the form of money rather than a ribbon. You go, or send, to collect it every three months, and that's all there is to it. The day you no longer want it, you write in to say you can do without it, and it will be transferred to somebody else, who probably needs it less than you.

In any case, I have mentioned your scruples and hesitations to Charmes, who will talk about them to the Chef de Cabinet; and I *think* they will offer you a pension, with no attendant publicity. If you absolutely don't want to accept, you will send your "No, thank you," to Monsieur Rambaud, the Chef de Cabinet. Since you have made no move yourself, it's easy for you. I'm eager to know what happens ...

1. François Marie Xavier Charmes (1849–1919), "directeur" at the Ministry of Education.

To Guy de Maupassant

[Croisset,] Sunday, 4 o'clock, 9 [March 1879]

Mon cher ami

Since you *assure* me that this pension will remain unknown to everybody, I resign myself, being driven to it by necessity.

But you say: "It's impossible that any newspaper will protest, the thing will seem so natural to everybody"; and: "I think no publicity will be given the matter." So you are not certain? How reconcile those two statements? And on the other hand, you tell me several times it will be a *secret.*

In short, if I can be *sure,* absolutely sure, that the entire thing will remain between the ministry and me—and only on that condition—I accept with gratitude, and on the condition (as I look on it) that it be a loan, a temporary grant.

This is what I intend to do. Once the pension is granted, and as soon as my brother returns from Nice,[1] I shall ask him for the equivalent of the pension. He, his daughter, and his grandson, who will soon be of age, have among the three of them an income of about a hundred thousand francs. They can perfectly well give me five. In that case, I'd go immediately to the minister and give up the pension. Otherwise I'd have to accept it until the time came when I could return it in a lump sum— i.e. all I had received. I would arrange to do this by taking appropriate measures. You cannot imagine how I suffer from being reduced to these expedients.

. . . To sum up: (1) No official title; (2) No publicity. *Absolute secrecy.* In this way I'll only have to say "Thank you." I trust you absolutely in this. Don't deceive me out of affection, I beg you. Be the guardian of what I consider (rightly or wrongly) my honor—my only wealth.

When I say "secret," I mean that even my most intimate friends (including the Commanvilles)[2] should know nothing. I will divulge it as I think proper.

And I don't thank you, my dear boy: that would offend you. But I embrace you affectionately.

Yours—

Thank M. Charmes for me. What have I done that your minister should be so good to me? I am astonished and moved by this.

1. Dr. Achille Flaubert, Flaubert's older brother, now sixty-six and retired from his post as chief surgeon at the Rouen Hospital, was convalescing at Nice following a stroke. On his return to Rouen, Flaubert made his financial request, and Achille granted it even before Flaubert finished speaking. But almost immediately the doctor's mental condition greatly worsened; he was never able to carry out his intention; and his wife and daughter showed no inclination to do so. Achille Flaubert died in 1882.

2. In a letter to Caroline written the following week, Flaubert would tell her only that

"I have every reason to believe I'm to be offered a pension"—without revealing the source either of the information or the possible pension itself. Perhaps he was apprehensive—not without reason—that the ill-fated Commanvilles might queer things. (He had learned that Caroline, doubtless "from the best of motives," had without consulting him played an interfering role in the fruitless appeal to Gambetta.) He would tell the Commanvilles of his pension only when it had become a certainty (see page 262).

❖-❖-❖-❖-❖

By the end of May Flaubert felt able to travel to Paris.

❖-❖-❖-❖-❖

To Edmond Laporte

[Croisset,] Thursday morning [May 29, 1879]

Mon Chéri

I leave tomorrow by the afternoon express. (What luck if I were to find my Bab[1] at the station!)

Guy wrote me yesterday that my nomination is signed, and that in Paris I'll find 750 francs, my first quarter. So the thing is certain.[2]

And you: what's up?

I count on seeing you in Paris very soon, no? We must give ourselves a "little family celebration": we've certainly earned it.

Quick answer, please, old chap.

Thank you for the magic names.

Your Giant

1. In 1877 Laporte had lost his position as manager of a lace factory in the Rouen suburb of Grand Couronne following the death of its owner, and he had since been unemployed, with diminished resources—one of his reasons for wanting to be relieved of further responsibility in the Commanville affair. With Flaubert's support he had applied for a government post, and was now about to receive official notification of his appointment as factory inspector at Nevers. Both before and after ministering to Flaubert as nurse and secretary he had been helping him with research for *Bouvard and Pécuchet* (most recently, for the chapter on magic). "Bab" would seem to be a Flaubertian shortening of the Turkish *baba* ("father").

2. Actually, although Flaubert's "nomination" for the pension of 3000 francs had probably been decided upon, he would be officially notified only in October (see page 262). This was apparently a normal bureaucratic delay. "You know how much time it takes for the slightest thing of this kind to be done," Maupassant had written him in the spring. If 750 francs, for his first quarter, was really already awaiting him in Paris, it was probably a special advance somehow made available. The reader will recall that Flaubert had other money awaiting him in Paris—a payment he had asked Charpentier to hold for him (see page 251), perhaps to avoid having to "share" it with the Commanvilles.

In further reference to Flaubert's pension, there exist portions of a correspondence between him and Frédéric Baudry concerning a suggestion by Baudry that Flaubert be given the title of "conservateur honoraire" at the Bibliothèque Mazarine, without duties, in addition to a pension. The aim would perhaps have been to make it seem that the pension was a salary—a gesture to his pride. Nothing seems to have come of it: Flaubert's name does not appear in the records of the Bibliothèque Mazarine.

❖❖❖❖❖

Flaubert stayed in Paris until June 25. He still limped badly, and stairs were difficult, but the Commanvilles had gone to Croisset, and he had his apartment to himself. He paid a courtesy call on "his" minister, Jules Ferry, and learned that the support of Victor Hugo had counted strongly for him in the matter of the pension; he did more research for *Bouvard and Pécuchet* in the Bibliothèque Nationale; he was pleased that Charpentier was preparing a new edition of *L'Éducation sentimentale;* he dined out; and, as before, was at home to his friends on Sunday afternoons. They poured in. "Monsieur is overwhelmed by courtesies," he wrote Caroline. "I'm quite surprised. It's evident that many people are glad to see me again, and that of all men I'm not the one least loved by his friends."

What would follow *Bouvard and Pécuchet,* the story of the two "woodlice"? The contrasts of Flaubert's creative temperament were never more apparent: "Do you know what is *obsessing* me now?" he wrote Caroline. "A longing to write the battle of Thermopylae. That idea again has me in thrall."

After spending the summer at Croisset, Flaubert returned to Paris in late August for a few weeks to correct proofs of the new printing of *L'Éducation,* to arrange for publication of Louis Bouilhet's complete poems, and to talk with the composer Ernest Reyer about music for an opera to be based on *Salammbô,* with libretto by Camille du Locle.[1]

1. The following appears in the English-language edition of *Capri, From the Stone Age to the Tourist Age,* by Arvid Andrén (Göteborg: Paul Aströms förlag, 1980), pp. 152–153:

"About 1880, a middle-aged Frenchman came to the island and settled down in the Villa Certosella by the Via Tragara in Capri. He soon became generally known for his recluse living, his shortness and his sharp tongue: the islanders called him variously 'U Francesiello,' 'the English,' or 'The Acid Drop.' No one knew why he settled on Capri and what he had been doing before he came. He was usually seen strutting about in an impeccable Parisian complet, which greatly increased his reputation for being somewhat eccentric. But one day he attracted everyone's attention by appearing in a suit and cape made from the handwoven, rough, and uncolored wool from Amalfi which otherwise was used only by fishermen. No innovation in clothing is so extravagant that it cannot become high fashion. Soon the English and Germans on Capri started appearing in more or less picturesque suits made from the same rustic material. Thus, 'the little Frenchman' gave rise to the production of handwoven wool fabrics on Capri which continued right up until a few decades ago, when machine-made products took over.

"Not until he died in 1903 was it discovered that he, Camille de [*sic*] Locle, had been the director of the Opéra Comique in Paris, that he had composed libretti for a great number of operas, among others the original text to Verdi's *Aïda,* and had launched several other operas, *Carmen* among them, which, however, received harsh reviews and did not become popular until afterwards. Perhaps it was disappointment which made him leave Paris and his career to hide himself on Capri."

Flaubert did not live to hear the Reyer-du Locle *Salammbô,* which had its "world premiere" only in 1890, in Brussels. It would be first sung at the Paris Opéra two years later, and at the Metropolitan Opera House in New York on March 20, 1901. And one wishes, too, that Flaubert, who had delighted in the gulf of Naples on his visit of 1851, might have had the pleasure of "strutting about" with his homespun-clad librettist on Capri—scene of Imperial Roman orgies and other excesses which, as "reported" by Suetonius, may well have entered into the inspiration for certain scenes of his Carthaginian novel.

EARLIER, in 1863–1866, in Russia, the young Modest Mussorgsky (1839–1881) had written a libretto and a voice-and-piano score for six scenes of an opera based on *Salammbô*. After orchestrating three of the scenes he abandoned the project, later using portions of the music in other works, including *Boris Godunov*. Some of Mussorgsky's *Salammbô* music was revised and orchestrated by Rimsky-Korsakov, and can be heard in a recording by the London Symphony Orchestra, conducted by Claudio Abbado (RCA: ARL 1-3988). Mussorgsky's entire score was recently revised, and its orchestration completed, by Zoltán Peskó, and the six scenes, with excellent soloists, were taped live at a concert of the Milan Symphony Orchestra and Chorus of the Radiotelevisione Italiana on November 10, 1980. The two-record album of this performance (CBS Masterworks 79253) includes Mussorgsky's libretto in the original Russian and in English, French, and German translation, and interesting notes by Zoltán Peskó and Rubens Tedeschi. There seems to be no evidence that Flaubert knew of Mussorgsky's *Salammbô*.

Saint Julien would also provide the subject of an opera, *Saint Julien l'Hospitalier, légende dramatique*, music by Camille Erlanger, libretto by Marcel Luguet, first produced at the Paris Conservatory in 1894. A symphonic excerpt from the score, entitled *La Chasse fantastique* [The Fantastic Hunt], became a popular orchestral number after being applauded at one of the Sunday "Concerts de l'Opéra" in 1895. (*Enciclopedia dello Spettacolo*.)

Additional details concerning scores inspired by Flaubertian texts can be found in the article "Flaubert" in the fifth edition of *Grove's Dictionary of Music and Musicians*.

◇◇◇◇◇

To GEORGES CHARPENTIER AND MADAME CHARPENTIER
Friday evening [Paris, September 1879?]

Monsieur Gustave Flaubert presents his respects to M. and Mme Charpentier. He will be proud and happy to appear next Friday in response to their honorable invitation.

He finds the fact that no bourgeois will be present a reassuring prospect. For he has now reached such a point of exasperation when he finds himself in the company of such persons that he is invariably tempted to strangle them, or rather to hurl them into the latrines (if such language be permitted)—an action whose consequences would be embarrassing to the publishing house of Charpentier—which, children and dog included, occupies a large place in his heart.

JULES FERRY TO FLAUBERT

> Ministère de l'Instruction Publique
> et des Beaux-Arts
> Paris, October 3, 1879

To Monsieur Gustave Flaubert
Croisset, near Rouen (Seine-Inférieure)
Monsieur,

I have the honor to inform you that I have decided you should be awarded an annual grant of three thousand francs, payable quarterly, from the funds available in my department for the encouragement of literature, to begin July 1, 1879.

I am happy, Monsieur, to be able to offer you this proof of the interest I take in your work in the field of letters.

> Very truly yours,
> The Minister
> Jules Ferry

◇◇◇◇◇

But the pleasure that those words from Ferry should have given him was blighted by what was the saddest event of Flaubert's old age—the sudden rupture of his long and close friendship with Edmond Laporte.

For both men this was nothing less than a tragedy. The circumstances (outlined in Appendix III) are not entirely clear, but they appear sordid. Apparently it was Caroline who insisted on the break, and the episode takes its place in the last act of the drama we have seen slowly unfolding and which could justly be called, in its effect on Flaubert, "The Curse of the Commanvilles." In this sad affair his loyalty—or subjection—to Caroline was complete; his suffering, acute. Immediately following the lines of his letter dated October 10, 1879, that are quoted in Appendix III, he finally told Caroline about his pension: "This story of Laporte fills me with such bitterness and so utterly spoils my life that I haven't the strength to enjoy a bit of good news that has come my way. Jules Ferry . . . wrote me yesterday that he was granting me an annual pension of 3000 francs beginning last July 1. His letter is ultra-amiable."

His distress overflowed in letters to others. He wrote to Guy de Maupassant from Croisset on October 8, 1879: *"Things aren't going well, my boy.* Something nasty happened recently that has affected my head and my stomach. I'll tell you about it. Suffice it to say that I've seldom been so fed up with existence . . ." And to Mme Roger des Genettes on the same day: "A man I considered my *intimate* friend has recently displayed the most crass selfishness in my regard. This betrayal is excruciating . . ."

December 12, 1879 was Flaubert's fifty-eighth birthday. It was his last, and one of his unhappiest. The winter at Croisset was long, lonely, laborious, and very cold. "The house isn't precisely warm," he wrote Caroline on December 16. "Just to walk through the big dining room is enough to numb you." And on December 21: "Don't come here now: it's too cold. You'd be too uncomfortable, and for Ernest it might even be dangerous. What a winter!"

The struggle to finish *Bouvard and Pécuchet* seemed endless, as he told Mme Adam in a letter dated December 2, 1879: "The first volume will be done this coming summer, but when? And the second will need a good six months more—if I'm not finished myself, before the book!"

◇◇◇◇◇

TO MRS. CHARLES TENNANT[1]

Croisset, Tuesday night [December 16, 1879]

. · .

What this book is? It's hard to say, in few words. The subtitle might be: "On lack of method in the sciences." In brief, I intend to pass in review all modern ideas. Women figure very little, and love not at all . . . I think the public won't have much understanding of it. People who read a book to discover whether the Baroness marries the Viscount will be disappointed, but I am writing for a few special spirits. Perhaps it will be a heavy-handed bit of foolishness? Or, on the contrary, something quite strong? I have no idea. And I am riddled with doubts and utterly exhausted.

. · .

1. Mrs. Tennant had been Gertrude Collier, daughter of a British naval officer stationed in Paris in the 1840s. The Flaubert and Collier families had become acquainted at Trouville at that time, and a correspondence had continued.

TO MADAME ROGER DES GENETTES

[Croisset,] Sunday, January 24, 1880

. · .

Do you know how many volumes I've had to absorb for my two characters? More than fifteen hundred! My pile of notes is eight inches thick. This superabundance of documents has enabled me to be free of pedantry: of that I'm sure.

I'm finally beginning my *last chapter*. When it's done (at the end of April or May), I'll go to Paris for the second volume, which won't take much more than six months. It's three quarters done, and will consist almost entirely of quotations. After which, I'll rest my poor brain, which is at the end of its tether . . .

I haven't suffered from the cold, but have burned eighteen cords of wood, plus a bag of coke a day. I've spent two and a half months absolutely alone, like a bear in its cave, and have come through perfectly well even though seeing no one: I've heard no stupid remarks. Inability to tolerate human stupidity has become a *sickness* with me, and that word is weak. Almost all human beings are endowed with the gift of exasperating me, and I breathe freely only in the desert.

. . .

◇◇◇◇◇

Turgenev, among others, did his best to cheer him.

◇◇◇◇◇

To Ivan Turgenev

[Croisset, December 28, 1879]

Your parcel came last night. The salmon is magnificent—but the caviar makes me groan with voluptuous delight. When shall we eat some of it together? . . . As for Tolstoy's novel,[1] send it in care of my niece. Commanville will bring it to me . . .

1. Turgenev had written to Flaubert on December 27 announcing the despatch of the "comestibles" and also of "a novel in three volumes, by Leo Tolstoy, whom I consider the foremost contemporary writer. You know who, in my opinion, might contest that place." The novel was *War and Peace.*

To Ivan Turgenev

[Croisset, December 30, 1879]

Thanks! triple thanks, O Saint Vincent de Paul of the Comestibles! Upon my word, you treat me like a bardash![1] These dainties are too much! I eat the caviar almost without bread, like jam.

As for the novel, I'm frightened by its three volumes. Three volumes just now, outside my work, is an undertaking. No matter, I'll set to . . .

1. Bardash, a catamite. (O.E.D.)

To Ivan Turgenev

[Croisset, January 21, 1880]

. . . Thank you for getting me to read Tolstoy's novel. It's first-rate. What a painter, and what a psychologist! The first two volumes are *sublime;* but the third falls off badly. He repeats himself and philosophizes: you see the man, the author, the Russian, whereas hitherto there had been only Nature and Mankind. Sometimes he seems Shakespearean. I cried aloud with admiration as I read—and it's a long novel. Tell me something about the author. Is it his first book? In any case, he has *balls!* Yes! it's very strong! very strong! . . .[1]

1. Turgenev replied: "Mon bon vieux, you cannot imagine the pleasure I was given by your letter and by what you say about Tolstoy's novel. Your approval confirms my view of him. Yes, he is very strong, and yet you have put your finger on the spot. He has also conceived a philosophical system at once mystical, childish and arrogant: this has doubly spoiled his second novel (*Anna Karenina*), which he wrote after *War and Peace*, and which also contains some first-class things."

◇◇◇◇◇

Another, much shorter, masterpiece that was sent to Flaubert gave him a different, more personal pleasure, for he could quite properly feel that he had played a role in its success:
◇◇◇◇◇

To Guy de Maupassant

[Croisset,] Sunday, February 1, 1880

I'm impatient to tell you that I consider "Boule de Suif" a *masterpiece.* Yes, young man! Nothing more, nothing less. It is the work of a master. It's quite original in conception, well constructed from beginning to end, and written in excellent style. One can see the countryside and the characters, and the psychology is penetrating. In short, I'm delighted; two or three times I laughed aloud . . .

I have written my schoolmasterly comments on a scrap of paper; consider them. I think they're sound.

This little story will *live:* you can be sure of it. How beautifully done your bourgeois are! You haven't gone wrong with one of them. Cornudet is wonderful and true. The nun scarred with smallpox, perfect! And the count saying "Ma chère enfant"—and the end! The poor prostitute weeping while Cornudet sings the *Marseillaise*—sublime. I feel like giving you little kisses for a quarter of an hour! No, really, I'm pleased. I enjoyed it and I admire it and you.

And now, *precisely* because it is fundamentally strong stuff and will annoy the bourgeois, I would take out two things that are not at all bad but which might bring complaints from idiots because they give the impression of saying "To hell with you." (1) . . . ;[1] and (2) the word *tétons* [tits]. If you do that, even the most prudish taste can find nothing to reproach you with.

Your prostitute is charming. If you could reduce her stomach a little at the beginning you'd give me pleasure.

Ask Hennique to excuse me. I am really overwhelmed by the reading I have to do, and my poor eyes are giving out. I still have a dozen books to read before beginning my last chapter. I'm now in phrenology and administrative law, to say nothing of Cicero's *De officiis* and the coitus of peacocks. You who are (or rather, were) a rustic, have you ever seen these birds celebrate their love-rites?

Certain parts of my book, I think, will be lacking in chasteness. I have an urchin with improper habits, and one of my protagonists petitions the authorities to establish a brothel in his village.

I embrace you more warmly than ever.

I have ideas on how to make "Boule de Suif" known, but I hope to see you soon. I want two copies. Bravo again! Nom de Dieu!

1. Flaubert's first suggestion is incomprehensible in the text.

❖❖❖❖❖

Flaubert's message to Léon Hennique (1851–1935), in the letter to Maupassant, referred to his delay in acknowledging and commenting on *Les hauts faits de Monsieur de Pontbau* [The Great Deeds of Monsieur de Pontbau] (1880), a satire on Romanticism, written in dramatic form, which Hennique, one of the young Naturalists, had sent him. Now he did so, in detail, and he added general observations on Realism and Naturalism.

❖❖❖❖❖

To Léon Hennique

Monday night, [February] 3 [1880]

. . .

This mania for thinking you've just discovered nature, and that you're more true than your predecessors, exasperates me. A storm in Racine isn't a whit less true than one described by Michelet. There is no "True." There are only ways of perceiving. Is a photograph a likeness? No more so than an oil painting, or about as much so.

Down with Schools, whatever they may be! Down with words devoid of sense! Down with Academies, Poetics, Principles! I'm astonished that a man of your worth should still let himself fall into such nonsense! . . .

God alone knows to what point I carry scruples regarding documents, books, information, travel, etc. Well, I regard all that as secondary and inferior. Material truth (or what is called such) must be only a springboard, to help one soar the higher. Do you think me fool enough to believe that in *Salammbô* I gave a true reproduction of Carthage, and in *Saint Anthony* an exact depiction of Alexandrianism? Ah, no! But I'm sure that I expressed the essence of each, as we conceive it today . . .

In brief, to finish with this question of reality, let me propose the following: assume that documents were discovered proving that Tacitus lied from beginning to end. What would that do to the glory and the style of Tacitus? Nothing whatever. Instead of one truth we would have two: that of History, and that of Tacitus . . .

To Madame Émile Husson[1]

[Croisset,] Monday, February 16, 1880

Kiss old Max for me—and then he should do the same to you. And tell him I'm sorry about his nephritis. I'm not always in top form myself; I've greatly aged in the past two years. But fundamentally I'm in sound shape.

As for the Academy, I fear he may fall foul of some machinations, such as happened to Taine the first time he ran. And if Max doesn't make a lot of visits he'll be defeated and remain a perennial candidate. He who desires the end desires the means. But why let oneself in for such nonsense? A great honor—to be proclaimed the equal of Messieurs Camille Doucet, Camille Rousselet, Mézières, Vieilcastel, etc.! Ah, no! Really too modest, to stoop so low . . . Now if being an Academician paid four thousand francs a year, I'd begin lowering myself at once.

Keep all this to yourself, mon Mouton. For nothing is in worse taste than to joke about the Academy. It's like the Legion of Honor. Money, yes: but "honor"—thanks!

1. A cultivated Parisian bourgeoise. She, her complacent husband, and Maxime Du-Camp formed a *ménage à trois* for many years. It was probably her curly white hair that caused her to be called "le Mouton" (the sheep). Through her, DuCamp had sent word to Flaubert that he was seeking election to the French Academy. It was, and remains, the custom for a candidate to visit Academicians and solicit their votes. DuCamp would win his chair without difficulty—a victory greeted with scorn and indignation by the Left, which never forgave him for his writings about the Commune and particularly for the Matillon incident.

To Maxime DuCamp

Croisset, February 27, 1880

First of all, it was good of you to tell me at once about your election, and I thank you for doing so.

Next, why should you think I would be "irritated"? Since it gives you pleasure, it also pleases me; but I am surprised, astonished, stupefied, and keep asking myself: "Why? For what purpose?"

Do you remember a skit that you, Bouilhet, and I once acted out at Croisset? We officially welcomed each other into the French Academy!

... Which "inspires me with curious reflections," as Joseph[1] would have put it.

Ask the Mouton to give the new academician a kiss from me.

Ton vieux.

1. Joseph (Giuseppe) Brichetti had been Flaubert and DuCamp's dragoman during their Egyptian journey in 1849–1850.

◇◇◇◇◇

Victor Hugo and others had at various times proposed to Flaubert that he stand for election to the Academy, but he always refused. When Taine and Renan entered the lists in 1878, he wrote to Princesse Mathilde (June 13): "I find both men exceedingly modest. In what respect can the Academy 'honor' them? When you are somebody, why wish to be some*thing*?" A little later, again to the princess: "You tell me that everybody, in his heart, wants to belong to the French Academy. Not everybody, I assure you, and if you could read my conscience you would see that I am sincere. Such protestations are in bad taste: no matter, I think I'll not give in. This honor isn't the subject of my dreams. What I dream of, men cannot give me. To tell the truth, I no longer have many dreams. My life has been spent grasping at chimeras. No more." And to Mme Roger des Genettes, apropos once more of his refusal to stand for election, he quoted from the proud—if possibly apocryphal—motto of the noble Rohan family:

> Roi ne puis
> Prince ne daigne
> Rohan suis

("King I cannot be, Prince I deign not be, Rohan I am.")

ABOUT THIS TIME, when Flaubert was nearing his death, a change seems to have entered his soul. What it was, one cannot definitely know; but perhaps the very brevity of the sensation of relief engendered by the pension—the almost instant, brutal destruction of that euphoria by the agonizing break with Laporte—made Flaubert resolve to strike out, to seek what pleasure, what comfort, was still possible for him despite the assaults of the Commanvilles.

In March 1880 Commanville had what Caroline reported as good financial news. Flaubert wrote her warmly about it; but even he must have regarded it, after all that had passed, as probably a will-o'-the-wisp; and in the same letter with his congratulations he made requests in which (as Enid Starkie says)[1] "one can sense ... the suppressed irritation of the past years." Apparently the Commanvilles were planning to move in the autumn to new Parisian quarters of their own; Flaubert, looking forward to more frequent visits to the city, demanded relief from the clutter they had made of his flat.

1. In *Flaubert the Master* (see Works of Related Interest).
◇-◇-◇-◇-◇

TO HIS NIECE CAROLINE

[Croisset,] Sunday, 4 o'clock [March 14, 1880]

.   .   .

And now let's talk a little about "our," or rather *my* apartment. Well, Madame, here are my wishes.

I ask to be liberated from my enemy, *the piano,* and from another enemy, which hits me on the forehead—the *stupid hanging lamp* in the dining room. It is very inconvenient when one has something to do at the table. So, since I'll need the table for my copyist this summer, remove that contraption and put back the simple lamp I had in the boulevard du Temple.

Free me also of *all the rest*—it will be simpler!—the sewing machine, the plaster casts, your *beautiful* glass-front bookcase, your chest. I was so inconvenienced by all that, the last time, that I had to keep my clothes on chairs. Store this superfluous furniture at Bedel's until your next move. But arrange things so I'll feel a bit at home and have some elbow room. Since this apartment is no longer to be of use to you, *empty it.* And please note that I'll need it in May and June, and that I'll probably be back there in September.

.   .   .

◇-◇-◇-◇-◇

He sent out invitations to a small festival at Croisset, to include Georges Charpentier, a few fellow writers whom Charpentier published, and his own "disciple":
◇-◇-◇-◇-◇

TO GUY DE MAUPASSANT

[Croisset,] Wednesday night [March 24, 1880]

My dear fellow,

I don't yet know what day Goncourt, Zola, Alphonse Daudet, and Charpentier are coming here for lunch or dinner and perhaps the night. They are to decide this evening, and I shall know on Friday morning. I think it will be Monday.[1] So if the condition of your eye permits, betake yourself to one of the aforesaid characters, find out when they are leaving, and come with them.

Assuming that all of them spend Monday night at Croisset, since I have only four beds available you will occupy the maid's room—she is absent at the moment.

Note: I have been hearing so many silly and implausible things about your illness that I should like very much, purely for my own satisfaction, to have you gone over by *my* doctor, Fortin. He is a simple health officer, but I consider him excellent.

Further observation: if you haven't the cash for the trip, I have a superb double louis at your service. A refusal on grounds of delicacy would be an insult to me.

Last item: Jules Lemaître, whom I told that you would recommend him to Graziani,[2] will call at your office. He has talent and is a real scholar, *rara avis*, worthy of a better post than the one he has at Le Havre.

He too may come to Croisset Monday; and since I intend to get you all drunk I have also invited Fortin, to "heal the sick."

The festival will be lacking in splendor if I don't have my disciple.

Your old
Gustave Flaubert

1. They arrived on Easter Sunday, March 28.
2. Probably Anton Graziani (1820–1906), "Chef de Division" in the Ministry of Justice.

◇–◇–◇–◇–◇

Edmond de Goncourt wrote about the Easter visit in his *Journal* for March 28:

> Maupassant meets us with a carriage at the Rouen station, and Flaubert welcomes us at the house, wearing a broad-brimmed hat and short jacket, with his big behind in pleated trousers, and his kind, affectionate face.
>
> It is really very beautiful, his place—I hadn't remembered it too well. The enormously wide Seine, with the masts of invisible ships passing by as though against a backdrop in a theatre; the splendid tall trees, their shapes tormented by the sea winds; the garden with its espaliers, the long terrace-walk facing full south: these all make it a fit dwelling for a man of letters—for Flaubert—after having been, in the eighteenth century, the country house of a community of Benedictines.
>
> The dinner is very good: a turbot in cream sauce that is truly a marvel. Many wines of all kinds; and we spend the evening telling broad stories that make Flaubert burst into laughter that is like a child's. He refuses to read from his novel—he can't, he's "all in."

And we retire to bedrooms that are rather cold and contain a number of family busts.

To the end, the Commanvilles did their best to spoil things.

❖❖❖❖❖

To His Niece Caroline

[Croisset,] Tuesday, 10 A.M. [March 30,] 1880

My Loulou

Do you understand anything about the enclosed letter? More threats! I'm beginning to get used to them, and since I defy anyone to seize my "property whether real or personal," I remain calm.

I absolutely did not know that I had borrowed fifty thousand francs. Who is M. Legendre? Whom should I consult about this, your lawyer in Rouen, or the one in Paris?

This letter from M. Mesnil has been sent on to me from the rue Murillo. Do what you think proper, as you undoubtedly have instructions.

My reception went off *admirably!*

To His Niece Caroline

[Croisset,] Thursday [April 1, 1880], April Fool's Day, 6 P.M.

Darling,

. . . I continue to receive legal documents addressed not only to me, but to others, including the servants! I don't know who has garnisheed the salary of your poor gardener (because of sums he does *not* owe, it seems). In all this I see only one thing: persecution of *me* by fate. Nothing in the world has ever been more intolerable to me. You would have to be in my skin to understand. Whenever anybody mentions money to me, I experience the aesthetic sensation of a person who has been flung into a Latrine!

It was not 400 francs that I advanced, at your husband's request, to Suzanne [the cook-housekeeper at Croisset], but 500. In addition, I gave her, quite apart from the ordinary house expenses, in order not to confuse accounts, 100 francs to pay in full for my reception last Sunday.

Your husband swore by all the gods that by mid-April he would reimburse me those 500 francs! (Note that last winter I paid 300 francs for wood and 300 francs for good wine.) If I advance you 500 more (which I will certainly do), and if it is impossible to reimburse me for that and for the rest, how am I to live in Paris this summer?

On the fifteenth of this month, we must find money to pay the quarter's rent. However, since I am "a man of order," whatever people may say, I have enough, now, to cover everything. So don't worry, poor kitten; but you *must* learn to be a little more regular about things. Because,

271

regarding these matters my nerves are at the end of their tether. Tuesday was made wretched—spoiled—by that letter from M. Mesnil.

. . .

To Ivan Turgenev

[Croisset,] Wednesday, April 7 [1880]

Mon bon cher vieux

I rejoice in the thought that in about a month I'll be seeing you . . .[1]

Did your ears burn on Easter Sunday? Here we drank a toast to Turgenev, regretting his absence. The following clinked their champagne glasses to your good health: first your humble servant, then Zola, Charpentier, A. Daudet, Goncourt, my doctor Fortin, and "that dirty-minded little Maupassant," as Lagier[2] calls him. Apropos of Maupassant, his condition isn't as serious as I thought; he has nothing organically wrong, but the young man is gouty and rheumatic to the nth degree, and totally neurotic.[3] After dining here, the aforesaid gentlemen spent the night, and left the next day after lunch. I was adamant about not reading them anything from *Bouvard and Pécuchet*.

Pradier, when he was working at the Invalides in 1848, used to say: "The Emperor's tomb will be my own," so exhausting did he find the task.[4] I can say: "It's time to reach the end of my book—otherwise, I know whose end will come." Frankly, I'm sick and tired of it. It's turning into a chore, and I still have three months to go, not counting the second volume, which will take me six. All in all, I'm afraid the result may not reward all the effort, and I feel so weary that the dénouement may well be anemic and botched. I've got to the point of scarcely knowing what I'm doing; every bone in my body aches, I have stomach cramps, and I scarcely sleep. But enough moaning.

Here are my plans: I hope to be in Paris about May 10, to remain until the end of June; then return to Croisset for two months to make the lists that will comprise most of my second volume; then back to Paris in September for a long stay . . .

My strongest indignation at present is directed against Botanists. Impossible to make any of them understand a question that I find very clear.[5] You'll see this for yourself, and will be amazed by the lack of *judgment* in those brains.

Try to find a few minutes to write to me: that would be good of you. And don't be too long about coming back here to all of us. A great embrace to you . . .

1. Turgenev was still in Russia.
2. The actress Suzanne Lagier (1833–1893), free and easy in life and language; friend of Flaubert and the Goncourts, and the subject of many a scabrous entry in the latters' *Journal*.

3. Limited contemporary medical knowledge apparently prevented Fortin, as well as other doctors, from recognizing Maupassant's early syphilitic symptoms.

4. James Pradier (1792–1852) had executed busts of Flaubert's father and sister. Readers of Volume I may recall that it was in Pradier's studio, where Louise Colet was posing, that she and Flaubert first met, in 1846. The twelve colossal figures of Victories surrounding Napoleon's tomb in the Invalides were in fact Pradier's last works.

5. For a passage in Chapter X of *Bouvard and Pécuchet.* In his indefatigable researches, Flaubert was seeking not only "exceptions to the rule" in botanical classification, but "exceptions to exceptions." He was to write Caroline on April 28 that Maupassant had found the answer for him by consulting "the professor of Botany at the Jardin des Plantes."

To His Niece Caroline

[Croisset,] Sunday night [April 18, 1880]

My Loulou,

. . . This morning I sent your husband yet another summons I have received from a process-server! If this is a bet, to see whether I'll die of pure rage, it's about won. Useless to say more about it, surely? I ask for no explanations, but, in heaven's name, give me some peace! Let me have some peace, and let this persecution stop!

.   .   .

Zola, Céard, Huysmans, Hennique, Alexis, and my disciple have sent me *Les Soirées de Médan,*[1] with a very pleasant collective inscription. I suppose Guy will have sent you a copy (unless he doesn't have one). I have reread "Boule de Suif," which I continue to consider a masterpiece.

.   .   .

1. This volume, in which "Boule de Suif" was first published, contained a preface by Zola, and one story by each of the writers named by Flaubert. All of them, for purposes of "publicity," labeled themselves "realist" or "naturalist." Each story recounted an episode of the Franco-Prussian War. The title, "Evenings at Médan," refers to Zola's house at Médan on the Seine, where the younger writers often gathered. " 'Boule de Suif' dwarfs the rest of the volume," Flaubert wrote Maupassant. "The title of the book is stupid." *Les Soirées* was expertly publicized and sold well.

❖❖❖❖❖

Maupassant's first and only volume of poetry, *Des Vers,* was published a week after *Les Soirées de Médan.* It was dedicated "To Gustave Flaubert, the illustrious and fatherly friend whom I love with all my heart, the irreproachable master whom I admire above all others."

❖❖❖❖

TO GUY DE MAUPASSANT

[Croisset, April 25, 1880]

Mon Jeune Homme,

You are right to love me, for this old man cherishes you. I read your volume at once—of course I was already familiar with three quarters of it. We'll go over it together. What pleases me especially is that it is personal. No chic! No pose! Neither parnassian nor realist (nor impressionist, nor naturalist).

Your dedication stirred up in me a whole world of memories: your uncle Alfred, your grandmother, your mother; and for a while this old man's heart was full, and there were tears in his eyes.

Save me everything that appears about "Boule de Suif" and about your volume of verse . . .

◇◇◇◇◇

Flaubert's last feast of St. Polycarp was celebrated at the Lapierres' in Rouen on April 27, 1880. This year it was embellished with a nonexistent orchestra and some farcical messages concocted by Maupassant.
◇◇◇◇◇

TO HIS NIECE CAROLINE

[Croisset,] Wednesday [April 28, 1880]

The St. Polycarp celebration left me speechless! The Lapierres surpassed themselves! I received more than *thirty* letters, sent from different parts of the world! and three telegrams during dinner. The Archbishop of Rouen, several Italian cardinals, some garbage collectors and members of the floor-waxers' guild, the proprietor of a shop selling religious statuettes, etc.—all sent me their greetings.

As presents, I was given a pair of silk socks, a foulard, three bouquets, a wreath, a portrait (Spanish) of St. Polycarp, a tooth (relic of the saint); and a box of flowers is on its way from Nice! An orchestra had been hired, but failed to put in an appearance. Letters from Raoul Duval and his two daughters. A poem by Mme Brainne's son. All the letters (including Mme Regnier's) were adorned with the likeness of my patron saint. I was forgetting a menu composed of dishes all named for my books.

Really, I was touched by the trouble everybody had taken to give me a good time. I suspect my disciple of having had a large hand in the farcical goings-on.

I'm glad you admire "Boule de Suif"—a true masterpiece, no more, no less: it stays in one's mind.

.   .   .

Ten days from now, will I have reached the point I'd like to attain before leaving my dear old Croisset? I doubt it. And when will the book be finished? That's the question. If it is to appear next winter, I haven't a minute to lose between now and then. But there are moments when I feel I'm liquefying like an old Camembert, I'm so tired. But a week spent chatting with "l'altière Vasthi"[1] will relax me.

. . .

1. See Appendix I, page 283.

To Maurice Sand[1]

[Croisset,] Tuesday morning [April 1880]

My dear Maurice

No: *omit* "Cruchard" and "Polycarp," and substitute for those names whatever you please. The public mustn't have our all: let's reserve something for ourselves. That seems to me more fitting (*quod decet*).

You don't say whether the edition will be complete? Ah! your dear mother—how I think of her, and how I need her! Not a day when I don't tell myself "If she were here, I'd ask her advice."

Until May 8 or 10 I'll be at Croisset. So—whenever you want to come you'll be welcome.

I embrace you all, from the oldest man to the youngest girl.

"Cruchard" to you.
"Polycarp" to the human race.
"Gustave Flaubert" in literature.

1. Maurice was preparing an edition of his mother's letters; Flaubert had sent him all those in his possession.

To Guy de Maupassant

[Croisset, May 3, 1880]

. . .

Eight printings of the *Soirées de Médan? Three Tales* had four. I'm going to be jealous.

You'll see me at the beginning of next week.

. . .

Guy de Maupassant to Ivan Turgenev

Paris, May 25, 1880

Dear Master and Friend,

I am still prostrated by this calamity, and his dear face follows me everywhere. His voice haunts me, phrases keep coming back, the disappearance of his affection seems to have emptied the world around me.

At three-thirty in the afternoon on Saturday, May eighth, I received a telegram from Mme Commanville: "Flaubert apoplexy. No hope. Leaving at six." I joined the Commanvilles at six o'clock at the station; but stopping at my apartment on the way I found two other telegrams from Rouen announcing his death. We made the horrible journey in the dark, sunk in black and cruel grief. At Croisset we found him on his bed, looking almost unchanged, except that his neck was dark and swollen from the apoplexy. We learned details. He had been very well during the preceding days, happy to be nearing the end of his novel; and he was to leave for Paris on Sunday the ninth. He looked forward to enjoying himself—having, he said, "hidden a nest-egg in a pot." It wasn't a very large nest-egg, and he had earned it by his writing. He had eaten a very good dinner on Friday, spent the evening reciting Corneille with his doctor and neighbor, M. Fortin; had slept until eight the next morning, taken a long bath, made his toilet, and read his mail. Then, feeling a little unwell, he called his maid; she was slow in coming, and he called to her out the window to fetch M. Fortin—but he, it turned out, had just left for Rouen by boat. When the maid arrived she found him standing, quite dizzy but not at all alarmed. He said, "I think I'm going to have a kind of fainting fit; it's lucky it should happen today; it would have been a great nuisance tomorrow, in the train." He opened a bottle of eau de Cologne and rubbed some on his forehead, and let himself down quietly onto a large divan, murmuring, "Rouen— we're not far from Rouen—Hellot—I know the Hellots—" And then he fell back, his hands clenched, his face darkened and swollen with blood, stricken by the death he had not for a second suspected.

His last words, which the newspapers interpreted as a reference to Victor Hugo, who lives in the Avenue d'Eylau, seem to me unquestionably to have meant: "Go to Rouen, we're not far from Rouen, and bring Dr. Hellot. I know the Hellots."

I spent three days beside him. With Georges Pouchet and M. Fortin I wrapped him in his shroud. And on Tuesday morning we took him to the cemetery, from which one has a perfect view of Croisset, with the great curve of the river and the house he so loved.

The days when we consider ourselves happy don't atone for days like those.

At the cemetery were many friends from Paris, especially his younger friends, *all* the young people he knew, and even some whom nobody knew; but not Victor Hugo, nor Renan, nor Taine, nor Maxime DuCamp, nor Frédéric Baudry, nor Dumas, nor Augier, nor Vacquerie, etc.

That's all, my dear master and friend. But I shall have many more things to tell you. We shall attend to the novel when the heirs have settled their affairs. You'll be needed for everything.

I wrote the very day of the calamity to Mme Viardot, asking her to tell you, because I didn't know your address in Russia. I preferred you should learn this sad news from friends rather than from a newspaper.

I shake your hands sadly, mon cher maître, and hope to see you soon.

Your entirely devoted

GUY DE MAUPASSANT

◇◇◇◇◇

The circumstances of Flaubert's death are known to us through those words by Maupassant.

Maupassant himself was to die insane eleven years later—a victim, at forty-three, of general paresis, one of the forms that can be taken by syphilis in its tertiary stage. Flaubert—who in a number of letters in the first volume of the present work refers to treatments for venereal infection, and to symptoms that are clearly syphilitic—was spared the prolonged wretchedness of such an end. But in modern medical opinion it was probably the same insidious disease, in its tertiary stage, that killed him, at the age of fifty-nine.

Drawing to its close, the nineteenth century thus bore away, as victims of its cruelest realities, one of its most powerful, and one of its most spirited, interpreters.

APPENDIX I

Flaubert's Niece Caroline

Flaubert's niece Caroline, one of his most frequent correspondents in the later part of his life, was named for her grandmother and her mother (Flaubert's mother and sister). Two months after Caroline was born, her mother died of puerperal fever. Her death came soon after that of her and Gustave's father, Dr. Achille-Cléophas Flaubert. The baby's father, Émile Hamard, had recently lost his own mother and brother, and in the tragic atmosphere of the household he soon showed signs of mental derangement. The child was brought up by her maternal grandmother (Mme Flaubert, Flaubert's mother), by Flaubert himself, and by English governesses—with one of whom, Juliet Herbert, Flaubert would have a long intimacy.

When Caroline superintended the publication of the first edition of Flaubert's general correspondence, in the late 1880s and early 1890s, she prefaced it with an account of her upbringing and her relations with her uncle. These introductory "Souvenirs intimes" are charming and informative, but leave much unsaid—and, as we know, Caroline suppressed many passages in the letters themselves. Some of the missing facts are supplied in another memoir, *Heures d'autrefois*, written later in her life. This she left unpublished on her death in 1931, and portions of it were printed, with commentary (not all of it reliable) by *her* niece, Mme Lucie Chevalley-Sabatier, only in 1971, in a volume entitled *Gustave Flaubert et sa nièce Caroline*.

From this and other sources we learn of the young girl's loneliness as she grew up almost entirely without companions of her own age; of the considerable culture she acquired from reading prescribed by Flaubert and from his conversation; and of her love, in late adolescence, for Johanny Maisiat, a young artist who had been engaged to give her drawing lessons. Mme Flaubert and the Flaubert relatives in Rouen quickly took alarm (Maisiat was "unsuitable," apparently something of a "bohemian"); and, deciding that an early, safe, bourgeois marriage was essential, they brought forward Ernest Commanville, a successful thirty-year-old lumber importer of Rouen and Neuville (near Dieppe). Intellectually there was nothing about Commanville to interest a seventeen-year-old girl who had been educated by Flaubert, and clearly she was not otherwise attracted to him. Nevertheless, the family promoted his candidacy without mercy, and the anguish of the bullied Caroline is pathetically mirrored in Flaubert's letter to her of [December 23, 1863]. (Her reply, written the next day, is no more mature than one might expect: "You'd always come to see me, wouldn't you? Even if you found my husband too 'bourgeois,' you'd come for your Liline's sake? You'd have your own room, with big armchairs, the kind you like," and so on.)

Flaubert seems to have taken no further steps in the matter beyond the affectionate expressions of "understanding" in his letter: much future grief might have been avoided had he successfully encouraged Caroline in her hesitation. She finally agreed to the marriage on securing from her grandmother a foolish promise that Commanville would be asked to agree that "there would be no children." After the wedding, still in her bridal dress, Caroline thanked her husband for his acceptance of that condition, only to learn that Mme Flaubert had simply not delivered the unrealistic message. The Commanvilles' Venetian honeymoon was a torment for both. Flaubert remained ignorant for years of the intensity of Caroline's unhappiness in her marriage.

For a time the Commanvilles seem to have lived rather largely, with a house at Neuville, a flat in Rouen, and a house in Paris. In *Heures d'autrefois* Caroline says that she was never "unfaithful" to Commanville, but that another infatuation was the reason she left France for England during the early months of the Franco-Prussian War. She does not reveal the name of her suitor. (M. Lucien Andrieu, secretary of the association "Les Amis de Flaubert" at Croisset, is at present investigating the possibility that he was Charles Henri Léon Rivoire, younger brother of two of Flaubert's "three angels," who was approximately Caroline's age.) He seems to have joined the army, and she could hope to correspond with him more freely from outside France. There is a certain irony here: Commanville seems to have been more or less aware of the situation, and encouraged his wife's departure for England, where she would be farther from her suitor. As the correspondence shows, Flaubert, apparently ignorant of all this, was puzzled both by Caroline's departure and by her husband's acquiescence in it.

After the war, despite painting lessons in Paris and the acceptance of some of her work by the Salon (thanks in part to Princesse Mathilde Bonaparte and other influential friends of her uncle's), despite dinners, the theatre, and other distractions, neurotic illness gradually overtook Caroline. Health spas were prescribed; and it was during one of her stays at Bagnères-de-Luchon during the summer of 1872, where Flaubert had accompanied her, that she told her uncle the story of her marriage, infatuation, and renunciation. (Rivoire had gone to Algiers, where he died, unmarried, on May 2, 1872.) By this time Caroline had sought consolation and counsel from a fashionable, "liberal" Dominican priest, Père Henri Didon, whose importance in her life Flaubert only now came to understand.

Commanville's lumber business suffered badly from the war. By the terms of her marriage contract under the dower system, Caroline could not legally pay debts contracted by her husband, and in 1871 the Commanvilles embarrassed Flaubert by persuading him to ask Princesse Mathilde to lend them 50,000 francs. The princess's lawyers advised her not to do so. In 1872 Caroline's capital came to include the house at Croisset, inherited from her grandmother with the proviso that Flaubert be allowed to spend the rest of his life there. The traditional Church advice to a troubled wife—"trust your husband"—had doubtless been part of Père Didon's counseling.[1] Loyal, therefore, to Commanville, who was "managing" Flaubert's own modest capital (actually, drawing on it constantly for his own purposes), Caroline displayed a hardness toward her uncle that was perhaps in part reluctant. She urged him to live more economically. The Commanville Paris house and Flaubert's pleasant flat in the rue Murillo were given up, and two small contiguous apartments were taken at the far end of the Faubourg St. Honoré.

Things went from bad to worse. In 1875 Commanville's creditors agreed to accept 35 percent of their claims rather than press for bankruptcy. To pay them in part, Flaubert sacrificed his only property, a farm at Deauville that was his chief source of income. Pending the sale of the sawmill and adjoining property, the bankers Faucon, Pécuchet, et Cie, of Rouen, who either were creditors themselves or represented the creditors, consented to accept 50,000 francs of the remainder in annual installments, to be paid by Caroline from her personal income. Because this was in fact illegal, they insisted on guarantors, and at Flaubert's plea his friends Raoul Duval and Edmond Laporte agreed to guarantee 25,000 francs each. Flaubert's anguish over this transaction arose from several causes. He feared that he and his beloved niece might be reduced to penury despite his sacrifice of the Deauville land that had come to him from his mother and held many memories; and that a way might be found to sell Croisset itself, despite the terms of his mother's will. It disgusted him that he should be involved in sordid business affairs and be called on to involve his friends as well.

In 1879, after four years of uncertainty, the Commanvilles' last hope, that the sale of the mill and adjoining property might realize more than enough to cover their remaining liabilities, was dashed. They gave up their Paris apartment and moved into Flaubert's, adjoining; Caroline sold silver inherited from an aunt; she gave drawing lessons and painted portraits and fans. Only during the last year of his life (1879–1880) did Flaubert regain a degree of financial comfort, thanks to a modest government pension. This was augmented by a minor commercial success with his volume *Three Tales* and by the reprinting of his earlier books. However, he continued to be persecuted by the creditors with whom Ernest Commanville had involved him. To the Commanvilles he sacrificed also a precious friendship, that of Edmond Laporte (see Appendix III).

The correspondence reflects Flaubert's constant concern for Caroline: he always remained devoted to her, even though during his last years his affection was sorely tried, and perhaps somewhat impaired,[2] by her steady reinforcement of her husband's financial demands. For her sake he remained on good terms with the rapacious Commanville, and to the end of his life did his incompetent best to suggest persons who might advance still more money to pay pressing creditors. Concerning his complaints about the Commanvilles' harassment, Mme Chevalley-Sabatier says: "Flaubert perhaps did not remember"—yet perhaps he did—"that he had, in this case, a certain responsibility. Had he forgotten Caroline's sobs and anger as she sought to refuse a marriage that her grandmother and uncle succeeded in imposing on her?"

Along with the sale of Croisset, one of Caroline's first concerns following Flaubert's death was to see to the publication of *Bouvard and Pécuchet*—that is, of what Flaubert had considered the first volume, left completed except for the final chapter. She and Maurice Sand together prepared portions of the Flaubert-George Sand correspondence for publication in *La Nouvelle Revue* in 1883–1884. In the latter year, a volume containing 122 of Flaubert's letters to George Sand was published by Charpentier, with a foreword by Guy de Maupassant.[3]

From 1886 to 1893 Caroline supervised the first edition of her uncle's general correspondence, omitting most passages reflecting unfavorably on her husband and herself, and—at Père Didon's insistence—many which showed Flaubert at his racy and irreverent best.[4] With the aid of Louis Bertrand, Caroline also published several volumes of Flaubert's youthful works that had hitherto remained in manuscript.

Ernest Commanville died in 1890. Enjoying a steady income from the worldwide sale of her uncle's works, Caroline moved to the south of France and built a house at Antibes which she christened Villa Tanit, from the name of the goddess in *Salammbô*.[5] In 1900 she married Dr. Franklin Grout, who until his retirement had been director of the celebrated private asylum founded by Dr. Esprit Blanche in Passy, where Maupassant had spent his last demented years. In 1907 she published a volume of Flaubert's letters to herself—again, many of them incomplete. She was widowed for the second time in 1921 and died at Antibes in February 1931. She bequeathed Flaubert's most important manuscripts and his correspondence to various French libraries; other manuscripts and some of Flaubert's personal belongings were sold at auction.

Caroline's personality as revealed in Flaubert's letters and in her own memoirs is a blend of the pathetic and the imperious. She had been completely deprived of a mother's affection, and barely knew her demented father; she was adored by her grandmother and uncle, and though often rebellious against their strict discipline, she knew it to be loving. At seventeen, her heart was broken when this accustomed authority suddenly showed itself ruthless, forcing her into a repellent marriage. From that time, with a momentary faltering when a likely suitor appeared as tempter, duty, "honor," and materialism ruled her, attended by neurasthenia, the consolations of religion, and a demeanor that many found cold. She could certainly be remorseless when she chose—to Flaubert among others. In his later letters her uncle took to calling her "l'altière Vasthi," after the haughty queen in the book of Esther. (For the impression that Caroline in her old age made on a sensitive, cultivated, talented—"innocent"—American woman, the reader may consult Willa Cather's charming essay, "A Chance Acquaintance," in her volume *Not Under Forty*. The two women met by chance at Aix-les-Bains during the last year of Caroline's life.)

Caroline's company and her letters were an incalculable boon to Flaubert, despite the distress that she and Commanville caused him. Her greatest services to us were the preservation of Flaubert's manuscripts, the publication of his youthful writings, and her edition, faulty though it was, of his correspondence. For Caroline's censoring of the latter, Mme Chevalley-Sabatier asks us to forgive her: "Let us not forget that we are in 1887."

It is perhaps comprehensible, as well, on grounds other than chronology. A consciousness of her role as reflected in the letters, and of her inability to present her own story in extenuation, no doubt weighed with her. Her role, as it touches Flaubert, is a painful one. And while certain of her actions are indefensible, it is ultimately impossible to judge her. In his preface to Mme Chevalley-Sabatier's memoir, Jean Bruneau adds his voice to hers in urging us to "understand" Caroline. This note is a brief attempt to do so.

1. The Church apparently retains this position in the present century. A Monsignor who is a professor of nineteenth-century history and literature, when asked by the present editor to comment on these remarks concerning Caroline's situation, replied: "I do not know what else can be said except a reference to St. Paul's injunction to wives that they be obedient to their husbands."

2. His friend Raoul Duval, who had witnessed much, being close to the scene, expressed this opinion in a letter to Maxime Ducamp, September 26, 1881. (J.B.)

3. Other editions of the Flaubert-Sand correspondence have since followed, most recently the admirable volume of 422 letters edited by Professor Alphonse Jacobs, published by Flammarion in 1981.

4. This, too, has been followed by many other editions, culminating in that of the Bibliothèque de la Pléiade (Gallimard) being prepared by Jean Bruneau, two volumes of which, out of a projected four, have already appeared at this writing.

5. This might be considered Caroline's second close connection with a Carthaginian name. The first had been a curious verbal coincidence: *Didon*, the name of her spiritual director, is the French form of *Dido*—name of the legendary queen and founder of the Punic city.

"Reply to a Friend"
by
George Sand

August, 1871—Nohant[1]

What! You want me to stop loving? You want me to say that I have been mistaken all my life, that mankind is contemptible, hateful, has always been so and always will be? And you reproach me for my anguish, calling it weakness, childish regret for a lost illusion? You say that the populace has always been savage, the priest always a hypocrite, the bourgeois always craven, the soldier always a brigand, the peasant always stupid? You say you have known all this since youth, and you rejoice in never having doubted it because that has spared you disillusionment in later life. You have never been young, then. Ah! You and I are very different, for I have never stopped being young—if to persist in loving is a sign of youth.

How should I isolate myself from my fellow beings, from my fellow countrymen, from my race, from the great family in whose bosom my private family is merely as one ear of corn in the earthly field? And if only this ear could ripen in a safe place, if only one might, as you say, live for a few privileged beings and withdraw from all the rest! But that is impossible, and your fine intelligence is adapting itself to a supremely unreal Utopia. In what Eden, in what fantastic El Dorado, will you hide your family, your little group of friends, your intimate happiness, so that the lacerations of society and the disasters of the country will not reach them? If you want to be happy through a few, then those few, your heart's elect, must be happy in themselves. Will they be? Can you guarantee them the slightest security?

Will you find me some refuge in my old age, which is drawing to its close? What do I care now about death or life for myself? Supposing that we die entirely, that love does not follow us into the other life, are we not tormented until our last breath by the longing, the imperious need, to assure the greatest possible happiness of those we leave behind? Can we go serenely to our rest when we feel the earth quaking, ready to engulf all those for whom we have lived?

To live along happily in the bosom of one's family despite everything

285

is without doubt a great good, relatively speaking—the sole consolation that one could, or would, enjoy. But even supposing that evil from without does not penetrate into our homes—an impossibility as you well know—I could never agree that we should reconcile ourselves to a source of public misery.

Everything that has come about was foreseen . . . Yes, of course. I had foreseen it as clearly as anyone! I saw the storm brewing; I was aware, as were all thinking people, of the unmistakable signals of the cataclysm. As you watch a sick man writhe in pain, is it any consolation that you are knowledgeable about his disease? When lightning strikes, are we any the calmer for having heard the thunder long before?

No, no, one doesn't isolate oneself, one doesn't sever the ties of blood, one doesn't curse and despise one's kind. Humanity is not an empty word. Our life is made of love, and to stop loving is to stop living.

The populace, you say! The populace is you and I: there is no escaping that. There are not two races; nowadays inequalities due to class distinctions are only relative and usually illusory. I don't know whether you have ancestors who were in the upper reaches of the bourgeoisie; as for me, on the maternal side my roots spring directly from the people, and I feel them ever alive in the very depths of my being. We all have such roots, no matter how much their memory may be obliterated: the first men were hunters and shepherds, then farmers and soldiers. Brigandage triumphant gave birth to the first social distinctions. There is perhaps no single title not acquired by the shedding of human blood. We must certainly endure our ancestors when we have them; but are those remote trophies of hate and violence a glory in which even the least philosophical mind can find a basis for presumption? "The populace is always savage," you say. I say, it is the nobility that is always ferocious.

Certainly, together with the peasant, the nobility is the class most obstinately set against progress, and thus the least civilized. Thinkers should congratulate themselves on not belonging to it; but if we are bourgeois, if we are the descendants of serfs and forced laborers, can we love and make reverence before our fathers' oppressors? No! Whoever denies the people degrades himself and displays to the world the shameful spectacle of apostasy. Bourgeoisie! If we want to rise again and recreate ourselves as a class, we have only one possibility: to proclaim ourselves the people, and struggle to the death against those who claim to be our superiors by divine right. For having failed to maintain the dignity of our revolutionary mandate, for having aped the nobility, usurped its insignia, adopted its playthings, for having been shamefully absurd and cowardly, we no longer matter, we are nothing: the people, who should be at one with us, spurn us, and would oppress us.

The populace savage? No: nor is it stupid. But at present it suffers from being ignorant and foolish. It is not the Parisian populace who massacred the prisoners, destroyed the monuments, and tried to set fire to the city. The Parisian populace comprises all who remained in Paris following the siege, since anyone with even the most modest means hastened to breathe the air of the provinces and embrace their absent families after the physical and moral hardships of the blockade. Those who stayed in Paris were the merchant and the workman, those two agents of labor and exchange without whom Paris would cease to exist. They are what directly constitutes the populace of Paris: a single, homogeneous family, whose relations and solidarity cannot be destroyed by political folly. It is now recognized that the oppressors in the turmoil were a minority. Thus the Parisian populace was not inclined to violence, for the majority displayed only weakness and fear. The movement was organized by men already inscribed in the ranks of the bourgeoisie and no longer sharing in the ways of life and the needs of the proletariat. These men were propelled by hatred, by thwarted ambition, deluded patriotism, fanaticism without an ideal, sentimental folly, or natural evil—there was something of all that in them, and even certain tenets of doctrinal pride unwilling to back down in the face of danger. They certainly did not rely on the middle class, which trembled, fled, or hid. They were forced to summon the real proletariat, who had nothing to lose. Well, that proletariat eluded them for the most part, divided as it was into very different shades of opinion, some wanting disorder for their own profit, others dubious of the consequences of involvement, most ceasing to reason because troubles had grown extreme and lack of work forced them to march into battle for thirty sous a day.

Why should you think that this proletariat, confined within Paris, and numbering at most eighty thousand soldiers of hunger and despair, represents the French populace? It doesn't even represent the Parisian populace, unless you want to maintain the distinction I reject, between the producer and the exploiter.

But I want to persist, and ask you on what this distinction rests. On more—or less—education? The dividing line is illusory. If you find men of cultivation and learning at the uppermost level of the bourgeoisie, and savages and brutes at the lowest grade of the proletariat, there nonetheless remains a vast number of people in between—intelligent and wise proletarians on the one hand, and, on the other, bourgeois who are neither wise nor clever. The majority of civilized citizens dates from yesterday, and many who can read and write have mothers and fathers yet living who can barely sign their names.

So it would be simply a greater or lesser amount of acquired wealth that would classify men into two distinct camps? In that case one wonders where the populace begins and where it ends, because affluence shifts every day: one man goes down in ruin, another comes into a fortune; roles change; he who was a bourgeois this morning will rejoin the proletariat this afternoon; and the proletarian of the moment will turn into a bourgeois if he finds a purse or inherits from an uncle.

Surely you see that these labels have become pointless, and that the task of classification, by whatever method, would be insoluble.

Men are above or below each other only in possessing more or less reason and morality. An education that develops only self-indulgence is inferior to the ignorance of a proletarian who may be instinctively and habitually honest. Compulsory education, which we all desire out of respect for human rights, is nevertheless not a panacea. Evil natures will discover in it merely more ingenious and better disguised ways to do wrong. Like all things misused by man, it will be both poison and antidote. The search for an infallible remedy for our ills is illusory. We must all seek, day by day, every means at hand. Today our only thought in practical life must be for improving ways of life and reconciling interests. France is in her agony, that is certain; we are all sick, all corrupt, all ignorant, all disheartened: to say that this was fated, that it must be so, has always been and always will be, is to recite again the fable of the pedagogue and the drowning child. One might as well say, straight out: "It's all the same to me." But if you add: "It doesn't concern me," you are mistaken. The deluge approaches, and death is gaining on us. In vain will you be prudent, and withdraw: your refuge will be invaded in its turn, and as you perish with human civilization you will be no more philosophical for not having loved than those who threw themselves into the flood to save a few shreds of humanity. They are not worth the trouble, those shreds: so be it! They will perish in any case: that is possible; we shall perish with them: that is certain. But we at least shall meet death as warm and living beings. I prefer that to a hibernation in ice, to an anticipated death. Besides, I could not do otherwise. Love does not reason. If I asked you why you have a passion for study, you could explain it no better than those with a passion for idleness could explain their laziness.

So you think me shaken in my convictions, that you preach me detachment? You tell me that in the newspapers you read some fragments by me that reveal a change in my ideas; and those newspapers which quote me benignly do their best to think me newly enlightened; whereas others, who do not quote me, perhaps believe that I am deserting the cause of the future. Let politicians think and say what they will. Let us leave them to their critical assessments. I have no need to object, no need to answer. The public has other matters to discuss than my personality. I have a pen; I have an honorable place for free discussion in a great newspaper; it is rather for me, if I have been incorrectly interpreted, to explain myself more clearly when occasion presents itself. To speak of myself as an isolated individual is something I do as infrequently as possible: but if you think me converted to false notions, I must say this to you and to others who interest themselves in me: Read me as a whole, and do not judge me by detached fragments: a mind independent of party requirements necessarily sees the pros and cons, and the sincere writer tells both, without concern for the blame or approval of partisan readers. However, every rational being maintains some consistency, and I think I have not departed from mine. In me, reason and feelings are always at one in making me repulse whatever seeks our reversion to infancy—in politics, in religion, in philosophy, in art. My feelings and my reason contest more than ever the concept of fictitious distinctions, the inequality of condition that is imposed as a right conferred on some, as a loss deserved by others. More than ever I need to raise what is low and lift what has fallen. Until my heart ceases to beat, it will be open to pity, it will espouse the weak, rehabilitate the despised. If today it is the populace who are under foot, I will hold out my hand to them; if they become the oppressor and the executioner, I will say they are cowardly and odious. What is this or that group of men to me, or these proper names that have become badges, or those personalities that are slogans? I recognize only wise men and fools, the innocent and the guilty. I need not wonder where my friends are, or my enemies. They are where the maelstrom has cast them. Those who have earned my love, yet do not see with my eyes, are no less dear to me for that. The thoughtless abuse of those who have abandoned me does not make me consider them my enemies. Any friendship unjustly withdrawn remains intact in the heart of the innocent. Such a heart is above empty pride; it knows how to await the rebirth of justice and affection.

Such is the rightful and simple role of a conscience not yoked by personal interest to the interests of a party. They who cannot say as much for themselves will surely succeed in their chosen sphere if they have the skill to avoid everything inimical to it; and the greater their talent in that direction, the more readily will they find means to requite their passions. But never summon them before history, to bear witness to absolute truth. From the moment they make a trade of their opinion, their opinion is worthless.

I know some tender, generous, and timorous souls who at this terrible moment of our history reproach themselves for having loved and served the cause of the weak. They see but one point in space, they think that the populace they loved and served no longer exists, because in its place a horde of bandits, followed by a little army of frenzied men, has momentarily taken over the theatre of the struggle. These good souls must make an effort to tell themselves that what was good in the poor, and of concern in the forsaken, still exists; it is only no longer apparent, political turmoil having driven it from the stage. When such dramas are enacted, those who rush in recklessly are the vain or greedy members of the family, and those who let themselves be dragged in are the idiots. That the greedy, the idiotic, and the vain exist by the thousand in France is something that no one can doubt; but there are as many of them, and perhaps more, in other countries. Only let there arise one of those all too frequent occasions that give rein to evil passions, and you will see whether or not other nations are better than we. Wait and see the German nation at work—that nation whose armies have just displayed brutal appetites in all their barbarous crudity, and you will see the nature of its unchained fury! The insurgent populace of Paris will strike you as sober and virtuous by comparison.

This must not be a so-called crumb of comfort: we shall have reason to pity the German nation for its victories, as we pity ourselves for our defeats, because for them this is the first act of their moral dissolution. The drama of their abasement has begun; they are working for it with their own hands, and matters will go very quickly. All those huge materialistic organizations in which right, justice, and respect for humanity go unrecognized are colossi made of clay, as we ourselves have discovered to our cost. Well, the moral abasement of Germany is not the future safety of France; and if we are called on to return evil for the evil she has done us, her defeat will not restore us our life! It is not by bloodshed that races are revitalized and rejuvenated. Some vital breath can still issue from the corpse of France; that of Germany will be a source of pestilence for all Europe. A nation whose ideals have died does not live on. Its death fertilizes nothing, and those who breathe its fetid emanations are struck down by the same pestilence that killed it. Poor Germany! The cup of Eternal wrath is spilt on you as on us; and while you reel in drunken joy, the philosophical spirit grieves for you and prepares your epitaph. This pale, torn, bloody thing called France still grasps a fold of the starry mantle of the future, while you drape yourself in a soiled flag that will be your shroud. Past grandeurs no longer belong in the history of men. It is all over with kings who exploit their peoples, all over with exploited peoples who consent to their own degradation.

That is why we are so ailing, and why my spirit is weary.

But it is quite without scorn that I survey the degree of our wretchedness. I do not wish to believe that this holy country, this cherished race, all of whose harmonious and conflicting chords vibrate within me, whose qualities and faults I love despite everything, all of whose responsibilities good and bad I choose to accept rather than disdain—no: I do not wish to believe that my country and my race are stricken unto death. I feel it in my suffering, in my mourning, even in my hours of deepest melancholy; I love; therefore I am alive: let us love and live.

Frenchmen, let us love one another! My God, my God! Let us love one another or we are lost. Let us destroy, deny, annihilate politics, since politics divides us and sets us in arms against each other: let us ask none what he was, or what he wanted, yesterday. Yesterday, everyone was mistaken; we must know what we want today. If it is not liberty for all and fraternity toward all, then let us not seek to solve the problem of equality: we are not worthy to define it, we are incapable of understanding it. Equality does not impose itself; it is a free plant that grows only in fertile soil, in healthy air. It takes no root on the barricades: we know that now! There, it is at once trodden down by the victor, whoever he may be. Let us have the desire to establish it in our way of life, the will to consecrate it in our ideas. Let us give it, for a start, patriotic charity, love! It is insane to think one can issue from a battle with respect for human rights. Each civil war has exacted and will exact its penalty.

Oh wretched International! Is it true that you believe the lie that force has primacy over right? If you are as multiple, as powerful, as one imagines, is it possible that you profess destruction and hatred as a duty? No: your power is then a phantom, born of fear. A great number of men of all nations could not deliberate and act on a principle of evil. If you are the savage arm of the peoples of Europe, something like the Anabaptists of Münster, like them you will destroy yourself with your own hands. If, on the contrary, you are a great and legitimate fraternal association, your duty is to enlighten your adherents and denounce those who debase and compromise your principles. I yet would like to believe that your body includes many men who are hard-working and humane, and that these men suffer and are ashamed to hear bandits take your name. In that case, your silence is foolish and cowardly. Have you not a single member capable of protesting ignoble crimes, idiotic principles, mad frenzy? Your chosen leaders, your administrators, your inspirers—are they all brigands and cretins? No! It is impossible! There are no groups, no clubs, no crossroads where the voice of truth could not make itself heard. Speak out! Justify yourselves! Proclaim your gospel! Disband and reconstitute, if there is discord among you. Hurl an appeal to the future, if you be something more than the barbarian invasions of antiquity. Tell those who still love the people what they must do on its behalf; and if you have nothing to tell, if you can utter no word of life, if the iniquity of your mysteries is sealed with fear, then renounce all hope of sympathy from noble souls, find your nourishment in the scorn of honest men, and have it out with the jailer and the police.

All France has been waiting for the word: the word of your destiny, which might well have decided her own. She has waited in vain. In my naiveté I too waited. Even while censuring the means, I did not want to prejudice the goal. There has always been a goal in revolutions, and the revolutions that fail are not always those least well grounded. Patriotic fanaticism seemed the first sentiment underlying this struggle. Those lost children of the democratic army would perhaps refuse to subscribe to an inevitable peace that they considered shameful: Paris had sworn to be buried in her own ruins. The democratic populace would force the bourgeois populace to keep its word. They seized the cannon; they were going to turn them against the Prussians. It was mad, but it was splendid . . . But no! The Commune's first act is to adhere to the peace; and throughout its entire administration it voices not one protest, makes not the slightest threat, against the enemy. It conceives and commits the dastardly act of destroying, under the enemy's eyes, the column commemorating that enemy's defeats and our victories. What it hates is the power derived from universal suffrage, and yet it invokes that suffrage in Paris, in order to establish itself. It is true that it does not obtain the vote: it dispenses with its desired appearance of legality and functions by brute force, invoking no right except that of hatred and scorn for everything other than itself. It preaches "positive social science," whose sole repository it claims to be, but not a word of which appears in its deliberations or decrees. It declares it has come to deliver man from his shackles and prejudices, and immediately it exercises unchecked power and threatens death to anyone not convinced of its infallibility. While claiming to revive the tradition of the Jacobins, it assumes the papacy of society and makes itself into a dictatorship. What kind of republic is that? I see nothing life-giving in it, nothing rational, nothing that is or could be constitutional. It is an orgy of self-styled renovators, who possess not an idea, not a principle; not the least solidarity with the nation or outlook to the future. Ignorance, cynicism, and brutality—that is all that emanates from this self-acclaimed social revolution. The unleashing of the lowest instincts, the debility of shameless ambitions, and the scandal of flagrant usurpations—that is the spectacle we have just witnessed. As a result, this Commune inspired the most ardent political men, those most devoted to democracy, with the uttermost disgust. After vain attempts, they realized that no conciliation was possible where principles did not exist; they withdrew from the Commune in distress and sorrow; and the next day the Commune declared them traitors and ordered their arrest. They would have been shot had they remained in its hands.

And you, my friend, you want me to see these things with stoical indifference! You want me to say: "Man is created thus: crime is his expression, infamy his nature"?

No: a hundred times no. Humanity is indignant with and within me.

We must not dissimulate that indignation, which is one of the most passionate forms of love, nor must we attempt to forget it. We must make immense efforts of brotherhood to repair the ravages of hate. We must exorcise the scourge, wipe out infamy with scorn, and inaugurate by faith the resurrection of our country.

George Sand

1. Published in *Le Temps*, October 3, 1871.

The Broken Friendship:
Flaubert and Laporte

From the correspondence, and with some light from other sources, it is possible to piece together an outline of the sad story of Flaubert's break in 1879 with Edmond Laporte, one of his few surviving close friends.

Laporte had repeatedly helped Flaubert with research, accompanied him on a tour of Normandy to find appropriate settings for *Bouvard and Pécuchet*, fetched him home from Switzerland after the "failure" of *The Temptation of Saint Anthony*, stood coguarantor for his nephew's debts, and nursed him after his accident. Flaubert called him his "Sister of Charity," along with many another affectionate nickname, and he was the only friend to whom Flaubert gave one of his manuscripts—the bound pages of *Three Tales*. As late as July 3, 1879, Flaubert wrote to him: "What's this, my dear fellow? You say that you are 'perhaps' my best friend? I'm crossing out 'perhaps' and writing 'certainly' instead."

A portion of Flaubert's letter to Caroline of January 18, 1879, makes it evident that he nevertheless allowed his nephew, Ernest Commanville, to use him, up to a point, for the purpose of harassing Laporte concerning renewal of the guarantee the latter had made in 1875. In September 1879 Commanville increased his pressure on Laporte. But Laporte, for at least two good reasons—his own reduced circumstances (he had himself been forced to accept a loan of 500 francs from Flaubert), and increased distrust of Commanville—knew that he must not, and could not, renew. Although he foresaw the possible consequences, he wrote to Commanville expressing his regrets. Whereupon Commanville, employing his usual method, persuaded Flaubert, who was incapable of refusing any service that might conceivably benefit Caroline, to beg Laporte to change his mind. On September 27 and 28, 1879, Flaubert wrote Laporte pleading letters (not included in the present volume), dense with commercial language obviously not his own. They make pathetic reading, especially in contrasting passages where Flaubert attempts to introduce his own usual tone of jaunty friendship. "Me no understand what keeps you from signing," the second letter ends. "Whatever you may decide, old fellow, nothing will be changed between the two of us; but before deciding, I beg you to reflect seriously."

Laporte wrote Flaubert on September 30, 1879:

> This is just what I feared, my good Giant. You have been made to intervene in a discussion from which you should have been excluded. I cannot accept you as judge in a matter concerning which your friend and your nephew are of different opinions. If we tell you all our grievances and justifications, what will happen? You will have to decide against one of us, and your affectionate relations with that one could be spoiled. So let me discuss this business with Commanville alone. If some temporary unpleasantness should result, at least you won't have to take sides. You must know, my dear Giant, that I shall always love you with all my heart.

To Commanville Laporte remained firm in his refusal; whereupon Caroline sent Flaubert a letter about which nothing is known except what can be gathered from Flaubert's replies.[1] He wrote Caroline on October 8*:

> I would very much like to know whether Faucon has wound things up with Laporte. It is *impossible* for me to work—to write, that is—in the intellectual state into which your deplorable story has plunged me. I can't stop thinking about it. I'm even more exasperated than tormented. I don't even dare go to Rouen (where I should see the oculist and the prefect and go to the library) lest I run into Laporte, not knowing how to act with him or what to say. So now I have to wait on Faucon's caprices to regulate my personal conduct!

And on October 13:

> I have just received a letter from Laporte. He has been at Couronne since Friday night, and counts on seeing me at the Prefect's dinner today. The tone is friendly, as before. Not seeing me there, he'll come here this week, I'm sure. Will he have received Faucon's letter between now and then? What shall I say to him? I'm confused and distressed. When will I ever be calm? When will I be left in peace, once and for all?

What was the "deplorable story" that Caroline related? And what role had been played by Faucon, the Commanvilles' banker-creditor, whose "caprices" Flaubert had to take into consideration in determining his "personal conduct"?

By "personal conduct" Flaubert can only have meant his conduct toward Laporte; and what that was is quickly told. Flaubert apparently never spoke or wrote to Laporte again—although, as we shall see, in his unhappiness he would have liked to.

A note in the 1954 *Supplément* to the Conard edition of Flaubert's correspondence (probably written by René Dumesnil, one of the editors of the *Supplément* and Laporte's former son-in-law) states that the Commanvilles, furious at Laporte's defection, extracted a promise from Flaubert that he break with his friend. If such was the case, then Flaubert's complaint about having to regulate his personal conduct according to Faucon's caprices makes it appear that the Commanvilles may have acted on orders from that banker, in whose power they now were; and that Flaubert's compliance—reluctant, it would seem—would have had the purpose of sparing them possible trouble with their creditor.

One previous December 31, during the years of their friendship, Laporte had spent the night at Croisset in order to be the first to wish his friend a happy new year. In 1879, probably on December 30, he sent a note:

> My old friend,
> Whatever feelings you may have been induced to have toward me, I don't want the New Year to begin without sending you all my affection and good wishes. Have no fear of accepting them: they come from someone who is perhaps your best friend. Je vous embrasse.
>
> E. Laporte
>
> My best respects to Mme votre nièce.

Flaubert wrote Caroline on December 31*: "By way of New Year's greeting, guess who has sent me a letter, received this morning. Monsieur Laporte! I enclose copy of same. What do you think of it? I'll not answer him, of course." And on January 4*: "You don't say anything about the letter from Laporte I sent you a copy of?"

Early in February, a portentous legal document arrived at Croisset. Ever since Flaubert had allowed himself to become involved in the Commanvilles' affairs, his letters to them had abounded in complaints about the flood of official forms that poured in on him: he hated the sight of them, understood none of them, and invariably turned them over to Commanville to deal with. By now his exasperation was close to the boiling point, and seeing on these most recent legal pages the name Laporte (now doubtless spoken only with abhorrence by the Commanvilles), along with the claim that he, Flaubert, was in some way liable for the sum of 13,000 francs, it overflowed in two letters, the second of which sounds almost mad. On February 5 he wrote Commanville*:

> You must have received, last night, a big envelope containing a legal summons for the thirteenth of this month? I have barely

skimmed through it, and what I understand is that it comes from Laporte ... I'm surprised that he doesn't pay me back my 500 francs before claiming 13,000 more ...

And the next day, to Caroline:

> The summons from the chivalrous Laporte shocked me, I confess. It's as though someone spat in my face. I haven't read it because of the handwriting and the length, but I saw my name several times on *stamped legal paper!* And from the last lines I understood the meaning. (You know the effect legal documents have on me.) Ah, he's going rather far, that gentleman ... It has put me into a torment again. Much as I try to be "lofty," as you say you are, in my view of the human race, this pains me nonetheless ... What I count on doing when things are finally cleared up (and it can't be long now) is to show Monsieur le Conseiller Général that I have Mohican blood in my veins, and that I can roar as loudly as any bear in its cave. The letter I shall send him will bring a good price later, if he keeps it. The rhetoric of that future letter is interfering with my work on *Bouvard and Pécuchet*, so I want to write it as soon as possible.

The terms of the summons received by Flaubert are unknown, and there is no certainty that it originated with Laporte. Flaubert, who "hadn't read it," but "understood it from its last lines," was almost certainly mistaken in taking it to mean that Laporte was suing him for 13,-000 francs. And perhaps the Commanvilles, even if they allowed him to retain that misapprehension, thought it best to dissuade him from writing to Laporte about his "Mohican blood": in any case, no such letter is known to exist.

On February 22* Flaubert wrote to Caroline that he was brooding about Laporte and the situation; on March 27* he wrote her: "Received the five hundred francs from Laporte, with a *pitiful* letter. It forms part of the dossier, and we'll decide together what my conduct should be."

Thus it would seem that Flaubert, despite everything, still envisaged the possibility of a reconciliation. But there was none: the Commanvilles, one may be sure, saw to that.

Laporte made one last appearance, in a scene that is not without its irony. The other male affection of Flaubert's later years had been Guy de Maupassant; there is no indication that relations between Maupassant and Laporte were anything but harmonious; together, they had supplied Flaubert with what he had said he longed for, in his letter of January, 1873 to Madame Regnier: "something nearer the heart." The day following Flaubert's death Laporte came to Croisset, wanting to pay his respects. It was Maupassant, delegated by Caroline, who went to the door—we do not know with what degree of willingness—and told Laporte he was not welcome.

1. Of the passages from Flaubert's letters to Caroline and Ernest Commanville included in this appendix, all or parts of those marked with an asterisk were omitted from editions of Flaubert's correspondence published during Caroline's lifetime.

In certain editions of the correspondence Caroline included a note: "Business difficulties had arisen between M. Laporte and my husband. This initiated a coldness between M. Laporte and my uncle, which ended in complete rupture." René Descharmes, an editor of the Conard edition of the correspondence (1926–1933), reprinted that note with a comment: "The truth is that there were never 'difficulties' of any kind between Flaubert and Edmond Laporte, his faithful friend until his death; but only what M. Lucien Descaves, very familiar with the facts, has properly called 'the consequences of a petty intrigue.' We have seen in earlier letters the services rendered by Laporte to Flaubert, or rather to his nephew Commanville and his niece, at the time of Commanville's financial disaster. The loss of Laporte's friendship was one of the last sorrows of Flaubert's life."

It might also be mentioned that among the many letters to Flaubert bequeathed by Caroline to the Institut de France, she included only one from herself.

APPENDIX IV

The Pavilion at Croisset

Flaubert died in May 1880. In a letter dated June 11, 1881, to Madame Roger des Genettes, preserved with other Flaubertiana in the Bibliothèque Lovenjoul at Chantilly, Caroline Commanville wrote: "We have sold Croisset, my husband was never well there,[1] and the property was a heavy charge on us. We were offered a good price for it . . . With only a few days' notice I had to leave all my childhood memories behind me, and—what was even dearer to me—those connected with my beloved uncle, and this seemed to me like a second death."

The house, with its gardens, terrace, old poplars, and Flaubert's beloved tulip tree, was at once demolished, and in 1882 a distillery (later transformed into a paper factory) opened on the site.

By chance, there survived beside the factory a small pavilion, dating from the seventeenth century, which the Flauberts had called "le petit salon" and used as a summerhouse. Neglected and falling into disrepair, it was rescued by a Rouen committee in the early years of the new century. Its purchase and restoration were paid for by public subscription; and, baptized "Le Pavillon de Croisset," it was presented to the city of Rouen and inaugurated as a Flaubert museum on June 17, 1907. Caroline did not attend the inauguration ceremonies. "My health is not good, and I am forbidden any form of agitation," she wrote to Paul Toutain, president of the committee. She subscribed a thousand francs and presented a copy in watercolor of a view of Croisset she had painted in oil at the age of twelve.[2]

Incongruous in its industrial setting on the riverbank, the pavilion is open to visitors.

---

1. Edmond de Goncourt, who attended Flaubert's funeral, makes several mentions in his *Journal* of Commanville's behavior on that occasion: pocketing a twenty-franc piece that Flaubert had left out to pay a locksmith, talking about his and Caroline's future income from Flaubert's works, referring repeatedly to letters from women that he had found in Flaubert's desk and had just been reading. The seeming obsession with this last

subject caused Goncourt to wonder whether Commanville might be capable of blackmailing the ladies.

Considering the role that Commanville had always played at Croisset, one can understand—and even take some satisfaction in the fact—that he "was never well there." Such a malaise perhaps implies a slight degree of sensitivity and conscience. Did Commanville—the Commanville we have read of in the letters and now find depicted by Goncourt—really possess even that minimum? One recalls George Sand's brief reference to the gentleman: "His forehead is *flat.*"

2. In an article in the May 1976 issue of the bulletin *Les Amis de Flaubert*, L. Andrieu says that for the most part it was the "bourgeoisie lettrée" who saved the Flaubert Pavilion, though what he calls "humble folk" also made contributions, including "Colange, Flaubert's former cook, and Cotelle, the [new] ferryman." A number of artists—Albert Lebourg, Robert Pinchon, Georges Rochegrosse, Kees Van Dongen, and Jacques Villon among the first—gave paintings, which were auctioned for the Pavilion's benefit.

Among later items presented to the Pavilion there is a clay urn, excavated at Carthage and said to be Punic. Flaubert would have enjoyed learning that on its importation into France it was classified, after "research" by customs officials, as an "objet de toilette, used by Salammbô for her ablutions," and that as such it was subjected to a ten percent luxury tax.

WORKS OF RELATED INTEREST

This brief bibliography is restricted to selected works in English or English translation. A number of other works are cited in the connecting texts and footnotes.

Barnes, Hazel E. *Sartre and Flaubert*. Chicago: University of Chicago Press, 1981.

Bart, Benjamin F., and Cook, Robert Francis. *The Legendary Sources of Flaubert's "Saint Julien."* Toronto: University of Toronto Press, 1977.

Brombert, Victor. *The Novels of Flaubert: A Study of Themes and Techniques*. Princeton: Princeton University Press, 1966.

Flaubert, Gustave. *Madame Bovary*. Translated with an introduction by Francis Steegmuller. New York: The Modern Library, 1957; revised edition, 1982.

Salammbô. Translated with an introduction by A. J. Krailsheimer. London and New York: Penguin Books, 1977.

Sentimental Education. Translated with an introduction by Robert Baldick. London and New York: Penguin Books, 1964.

The Temptation of Saint Anthony. Translated with an introduction and notes by Kitty Mrosovsky. London: Secker & Warburg, 1980

Three Tales. Translated with an introduction by Robert Baldick. London and New York: Penguin Books, 1961.

Bouvard and Pécuchet. Translated with an introduction by A. J. Krailsheimer. London and New York: Penguin Books, 1976.

The Dictionary of Accepted Ideas. Translated with an introduction and notes by Jacques Barzun. New York: New Directions, 1954

The Letters of Gustave Flaubert, 1830–1857. Selected, edited, and translated by Francis Steegmuller. Cambridge: The Belknap Press of Harvard University Press, 1980.

Levin, Harry. *The Gates of Horn: A Study of Five French Realists*. New York: Oxford University Press, 1963.

"A Literary Enormity: Sartre on Flaubert." In *Memories of the Moderns*. New York: New Directions, 1980.

Maurois, André. *Lélia: The Life of George Sand*. Translated by Gerard Hopkins. New York: Harper, 1953.

Oliver, Hermia. *Flaubert and an English Governess: The Quest for Juliet Herbert.* Oxford: Clarendon Press, 1980.

Richardson, Joanna. *Théophile Gautier: His Life and Times.* London: Max Reinhardt, 1958.

Princesse Mathilde. New York: Charles Scribner, 1969.

Sartre, Jean-Paul. *The Family Idiot.* Translated by Carol Cosman. Volume I. Chicago: University of Chicago Press, 1981. Only the first volume has appeared. A revised and completed translation is awaited.

Starkie, Enid. *Flaubert the Master: A Critical and Biographical Study (1856–1880).* New York: Atheneum, 1971.

Zeldin, Theodore. *France 1848–1945. Volume I: Ambition, Love and Politics. Volume II: Intellect, Taste and Anxiety,* Oxford: Clarendon Press, 1973, 1977.

Index

Obry, 24
Osmoy, Charles d', 74, 132, 133, 210

Pascal, 155, 157
Passalacqua, 57
Pausanius, 55
Pelletan, Eugène, 30, 214
Pennetier, 220
Pericles, 162, 181
Person, Béatrix, 121n
Philostratus, 57
Plauchut, Edmond, 138–139
Platus, 54, 151n
Plessy, Sylvanie, 120
Pliny, 42, 56, 57
Plutarch, 13, 29, 147, 150
Polyaenus, 42–43
Polybius, 2, 3, 40, 41, 54, 56
Popelin, Claudius, 224, 253; letter to, 249–250
Pouchet, Georges, 196, 218n, 220, 224, 276
Pradier, James, 272
Proudhon, 14, 76, 89, 116, 117, 120, 185
Proust, Marcel, xvii–xviii
Pushkin, 224

Racine, 31, 49n, 266
Regnier, Mme, 78–79, 274; letters to, 203, 297
Renan, 16, 65, 74, 107n, 176, 177, 183, 187, 212, 238, 268, 276
Reyer, Ernest, 260
Ribera, 32
Rimsky-Korsakov, 261n
Ritter, Karl, 13
Rivoire, Charles Henri Léon, 280–281
Rollin, Charles, 42
Ronsard, 154
Rousseau, 107n, 111
Rousselet, Camille, 267
Roux, 249

Sacy, Silvestre de, 251–253
Sade, Marquis de, 13n, 45, 84n, 118, 136
Sainte-Beuve, Charles Augustin, xii, 65n, 86–87, 102, 103–104, 178n; and criticism of *Salammbô*, xiv, 37–51, 60, 62; as critic, 38, 125–126; as Senator, 105, 107–108, 125–128; death of, 134, 148; letters to, 38, 39–48, 68, 81, 107
Saint-Germain, Giles de, 206, 208
Saintsbury, George, 211n

Saint-Simon, 76
Saint-Taillandier, René, 212
Saint-Victor, Paul de, 63, 86, 136, 212
Salzman, August, 64
Sand, Aurore, 87, 93, 123, 127n, 138–140, 155, 179, 180, 209, 235
Sand, Gabrielle, 139n, 155, 179, 180, 209
Sand, George, xiii, xiv, 49n, 68n, 78, 107n, 194n, 201, 239, 244n, 275, 282, 300n; and *Salammbô*, 37, 84–86, 210; *Histoire de ma vie*, 83, 87, 123, 128; and *Madame Bovary*, 83, 86, 210, 229; and visits to Croisset, 86, 90–91, 115–116; and *La Tentation de Saint Antoine*, 86, 202; journal entries, 90n, 115, 138–139, 159–160, 202–203; and *L'Éducation sentimentale*, 91, 103, 108, 110n, 117–118, 130, 135, 137–138, 140–141, 226, 228–229; *Malgrétout*, 138, 143–146; and Flaubert's visits to Nohant, 138–140, 202–203; "Reply to a Friend," 181–184, 285–293; and *Le Candidat*, 206–210; and *Bouvard et Pécuchet*, 209–210, 222, 241–242; death of, 232, 234–235; letter to, from Turgenev, 218–219; correspondence with, xii, 83–95, 100–106, 108, 110, 112–114, 116, 119, 120, 122–123, 125–129, 135–141, 143–151, 154–159, 160–165, 170–172, 174–185, 187, 189, 191–192, 197–200, 206–210, 211n, 212–213, 214n, 221–223, 225–234
Sand, Lina, 87n, 128, 138, 140, 155, 234, 239
Sand, Maurice, 87n, 88n, 128, 130, 139, 155, 160, 163, 180, 234, 282; letters to, 236, 239, 275
Sandeau, Jules, 68n
Sarcey, 135, 136
Sardou, Victorien, 207n, 209
Sasse, Marie, 151
Saulcy, Félicien de: letter to, 64
Schlesinger, Elise (Mme Maurice), 19n, 130, 151n, 194, 196; letter to, 195
Scott, Sir Walter, xvi, 102n, 237
Scribe, Augustin, 78n
Selden, John, 42, 54
Senard, Jules, 252
Seneca, 216
Séon-Pasquier, Alice, 194n
Shakespeare, 15, 181, 182, 223, 225, 226, 264
Simon, Jules, 200
Socrates, 24, 25

Soulié, Eudore, 63, 177
Sozomen, 24
Spendius, 43, 45, 47
Spinoza, 131, 147, 150
Stendhal, 87n
Strabo, 54
Suetonius, 261n
Swift, 214
Swinburne, 224

Tabarin, 12
Tacitus, xii, 213, 267
Taine, Hippolyte, 65, 126, 213, 224, 251–252, 276; *De l'intelligence,* xiv, xvi, 95–99; and French Academy, 267–268; letters to, 96–99
Talleyrand, 88
Tennant, Mme Charles: letter to, 263
Theophrastus, 42, 43, 56, 57
Thibaudet, Albert, xvii
Thiers, Adolphe, 106, 111, 112–114, 117n, 201n
Tolstoy, 264–265
Toudouze, Gustave, 224
Trochu, Louis-Jules, 106, 160n
Troubat, Jules, 107, 117, 252
Tourbey, Jeanne de, 65
Turgan, 199

Turgenev, Ivan, 78, 128, 149, 168, 205, 208, 212, 221, 223–224, 232, 233, 252–254; visits to Nohant, 192, 197, 202–203; comments on *Bouvard et Pécuchet,* 214, 241; letter to George Sand, 218–219; letter to Flaubert, 214; letter to, from Guy de Maupassant, 275–277; letters to, 73, 126n, 200–201, 213–215, 217–218, 235–236, 238, 242, 264–265, 272
Turgot, 89

Vallès, Jules, 183
Vegetius, 24
Veuillot, Louis, 116
Viardot-Garcia, Pauline, 129n, 192, 197, 212, 217, 277
Vieilcastel, 267
Vigny, Alfred de, 64n
Voltaire, xvi, 69, 79, 111, 116, 214, 237; *Candide,* 18, 41, 107n, 239

Xenophon, 13

Zola, Émile, 136n, 214, 223–224, 231–233, 238n, 242, 247n, 254–256, 269, 272; *Les Soirées de Médan,* 273; letter to Flaubert, 254–255; letters to, 188, 249, 255